THE
DISNEYLAND®
BOOK
OF LISTS

UNOFFICIAL, UNAUTHORIZED, AND UNPRECEDENTED!

CHRIS STRODDER

AUTHOR OF THE DISNEYLAND® ENCYCLOPEDIA

SANTA
MONICA
PRESS

Published by: Santa Monica Press LLC
P.O. Box 850
Solana Beach, CA 92075
1-800-784-9553
www.santamonicapress.com
books@santamonicapress.com

Printed in the United States

Santa Monica Press books are available at special quantity discounts when purchased in bulk by corporations, organizations, or groups. Please call our Special Sales department at 1-800-784-9553.

ISBN-13 978-1-59580-081-7

Library of Congress Cataloging-in-Publication Data

Strodder, Chris
  The Disneyland book of lists / Chris Strodder.
    pages cm
  Summary: The Disneyland® Book of Lists offers a new way to explore six decades of Disneyland history. Hundreds of fascinating lists cover the past and present and feature everything from the park's famous attractions, shops, restaurants, parades, and live shows to the creative artists, designers, characters, and performers who have made Disneyland the world's most beloved theme park.
  ISBN 978-1-59580-081-7 (paperback)
  1. Disneyland (Calif.)—Miscellanea. I. Title.
  GV1853.3.C22D57825 2015
  791.06'879496—dc23
                    2014045519

Cover and interior design and production by Future Studio

A LIST OF THE LISTS

LISTS OF BACKGROUND INFORMATION ABOUT THIS BOOK

WALTLAND
The Man and His Park

HISTORY
Here You Leave Today and Enter the World of Yesterday

GEOGRAPHY
Around the Park in 29 Lists

ATTRACTIONS
Rides, Glides, Zooms, and Flumes

DISNEYLAND BY DESIGN
Imagination Brought to Life

SHOPS AND RESTAURANTS
You Can Buy! You Can Buy! You Can Buy!

ATTENDANCE, TICKETS, AND OPERATIONS
The Business of Fun

THE GUEST LIST
Disneyland Is Your Land

MEDIAPEDIA
Disneyland in Popular Culture

IMAGINEERS, CAST MEMBERS, AND PERFORMERS
Making the Dream a Reality

LIVE SHOWS, EXHIBITS, AND SPECIAL EVENTS
A New Concept in Entertainment

MOUSCELLANEOUS
Assorted Tails

LISTS OF
BACKGROUND
INFORMATION
ABOUT THIS BOOK

A Dozen Historical Lists

Ordering things into lists—"listing"—has a long history. As proof, here are some memorable lists from the past, presented in chronological order.

1. The Ten Commandments in the Old Testament's *Book of Exodus*, first written circa 600–500 B.C. according to some scholars.

2. Seven Wonders of the Ancient World, compiled circa 200–100 B.C.

3. The Seven Deadly Sins, written by Pope Gregory I, 590 A.D.

4. Charles Messier's landmark list of astronomical objects, first published by the French astronomer in 1771.

5. Santa is "making a list" and "checking it twice" in the 1934 Christmas song "Santa Claus Is Coming to Town."

6. The Hit Parade, *Billboard* magazine's ranking of popular tunes that made its debut in 1936.

7. The Hollywood Blacklist of supposed Communist sympathizers in the 1940s and '50s.

8. *The List of Adrian Messenger*, John Huston's 1963 movie with an all-star cast.

9. Nixon's Enemies List, the disgraced president's list of political enemies in the early 1970s.

10. "50 Ways to Leave Your Lover," Paul Simon's 1975 hit song.

11. *Schindler's List*, Thomas Keneally's 1982 historical novel (originally titled *Schindler's Ark*), later made into an Oscar-winning movie by Steven Spielberg.

12. *The Bucket List*, Rob Reiner's 2007 movie with Jack Nicholson.

A Dozen of Disney's Own Lists

There are some historical precedents for Disney-related lists.

1. Disneyland's first nationally televised "list" came on July 17, 1955, during the Opening Day festivities. After christening the *Mark Twain*, actress Irene Dunne quickly yelled, "We're listing!" when she noticed that the overloaded boat was starting to tilt to one side.

2. Disneyland's pictorial souvenir books from the 1950s and '60s include long lists relating to practically everything in the park. (The old A–E ticket books have similar checklists on the inside back cover, cataloging all the "Adventures in Disneyland.")

3. A list of Disney's seven dwarfs becomes a bar bet in Robert Altman's *California Split* (1974).

4. "You got a list that's three miles long," sings the Genie in "Never Had a Friend Like Me" in 1992's *Aladdin*.

5. "If I were on his boogie list, I'd get out of town"—a lyric from "Kidnap the Sandy Claws" in 1993's *The Nightmare Before Christmas*.

6. Napa Rose, the award-winning restaurant that opened inside Disney's Grand Californian Hotel in 2001, is inspired by Napa Valley's wine country and features an extensive wine list.

7. The spring 2002 issue of *Disney Magazine* lists 125 theme park tips, including fourteen for Disneyland.

8. The summer 2005 issue of *Disney Magazine* lists twenty-nine milestones from Disneyland's fifty-year history.

9. In 2005, Disneyland's City Hall offered a list of locations for the "Hidden 50" emblems placed throughout the park for its fiftieth anniversary.

10. In 2011, the young actress Peyton List made her debut as Emma Ross on the Disney Channel's show *Jessie*.

11. Ask for a list in City Hall today, and you might be handed a map with a list of Disneyland's coin-press (aka "penny-press" or "pressed-penny") machines, which transform ordinary coins into Disneyland souvenirs by stamping new images onto them.

12. For the "Radio Disney Top 30" list, visit www.music.disney.com/radio-disney-top-30.

A List About This List Book

1. Disneyland history is a well-plowed field sprouting scores of new travel guides, trivia books, picture books, self-published novels, and e-books every year. However, to our knowledge, this is the first list book ever published about "The Happiest Place on Earth." So, the book you're holding is listorical.

2. The information presented in this book comes from forty-nine years of Disneyland visits. I have been visiting the park since 1966, keeping notes since the 1970s, taking frequent photo safaris since the 1980s, and compiling simple lists since the 1990s. Research for this list book has also paralleled research I was doing for my two editions of *The Disneyland Encyclopedia*, published in the 2000s. Additionally, the lists in this book are informed by decades of collecting and studying almost everything ever printed on the topic of Disneyland history (most of the lists in this book identify my sources and research materials; more detailed information can be found in the bibliography).

3. *The Disneyland Book of Lists* is not a book of "top tens," which was already a clichéd term when David Letterman started doing them on his late-night talk show in the 1980s. Our Disneyland lists are rarely confined to ten items. They *are*, however, confined to Disneyland; there are no lists devoted to Disney California Adventure, Downtown Disneyland, the Disney-owned hotels, or Disney parks outside of Anaheim. Also note that our Disneyland lists celebrate the park's long history, its innovative design, and its singular experiences, but they don't include many travel tips. There are no lists of the best nearby motels or the best ways to get from the airport to Disneyland, because it's just not that kind of book.

4. The lists are grouped by subject ("Geography: Around the Park in 29 Lists," "Attractions: Rides, Glides, Zooms, and Flumes," etc.) and there are two main types of lists: lists of interesting facts (for example, "13 Movies Inspired by Disneyland's Attractions") and lists of informed opinions ("Ranking Disneyland's Thrill Rides"). Short intros preface the lists to give them some context. The strangest list? There's some tough competition, but the winner might be "50 Projects, Organizations, and Locations That Were Compared to Disneyland," a list of non-Disney things (gun ranges? dog apps? the Wall Street lifestyle?) that were described as the "Disneylands" of their fields.

5. Other lists books always feature lists, but they don't always provide explanations. For example, one of the lists in Sugar and Atlas's *The Ultimate Book of Boxing Lists* (see bibliography) is "Bert's Top Ten All-Time Heavyweights," which ranks Sam Langford (#9) ahead of Joe Frazier (#10). Undoubtedly, there's a compelling reason why Langford, who was never heavyweight champion, is preferred over Smokin' Joe Frazier, who was the heavyweight champ in the early 1970s, but the authors don't explain their reasoning. (Turns out, Langford never got a shot at the heavyweight crown because other early twentieth-century boxers simply refused to fight him. He was *that* devastating.) Likewise, Marsh and Stein's *The Book of Rock Lists* places Linda Ronstadt on the list of "10 Most Forgettable Performers," and the Drifters' "Save the Last Dance for Me" beats the Rolling Stones' "(I Can't Get No) Satisfaction" on "The 40 Greatest Number 1 Hits" list. A little reasoning would have made those choices easier to accept. For *The Disneyland Book of Lists*, I wanted to make sure the *why* was as clear as the *what*. To that end, I've included my rationalizations for as many of the lists as possible. Ideally, the Disneyland novice will be as enlightened as the expert will be convinced.

6. *The Disneyland Book of Lists* complements my other book about Disneyland, *The Disneyland Encyclopedia* (Santa Monica Press). The information sketched briefly in this list book is given a detailed description and history in *The Disneyland Encyclopedia*.

7. With just two exceptions, we have not included the lists that Disney-land itself has posted around the park. For example, there are three lists mounted on poles at the Big Thunder Mountain Railroad—one record-ing the nearby town's dwindling population, the other two showing dis-tances to various landmarks (exception #1—we've included one of the latter in our "Geography: Around the Park in 29 Lists" section). There's another list inside Roger Rabbit's Car Toon Spin that itemizes ingredi-ents in the infamous Dip (Judge Doom's lethal toon-dissolver, not the good kind of dip for potato chips). Nearby, Goofy's Gas Station has a board that lists the kinds of water available (Liquid, Wet, High, etc.), and posted on the door of the Toontown Insurance Co. is a humorous list of the accidents it covers (exception #2—in the "Disneyland By Design" section, we've included Minnie's easy-to-miss shopping list from her re-frigerator door). In Tomorrowland, the Status Board posted at the exit of Buzz Lightyear's Astro Blasters displays scores and rankings. Most of these lists (and more) are conspicuous, so we'll let you discover and en-joy them on your own.

8. Having written articles, nonfiction books, short stories, children's books, and novels, I found the list book to be a unique, fascinating, and reward-ing genre. "Listmaking," according to Segalove and Velick's *List Your Self*, "is an elegant, complete, and artful act in and of itself. The very process is a breakthrough change of mind. . . . Listmaking turns on the juices. Your memory will start to dance. . . . It's an exercise that flexes a muscle you may not have used in a while." Or ever. I began this book in earnest in 2012 and have been happily making lists of non-Disneyland things ever since. I highly recommend it. Actually, you might already be list-ing—ever write down items to shop for at the grocery store? Keep track of things you have to do during the day? Organize songs into a playlist? What you've got there are lists, my friend, making you a "lister."

9. *The Oxford English Dictionary* defines archaic forms of the word "list": the first time it was used in the sense of "cataloguing" was in the 1500s. (Other usages include a variation of "listen"; a variation of "lust"; a strip of cloth; a boundary or site of a contest; and "listy," which in the *OED* means "pleasant" or "delightful." Hopefully you'll find this list book listy.)

10. "Listless"—you sure can't say that about ever-changing, ever-abundant Disneyland. Read on, and be listful.

Chris Strodder
Mill Valley, CA

WALTLAND

The Man and His Park

30 Walt Disney Quotes About Disneyland

Of the many things Walt Disney said about Disneyland, here are thirty of the most memorable quotes. See page 36 for thirty more Disneyland quotes from a range of prominent speakers.

1. "[Disneyland] came about when my daughters were very young, and Saturday was always Daddy's day with the two daughters. So we'd start out and try to go someplace, you know, different things, and I'd take them to the merry-go-round and . . . as I'd sit while they rode the merry-go-round . . . I felt that that there should be something built, some kind of an amusement enterprise where the parents and the children could have fun together. So that's how Disneyland started. . . . A daddy with two daughters wondering where he could take them where he could have a little fun with them too." (Interview with Fletcher Markle, 1963; Jackson, *Walt Disney Conversations*)

2. "Disneyland would be a world of Americans, past and present, seen through the eyes of my imagination—a place of warmth and nostalgia, of illusion and color and delight." (Walt Disney Corporation, *Walt Disney: Famous Quotes*)

3. Conversation with his wife, Lillian:

   "Why would you want to get involved with an amusement park?" she asked. "They're so dirty and not fun at all for grown-ups. Why would you want to get involved in a business like that?"

   "That's exactly my point," Walt replied. "Mine isn't going to be that way. Mine's going to be a place that's clean, where the whole family can do things together." (Bright, *Disneyland: Inside Story*)

4. Pitching the Disneyland concept to board members:

   "There's nothing like it in the entire world. I know, because I've looked. That's why it can be great: because it will be unique. A new concept in entertainment, and I think—I know—it can be a success." (Thomas, *Walt Disney: An American Original*)

5. To artist Herb Ryman as he drew the first map of what Disneyland could look like:

   "I've been studying the way people go to museums and other entertainment places. Everybody's got tired feet. I don't want that to happen in this place. I want a place for people to sit down and where old folks can say, 'You kids run on. I'll meet you there in a half hour.' Disneyland is going to be a place where you can't get lost or tired unless you want to." (Bright, *Disneyland: Inside Story*)

6. "Disneyland is not just another amusement park. It's unique, and I want it kept that way. Besides, you don't work for a dollar—you work to create

and have fun." (Smith, *The Quotable Walt Disney*)

7. "I had all my drawing things laid out at home, and I'd work on plans for the park, as a hobby, at night. . . . I talked Disneyland, but no one could see it." (De Roos, "The Magic Worlds of Walt Disney," *National Geographic*)

8. "It's no secret that we were sticking just about every nickel we had on the chance that people would really be interested in something totally new and unique in the field of entertainment." (Ballard, *The Disneyland Hotel*)

9. "One thing it takes to accomplish something is courage. Take Disneyland for an example. Almost everyone warned us that Disneyland would be a Hollywood spectacular—a spectacular failure." (Sklar, *Dream It! Do It!*)

10. To his designers:

    "All I want you to think about . . . is that when people walk through or ride through or have access to anything that you design, I want them, when they leave, to have smiles on their faces. Just remember that; it's all I ask of you as a designer." (Thomas, *Walt Disney: An American Original*)

11. "You've got to have a wienie [an alluring element, usually a vivid visual landmark] at the end of every street!" (Finch, *The Art of Walt Disney*)

12. "I don't want the public to see the real world they live in while they're in the park. I want them to feel they are in another world." (De Roos, "The Magic Worlds of Walt Disney," *National Geographic*)

13. "It has that thing—the imagination, and the feeling of happy excitement—I knew when I was a kid." (Greene, *The Man Behind the Magic*)

14. "[A] cute movie set is what it really is." (Gabler, *Walt Disney: The Triumph of the American Imagination*)

15. "Give the people everything you can give them. Keep the place as clean as you can keep it. Keep it friendly, you know. Make it a real fun place to be." (Bright, *Disneyland: Inside Story*)

16. To the Disneyland Merchant's Association at Disneyland's Red Wagon Inn:

    "We must build Disneyland into an attraction that will never be in competition with anything else. It must be made impossible to duplicate. . . . We need things that are unique—things that are 'Disneylandish'." (Minutes presented by Sherry Barkas, reporting for the *Desert Sun*, December 2013)

17. To cast members:

    "Above everything, always give them full value for their money. If a boat ride is supposed to last twelve minutes and they only get eleven minutes thirty seconds, they've a right to feel cheated. Thirty seconds shy, and they hate us for selling them short. Thirty seconds extra, and they feel they've gotten away with something. That's the way we want them to feel. Contented, even smug." (Mosley, *Disney's World*)

18. "I come down here to get a real rest. . . . This is my amusement. This is where I relax." (Green and Green, *Remembering Walt*)

19. "Disneyland was a natural. . . . It was so close to what we were doing in film. I thought of it a long time, but very few people believed in it at first. Now look at it [in 1959]. Five years ago, Disneyland was just a flat plain of orange groves. It cost us $4,500 an acre. The bank recently appraised it [at] $20,000 an acre. Imagine, $20,000 an acre." (Interview with Lee Edson, 1959; Jackson, *Walt Disney Conversations*)

20. When asked if anyone else was working on Audio-Animatronics:

    "I don't know anyone crazy enough," Walt laughed. . . . "The fun is in always building something. . . . We never do the same thing twice around here. We're always opening up new doors." (De Roos, "The Magic Worlds of Walt Disney," *National Geographic*)

21. "The park means a lot to me. It's something that will never be finished, something I can keep developing, keep 'plussing,' and adding to. It's alive. It will be a live, breathing thing that will need changes. When you wrap up a picture and turn it over to Technicolor, you're through. *Snow White* is a dead issue with me. . . . I want something live, something that would grow. The park is that. Not only can I add things to it, but even the trees will keep growing. The thing will get more beautiful year after year. And it will get better as I find out what the public likes. I can't do that with a picture. It's finished and unchangeable before I find out if the public likes it or not." (Mosley, *Disney's World*)

22. "The one thing I learned from Disneyland was to control the environment." (Walker, *Los Angeles: Architectural Digest Profile*)

23. "No other place has as high a quality. I stand here in the park and talk to people. It's a most gratifying thing. All I've got from the public is thank-yous." (Bright, *Disneyland: Inside Story*)

24. "Though people don't realize it, Disneyland is designed by the same staff that has done *Snow White* and all the pictures. I have that reservoir of talent that I can draw on, and that's why, when people talk about making another Disneyland, they better first see what reservoir of talent they have to draw on like I have." (Lefkon, *Disney Insider Yearbook 2005*)

25. "Disneyland is the star. Everything else is in the supporting role." (Smith, *The Quotable Walt Disney*)

26. "You've got to keep it fresh and new and exciting. And when people come back, you always want to have something new they hadn't had a

chance to see before." (Interview for *Look* magazine, 1964; Jackson, *Walt Disney Conversations*)

27. To employees at Disneyland's Tencennial Celebration in 1965:

"The past ten years have just sort of been a dress rehearsal. We're just getting started, so if any of you start to rest on your laurels, just forget it!" (Bright, *Disneyland: Inside Story*)

28. "Disneyland is a work of love." (Kurtti and Gordon, *The Art of Disneyland*)

29. "Anything is possible in Disneyland." ("Disneyland's Tenth Anniversary" episode of *Walt Disney's Wonderful World of Color*, January 3, 1965)

30. "Disneyland will never be completed. It will grow as long as there is imagination left in the world." (De Roos, "The Magic Worlds of Walt Disney," *National Geographic*)

A Dozen Sites Walt Disney Considered Before Building Disneyland

In the early 1950s, before consultant Harrison "Buzz" Price pointed Walt Disney toward Anaheim as the best location for Disneyland, Disney thought about (but ultimately rejected) other Southern California locations. They're listed here in the approximate chronological order in which he considered them. (Sources: Bright, *Disneyland: Inside Story*; Price, *Walt's Revolution! By the Numbers*; Thomas, *Walt Disney: An American Original*)

1. Burbank: "A small playground for kids on the corner of the studio property" would have been called "Walt Disney's America," but Walt Disney's ideas quickly outgrew this tiny seven-acre plot.

2. Burbank: Announced in 1952, a $1.5-million park would have been built on sixteen acres across the street from Disney's movie studio. However, Burbank officials eventually cooled to the idea, so Disney began looking elsewhere (the Burbank land was engulfed by the Ventura Freeway's expansion).

3. La Cañada Flintridge: Nestled in this small town about forty miles north of Anaheim, the grounds of Descanso Gardens are beautiful and lush, but summer temperatures are slightly hotter.

4. Chatsworth: At the time, this was a quiet, undeveloped area in the San Fernando Valley with a police pistol range; however, summer temperatures are about ten degrees higher than in Anaheim.

5. Calabasas: This dry, hilly region is about sixty miles northwest of Anaheim, but like Chatsworth, the summer temperatures run about ten degrees hotter than Anaheim's.

6. Beaches: There's a long tradition of beach towns on both coasts hosting amusement parks, but Walt Disney "reasoned that the ocean would eliminate half the access." Disney also "disliked the honky-tonk atmosphere of amusement piers" and "didn't want people coming to Disneyland in bathing suits."

7. Palos Verdes: Although it was the site of Marineland of the Pacific from 1954 to 1987, this scenic peninsula about thirty-five miles west of Anaheim was deemed undesirable because of its narrow roads and expensive real estate.

8. Chavez Ravine: The Dodgers would eventually build their stadium on this site north of downtown Los Angeles, which Walt Disney briefly considered but dismissed as too expensive.

9. Downtown Los Angeles: In some ways, the historic railroad terminal here was considered "the ideal" site for the park, but it was also "obviously the wrong place to acquire reasonably priced land."

10. Buena Park: The home of Knott's Berry Farm, this area was a close finalist for the Disneyland location. However, the available land would have been only about two miles (as the crow flies) from Knott's, which was already established and growing.

11. Los Alamitos: This suburb, twelve miles west of Anaheim and halfway to Long Beach, was also worthy of serious consideration.

12. Santa Ana: As Price narrowed his search to a corridor along Interstate 5 in Orange County, he looked at a golf course five miles south of Anaheim, but it didn't have easy freeway access.

7 Reasons Why Walt Disney Chose Anaheim as the Site for Disneyland

In the report he finalized on August 28, 1953, consultant Harrison "Buzz" Price (who is profiled on page 272) recommended that Walt Disney build Disneyland on a 160-acre spread in Anaheim. It was not an obvious choice. Orange County's oldest incorporated city, Anaheim was at that time a sleepy agricultural area—nothing like the crowded city it is now—and it seemed unreasonably far from glamorous Hollywood and other familiar L.A. areas. There were fewer than a hundred hotel and motel rooms in all of Anaheim (in 2011, the Disney hotels at the Disneyland Resort alone contained over 2,200 rooms). "I first saw the [possible] site for Disneyland back in 1953," Disney said. "In those day, it was all flat land—no rivers, no mountains, no castles or rocket ships—just orange groves and a few acres of walnut trees."

At the time, most West Coast amusement parks, including eight between San Diego and Santa Monica, were built along scenic Pacific Ocean beaches. Price was bucking tradition with his inland selection. Additionally, Walt Disney had hoped to buy flat, undeveloped land from a single owner, but the Anaheim property (formally called the Ball Road Subdivision) had seventeen different owners. Still, Price had at least seven good reasons for choosing Anaheim . . .

1. Price declared that, within a few decades, Anaheim would be the epi-center of Southern California's spreading population (an amazing pre-diction—the actual center is Fullerton, just one town over and only four miles away).

2. Growth in Orange County, Price felt, would continue as it had in the 1940s and early '50s, when its population had almost doubled (right again—Anaheim's population of 14,000 multiplied by a factor of seven during the 1950s and became the "fastest growing city in America," ac-cording to Faessel's *Images of America: Anaheim 1940–2007*).

3. An unfinished north-south freeway project would soon pass right through Anaheim, putting Disneyland within easy reach of millions of drivers (Interstate 5 was completed three months after Disneyland opened).

4. With an annual rainfall averaging only an inch a month, Anaheim stays drier than much of L.A. County.

5. Anaheim's Mediterranean climate offers average summertime tempera-tures in the mid-80s and lows in the mid-60s, milder than many other inland areas of L.A. County.

6. Anaheim's winters are also relatively calm, with average highs in the mid-60s and lows in the upper 40s.

7. Back then, Anaheim land was still relatively cheap—under $5,000 per acre.

10 Pieces of Advice Walt Disney Ignored Before Opening Disneyland

While he was planning Disneyland, Walt Disney and his staff consulted numerous amusement park "experts" who generally disparaged his ideas. "Most of the people I talked to thought it would be a financial disaster—closed and forgotten within the first year," Disney said. Compiled from mul-tiple sources (notably the *Walt Disney Treasures: Disneyland Secrets, Stories & Magic* DVD, Thomas's *Building a Company*, and Bright's *Disneyland: Inside Sto-ry*), some of the suggestions he received are paraphrased here.

1. Advertise what's in the park by making everything completely visible from the street.

2. For customer convenience, offer multiple entrances and exits.

3. Increase profits by selling alcohol.

4. Offer what customers expect to see in an amusement park, such as a midway with simple carnival games, a Ferris wheel, and a traditional roller coaster.

5. Don't waste money on landscaping and detailed interiors for shops and restaurants; nobody will be impressed.

6. Don't waste money on non-revenue-generating structures like Sleeping Beauty Castle.

7. Don't offer any food other than basic hot dogs, candy, and ice cream.

8. Don't include beautiful old-fashioned vehicles for customers to vandalize.

9. Don't stay open more than four months a year—summer is the busy season.

10. Anticipating the worst, some of Walt Disney's top lieutenants even urged him to board up the incomplete Tomorrowland or move Disneyland's grand opening from mid-summer to autumn.

10 Other Projects Walt Disney Was Working on While Planning and Building Disneyland

During the mid-1950s—when he was so deeply immersed in detailed Disneyland planning and construction that he was living in an apartment at the site much of the time—Walt Disney also oversaw a number of other projects. Here are a few highlights from 1953, '54, '55, and '56, listed chronologically.

1. *Peter Pan*: Released in 1953, the film was nominated for the Cannes Film Festival's Grand Prize.

2. *True-Life Adventure* documentaries: Between 1953 and 1956, Disney produced four key entries in this Oscar-winning series—*Bear Country*, *The Living Desert*, *The Vanishing Prairie*, and *The African Lion*.

3. Cartoons: Between 1953 and 1956, Disney also produced dozens of short cartoons, notably the Oscar-winning *Toot, Whistle, Plunk and Boom*.

4. *Disneyland* TV series: The first episode of this long-running series (later renamed *Walt Disney's Wonderful World of Color*, among other titles) was broadcast on October 27, 1954; the first episode about Davy Crockett, "Davy Crockett: Indian Fighter," aired seven weeks later (the film *Davy Crockett: King of the Wild Frontier* hit theaters soon after, in May 1955).

5. 20,000 *Leagues Under the Sea*: A box-office hit in December 1954, this live-action movie won Oscars for Art Direction and Special Effects.

6. *Man in Space*: This memorable Oscar-nominated series debuted on March 9, 1955.

7. *Lady and the Tramp*: Another big box-office success, released in 1955.

8. *The Mickey Mouse Club*: The Mouseketeers' popular afternoon series debuted on October 3, 1955.

9. *People and Places* documentaries: In 1953, Disney began producing these Oscar-winning travelogues. *Disneyland, U.S.A.*, a 42-minute featurette, was released into theaters in 1956.

10. *Westward Ho, the Wagons!*: Between 1953 and 1956, Walt Disney oversaw several historical live-action dramas, including this one from late 1956 with Fess Parker. Others included *The Sword and the Rose* (1953) and *The Great Locomotive Chase* (1956).

2 Dozen Reminders of Walt Disney in Disneyland

"Disneyland is the roadmap of Walt Disney's life," said Disney Legend Martin Sklar in Van France's *Window on Main Street*. Guests can easily find Disney's name and likeness everywhere in the park. The 1970s exhibit area on Main Street called Legacy of Walt Disney and (later) the displays inside Town Square's Opera House have been the primary showcases for various photographs and items of Disney memorabilia. In addition, the unavoidable *Partners* statue in the Disneyland Hub is probably the most photographed representation of Walt Disney in this century. Here are two dozen more locations referencing Walt Disney, his family members, and Marceline, the Missouri town where he spent part of his childhood.

1. Entrance: At the east-side pedestrian entrance on Harbor Boulevard, a star in the Anaheim Walk of Fame honors Walt Disney.

2. Fantasyland: The mural in the queue area for Mr. Toad's Wild Ride includes a train in the upper-right corner marked WED RAIL (WED = Walt Elias Disney). Some guests claim that Disney is depicted as the train's engineer, though that's probably wishful thinking.

3. Fantasyland: Peter Pan's Flight begins with a flight out of a bedroom window, and occasionally the alphabet blocks on the bedroom floor are arranged to spell "Disney."

4. Fantasyland: Since the mid-1960s, a heraldic crest (*right*) has adorned the entranceway to Sleeping Beauty Castle. According to Disneyland, this is the official Disney family crest (some heraldry researchers denounce this claim as being apocryphal; comedian Steve Martin, who worked at Disneyland once upon a time, calls it "a made-up Disney family crest" in his book *Born Standing Up*).

5. Fantasyland: At the Storybook Land Canal Boats, some of the boats (*Alice, Faline, Snow White*, and *Wendy*) have the words "Walt Disney Limited" painted on the side of their cabins.

6. Frontierland: Equestrian-themed photographs of Walt Disney have been displayed inside Miss Chris's Cabin and along construction walls surrounding the Big Thunder Mountain Railroad.

7. Frontierland: At the train station, a landline telegraph clicks out lines from Walt Disney's Disneyland dedication speech (more of the text is displayed at the base of the flagpole in Town Square).

8. Frontierland: Walt Disney presented the mineralized Petrified Tree as an anniversary gift to his wife, Lillian (who then gave it to Disneyland in 1957).

9. Frontierland: From 1955 to 1956, a small one-story Marshal's Office (primarily a backdrop for photos) had a sign on its slanted roof identifying Walt Disney's father-in-law, "Willard P. Bounds, Blacksmith and U.S. Marshal."

10. Hub: Walt Disney's baby photo is inside the Baby Care Center (*right*).

11. Hub: Doc Sherwood M.D., Walt Disney's boyhood neighbor who encouraged young Disney to draw, has a tribute window at the First Aid building.

12. Main Street: Christopher D. Miller, Walt Disney's grandson, has a tribute window on West Center Street.

13. Main Street: Elias Disney, Walt Disney's father, has a tribute window above the Emporium.

14. Main Street: There is a conspicuous but inaccessible structure on East Center Street called Hotel Marceline.

15. Main Street: Tilly, the Main Street Cinema's ticket taker, wears a nametag identifying her hometown as "Marceline, MO."

16. Main Street: Walter Elias Disney is identified as the "Founder & Director Emeritus" of the Disneyland Casting Agency on the door next to the Main Street Cinema.

17. Main Street: The giant penny above the Penny Arcade is dated 1901, Walt Disney's birth year.

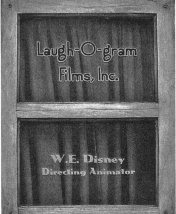

18. Mickey's Toontown: A tribute window (*right*) above the library reads "Laugh-O-Gram Films, Inc., W. E. Disney, Directing Animator."

19. Mickey's Toontown: One of the books displayed inside Mickey's House is called *My Pal Walt: A Tribute* by Mickey Mouse, from the Marceline Publishing Company.

20. New Orleans Square: Ornamental designs (*right*) of "WD" and "RD" (for Walt Disney and Roy Disney, respectively) are in the railing above Pirates of the Caribbean—the location for what would have been the Disney family's private apartment.

21. Town Square: The most popular guided tour at the park is called "Walk in Walt's Disneyland Footsteps," a three-hour walk-and-talk that includes recordings of Walt Disney's voice.

22. Town Square: Often seen at the train station, the Disneyland Railroad's lavishly appointed Presidential Parlor Car (filled with family photos and used for VIP trips) is named the *Lilly Belle*, after Lillian Disney. Lilly Belle was also the name of one of the tiny Shetland ponies in 1955's Miniature Horse Corral.

23. Town Square: Inside the train station are photos and memorabilia evoking Walt Disney's lifelong love of trains.

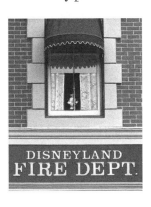

24. Town Square: Above the Fire Department is Walt Disney's private apartment, recognized by the lamp lit in the second-floor window (*right*).

Let's Get Small: 17 Examples of Walt Disney's Love of Miniatures

Walt Disney's well-chronicled love of miniatures was most famously expressed in his private life by his elaborate miniature train on a half-mile of track in his Holmby Hills backyard. Long before Disneyland was built, Disney even toyed with the idea of sending "Disneylandia" exhibits of miniatures around the country. Instead, miniatures have become a prominent part of Disneyland's past and present. Here are seventeen examples.

1. In Adventure Thru Inner Space (1967–1985), guests "shrank" as the atomic realm enlarged around them.

2. Disneyland Presents a Preview of Coming Attractions (1973–1989) offered detailed models of future projects.

3. At the Emporium (1955-ongoing), small, elaborate dioramas began appearing in the windows in 1969, and they continue to delight guests today.

4. Flight Circle, aka Thimble Drome Flight Circle (1955–1966) featured demonstrations of motorized model planes, boats, and cars in Tomorrowland.

5. Frontierland Miniature Museum (never built) would have displayed miniature buildings.

6. Gadget's Go Coaster (1993–ongoing) takes guests on a ride past oversized toys and objects.

7. In *Honey, I Shrunk the Audience* (1998–2010), the movie theater was accidentally miniaturized to the size of a lunch box.

8. Lilliputian Land (never built) would have featured rides past small-scale structures located between Fantasyland and Tomorrowland.

9. In the Midget Autopia (1957–1966), young children drove diminutive versions of the bigger Autopia cars on a track that went through a small building.

10. The Miniature Horse Corral (1955–1957) in Frontierland featured live miniature horses from the Shetland Islands.

11. Since the 1970s, a large replica of the U.S. Capitol at a 1:64 scale has been displayed inside the Opera House (1955–ongoing), joined in recent years by an impressive model of Disneyland.

12. Pixie Hollow (2008–ongoing) guides guests on a walk into Tinker Bell's fairy-sized world.

13. Located on the second level of Tomorrowland's Carousel Theater above the Carousel of Progress, Progress City (1967–1973), a huge model of a

futuristic metropolis, included over 4,000 small buildings and 20,000 tiny trees.

14. Rainbow Ridge (1956–1977, 1979–ongoing) is a miniature town originally located in the loading areas of the extinct Mine Train before it was moved to the Big Thunder Mountain Railroad.

15. In the Sleeping Beauty Castle Walk-Through (1957–2001 and 2008–ongoing), miniature settings re-tell the *Sleeping Beauty* storyline.

16. The Storybook Land Canal Boats (1956–ongoing) feature exquisite landscaping that enhances meticulously detailed settings from Disney animation.

17. The 20,000 Leagues Under the Sea Exhibit (1956–1966) featured props from the movie, including a realistic *Nautilus* model.

13 of Walt Disney's Disneyland Favorites

So what were Walt Disney's most treasured activities, attractions, and even time of day at Disneyland? These thirteen were among his favorites.

1. **Land: Fantasyland**
   "Fantasyland, which he admitted was his favorite." (Thomas, *Walt Disney: An American Original*)

   "[Fantasyland was] Walt's favorite land." (Imagineer Bruce Gordon on the *Walt Disney Treasures: Disneyland Secrets, Stories & Magic* DVD)

2. **Attraction: Steam Trains**
   "For him, the main attraction at Disneyland was the steam trains." (Ollie Johnson, animator/Disney Legend, writing in Broggie's *Walt Disney's Railroad Story*)

3. **Attraction: Storybook Land Canal Boats**
   "This tiny childhood world [of the Storybook Land Canal Boats] was one of Walt's personal favorites." (Anonymous, *Disneyland: The First Thirty Years*)

4. **Attraction: Great Moments with Mr. Lincoln**
   Reflecting his "attempts as a boy in school to make the great president come alive for his listeners," Great Moments with Mr. Lincoln was "one of Walt's favorite attractions." (Hammontree, *Walt Disney: Young Movie Maker*)

5. **Attraction: King Arthur Carrousel**
   In *Saving Mr. Banks*, Tom Hanks (playing Walt Disney) tells Emma Thompson (playing P. L. Travers), "I'm just going to take you on one ride,

my favorite amusement," as he leads her to the King Arthur Carrousel.

6. **Attraction: It's a Small World**

   "This is our Imagineering Department. It is here where we dream up all of the future things for Disneyland . . . especially one that I'm in love with, the story of the children of the world. We call it It's a Small World." (Walt Disney on 1965's "Disneyland's Tenth Anniversary" episode of *Walt Disney's Wonderful World of Color*)

   "Among the attractions at Disneyland, a personal favourite of Walt's was It's a Small World." (Moore, *Why We Build*)

7. **Attraction: Pirates of the Caribbean**

   When asked at a press conference to name his favorite attraction, Walt "launched into a long description of a ride that would include pirate ships and treasure. The journalists didn't know what he was talking about. It was Pirates of the Caribbean, which wouldn't be finished for another few years. Walt's favorite ride always was the next one." (Greene, *The Man Behind the Magic*)

8. **Favorite Fantasyland dark ride: Peter Pan**

   "His favorite was the Peter Pan, because it was an entirely new concept—a fly-through with cars suspended from the ceiling." (Thomas, *Walt Disney: An American Original*)

9. **Favorite show: *Golden Horseshoe Revue***

   The *Golden Horseshoe Revue* "was always one of Dad's very favorite things." (Diane Disney Miller on the *Walt Disney Treasures: Disneyland Secrets, Stories & Magic* DVD)

   "This show was a favorite of Walt's, as he would often watch from one of the private boxes next to the stage." (Kurtti and Gordon, *The Art of Disneyland*)

   According to the spring 2002 issue of *Disney Magazine* and the official Disney website, Walt Disney's favorite box for watching the show was the lower one at stage left (viewed from the audience, it's the lower-right box). A few sources claim the upper box was his favorite.

10. **Favorite restaurant: The Plaza Inn**

    The Hub's opulent Plaza Inn "is the one Walt Disney was most proud of." (Disney Editions' *Birnbaum's 2014 Official Guide to the Disneyland Resort*)

11. **Favorite times of day: Morning and sundown**

    "This is one of my favorite times of the day here—just about sundown. I like to be around when the lights come on. Seems like a new kind of magic takes over in Disneyland after dark. . . . Morning comes around early—and that's one of my favorite times here too!" (Walt Disney on the "Disneyland After Dark" episode of *Walt Disney's Wonderful World of Color*)

12. Favorite activity: Watching the *Mark Twain*

"One of the biggest joys of my life is sitting on the levee in the Frontierland section of our park . . . watching the steamboat *Mark Twain* [*below*] belching smoke and skirting along toward the tip of Tom Sawyer Island." (Walt Disney, quoted in Jackson and West's *Disneyland and Culture*)

13. Favorite activity: Meeting Disneyland guests

"I think he loved meeting the people, and he often asked them a lot about what they thought. Many of his ideas came from every corner, including the guests." (Disney Legend Tony Baxter, adding commentary to the *Disneyland, U.S.A.* documentary on the *Walt Disney Treasures: Disneyland Secrets, Stories & Magic* DVD)

HISTORY

Here You Leave Today and Enter the World of Yesterday

30 Quotes About Disneyland from Prominent Sources

Of the millions of printed and recorded quotes about Disneyland, here are thirty from famous speakers and publications.

1. Julie Andrews, actress: "Disneyland was Walt's gift to a weary world. Once you pass through its gates, the stress and strife of our everyday reality seems to melt away, and we enter a truly timeless realm that has withstood trends and fads to become a national treasure." (Gordon and O'Day, *Disneyland: Then, Now, and Forever*)

2. *Better Homes and Gardens*: "Parents entering Disneyland with their children are due for the same surprise they got from other Walt Disney creations. What is planned as a dutiful pilgrimage for the sake of the children turns out to be an eye-opening day of adult entertainment and education." (February 1, 1956)

3. Ray Bradbury, author: "I found, in Disneyland, vast reserves of imagination before untapped in our country." (Sklar, *Walt Disney's Disneyland*)

4. Ray Bradbury, author: "When you enter Disneyland you're entering . . . a fabulous time machine with a series of doors you can open and go into the past or into the future." (*Walt Disney Treasures: Tomorrow Land* DVD)

5. *BusinessWeek* magazine: "Welcome to a revolution in family entertainment—and travel destinations." (July 9, 1955)

6. Bob Cummings, actor, at the Opening Day ceremonies on July 17, 1955: "I think that everyone here will one day be as proud to have been at this opening as the people who were at the dedication of the Eiffel Tower." (*Disneyland: The First Thirty Years*)

7. Roy O. Disney, Walt Disney's brother: "It sounded crazy. We were in the movie business, not the amusement-park business. We didn't know a thing in the world about amusement parks. None of us around Walt wanted any part of his amusement park. His banker used to hide under the desk when Walt started talking about that park. But you couldn't stop him. He was confident it would be wonderful." (Eddy, "The Amazing Secret of Walt Disney," *American Magazine*)

8. Lawrence Durrell, author of *The Alexandria Quartet*: "I had a day in Disneyland. . . . Magnificent exhibitions, and the rides! I don't remember when I had such fun." (*New York Times*, March 29, 1968)

9. Dwight Eisenhower during a family visit on December 26, 1961: "I suppose you might say I'm enjoying this as much as the grandchildren. No! More! . . . I never dreamed it would be this much fun." (Hillinger, *Hillinger's California*)

10. Michael Eisner, former chairman and CEO of the Walt Disney Company,

speaking in 1993 at the Mickey's Toontown dedication: "[Disneyland is] the temple of the entire Walt Disney Company." (Dunlop, *Building a Dream*)

11. Billy Graham, evangelist: "What a fantastic world! What a marvelous fantasy world!" (Green and Green, *Remembering Walt*)

12. *Life* magazine: "It may be more than the kids can bear. . . . It is easily the most lavish amusement park on earth." (August 15, 1955)

13. *Look* magazine: "A fantastic monument to the imagination and genius of one man. . . . Disneyland is sixty acres of pure whimsy." (July 26, 1955)

14. *Los Angeles Times* headline and first line of an article about Disneyland's opening:

Dream Realized—Disneyland Opens

$17,500,000 World of Fantasy Dedicated to Children and Hope

Once-upon-a-time land—that magical land of fantasy and faraway places in the minds of little children—became a dream come true yesterday. (July 18, 1955)

15. Steve Martin, comedian, remembering the opening of Disneyland when he was ten years old: "Disneyland, and the idea of it, seemed so glorious that I believed it should be in some faraway, impossible-to-visit Shangri-la, not two miles from the house where I was about to grow up." (Martin, *Born Standing Up*)

16. *McCall's* magazine: "Walt Disney's cartoon world materializes bigger than life and twice as real." (January 1955)

17. *National Geographic* magazine: "Shrieks of joy resound. . . . Disneyland, on a fall day, is full of warmth and zest." (August 1963)

18. *Newsweek* magazine: "The gamble paid off." (December 31, 1962)

19. *The New Yorker* magazine: "Our Mecca . . . [we] all delighted in Disneyland like small children. . . . Uncritical euphoria . . . had possessed us." (September 7, 1963)

20. *The New Yorker* magazine: "Disneyland . . . is surely one of the wonders of the world, and no tourist, foreign or domestic should miss it." (December 9, 1967)

21. *New York Times*: "Mr. Disney has tastefully combined some of the pleasantest things of yesterday with the fantasy and dreams of tomorrow." (January 22, 1955)

22. Richard Nixon, visiting Disneyland in 1955: "This is a paradise for children and for grown-ups, too." (Watts, *The Magic Kingdom*)

23. Ronald Reagan, commemorating Disneyland's thirty-fifth anniversary

in 1990: "[It's] a place that has captured the imagination and earned the affection of four generations of Americans ... and a place that has served as host and goodwill ambassador to millions of visitors from abroad." ("Disneyland Celebrates 50 Magical Years," *PR Newswire*)

24. Astronaut Sally Ride, on board a 1986 Space Shuttle flight: "Have you ever been to Disneyland? . . . This is definitely an 'E' ticket!" (Hurwitz, *Sally Ride: Shooting for the Stars*)

25. Entertainer Danny Thomas, ad-libbing during the Opening Day TV broadcast: "I'm absolutely flabbergasted at this fantastic place!" (*Walt Disney Treasures: Disneyland U.S.A.* DVD)

26. *Time* magazine: "By the time Walt gets through, this will not only be the seventh wonder of the world, but the eighth, ninth, and tenth as well." (July 29, 1957)

27. *Time* magazine: "The theme park was Disney's masterwork ... a bet-the-farm risk," and its "design . . . anticipated many of the best features of modern urban planning." (December 7, 1998)

28. Earl Warren, Supreme Court Chief Justice: "Everywhere I travel in the world people ask me about Disneyland." (Sklar, *Walt Disney's Disneyland*)

29. *Woman's Home Companion* magazine, Volume 81, 1954: "Probably the closest yet to life-as-we-wish-it-were compared with life-as-it-is."

30. Herman Wouk, author of *The Winds of War*: "There are few things more worth seeing in the United States, or indeed anywhere in the world." (Sklar, *Walt Disney's Disneyland*)

A Dozen Details in Herb Ryman's Drawing of Disneyland That Didn't Make It Into the Park

Few artists who contributed to Disneyland were as significant as Herb Ryman, whose work helped shape Sleeping Beauty Castle, the Jungle Cruise, the Main Street buildings, and New Orleans Square. In addition, on September 26 and 27 of 1953, he drew a detailed aerial view of the unbuilt park as Walt Disney described it to him (*opposite*). That landmark drawing—which included two pedestrian tunnels at the entrance, a recognizable Main Street, a Hub with various lands radiating outward from it, a castle, a berm with a train, a river with a riverboat, and a Jungle Cruise-style attraction—was a key component of the successful presentations Roy Disney made to potential investors. In the 2005 film *Disneyland: The First 50 Magical Years*, Steve Martin calls Ryman's drawing "the most rare and valuable piece of art in the Disney Archives."

Even though Walt Disney was personally giving detailed instructions about Disneyland's layout and structures to Ryman, many things in the

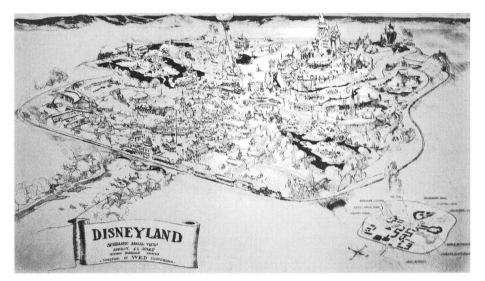

DISNEYLAND

drawing changed dramatically by the time the park opened less than two years later. Here are a dozen details Walt Disney told Herb Ryman to draw, but later changed.

1. Ryman's drawing defines Disneyland as a forty-five-acre square with rounded corners. In reality, Disneyland originally covered sixty acres and is shaped more like a triangle with rounded corners.

2. Unlike the train that has circled Disneyland since 1955, the train in Ryman's drawing goes around the park counterclockwise, with several S-curves along the track.

3. In Ryman's drawing, a hot-air balloon is tethered high above Disneyland's center.

4. By far the tallest building in Ryman's drawing is the towering castle, which is surrounded by intimidating walls and fortifications. However, when Disneyland opened, Sleeping Beauty Castle was just one foot taller than the seventy-six-foot *Moonliner* rocket in Tomorrowland (Ryman's rocket in "World of Tomorrow" is only half the size of the castle).

5. The park's Center Street currently divides Main Street into separate retail blocks; in Ryman's drawing, West Center Street ends at a large church.

6. Ryman drew a large circus on the west side of Disneyland with two tents. The short-lived Mickey Mouse Club Circus opened on Disneyland's east side in November 1955.

7. Ryman's drawing depicts two big paddlewheelers, not one, circling a "Frontier Country" island.

8. Ryman's oval wilderness island in an area called "Frontier Country" is

marked "Mickey Mouse Club." In reality, Frontierland's island is elongated, runs north to south, and is called Tom Sawyer Island.

9. In Ryman's "Fantasy Land," the carousel is located in front of the castle (the south side) instead of behind it (the north side, where the King Arthur Carrousel has been since 1955).

10. Ryman's northeast section of Disneyland is dominated by several acres of "Lilliputian Land," an area that would have been filled with miniatures.

11. Ryman's northwest section of the park is dominated by largely undeveloped acreage with an entrance that says "Holiday Park" (called "Recreation Park" on the legend).

12. Ryman's southeast section (where today's Space Mountain is located) is marked "True-Life Adventureland" and includes a jungle boat ride, which was actually built in Disneyland's southwest corner (Adventureland).

A Dozen Dilemmas on "Black Sunday"

Disneyland's Opening Day, when the park welcomed its first invited guests and a national TV audience, has nearly always been declared a failure. That's certainly how it was reported by some of the press the next day. Walt Disney, ever the demanding perfectionist, even nicknamed it "Black Sunday." For decades, the troubles that occurred on July 17, 1955, have been well-chronicled, the park's early flaws and deficiencies well-documented, and the failure of Opening Day generally accepted.

Historic accounts of Opening Day often present such hyperbolic pronouncements as "anything that could go wrong did," "nothing was working," and "a disaster from start to finish"—none of which is actually true. Looking back, Opening Day had minor inconveniences, not major traumas. Glitches are not catastrophes: there was no riot, no natural disaster, no park-emptying pandemonium, and not a single significant injury. The crowds of guests and dozens of celebrities shown in the TV coverage are generally smiling, excited, and unaware of any crisis. Still, Disneyland was an unfinished, untried, unrehearsed idea, and it did have a few problems on Opening Day.

1. Out of plants, the park landscapers resorted to decorating existing weeds with little signs adorned with important-sounding Latin names.

2. Out of time, designers put the Rocket to the Moon and Casey Jr. Circus Train attractions on view, but not in operation.

3. Out of money, Walt Disney left Tomorrowland undone, its incompletion hidden behind a distraction of balloons and bunting.

4. Attendance that first sunny Sunday was supposed to be 10,000, and the invited guests—dignitaries, celebrities, reporters, Disney employees,

and Disneyland sponsors—all held special invitations with different entrance times so attendance would be staggered. However, many guests arrived early, supplemented by an additional 20,000 people who hoped to get in. Traffic was jammed for miles around.

5. A huge vanguard of unsolicited guests managed to enter the park, either by presenting counterfeit invitations or by sneaking over the berm. By mid-afternoon, the massive crowd was working its way up Main Street shoulder-to-shoulder before streaming off to the different lands.

6. With attendance suddenly tripled in size, the inexperienced cast members were immediately confronted with food and beverage shortages . . .

7. . . . and an inadequate number of restrooms . . .

8. . . . and not enough trash cans.

9. The intense summer heat caused some of the newly poured pavement to soften and trap the high heels of women who had dressed up for the event.

10. Attraction lines quickly filled up, and some rides either became overloaded with guests or stopped working altogether. At least one of the watercraft came close to calamity—the *Mark Twain* was so weighted down with extra guests that water splashed onto its tilting decks.

11. According to Disney Legend Van France's book, *Window on Main Street*, Sleeping Beauty Castle's doors were inadvertently left unlocked, allowing inquisitive guests to roam through the incomplete interior.

12. Compounding the inexperience of the cast members was the inexperience of the TV crews broadcasting the live coast-to-coast show. Nobody had ever televised anything so big, so spread out, and so complex before, and it showed. Cues were missed and stars missed their marks; occasionally no sound accompanied the visuals; and cameras caught activity not intended for television. During a year when the total U.S. population was only about 165 million, 90 million Americans tuned in to see a humorous, confusing, spontaneous (but non-catastrophic) TV spectacle of unprecedented proportions.

Lonnie Burr's Opening Day Mousekememories

To find out what Disneyland's Opening Day was really like, we asked someone who was actually there. As an original Mouseketeer, twelve-year-old Lonnie Burr (*page 42*) performed at Disneyland on July 17, 1955, along with Annette Funicello and all the other Mouseketeers. After staying with *The Mickey Mouse Club* show for its entire run on TV (1955–1959), Lonnie later earned his M.A. from UCLA, appeared in numerous TV shows, movies, and stage productions, became an acclaimed theater director and playwright, wrote a book about the great comedy teams, and recently updated his memoir, *The Accidental Mouseketeer*. Keep up with Lonnie at www.mouseketeerlonnieburr.com, aka "Mouseketeer Lonnie's Clubhouse."

1. **How did Walt Disney seem to you on Opening Day?**

   "He seemed to have a combination of moods and emotions that day—excited yet also calm, intense but also distracted. He did not say anything to us. There were too many things for him to worry about, like not having enough toilets."

2. **What was the mood backstage among the Mouseketeers before you were introduced on live TV?**

   "It was the first time the Mouseketeers had been on TV as a group, and there were butterflies in a few stomachs. I had done a lot of TV already, so for me it was not much of a problem. I did have to watch myself vis-à-vis Annie [Annette Funicello], since we had been in love since early on in the show. This is noted in her 1994 autobiography, in my recent memoir *The Accidental Mouseketeer*, and on talk shows *like Sally Jesse Raphael* in 1994. On our trips back and forth to Disneyland, Annie and I got to hold hands all the way down to Anaheim and home IN THE DARK!"

3. **How did the Mouseketeers entertain at Disneyland that day?**

   "We did the parade on Main Street and then did roll call at Fantasyland's Mickey Mouse Club Theatre [the *only* roll call that had *all* the Mice—twenty-four at the time], followed by a dance number. Some of us wore the usual short-sleeved turtlenecks, others wore the cowboy outfits that would be seen on the show's Friday 'Talent Round-Up.'"

4. **The crowd that greeted the Mouseketeers had never seen you all before. How did they react as you were all introduced?**

   "Everyone was smiling from ear to ear, if you'll forgive the hackneyed phrase. They were keen on waving in the parade and watching us dance live on TV."

5. **Many articles and books have described Opening Day as a total disaster—"Black Sunday." Were you aware of any problems elsewhere in the park?**

   "At the time, no; anyone with a brain does *not* tell performers about something bad that will not concern them and they could do nothing about. I doubt that most people were aware of any problems. I only became aware of the toilet problem years later, and didn't know about any of the other malfunctions. I think reporters sometimes look feverishly for *anything* they can find that is negative."

6. On Opening Day, did you get a chance to visit any attractions?
"No. We were working. After doing the first season of our TV show, we were part of the Mickey Mouse Club Circus behind Fantasyland from late November through January 10, 1956. Walt loved the circus, which is why there was (and still is) a carousel in Fantasyland. When we did the circus, we got to go on rides *with no lines* before Disneyland was open each day. My favorites were the Autopia cars that, with their 'governors' off, went fifteen miles per hour! My second favorite was the teacups, which spin independently from the already-spinning plate on the main revolving table, so you could be going three ways at once and make one of the other guys upchuck. This was not the girls' favorite ride."

7. As a kid, did you have any favorite foods or treats at Disneyland?
"Not really a favorite, but I did find myself in the Refreshment Corner on Main Street on occasion."

8. As a kid, what was your favorite thing to do at Disneyland?
"As mentioned above, it was fun to pass on the lines and go on those two rides. It was definitely *not* fun riding on the circus's camels and elephants, which have long, very stiff hair growing where you sit and piercing through your pants. Fortunately, those particular feats were rare and usually just for photos."

9. As you made visits in later years, what became your favorite attraction?
"Club 33, which is still my favorite thing at Disneyland."

10. Describe 1950s Disneyland in a single word or phrase.
"Uniquely happy and relaxing."

11. Describe today's Disneyland in a single word or phrase.
"Uniquely crowded and happy if you can take that; I cannot very often."

12. Many critics predicted that Disneyland would quickly fail. Why do you think it has thrived for so long?
"Many reasons. There is no other park like it; it is very clean, unlike a fair, circus, or carnival. The 'synergy' department does a great job of interlocking all of the films, TV, parks, merchandising and so on, making it unlike anything else for both kids *and* their parents. It harkens back to a time [the 1950s] when things were simpler and better, before there was the Internet and violence on TV and in films and everywhere else. You can go to Disneyland for a day or stay at their great hotels for longer, for a week. You can also go without kids and accomplish that same feeling, allowing yourself to be that 'inner child' and getting away from your problems, your neighbor's problems, the country's problems, and the world's problems. Who does not want a place like that to go to?"

Disneyland's Opening Day Attractions

For its Opening Day festivities on July 17, 1955, Disneyland had these seventeen attractions up and running (asterisks note those still in operation today).

Adventureland

1. Jungle Cruise*

Fantasyland

2. Canal Boats of the World
3. King Arthur Carrousel*
4. Mad Hatter's Mad Tea Party*
5. Mr. Toad's Wild Ride*
6. Peter Pan Flight*
   (now Peter Pan's Flight)
7. Snow White Adventures*
   (now Snow White's Scary Adventures)

Frontierland

8. *Golden Horseshoe Revue*
9. *Mark Twain* Riverboat*
10. Mule Pack
11. Stage Coach

Main Street

12. Main Street Cinema*
13. Main Street Vehicles*
14. Santa Fe & Disneyland Railroad
    (now the Disneyland Railroad)*

Tomorrowland

15. Autopia*
16. Hall of Chemistry
17. Space Station X-1

111 Disneyland Debuts After Opening Day

"Disneyland will never be completed," said Walt Disney. He began to prove this statement on July 18, 1955, one day after the nationally televised opening. Disneyland has continued to evolve ever since.

1955 July: Circarama theater, Rocket to the Moon (Tomorrowland); Casey Jr. Circus Train (Fantasyland)

August: Conestoga Wagons (Frontierland); 20,000 Leagues Under the Sea Exhibit, Phantom Boats (Tomorrowland); Dumbo the Flying Elephant, Mickey Mouse Club Theater, Pirate Ship Restaurant (Fantasyland)

September: Flight Circle (Tomorrowland)

October: A-B-C ticket books

December: Mike Fink Keel Boats (Frontierland)

1956 March: Astro-Jets (Tomorrowland)

June: Tom Sawyer Island (Frontierland); Storybook Land Canal

Boats (Fantasyland); Skyway (Fantasyland and Tomorrowland)

July: Mine Train, Indian War Canoes (Frontierland); Junior Autopia (Fantasyland)

1957 April: Sleeping Beauty Castle Walk-Through (Fantasyland)

June: Motor Boat Cruise (Fantasyland); House of the Future (Tomorrowland); Holidayland (near Frontierland)

July: Frontierland Shooting Gallery (Frontierland)

December: First New Year's Eve Party

1958 March: Grand Canyon Diorama (near Tomorrowland)

April: Midget Autopia (Fantasyland)

June: Alice in Wonderland (Fantasyland); Sailing Ship Columbia (Frontierland); Viewliner (Tomorrowland)

December: First Candlelight Procession

1959 January: Fantasyland Autopia (Fantasyland)

June: Matterhorn Bobsleds, Monorail, Submarine Voyage (Tomorrowland)

1960 May: Western Mine Train Through Nature's Wonderland (Frontierland)

June: Pack Mules Through Nature's Wonderland (Frontierland)

December: Skull Rock (Fantasyland)

1961 June: First Grad Nite

August: Flying Saucers (Tomorrowland)

December: Babes in Toyland Exhibit (Town Square)

1962 June: Big Game Safari Shooting Gallery (Adventureland)

November: Swiss Family Treehouse (Adventureland)

1963 June: Enchanted Tiki Room (Adventureland)

1965 July: Great Moments with Mr. Lincoln (Town Square)

1966 May: It's a Small World (Fantasyland)

July: Primeval World (near Tomorrowland); New Orleans Square

1967 March: Pirates of the Caribbean, Blue Bayou (New Orleans Square)

July: PeopleMover, Carousel of Progress, Rocket Jets, Tomorrowland Terrace (all in the newly remodeled Tomorrowland)

August: Adventure Thru Inner Space (Tomorrowland)

1969 August: The Haunted Mansion (New Orleans Square)

1970 January: Legacy of Walt Disney (Town Square)

1972 March: Country Bear Jamboree and the new Bear Country

June: Main Street Electrical Parade

1973 April: Disneyland Presents a Preview of Coming Attractions (Main Street); The Walt Disney Story (Town Square)

1974 June: America Sings (Tomorrowland)

1975 March: Mission to Mars (Tomorrowland)

June: The Walt Disney Story Featuring Great Moments with Mr. Lincoln (Town Square)

1977 May: Space Mountain (Tomorrowland)

1979 September: Big Thunder Mountain Railroad (Frontierland)

1983 May: Pinocchio's Daring Journey (in the newly remodeled Fantasyland)

1985 May: Magic E96ye Theater (Tomorrowland)

June: Videopolis (Fantasyland)

1986 June: Big Thunder Ranch (Frontierland)

September: *Captain EO* (Tomorrowland)

1987 January: Star Tours (Tomorrowland)

July: Disney Gallery (New Orleans Square)

1988 November: Critter Country

1989 July: Splash Mountain (Critter Country)

1991 March: Disney Afternoon Avenue (Fantasyland)

1992 May: Fantasmic! (Frontierland)

1993 January: Fantasia Gardens (Fantasyland); Chip 'n Dale Tree House, Donald's Boat, Gadget's Go Coaster, Goofy's Bounce House, Jolly Trolley, Mickey's House, Minnie's House (all in the new Mickey's Toontown)

July: Aladdin's Oasis (Adventureland)

November: *Partners* (Hub)

1994 January: Roger Rabbit's Car Toon Spin (Mickey's Toontown)

1995 March: Indiana Jones Adventure (Adventureland)

1996 January: Toy Story Funhouse (Tomorrowland)

1998 May: Astro-Orbitor, Observatron, Rocket Rods, and *Honey, I Shrunk the Audience* (all in the newly remodeled Tomorrowland)

July: Innoventions (Tomorrowland)

1999 June: Tarzan's Treehouse (Adventureland)

November: FASTPASS tickets

2003 April: Many Adventures of Winnie the Pooh (Critter Country)

2005 March: Buzz Lightyear Astro Blasters (Tomorrowland)

2006 September: Halloween Time

2007 May: Pirate's Lair on Tom Sawyer Island (Frontierland)

June: Finding Nemo Submarine Voyage (Tomorrowland)

2008 October: Pixie Hollow (Hub)

2010 October: Tangled (Fantasyland)

2011 June: Star Tours: The Adventures Continue (Tomorrowland)

2013 March: Fantasy Faire (Hub)

A Dozen Key Years
for New Lands and Attractions

After opening in 1955, Disneyland has steadily added new lands and attractions. Here are a dozen key years in which there was a significant surge in the park's list of attractions.

1. 1956: This was a busy year construction-wise, as the Astro-Jets, Indian War Canoes, Junior Autopia, Mine Train, Skyway, Storybook Land Canal Boats, and Tom Sawyer Island all opened.

2. 1959: "E tickets" joined the ticket books, and major new attractions opened in the park—the Fantasyland Autopia, Matterhorn Mountain (with its Matterhorn Bobsleds), the Monorail, and the Submarine Voyage.

3. 1960: Fantasyland welcomed Skull Rock and Pirate's Cove as dramatic new backdrops, and Frontierland got a makeover with its much-publicized Nature's Wonderland (replaced by the Big Thunder Mountain Railroad in 1979).

4. 1966: It's a Small World, the Primeval World Diorama, and New Orleans Square (the park's first new land) all debuted.

5. 1967: After Pirates of the Caribbean debuted in March, a remodeled Tomorrowland opened over the summer, bringing with it Adventure Thru Inner Space, the Carousel of Progress, the PeopleMover, and more.

6. 1969: Only one major new attraction opened this year, but it was a doozy—the eagerly anticipated Haunted Mansion.

7. 1972: Debuts of the long-running Main Street Electrical Parade and another new land, Bear Country (with its Country Bear Jamboree).

8. 1977: Space Mountain took over a big corner of Tomorrowland.

9. 1983: A dramatically remodeled Fantasyland showed off enchanting architecture and a new attraction, Pinocchio's Daring Journey.

10. 1989: Splash Mountain added a new peak to Critter Country, which had opened late in 1988 as a reinvention of Bear Country.

11. 1993: In this toontastic year, Mickey's Toontown expanded the park northward with many new attractions; elsewhere, Aladdin's Oasis (Adventureland) and the *Partners* statue (Hub) debuted.

12. 1998: Tomorrowland got a major facelift and new attractions, including the Astro-Orbitor, *Honey, I Shrunk the Audience*, Innoventions, and Rocket Rods.

A Dozen Attractions and Exhibits That Permanently Closed Within 1 Year of Debuting

Walt Disney wasn't afraid of risk and failure. "You do big things, you make big mistakes," he says in Van France's *Window on Main Street*. Thus, as magical as it usually is and as perfect as it often seems, Disneyland hasn't had an unbroken streak of successes. Some ideas just didn't work out and were either pulled or completed remodeled soon after opening; a few others were probably never intended to enjoy a long run in the park, and they clearly fulfilled that expectation. Whatever the reason, to the following attractions and exhibits (listed in order from shortest duration to longest) we sang, "So here's goodbye so soon," just like in *The Great Mouse Detective*.

1. Two months: Mickey Mouse Club Circus
   Extremely low attendance drove out this tented Fantasyland circus soon after its November 1955 opening.

2. Two months: Dalmatian Celebration
To promote Disney's live-action version of *One Hundred and One Dalmatians*, this Town Square exhibit enabled guests to get their faces painted, meet Cruella De Vil, and see some puppies from November 1996 to January 1997.

3. Three months: Canal Boats of the World
Opened in July 1955, this attraction took riders past un-landscaped dirt banks before it was completely remodeled into the long-running Storybook Land Canal Boats.

4. Four months: Light Magic
This "street spectacular" was the expensive successor to the Main Street Electrical Parade, but a disappointing debut in May 1997 preceded "lights out" at the end of the summer.

5. Four months: Davy Crockett Frontier Museum
Opened in July 1955, this Frontierland building capitalized on TV's Davy Crockett craze with displays and exhibits, but by October it had transformed into the Davy Crockett Arcade.

6. Five months: Phantom Boats
These troublesome "speedboats" cruised Tomorrowland's lagoon from August 1955 to January 1956 (they briefly reappeared in mid-1956).

7. Five months: Toy Story Funhouse
With *Toy Story* a hit in theaters, guests explored this interactive Tomorrowland exhibit from January to May 1996.

8. Six months: Disney Afternoon Avenue
From March to September 1991, characters from the *Disney Afternoon* TV series met with guests in cartoony structures near It's a Small World.

9. Seven months: Keller's Jungle Killers
When the Mickey Mouse Club Circus left in early 1956, this trained animal act featuring sedated jungle cats remained in Fantasyland until September.

10. Eight months: Court of Honor
Opened in July 1955 and closed the following March, this "court" was a display of state flags in the Tomorrowland plaza, west of today's Innoventions.

11. Nine months: Fashions and Fabrics Through the Ages
From March to December 1965, this odd exhibit brought the history of fashion to Tomorrowland.

12. Twelve months: Marshal's Office
Opened in July 1955 and lasting for just a year, this small structure was used mostly for photo ops.

The Dozen Oldest Attractions to Be Retired

"Disneyland will never be completed," according to Walt Disney; "life is flux," according to Heraclitus; "I can't go back to where I used to be," according to Jasmine's "A Whole New World" song in *Aladdin*. Hence, even the following venerable classics, listed with the oldest first, were finally retired after serving lengthy runs in the park.

1. The Circarama/Circle-Vision theater, a Tomorrowland staple for forty-two years (1955–1997), was located in the circular building now occupied by Buzz Lightyear Astro Blasters.

2. Tomorrowland's original Autopia was so popular that a Fantasyland Autopia was added in 1959. It lasted for forty years, until the land was used to expand the Tomorrowland version.

3. After a splashy 1959 debut, the classic Submarine Voyage was sinking in popularity when it was retired in 1998 after thirty-nine years. The attraction resurfaced in 2007 as the Finding Nemo Submarine Voyage.

4. Great Moments with Mr. Lincoln opened in Town Square in 1965, and was temporarily retired in 1973. Insistent fans demanded the return of the landmark Audio-Animatronic attraction, spurring its re-opening two years later. Mr. Lincoln performed until what seemed like a permanent retirement in 2005 after thirty-eight years; however, four years later, Mr. Lincoln came back. He's still going strong today.

5. The Skyway running between Fantasyland and Tomorrowland offered spectacular aerial views, but a desire to remove its tall towers as well as concerns about falling objects (and falling guests) led to its 1994 removal after thirty-eight years.

6. The opening of the Swiss Family Treehouse in 1962 saluted a beloved Disney movie; however, after thirty-seven years, that reference seemed dated. With *Tarzan* a box-office hit, the animated jungle hero moved into the treehouse in 1999.

7. For thirty-six years (1957–1993), the Motor Boat Cruise was a gentle boat ride on a submerged track through Fantasyland waters. Today, the boats are gone, but the loading dock still exists as a pleasant sitting area.

8. The *Golden Horseshoe Revue* was the original show in Frontierland's beautiful saloon; after thirty-one years of performances by its popular stars and fetching can-can dancers, the *Revue* finally closed in 1986.

9. Rocket Jets zoomed high above the heart of Tomorrowland starting in 1967. Thirty years later they returned to Earth, and the Astro-Orbitor (now at Tomorrowland's entrance) became the new spinning attraction.

10. The Country Bear Jamboree (and various versions of the ursine show) played in Bear Country for twenty-nine years (1972–2001), until Many

Adventures of Winnie the Pooh moved in (*right*).

11. PeopleMover trains gave Disneyland guests quiet, scenic tours of Tomorrowland for twenty-eight years (1967–1995). Today, the graceful tracks remain as tantalizing reminders of one of Disneyland's most splendid and efficient transportation systems.

12. For twenty-one years (1956–1977), Mine Train cars gave slow but fun looks at imaginatively developed Frontierland acreage. The need to please a thrill-hungry audience with a rowdy roller coaster led to the installation of the Big Thunder Mountain Railroad in this area.

Gone/Not Gone: A Dozen Locations That Closed "Permanently" But Later Returned

Just when we thought they were gone, back they came! These twelve attractions, shops, and eateries all closed "permanently" (not just for a remodeling), but reopened later in the same location with essentially the same names.

1. Arts and Crafts Shop (Fantasyland): ca. 1958–ca. 1963; ca. 1970–1982

2. Briar Patch (Critter Country): 1988–1996; 1996–ongoing

3. *Captain EO*; *Captain EO* Tribute (Tomorrowland): 1986–1997; 2010–2014

4. Fantasyland Theatre (Fantasyland): 1995–2006; 2013–ongoing

5. Flower Mart/Flower Market (Main Street): 1957–1995; 2013–2014 (the twenty-first-century flowers were not for sale)

6. Great Moments with Mr. Lincoln (Town Square): 1965–1973; 1975–2005; 2009–ongoing

7. L'Ornement Magique (New Orleans Square): 1998–February 2012; November 2012–October 2013

8. Mlle. Antoinette's Parfumerie (*above right*) (New Orleans Square): 1967 1997; 2011 ongoing

9. Phantom Boats (Tomorrowland): August 1955–January 1956; July 1956–October 1956

10. Sleeping Beauty Castle Walk-Through
    (Fantasyland): 1957–2001; 2008–ongoing

11. Submarine Voyage/Finding Nemo Submarine Voyage (Tomorrowland):
    1959–1998; 2007–ongoing

12. Town Square Café (Town Square): 1976–1978; 1983–1992

13 Never-Built Areas and Attractions

Many never-built attractions have been announced as "coming soon." Some
have even been shown on the poster-size maps sold in Disneyland, seemingly cementing them as real developments in specific locations. However,
none of the following ideas actually came to fruition.

1. Airboats: To replace 1955's troublesome Phantom Boats (mechanical nightmares that continually broke down throughout their first six
   months in Tomorrowland's lagoon), new boats styled after the shal-
   low-draft, propeller-driven boats used in the Everglades were advertised as an exciting new attraction coming in June 1956. One boat was
   even built and successfully tested, but concerns about high speeds and
   that big dangerous propeller scuttled the plans, so the Phantom Boats
   were brought back to lurch through one more summer.

2. Botanical Garden: Very early in the Disneyland planning process, Walt
   Disney considered building a botanical garden in "True-Life Adventureland" on the southeast side of the Hub, where Space Mountain is
   located today (Adventureland was eventually built on the *southwest* side
   of the Hub).

3. Discovery Bay: Planned in the 1970s, a new body of water was to be
   constructed between Fantasyland and Frontierland, possibly in the
   area that became Big Thunder Mountain. Small waterfront buildings
   would have evoked the spirit of the nineteenth-century Barbary Coast,
   a half-submerged *Nautilus* (from *20,000 Leagues Under the Sea*) might have
   been a restaurant, and a giant hangar with the sleek airship *Hyperion*
   (from *Island at the Top of the World*) looked to be some kind of attraction
   or exhibit.

4. Duck Bumps: Concept drawings in the 1950s showed a new watery attraction for Fantasyland with boats and "bumper-car" maneuvering.
   Adjacent to this attraction was a twenty-foot windmill called *The Old Mill*
   (in reference to the 1937 Disney cartoon).

5. Dumbo's Circusland: This five-acre circus-themed area near It's a Small
   World was discussed in the 1970s. Plans included a thrilling indoor attraction called Mickey's Madhouse and a fountain featuring the wacky
   firemen from *Dumbo*.

6. Edison Square: Had it been built in the late 1950s/early 1960s, this Thomas Edison-themed area at the north end of Main Street would have headed eastward toward Tomorrowland. A series of theaters (designed to look like old-fashioned homes) populated with Audio-Animatronic figures would have displayed decades of technological advancements (as with the Carousel of Progress, opened in 1967).

7. Garden of the Gods: Hoping to enhance Fantasyland's slow-moving Motor Boat Cruise, in the 1960s Disney designers considered adding pastoral design elements from the movie *Fantasia*, including Olympian sculptures, peaceful fountains, boats shaped like swans, rail cars that looked like steeds, and the movie's classical music.

8. International Street: Announced in the 1950s and shown on early poster-sized Fun Maps, this ambitious area alongside Main Street's eastern blocks would have offered architecture and shops inspired by a half-dozen countries. When enthusiasm waned, a patriotic replacement, Liberty Street, was announced in 1958 with a sign in Town Square. Liberty Street culminated in a cobblestone cul-de-sac called Liberty Square, a quaint area echoing American colonies of the 1700s. Themed shops and a blacksmith would have joined Liberty Hall, the Hall of Presidents, the Declaration of Independence Diorama, and other historical exhibits.

9. Lilliputian Land: Long before the Storybook Land Canal Boats cruised past tiny buildings, Walt Disney wanted to devote an entire land to miniatures. Named after the *Gulliver's Travels* kingdom, Disney's Lilliputian Land was shown on several 1953 concept drawings as a 2.5-acre rounded triangle sandwiched between Fantasyland and Tomorrowland. The area included a curving track for a small railroad, a winding river for boats, and plenty of small hills and trees. When plans expanded to include mechanical figures, Walt Disney realized the requisite Audio-Animatronic technology was still years away, so Lilliputian Land was tabled. Within five years, some of its acreage would be occupied by the Matterhorn, the Submarine Voyage, and the Fantasyland Autopia.

10. Paul Bunyan's Boot: In January 1956, Walt Disney mentioned to a merchant's group something he called Paul Bunyan's Boot, a twenty-five-foot-tall Frontierland structure that he claimed would open in the late 1950s.

11. Peter Pan Crocodile Aquarium: If Bruce Bushman's concept art had made it off the drawing table, a large aquarium with a *Peter Pan* theme would have been built in Fantasyland, possibly in the King Arthur Carrousel courtyard or in the open area where the Matterhorn is located. Bushman's 1953 drawings for the Peter Pan Crocodile Aquarium depicted a giant crocodile stretched out in a pool, with the croc's head and tail protruding from the surface. After walking through its gaping jaws and down below the waterline, guests would have entered an aquarium area with live fish swimming behind large windows.

12. Reel-Ride: If the intriguing legend is accurate, Willis O'Brien, the wizard behind the stop-motion special effects for *King Kong*, drew the concept art for a Frontierland attraction called the Reel-Ride. As shown in a 2006 museum exhibition called *Behind the Magic: 50 Years of Disneyland*, a color illustration (purportedly O'Brien's) depicted ten kids on mechanical horses facing a movie screen. The young buckaroos would have ridden their horses while a rollicking movie of a mounted cowboy star rolled in front of them. Had it been constructed, the three-to-five-minute Reel-Ride might have been the world's first melding of film, motion-simulation, and an amusement-park attraction (making it a precursor of Star Tours).

13. Rock Candy Mountain, aka Candy Mountain: The Burl Ives ballad "Big Rock Candy Mountain" was a 1949 hit, so the idea of an abundantly sweet wonderland was still fresh when Disney designers began drawing concept illustrations in the early 1950s. Although the project gathered momentum late in the decade and was worked on by several Disney Legends, ultimately no mountain of candy ever materialized. It would have been incorporated into the Storybook Land Canal Boats attraction, where the boats would have entered the mountain's caverns and wound past scenes from a new Disney movie based on one of L. Frank Baum's many *Wizard of Oz* sequels (not to be confused with the 1939 Judy Garland classic). The mountain's six-story exterior was originally going to be transparent, but was later revised to carry a thick coating of artificial candy canes, gumballs, lollipops, and more, with the Casey Jr. Circus Train wrapping around the base. When Disney's plans for an Oz movie plans collapsed, so did plans for the mountain.

33 Remaining Signs and Structures from Disneyland's Past

In recent years, these thirty-three locations have reminded guests of things that used to be in Disneyland.

1. Adventureland Bazaar: As noted in Jeff Kurtti's *Walt Disney's Imagineering Legends and the Genesis of the Disney Theme Park*, "Victorian posts from the long-demolished Swift Chicken Plantation restaurant" (1955–1962) still stand in the Bazaar's back corner closest to the Enchanted Tiki Room.

2. Alice in Wonderland: Fantasyland still has several structures that used to be ticket booths. One of these is the giant mushroom underneath the

big book (*right*) at the Alice in Wonderland attraction (the lighthouse at the nearby Storybook Land Canal Boats is also a former ticket booth).

3. Along the Autopia road, drivers will see a small bronze-colored car (*below left*) on their right-hand side that once belonged to the Midget Autopia (1957–1966).

4. Bibbidi Bobbidi Boutique: The wood carvings in front of the boutique depict characters from *Peter Pan*, a reminder of the Tinker Bell Toy Shoppe formerly at this location.

5. Big Thunder Mountain Railroad: Up until 2010, a derelict engine and some cars from the old Mine Train (1956–1977) were crashed near the Rivers of America (*below right*).

6. Casey Jr. Circus Train: Two decades after it closed, the Fantasyland terminal of the old Skyway (1956–1994) still stood, unused and hidden by trees, near the Casey Jr. Circus Train.

7. Emporium: Formerly located in the northern corner of the Emporium behind the old Upjohn Pharmacy, the Story Book Shop sold comics, picture books, and Disneyland's pictorial souvenir books; today, a conspicuous sign on the shelf still shows the Book Shop name (though the area is now for toys).

8. Fairytale Arts: Next to this spot by Matterhorn Mountain is a quiet dock that was once the loading area for the gentle Motor Boat Cruise (1957–1993).

9. Fantasy Faire: The Plaza Gardens/Carnation Plaza Gardens, which was here from 1955 to 2012, is represented with a CPG symbol on a rooftop spire.

10. Fire Department: The beautifully appointed horse-drawn Fire Engine

was one of the original Main Street Vehicles, but it was withdrawn from service in mid-1960 and permanently parked inside the Fire Department, where it's still on view.

11. Fortuosity Shop: Main Street Tribute Windows identify important people from Disneyland's history, but two of the Fortuosity Shop's windows also identify an extinct location. W. F. Allen, D. S. Gilmore, C. V. Patterson, and E. G. Upjohn, all former Upjohn executives, are identified on windows of this corner building that used to be the Upjohn Pharmacy.

12. The Haunted Mansion: In the ballroom, a ghost plays the pipe organ that formerly sat inside Tomorrowland's 20,000 Leagues Under the Sea Exhibit (1955–1966).

13. Indiana Jones Adventure: Up by the projector in Indy's queue area is a hard-to-detect sign that shows Eeyore—a leftover marker from the massive parking lot that spread in front of Disneyland until 1998.

14. Innoventions: Occasionally the banners hanging outside the building spotlight extinct Tomorrowland attractions.

15. Innoventions: Images painted on the side of the building have sometimes shown the Clock of the World (1955–1966), the old Bandstand (*below left*) (1955–1962), and the House of the Future (1957–1967). Inside, a model of the House of the Future has been used as a table.

16. Jolly Trolley: No longer running, the bouncy Jolly Trolley (*below middle*) now sits quietly in the heart of Mickey's Toontown.

17. La Mascarade d'Orleans: An exterior mural identifies the Marché aux Fleurs, Sacs et Mode shop that was here from the mid-1970s to the mid-1980s.

18. Little Green Men Store Command: Several of the vertical display cases

are repainted rockets (*opposite, bottom right*) formerly used in Tomorrow-land's Rocket Jets attraction (1967–1997).

19. Many Adventures of Winnie the Pooh: The heads of Max the deer, Melvin the moose, and Buff the buffalo, performers in the old Country Bear Jamboree/Country Bear Playhouse (1972–2001), are still mounted on a darkened wall just past the Woozles inside today's Winnie the Pooh attraction (*above left*).

20. Pieces of Eight: Fortune Red, the fortune-telling arcade machine just outside today's Pieces of Eight, is a hold-over from the Pirate's Arcade Museum that was here from 1967–1980.

21. Pooh Corner: Painted on an exterior second-story wall are the words "Teddi Barra's Swingin' Arcade," naming a former attraction located in this building from 1972 to 2002.

22. Rancho del Zocalo Restaurante: The "*mi casa es su casa*" sign (*above right*) at the front of this Frontierland restaurant honors Casa Mexicana, a popular restaurant located here until 2001.

23. Rancho del Zocalo Restaurante: A window behind this restaurant identifies a fondly remembered store and exhibit space called the Mineral Hall (1956–1962).

24. Rancho del Zocalo Restaurante: One wall by the Big Thunder Mountain Railroad tracks is painted with text announcing "Pack Mules Bought, Sold & Traded"—a reference to an extinct attraction once based in this location.

25. Space Mountain: "DL 05"—presumably a reference to Disneyland's fiftieth anniversary in 2005 (and the year of a huge update to Space Mountain)—is painted on both sides of the queue area's giant spaceship.

26. Splash Mountain: Many of the Audio-Animatronic animals in this attraction first appeared in America Sings, a Tomorrowland musical extravaganza from 1974 to 1988.

27. Star Tours: Armatures of several robotic geese from America Sings were transformed into high-tech droids for the queue leading into Star Tours.

28. Tarzan's Treehouse: A gramophone plays the "Swisskapolka" song used in the *Swiss Family Robinson* movie and the Swiss Family Treehouse (1962–1999).

29. Tomorrowland: A stark reminder of a beloved attraction, the unused track of the classic PeopleMover (1967–1995) still weaves through Tomorrowland.

30. Tom Sawyer Island: Parked at the north end of the island since 2010 is a leftover boat from the Mike Fink Keel Boats attraction (1955–1997).

31. Tom Sawyer Island: Still standing on the island are two conspicuous structures that guests used to explore—a rebuilt Fort Wilderness (closed to guests for over a decade) and Tom & Huck's Treehouse (sealed off since 2013, ostensibly for safety concerns).

32. 20th Century Music Company: A traditional cigar-store Indian (*near right*) has been standing in front of this shop since it was called Fine Tobacco (1955–1990).

33. Village Haus: A Geppetto mural (*far right*) inside this Fantasyland restaurant recognizes Geppetto's Arts & Crafts, an extinct shop from the 1980s.

The New Tomorrowland of 1967

One of the most fondly remembered summers in Disneyland history was in 1967, with the debut of an expensively remodeled Tomorrowland. The individual elements (listed alphabetically below) didn't open simultaneously, but by mid-August everything was up and running in Disneyland's exciting new "world on the move." They joined some familiar Tomorrowland landmarks already in existence, including the House of the Future, Monorail, Skyway, and Submarine Voyage. All of this, by the way, directly followed the opening of the Pirates of the Caribbean in March, making 1967 one of the park's most ambitious years ever.

1. **Adventure Thru Inner Space:** Located where Star Tours is now, this imaginative attraction toured the atomic realm.

2. **Autopia:** Tomorrowland's Autopia had originally opened in 1955, but in 1967 it got a big upgrade—new Mark VII cars that were, at over $5,000 apiece, the most expensive Autopia cars yet (by comparison, guests could have bought two brand-new, full-size Ford Mustangs for that price). Looking like little Corvette Stingrays, these sturdy vehicles rode the track until 1999.

3. **Carousel of Progress:** Today's Innoventions used to be the Carousel of Progress, which presented a revolving tour of innovations in electricity.

4. **Character Shop:** Opening next to Adventure Thru Inner Space was one of Disneyland's largest stores, a must-visit for guests searching for Disney-themed clothes, futuristic gifts, and, surprisingly, stuffed animals.

5. **Circle-Vision 360:** The theater formerly called Circarama and Circle-Vision got a makeover that included a new name, a new and improved version of its film, *America the Beautiful*, and a new pre-show area.

6. **Corridor of Murals:** Huge tiled mosaics were added to the two large, curving Tomorrowland buildings that still face each other today. Created by Mary Blair, one of the principal designers behind It's a Small World, the work was called *The Spirit of Creative Energies Among Children* and depicted frolicking children in international garb.

7. **Flight to the Moon:** The original Rocket to the Moon got a huge makeover, including new special effects and a sophisticated new pre-flight area.

8. **Mod Hatter:** The Mad Hatter of Tomorrowland got remodeled into the hip Mod Hatter, with a new location near the Carousel of Progress.

9. **PeopleMover:** "Tomorrow's transportation . . . today" was the slogan for this futuristic new system of ramps and quiet little trains that took guests on leisurely scenic tours above Tomorrowland and through some of the buildings.

10. **Rocket Jets:** The old Astro Jets/Tomorrowland Jets got dramatic new styling (echoing Apollo rockets) and a new home above the PeopleMover's loading platform.

11. **Tomorrowland Stage:** A big stage for big shows, this new structure was built where the Flying Saucers had been (and where Space Mountain now sits) and could seat over a thousand guests in an outdoor setting.

12. **Tomorrowland Terrace:** Guests didn't know what to expect when they first saw this abstract sculpture sitting out in the open. Its purpose became clear, however, once the subterranean stage rose out of the ground with a pop group already playing.

A Dozen Changes to Make Way for the New Tomorrowland of 1967

To make room for all the changes in the previous list, a few things had to go.

1. Avenue of the Flags: This 150-foot-long, flag-lined walkway into Tomorrowland was replaced by beautiful landscaping and a futuristic aluminum entrance.

2. Art of Animation: This exhibit space was lost when the Circle-Vision theater expanded and became the larger Circle-Vision 360.

3. Clock of the World: The tall clock with a world map stood near the new entrance and PeopleMover ramps.

4. Flight Circle: This seventy-five-foot-wide circle for model airplanes was replaced by a walkway and the PeopleMover's loading platform.

5. Flying Saucers: The outdoor Tomorrowland Stage took over this large space.

6. Hobbyland: The outdoor sales tables with model kits were replaced by a walkway and the PeopleMover's loading platform.

7. *Moonliner*: This iconic symbol was removed when the expanded Flight to the Moon replaced the old Rocket to the Moon attraction.

8. Rocket to the Moon: Flight to the Moon updated and expanded upon the Rocket to the Moon concept.

9. Space Bar: When the huge Carousel Theater (with the Carousel of Progress) was built, this large restaurant with its own dance area shrank to a mere snack stand located under the PeopleMover's loading platform.

10. Tomorrowland Jets: In 1967, this whirling attraction got a new theme and a new name—the Rocket Jets, with a new location on top of the PeopleMover's loading platform.

11. 20,000 Leagues Under the Sea: The building containing these movie sets and props was thoroughly remodeled for Adventure Thru Inner Space.

12. Yacht Bar: This free-standing counter-service eatery was in the general location of the new Tomorrowland Terrace.

The New Tomorrowland of 1998

After a "New Tomorrowland" was introduced in 1967, the next "New Tomorrowland" ("New New Tomorrowland"?) arrived in 1998, featuring bronze and green paint, edible landscaping, and these ten alphabetically listed attractions.

1. American Space Experience: NASA sponsored this space exhibit, located near the Rocket Rods.

2. Astro-Orbitor: This eye-catching attraction—equal parts kinetic sculpture and whirling ride—stands at Tomorrowland's entrance.

3. Cosmic Waves: An interactive fountain near Innoventions probably seemed like a good idea until someone had to deal with all the soaking-wet kids. The big stone ball can still be taken for a spin.

4. *Honey, I Shrunk the Audience*: This new 3-D movie with Rick Moranis and Eric Idle replaced *Captain EO*.

5. Innoventions: This import from Walt Disney World brought ever-changing edutainment to the revolving Carousel Theater.

6. *Moonliner*: The seventy-six-foot-tall rocket—a Tomorrowland icon from 1955 to 1966—reappeared in 1998 at two-thirds the size.

7. Observatron: The mechanized jumble atop the old PeopleMover loading platform was once a spinning timepiece, but most days it sits inert like a collapsed spacecraft.

8. Redd Rockett's Pizza Port: This new restaurant took over the Mission to Mars building.

9. Rocket Rods: A famous disappointment, this high-speed ride on the PeopleMover tracks was so jarring and undependable that it closed after two years.

10. Spirit of Refreshment: This beverage stand underneath the revived *Moonliner* shares the same red-and-white livery as its sponsor, Coca-Cola.

7 Changes to Make Way for the New Tomorrowland of 1998

To make room for all the changes in the previous list, a few things had to go.

1. America Sings: After this patriotic show closed in 1988, offices filled some of the Carousel Theater until Innoventions arrived in 1998.

2. *Captain EO*: Michael Jackson's movie enjoyed a long run from 1986 to 1997, until *Honey, I Shrunk the Audience* took over. In 2010, however, the *Captain EO* Tribute opened, much to the delight of its nostalgic fans.

3. Circle-Vision: This prominent theater underwent several name changes before it was replaced by Rocket Rods.

4. PeopleMover: The graceful tracks of this attraction were used by the short-lived Rocket Rods.

5. Rocket Jets: The whirling jets atop the PeopleMover's loading platform were replaced by the futuristic Observatron device.

6. Submarine Voyage: The classic subs were retired to make room for Tomorrowland, but they returned in 2007.

7. Toy Story Funhouse: Redd Rockett's Pizza Port, the newer and smaller *Moonliner*, and the Spirit of Refreshment took over the space formerly occupied by a temporary *Toy Story* exhibit and the old Mission to Mars.

The New Fantasyland of 1983

In 1983, a massive two-year, $50-million remodel transformed the heart of Fantasyland. Here are ten of the many changes.

1. Eliminated: The Fantasyland Theatre, Merlin's Magic Shop, the Pirate Ship Restaurant, and Skull Rock.

2. Relocated: Dumbo the Flying Elephant, from the western corner of Fantasyland towards the center; the Mad Hatter's Mad Tea Party, from the castle courtyard to the Alice in Wonderland area; and the King Arthur Carrousel, away from the castle by about sixty feet.

3. Replaced: The old "medieval tournament" exterior façades, with new architecture corresponding to each attraction (for instance, the exterior of Mr. Toad's Wild Ride really looked like Toad's English manor).

4. Returned: A flying Tinker Bell in the fireworks shows, after a six-year absence.

5. Updated with new technology and characters: Mr. Toad's Wild Ride, Snow White's Adventures, Peter Pan's Flight, and Alice in Wonderland.

6. New attraction: Pinocchio's Daring Journey.

7. New entertainment: The Sword in the Stone Ceremony.

8. New restaurant: The Village Inn (now the Village Haus), replacing the quick-snack eateries in Fantasyland's western corner.

9. New shops: Geppetto's Arts & Crafts opened next to Pinocchio's Daring Journey, and Mickey's Christmas Chalet filled Merlin's Magic Shop.

10. New carts: Stromboli's Wagon and Carrousel Candies.

50 Disneyland Acronyms and Initials

Listed alphabetically, here are fifty acronyms and initials relating to the park.

1. AAA: The American Automobile Association's Touring and Travel Services Center kiosk in Town Square offered maps, free towing, and flat tire repair.

2. **ABC:** The American Broadcasting Company gave Walt Disney a loan towards Disneyland's construction and enabled him to promote the park via a weekly *Disneyland* TV series.

3. **AED:** Locations for sixteen automated external defibrillators are indicated on the free maps available at the turnstiles.

4. **Alweg:** Named after the initials of its founder, Dr. Axel Lennart Wenner-Gren, Alweg is a design company Walt Disney hired to construct a new, streamlined Monorail, after Disney saw an Alweg monorail train running on a test track near Cologne while on vacation in 1957.

5. **AMC:** The American Motors Corporation sponsored Tomorrowland's Circarama theater from 1955 to 1960 (AMC cars were displayed in the exhibit area).

6. **ASIMO:** Designed by Honda, Innoventions' humanoid robot's name stands for "Advanced Step in Innovative Mobility."

7. **ATM:** Guests have been able to get cash at automated teller machines, located near the entrance and in Town Square, Fantasyland, Frontierland, and Tomorrowland.

8. **AT&T:** In the 1970s, American Telephone & Telegraph presented *America the Beautiful* inside Tomorrowland's Circle-Vision 360 theater. Two decades later, AT&T created decoder cards for the "Maraglyphics" inside the Indiana Jones Adventure tunnels. In 2013, AT&T became Disneyland's "official wireless provider."

9. **B of A:** Bank of America helped finance *Snow White and the Seven Dwarfs*, sponsored It's a Small World, and even had a branch in Town Square from 1955 to mid-1993.

10. **BPOM:** The emblem for the Benevolent & Protective Order of Mouse is above the entrance to Mickey's Toontown.

11. **BTM:** The Big Thunder Mountain Railroad engines carry these initials on their sides.

12. **BTR:** The Big Thunder Ranch logo is displayed throughout this area in Frontierland (*right*).

13. **C & H:** This sugar company named after California and Hawaii has been one of the sponsors of Main Street's Market House.

14. **CJr.RR:** These initials appear on the side of Fantasyland's Casey Jr. Circus Train.

15. **DAR:** The emblem for the Daughters of the Animated Reel is located above the entrance to Mickey's Toontown.

16. **DAS:** The Disability Access Service Card, introduced in October 2013, replaced the GAC (see below); the new card included a photo of the disabled guest and reserved special access to one attraction at a time (the GAC provided all-day special access to attractions).

17. **DCA:** Disney California Adventure, the big park across the esplanade from Disneyland, opened on February 8, 2001.

18. **DKC:** The initials of the Disneyland Kennel Club are located east of the main gate.

19. **DRD:** Guests can make restaurant reservations with Disneyland Resort Dining (714-781-DINE; 714-781-3463; www.disneyland.disney.go.com/dining).

20. **DVC:** Kiosks for the Disney Vacation Club have been found at the Hub and in Frontierland, Mickey's Toontown, New Orleans Square, and Tomorrowland.

21. **ECVs:** Available for rent near the entrance to the park, electronic convenience vehicles can be seen throughout Disneyland.

22. **EMS:** The advanced technology of the Enhanced Motion System is what puts the bounce into the Indiana Jones Adventure's vehicles.

23. **F:** During the *Legends of Frontierland* interactive game that installed in summer 2014, signs and small flags with Frontierland's initials appeared throughout the area.

24. **GAC:** From 2004 to 2013, Disneyland made Guest Assistance Cards available at City Hall. A GAC enabled a disabled guest and his or her party to utilize special accommodations all day long, which included preferential seating and alternate entrances to attractions.

25. **GAF:** The General Analine Film Corporation sponsored Main Street's GAF Photo Salon from 1970 to 1977.

26. **G.E.:** General Electric sponsored Tomorrowland's electricity-themed Carousel of Progress from 1967 to 1973.

27. **INA:** The Insurance Companies of North America sponsored Main Street's Carefree Corner from 1956 to 1974.

28. **KAP:** From 1955 to 1960, the Kaiser Aluminum & Chemical Company sponsored Tomorrowland's Hall of Aluminum Fame and displayed the mascot Kap, an acronym for "Kaiser Aluminum Pig" ("pig" being the term for the impure base alumina that is refined into pure aluminum).

29. **LAX:** Fifteen-minute helicopter flights between Los Angeles International Airport and Disneyland were offered until 1972. These helicopters transported over a million guests to a heliport outside the berm, where trams picked them up. Two 1968 chopper crashes (killing

forty-four people) eventually brought the service to a halt.

30. MAPO: With *Mary Poppins* a blockbuster hit in 1964, the movie's first letters were given to a new manufacturing division formed in 1965 to work with Imagineers on Disneyland attractions.

31. MM: Mickey Mouse's initials appear inside Mickey's House.

32. MT: These large initials are on display at the entrance gates to Mickey's Toontown.

33. NASA: Engineers from the National Aeronautics and Space Administration helped construct the new *Moonliner* added to Tomorrowland in 1998. NASA also sponsored Tomorrowland's American Space Experience exhibit from 1998 to 2003.

34. NGE: Disneyland's long-rumored NextGen Experience was meant to include MyMagic+, Fastpass+, and MagicBands to enhance the park experience, but difficulties with these programs at Walt Disney World have put the NGE on hold.

35. N.W.R.R.: The acronym for Nature's Wonderland Railroad graced the sides of Frontierland's old Western Mine Train Through Nature's Wonderland (1960–1977).

36. ODV: Outdoor Vending is the official name of the small (but usually well-themed) carts selling snacks, ice cream, candy, beverages, and other treats throughout Disneyland.

37. PSA: Pacific Southwest Airlines sponsored Tomorrowland's World Premiere Circle-Vision theater from 1984 to 1989.

38. RD: Roy Disney's initials are worked into the railings above Pirates of the Caribbean.

39. Retlaw: It looks like an acronym, but it's really "Walter" spelled backwards. After Walt Disney sold most of his WED Enterprises (see below) to Walt Disney Productions in 1965, he created a new name, Retlaw, for the remainder that he still owned; Retlaw controlled the Disneyland Railroad and Monorail until the Disney family sold the company to Walt Disney Productions in 1981.

40. RMM & E Co.: The initials for the Rainbow Mountain Mining and Exploration Company graced the sides of Frontierland's old Rainbow Caverns Mine Train (1956–1959).

41. Rocket Rods XPR: XPR stood for "Experimental Prototype Rocket," but these initials were dropped before guests could start inventing their own interpretations of the acronym (Extremely Problematic Ride, Exceptional Patience Required) for this short-lived (1998–2000) Tomorrowland attraction.

42. **RR:** During the run of 2014's *Legends of Frontierland* interactive game, signs and small flags with the Rainbow Ridge initials appeared throughout Frontierland.

43. **SF&DRR:** These initials appeared on the sides of some of the passenger cars of the old Santa Fe & Disneyland Railroad (riders today will see "DRR").

44. **STR:** These letters appear on Walt Disney's necktie in the *Partners* statue; they stand for "Smoke Tree Ranch," the site of his Palm Springs vacation home.

45. **T:** Guests will find this single letter on the side of Tomorrowland's trash cans and on a shield inside Toad Hall, near the exit of Mr. Toad's Wild Ride.

46. **TDA:** Team Disney Anaheim is the park's administrative headquarters, located in a four-story Frank Gehry-designed building just north of Disneyland.

47. **TWA:** Trans World Airlines sponsored Tomorrowland's *Moonliner* rocket from 1955 to 1962.

48. **WD:** Walt Disney's initials are worked into the railings above Pirates of the Caribbean.

49. **WDI:** The group incorporated in December 1952 that became known as WED Enterprises (see below) eventually evolved into WDI, short for Walt Disney Imagineering, based in Glendale, California.

50. **WED Enterprises:** Incorporated in December 1952 as Walt Disney Enterprises, this group was renamed Walt Disney Incorporated three months later and then Walter Elias Disney Enterprises (or WED Enterprises) in November 1953. The WED team of craftspeople, artists, architects, engineers, and designers were gathered together by Walt Disney to create Disneyland and its attractions.

A Snapshot of Disneyland's Opening Year (1955)

These twenty-five factoids help paint a picture of what life was like in America sixty years ago.

1. White House: President Dwight Eisenhower, Vice President Richard Nixon

2. Number of U.S. states: 48

3. First-class postage stamp: 3 cents

4. Gallon of gas: 23 cents

5. Movie ticket: 45 cents

6. Average cost of a new car: $1,900

7. Average home price: $11,000

8. Average annual salary (according to the national wage index used to calculate Social Security): $3,300

9. Academy Award for Best Picture of 1955: *Marty*

10. Academy Award for Best Actor of 1955: Ernest Borgnine

11. Academy Award for Best Actress of 1955: Anna Magnani

12. Emmy Award for Best Comedy Series of 1955: *The Phil Silvers Show*

13. Emmy Award for Best Dramatic Series of 1955: *Producers' Showcase*

14. Emmy Award for Best Action or Adventure Series of 1955: *Disneyland*

15. Pulitzer Prize for Drama: Tennessee Williams's *Cat on a Hot Tin Roof*

16. Pulitzer Prize for Fiction: William Faulkner's *A Fable*

17. Miss America: Sharon Kay Ritchie, Miss Colorado

18. NCAA Basketball Champions: University of San Francisco

19. NCAA Football Champions: University of Oklahoma

20. NBA Champions: Syracuse Nationals

21. NFL Champions: Cleveland Browns

22. World Series Champions: Brooklyn Dodgers

23. Number of Baseball Hall of Fame Inductees: Six, including Frank "Home Run" Baker and Joe DiMaggio

24. Kentucky Derby Winner: Swaps

25. *Time* magazine's "Man of the Year" for 1955: General Motors' President Harlow Curtice

Then and Now at Disneyland

My, how things have changed in the Magic Kingdom . . .

1955 1. Address: 1313 South Harbor Boulevard (on Disneyland's east side)

2. Hours: 10 AM to 10 PM; open daily all summer; closed most Mondays the rest of the year

3. Annual attendance (July 1955 to July 1956): Approximately 3.6 million

4. Adult admission: $1 (plus additional charges for attractions)

5. Cost to park one car: 25 cents

6. Average guest expenditure per person: $2.37 (according to a 1956 Disneyland press release, this figure included parking, admission, rides, amusements, and souvenirs)

7. Number of lands: Five (Adventureland, Fantasyland, Frontierland, Main Street, and Tomorrowland)

8. Number of main attractions: Seventeen on Opening Day

9. Number of other Disney parks around the world: Zero

2015 1. Address: 1313 South Harbor Boulevard (sometimes listed online and in travel guides as 1313 Disneyland Drive and 1313 South Disneyland Drive—addresses located on the west side of the park)

2. Hours: Varied, often from 8 or 9 AM to 10 PM or midnight; open daily

3. Annual attendance: Approximately 16 million

4. Adult admission: $99 (no additional charges for attractions)

5. Cost to park one car: $17

6. Average guest expenditure per person: Disneyland no longer issues press releases about attendance and expenditures, but our conservative estimate puts this daily figure at almost 83 times the 1955 average (2015 parking + admission + $50 meals/snacks +$30 souvenirs = $196)

7. Number of lands: Eight (the original five, plus Critter Country, Mickey's Toontown, and New Orleans Square)

8. Number of main attractions: Sixty-plus

9. Number of other Disney parks around the world: Five (Disneyland Paris, Hong Kong Disney Resort, Shanghai Disney Resort opening in 2016, Tokyo Disney Resort, and Walt Disney World Resort)

16 60th Anniversaries in the Walt Disney Company

This chronological list presents significant names in the Disney universe that have already celebrated, or will someday celebrate, turning sixty.

1. 1953: Roy O. Disney's sixtieth birthday (Walt's older brother, the financial wizard who co-founded what is today called the Walt Disney Company, born June 24, 1893)

2. 1961: Walt Disney sixtieth birthday (born December 5, 1901)

3. 1983: Disney Brothers Cartoon Studio opening (the Hollywood animation studio that would later become Walt Disney Productions, founded in 1923)

4. 1985: Walt and Lillian Disney's sixtieth wedding anniversary (they were married in 1925)

5. 1988: Mickey Mouse's first appearance in a theatrically-released cartoon (in *Steamboat Willie*, 1928)

6. 1988: Minnie Mouse's first appearance in a theatrically-released cartoon (in *Steamboat Willie*, 1928)

7. 1990: Pluto's first cartoon appearance (in *The Chain Gang*, 1930)

8. 1992: Goofy's first cartoon appearance (in *Mickey's Revue*, 1932)

9. 1994: Donald Duck's first cartoon appearance (in *The Wise Little Hen*, 1934)

10. 1997: *Snow White and the Seven Dwarfs* debut (1937)

11. 2000: Walt Disney Studios official opening in Burbank (1940)

12. 2015: Disneyland celebrates its sixtieth anniversary

13. 2031: Walt Disney World opening (October 1, 1971)

14. 2043: Disney Channel launch (April 18, 1983)

15. 2058: Disney Cruise Line launch (Disney's first ship, *Disney Magic*, took its maiden voyage in 1998)

16. 2061: Disney California Adventure opening (February 8, 2001)

11 Tributes to Disneyland

Some of these are on view as elaborate certificates in City Hall.

1. 1965: The County of Los Angeles and supervisors congratulated Disneyland's "Tencennial Celebration" and the park's "fabulous creator, Walt Disney" for generating "untold joy and wholesome recreation."

2. 1980: A County of Orange Resolution by the Board of Supervisors recognized Disneyland's twenty-fifth anniversary.

3. 1980: A City of Los Angeles Resolution by Mayor Tom Bradley and supervisors recognized the park's twenty-fifth anniversary and wished "every continued success in the many years ahead."

4. 1985: California Legislative Resolution No. 246, introduced by Senator John Seymour and Assemblyman Richard Robinson, congratulated Disneyland on its thirty-fifth anniversary.

5. 1997: *The Architecture of Reassurance*, an extensive exhibition, toured major museums for three years and spotlighted Disneyland's design innovations.

6. 1998: This year, the California Assembly officially congratulated Disneyland's success.

7. 2003: A tribute from Anaheim's police department extended "appreciation to our friends at the Disneyland Resort" for "joining the force" and "helping to recognize Anaheim's everyday heroes."

8. 2005: Congressional Resolution No. 142, introduced by California Representative Loretta Sanchez (and fifty-one co-sponsors) to the 109th Congress, congratulated "Disneyland and the Walt Disney Company on the fiftieth anniversary of the opening of Disneyland."

9. 2005: *Behind the Magic: 50 Years of Disneyland*, an artifact-filled exhibit, debuted at Michigan's Henry Ford Museum before coming to the Oakland Museum of California in 2006.

10. 2005: To commemorate Disneyland's fiftieth anniversary, the Smithsonian's National Museum of American History temporarily displayed park photos, attraction posters, an elephant from Dumbo the Flying Elephant, and a teacup from the Mad Hatter's Mad Tea Party.

11. 2005: Disneyland received a star on the Hollywood Walk of Fame in front of the El Capitan Theater (6874 Hollywood Boulevard).

15 Historic Disneyland Firsts

Here are fifteen Disneyland firsts, listed in chronological order.

1. First employee: Milt Albright, hired as manager of accounting in 1954 and named a Disney Legend in 2005, is usually acknowledged as Disneyland's first-ever employee.

2. First female Imagineer: Harriet Burns, a model-maker who began working on Disneyland projects in 1955.

3. First major structure to be built: Opera House (in Disneyland's first years, this spacious building housed a working lumber mill filled with projects destined for other park locations).

4. First paddlewheeler built in the United States in fifty years: The *Mark Twain* Riverboat (according to Disney lore and Randy Bright's *Disneyland: Inside Story*, though at least two famous paddlewheelers, the *Belle of Louisville* [1914] and the *Delta Queen* [1927], were built in America after 1905).

5. First Disneyland postcard: In this postcard picture, Walt Disney stands in front of artist Peter Ellenshaw's majestic four-by-eight-foot painting that shows an overhead view of the park.

6. First Main Street store to fold: Grandma's Baby Shop, closed in September 1955 after three months and replaced by the Silhouette Studio.

7. First major attraction added after Opening Day: Tomorrowland's Astro-Jets, on March 24, 1956.

8. First ski-resort-style aerial lift (using multiple gondolas on a cable) in the U.S.: Skyway, opened in 1956.

9. First roller coaster in the world with steel tubes for tracks: Matterhorn Bobsleds, opened in 1959.

10. First monorail to run on a daily schedule in the Western Hemisphere: Disneyland-Alweg Monorail, opened in 1959 (also the first monorail to pass over a public roadway).

11. First time Disneyland unexpectedly closed all day because of a national tragedy: November 23, 1963, the day after President John F. Kennedy's assassination.

12. First permanent "land" added after 1955: New Orleans Square, 1966.

13. First Disneyland attraction that cost more to build than Disneyland itself: Space Mountain for $20,000,000 in 1977 (Disneyland cost $17,000,000 to build in 1955).

14. First Disneyland attraction to get FASTPASS ticket distribution: It's a Small World, 1999.

15. First time Disneyland and Walt Disney World remained open to the public all night long on the same date: The twenty-four-hour One More Disney Day event, February 29–March 1, 2012.

11 Historic Disneyland Lasts

Here are eleven Disneyland lasts, listed in chronological order.

1. Last Disneyland attraction Walt Disney worked on before Opening Day: According to Neal Gabler's biography of Walt Disney, Disney and Disney Legend Ken Anderson spray-painted Tomorrowland's 20,000 Leagues Under the Sea Exhibit late into the night of July 16, 1955, rushing to finish it before the next day's televised opening.

2. Last major Disneyland project opened in Walt Disney's lifetime: New Orleans Square, July 24, 1966—144 days before his death on December 15.

3. Last attraction built under Walt Disney's direct supervision: Pirates of the Caribbean, according to *Birnbaum's 2014 Official Guide to the Disneyland Resort*.

4. Last day Walt Disney visited Disneyland: Most likely October 14, 1966, sixty-two days before his death.

5. Last performance of the *Golden Horseshoe Revue*: October 12, 1986, after a record-setting thirty-one years.

6. Last flight of the Skyway: Mickey and Minnie took this thirty-eight-year-old attraction's ceremonial final trip on November 10, 1994.

7. Last performance of the Main Street Electrical Parade: After debuting in 1972, Disneyland's beloved parade finally ended on November 25, 1996.

8. Last cast member to retire who had worked at Disneyland on Opening Day: Bob Penfield retired in 1997 and later received a tribute window on Main Street.

9. Last day Disneyland's hundred-acre parking lot was open to the public: Opened in 1955, the gigantic parking lot was eventually capable of holding over 15,000 cars before it was lost to Disney California Adventure construction on January 21, 1998.

10. Last day of Disneyland's giant marquee along Harbor Boulevard: The sixty-seven-foot-tall marquee was lost to Disney California Adventure construction on June 14, 1999.

11. Last time Disneyland closed unexpectedly all day because of a national tragedy: September 11, 2001, after the terrorist attacks in New York City earlier that day.

13 World Records Set at Disneyland

Many of these records have since been eclipsed, but all were established at Disneyland.

1. Approximately ninety million viewers, the world's largest TV audience at that time, watched the July 17, 1955 Opening Day broadcast.

2. The Grand Canyon Diorama opened in 1958 as the world's longest diorama (305 feet).

3. In honor of Disneyland's thirtieth anniversary and what would have been Walt Disney's eighty-fourth birthday, on December 5, 1985, Disneyland teamed up with the City of Anaheim to set the record for the largest helium balloon release. Skyfest's "Million Balloon Salute" was launched from nearby Katella Avenue.

4. *Guinness World Records 2004* declared that the *Golden Horseshoe Revue* was "the longest theatrical run for a revue," with 47,250 performances in front of over sixteen million viewers between 1955 and 1986.

5. Hula hooping: The March 25, 1988 Super Hooper Duper event set a

world record for having the most simultaneous hula-hoopers (1,527) in a single location (in front of Sleeping Beauty Castle).

6. Disneyland's "Let's Twist Again" event brought Chubby Checker and 2,248 dancers together on March 31, 1989 to set the record for the world's largest "twist party."

7. Splash Mountain opened in July 1989 as the world's longest water-flume chute (fifty-two feet).

8. *Disneyland: Then, Now, and Forever* claims that the Main Street Electrical Parade's 3,500 performances played to 75 million guests, the largest audience ever for a live show.

9. When it opened in 2000, Disneyland's six-story Mickey and Friends parking structure, with over 10,000 spaces, was the world's biggest.

10. To celebrate the Mickey Mouse Club's fiftieth anniversary on October 3, 2005, about 1,000 people arranged themselves in front of Sleeping Beauty Castle to form the world's largest pair of mouse ears, a pattern approximately 100 feet across.

11. Pirates of the Caribbean has entertained something like a third of a *billion* riders, more than any attraction ever, according to *Birnbaum's 2014 Official Guide to the DL Resort*.

12. It's a Small World's theme song may hold an unverifiable world record; according to www.songfacts.com, it is "the most performed and translated song of all time." While the attraction and song made their first appearances in a Disney park at Disneyland, they've spread to Disney parks around the globe, so any record could truly be a "world" record.

13. Not exactly a world record, but an impressive statistic nonetheless: In December 2014, Instagram reported that the world's most geo-tagged location (the place where people shared a photo and simultaneously tagged their location) was Disneyland. By comparison, Times Square was third on that list, and Paris's Louvre Museum was sixth.

10 Other Amusement Park Debuts

1. Cedar Point, Ohio: A nirvana for fans of thrilling roller coasters, this much-honored park opened in 1870 and added its first coaster in 1892.

2. Coney Island, New York: America's most-visited amusement area for half a century, Coney Island's three main parks— Steeplechase Park, Dreamland, and Luna Park—were built between 1897 and 1904.

3. Kennywood, Pennsylvania: This nostalgic favorite opened in 1898 as a working-class picnic area (a "trolley park" at the end of a railway line),

but within a few decades new owners had added rides and an influential Kiddieland area.

4. Knott's Berry Farm: A tiny berry stand in the 1920s and a restaurant serving famous chicken dinners in the 1930s, Knott's began to grow after adding Ghost Town in 1940, establishing itself as an up-and-coming theme park.

5. Magic Mountain, California: Opened in 1971, this coaster-packed park an hour north of Disneyland became Six Flags Magic Mountain in 1979.

6. Marineland of the Pacific, California: With its pioneering shows and exhibits, this was the world's largest oceanarium when it opened in Palos Verdes (about forty miles west of Disneyland) in 1954. Marineland closed in 1987, and its popular killer whales were moved to San Diego's SeaWorld.

7. Schlitterbahn Water Park, Texas: One of America's best water parks, the original Schlitterbahn park opened in 1979 and boasts sixty-five acres of beaches, pools, and slides.

8. Six Flags Over Texas: The first Six Flags theme park—and the first major theme park to charge a single price for admission with rides included—opened in 1961, fifteen miles from Dallas.

9. Tivoli Gardens, Copenhagen: In some important ways, Disneyland was patterned after this beautifully landscaped amusement park that opened in 1843. In 1914, Tivoli added what is now the world's oldest wooden roller coaster still in operation.

10. Universal Studios: Guests had taken simple tours of the studio lot in the 1920s and 1930s, but starting in 1964 they could ride trams and watch staged events—precursors of the major rides and shows that would be added later.

Bob Gurr's
10 Most Memorable Events at Disneyland

Any guest who's ever ridden in a Disneyland train or car knows Bob Gurr's work, because he's the man who created and engineered the park's transportation. As a young industrial designer fresh out of college, Gurr started designing automobiles for Disneyland's Autopia after a stint as a Ford Motor Company auto stylist. He worked full time to make realities out of the elaborate vehicles dreamed up by Walt Disney, including such diverse devices as the hovering Flying Saucers, the sleek Monorail, the speedy Matterhorn Bobsleds, and Adventure Thru Inner Space's revolutionary Omnimover pods. A Disney Legend who has been part of all sixty years of Disneyland's history, he recalls his ten most memorable Disneyland events with this list, written exclusively for this book.

1. July 17, 1955: "At Disneyland's opening—I was thrilled to be part of the launch of a whole new generation of parks."

2. June 1957: "Testing Tomorrowland's new Viewliner train with Walt Disney—it was exciting to drive my very first train design with Walt in the cab with me."

3. July 1958: "I designed, built, and delivered my very own design of a fire engine as one of the new Main Street vehicles."

4. June 1959: "Dedicating the Monorail with Walt and Richard Nixon, the vice president of the United States."

5. July 1980: "I was honored to be a part of the celebration for Disneyland's twenty-fifth anniversary."

6. June 1986: "At the ceremony that designated the Monorail as an engineering landmark, it was a wonderful feeling to know I had helped design America's first daily operating monorail system."

7. July 2005: "It was amazing to participate in the celebration for Disneyland's fiftieth year.

8. March 2007: "This was the first time I rode in a Main Street parade, and it was especially nice because I was in the fire engine I designed!"

9. March 2008: "Receiving the highest honor Disneyland bestows—a window on Main Street."

10. August 2012: "The first Bob Gurr Disneyland tour for auction winners. Beginning in August 2012, I started donating my time for private tours of Disneyland through fund-raising auctions to support RymanArts and Walt Disney's Barn in Griffith Park. Disney fans have donated as much as $5,000 to walk in Walt's footsteps and hear tales of the early days of Disneyland from a Disney Legend. I've continued to do these tours ever since."

GEOGRAPHY
Around the Park in 29 Lists

Distances from Disneyland to Other Disney Parks

In March 2014, a new sign appeared at the Big Thunder Mountain Railroad showing the distances to similar locations in three other Disney parks. The towns listed below are the local equivalents of Rainbow Ridge, the miniature town that decorates the Big Thunder loading area at Disneyland (according to the sign, Disneyland's Rainbow Ridge is just 76 feet away). The sign gives the distance to Florida in miles and to the two international locations in kilometers (our mileage conversions are in parentheses). Tokyo Disneyland and Shanghai Disneyland, by the way, are not included on Disneyland's list, but they're approximately 5,500 miles and 6,500 miles (respectively) from Anaheim.

1. Tumbleweed (Walt Disney World) = 2,496 miles
2. Thunder Mesa (Disneyland Paris) = 9,258 kilometers (5,753 miles)
3. Grizzly Gulch (Hong Kong Disneyland) = 11,743 kilometers (7,297 miles)

Distances from Disneyland to Other Prominent Locations

These are the walking and driving distances from "The Happiest Place on Earth" to other locations of note. (Distances were either paced off at the park or calculated using www.mapquest.com.)

Walking from Disneyland's turnstiles to . . .

1. Disney California Adventure's turnstiles: 300 feet
2. Mickey and Friends tram stop by World of Disney: 600 feet
3. East-side pedestrian entrance at Harbor Boulevard: 800 feet
4. Monorail station at Downtown Disney: 1,800 feet
5. Disneyland Hotel: 2,500 feet

Driving from Disneyland to . . .

6. Knott's Berry Farm, Buena Park, California: 7 miles
7. John Wayne Airport, Santa Ana, California: 13 miles
8. Nearest beach (Bolsa Chica State Beach in Huntington Beach, California): 18 miles
9. Walt Disney's final resting place, Forest Lawn Memorial Park, Glendale, California: 32 miles
10. Walt Disney Studios, Burbank, California: 38 miles

11. Walt Disney's last home address, 355 Carolwood Drive, Holmby Hills, California: 45 miles

12. California Institute of the Arts (the institution Walt Disney helped found), Valencia, California: 59 miles

13. Walt Disney's vacation retreat at Smoke Tree Ranch, 1850 Smoke Tree Lane, Palm Springs, California: 96 miles

14. Walt Disney Family Museum at the Presidio in San Francisco, California: 411 miles

15. Marceline, Missouri, where Walt Disney lived on a farm just outside of town from 1906 to 1910: Approximately 1,740 miles

16. The house where Walt Disney was born on December 5, 1901 (today's address is 2156 North Tripp Avenue, Chicago, Illinois): Approximately 2,080 miles

17. The site of the 1964–1965 New York World's Fair in Flushing Meadows, Queens: Approximately 2,835 miles

7 Thoroughfares Around Disneyland

Some of the roads that Disneyland-goers drive on today (*shown below, on a Harbor Boulevard sidewalk map*) didn't even exist in 1955. Here's a list of the thoroughfares that have been around Disneyland since Opening Day.

1. Disneyland Drive: The primary thoroughfare immediately west of Disneyland, this route guides guests into today's Mickey and Friends parking structure. The road was originally called West Street until 1999, when the area was redeveloped. The Disneyland Hotel is on the west side of the street.

2. Disney Way: Called Freedman Way until 1998, this east-west road curves from Harbor Boulevard (opposite Disney California Adventure's Tower of Terror) toward the Santa Ana Freeway one-third of a mile away.

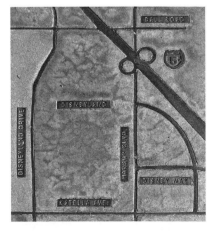

3. Harbor Boulevard: This busy east-side thoroughfare used to guide drivers straight to Disneyland's memorable marquee and huge parking lot. The Monorail runs parallel to Harbor Boulevard for about one-eighth of a mile.

4. Katella Avenue: This primary east-

west thoroughfare immediately south of Disneyland passes what used to be the main parking lot. Located four miles west of Disneyland on Katella is Rancho Alamitos High, one of Steve Martin's old schools (Martin worked at Disneyland for about a decade).

5. Magic Way: This quarter-mile east-west road was laid down just west of Disneyland in 1999 during major construction at the Disneyland Resort. The Disneyland Hotel is on this street, at 1150 Magic Way.

6. Santa Ana Freeway: Completed in 1955, Interstate 5 is the central artery connecting downtown Los Angeles to Orange County. Passing within about 400 feet of Tomorrowland, the I-5 gives drivers a glimpse of Matterhorn Mountain.

7. West Ball Road: This primary east-west thoroughfare immediately north of Disneyland houses the Disney Casting Center for employment, at 700 West Ball Road (the corner of Ball and Cast Place).

17 Thoroughfares Inside Disneyland

Everybody recognizes Main Street, of course, but Disneyland has many other named roads, streets, and lanes.

1. Big Thunder Trail: Wide walkway connecting Fantasyland and Frontierland.

2. East Center Street/West Center Street: Short street intersecting Main Street at the Market House.

3. East Plaza Street/West Plaza Street: Separates the Hub from Main Street.

4. Esplanade: Wide walkway between New Orleans Square and the Rivers of America.

5. Front Street: North-south alley on the west side of New Orleans Square.

6. London Lane: Named on a street sign inside Mr. Toad's Wild Ride.

7. Matterhorn Way: North-south walkway between Alice in Wonderland and Matterhorn Mountain.

8. Meadow View: Named on a street sign inside Mr. Toad's Wild Ride.

9. Mill View Lane: Narrow walkway around Fowler's Harbor.

10. Neighborhood Lane: Mickey and Minnie's respective houses are on this residential street in Mickey's Toontown.

11. New Orleans Street: East-west walkway connecting the Golden Horseshoe and the River Belle Terrace.

12. Orleans Street: Diagonal street in the center of New Orleans Square.

13. River Road to London: Named on a street sign inside Mr. Toad's Wild Ride.

14. Route 55: The Autopia roadway, as identified on a sign along the route ("55" is a tribute to Disneyland's opening year).

15. Royal Street: Southernmost street in New Orleans Square.

16. Small World Way: Wide walkway connecting the Storybook Land Canal Boats with It's a Small World.

17. Wilderness Road/Wilderness Trail: Identified on free Tom Sawyer Island maps (the "brown one" seen on page 125) as routes to Fort Wilderness.

19 Sections of the Old Disneyland Parking Lot

From 1955 to 1998, a huge parking lot offered about 15,000 spaces on a hundred acres south of Disneyland (Disney California Adventure now occupies much of this land). The lot was divided into nineteen main sections, each marked with character signs to help guests remember where they had parked. All the sections are listed east to west (which is also their alphabetical order). The streets named below are on the east (Harbor Boulevard) and south (Katella Avenue).

Northern-most row (closest to Disneyland's turnstiles)

1. Alice (next to Harbor Boulevard)

2. Bambi (near the ticket booths)

3. Donald (near the ticket booths)

4. Eeyore (for buses and motor homes)

5. Flower (across from the Disneyland Hotel)

North-center row

6. Goofy (next to Harbor Boulevard)

7. Happy

8. Jiminy Cricket (the entrance to Disney California Adventure is here now)

9. Kanga

10. King Louie

South-center row

11. Mickey (next to Harbor Boulevard)

12. Minnie

13. Owl

14. Pinocchio

15. Robin Hood

Southern-most row (there's reverse alphabetical order in the T's)

16. Sleepy (next to Katella Avenue, the next section to the east was the toll plaza for cars)

17. Tinker Bell (next to Katella Avenue)

18. Thumper (next to Katella Avenue)

19. Winnie the Pooh (far southwest corner)

Disneyland's Original 160 Acres in a Dozen Prominent Locations

Disneyland opened in 1955 on 160 Anaheim acres (60 for the park, 100 for the adjacent parking lot). How many 160-acre plots could fit in other well-known locations?

187.5: Walt Disney World, Florida (approximately 30,000 acres)

30: Disneyland Paris (4,800 acres)

7.5: 1904 St. Louis World's Fair (the Louisiana Purchase Exposition), Missouri (1,200 acres)

6.3: Golden Gate Park, San Francisco, California (1,017 acres)

5.25: Central Park, New York (840 acres)

4: 1964–1965 New York World's Fair, Flushing Meadows, Queens (featuring popular Disney attractions; 646 acres)

2.5: 1939 Golden Gate International Exposition, San Francisco, California (attended by Walt Disney; 400 acres)

2.2: Dodger Stadium and its surrounding parking lots, Los Angeles, California (352 acres)

1.93: National Mall, Washington, D.C., Grant Memorial to Lincoln Memorial (309 acres)

1.7: Meteor Crater, aka Barringer Crater, Arizona (America's largest known impact crater; 274 acres)

1.4: New South China Mall in Dongguan, China (world's largest shopping center; 220 acres)

1: Knott's Berry Farm, California (160 acres)

A Dozen Prominent Locations That Would Fit in Disneyland's Original 160 Acres

Conversely, how many of these well-known locations could the original 160-acre Disneyland property hold?

57.1: St. John the Divine Cathedral, New York (one of the world's largest cathedrals; 2.8 acres)

25: Madison Square Garden, New York (6.4 acres)

12.3: Great Pyramid of Khufu, Egypt (world's largest pyramid; 13 acres)

10.6: Louvre Museum, Paris (15 acres)

8: Crystal Lagoon, San Alfonso del Mar Resort, Chile (world's largest swimming pool; 20 acres)

7.6: Aulani, Oahu (Disney's Hawaiian resort; 21 acres)

4.8: Pentagon, Virginia (world's largest administrative building; 33.5 acres)

3.8: Taj Mahal tomb and gardens, India (42 acres)

2.5: Kremlin, Moscow (68 acres)

1.5: Tiananmen Square, Beijing, China (one of the world's largest city squares; 109 acres)

1.4: MGM Grand Hotel and Casino, Las Vegas, Nevada (America's largest hotel; 112 acres)

1.3: Hearst Castle, California (William Randolph Hearst's home and gardens; 127 acres)

Disneyland Measured in Football Fields

To grasp the scale of Disneyland's dimensions, it helps to think of the park in terms of football fields. Here are some approximate measurements, listed in order of increasing distance (1 FF = 100 yards).

1. North–south length of each Main Street block = .5 FF

2. Width of Town Square (City Hall to Opera House) (*below*) = .75 FF

3. Distance from Main Street's Emporium to Coke Corner (main entrance to main entrance) = 1 FF

4. Length of Adventureland (Enchanted Tiki Room to Tarzan's Treehouse) = 1 FF

5. Distance from the Hub to Frontierland's Golden Horseshoe = 1 FF

6. Distance from Disneyland to Disney California Adventure (turnstiles to turnstiles) = 1 FF

7. Length of the Grand Canyon Diorama = 1 FF

8. Length of the Primeval World Diorama = 1.5 FF

9. The walk from Tom Sawyer Island's rafts to the *Mark Twain* dock = 1.5 FF

10. East-west distance across the esplanade in front of Disneyland (check-point to checkpoint) = 1.75 FF

11. Distance from the Hub to Tomorrowland's Innoventions = 2 FF

12. Distance from the Hub to Pirates of the Caribbean = 2 FF

13. Distance from Pirates of the Caribbean to Splash Mountain = 2 FF

14. North-south length of Tom Sawyer Island = 2.5 FF

15. Distance from Town Square's train station to the Hub = 2.5 FF

16. Length of Indiana Jones Adventure's queue = 3 FF (Disneyland's longest queue—one FF longer than Space Mountain's)

17. Distance from Town Square's train station to the Mickey's Toontown entrance (the maximum south-north length of the original park) = 6 FF

18. Distance from Critter Country's train tracks to Tomorrowland's train station (the maximum west-east width of the original park) = 7 FF

8 Attractions and Lands Beyond the Berm

The embankment surrounding Disneyland's original acreage is called the berm. Approximately twenty feet high at its tallest point, the berm helps keep out trespassers, blocks views outside the park, and gives Disneyland its recognizable "rounded triangle" shape. Some attractions, however, actually extend outside this embankment; they may start inside the berm, but at some point they go through or under it to an area (often a "show building") where most of the attraction is actually staged.

1. Bear Country/Critter Country: Today's guests explore Critter Country (formerly Bear Country) by walking under the train tracks (essentially walking through a gap in the berm) to reach an area added in 1972.

2. The Haunted Mansion: The iconic mansion is located inside the berm, but the elevator in the "stretching room" and the subterranean hallway take guests west of the berm to a show building containing the Doom Buggies.

3. Holidayland: Nine acres of outdoor family fun, located west of Frontierland's berm from 1957 to 1961.

4. Indiana Jones Adventure: Entered from Adventureland, this attraction's long queue travels outside the berm to a show building where the jungle jeeps roam.

5. It's a Small World: The famous façade of this attraction is located at the berm, while the cruise's show building is north of the berm.

6. Mickey's Toontown: Guests dip under the train tracks at Fantasyland's northern boundary and come up north of the berm to get to Mickey's Toontown, where a road, the Pony Farm, and storage facilities used to be located.

7. Monorail: Much of this train's beam is outside the berm. The Monorail runs along Harbor Boulevard, goes past Disney California Adventure to the Downtown Disney station, crosses in front of Disneyland's entrance, and re-enters the park in Tomorrowland.

8. Pirates of the Caribbean: Two waterfalls and the early cruise take guests under the berm to a show building southwest of the original park.

8 Ways to Look Outside the Berm from Inside the Park

The thickly planted berm around Disneyland enhances the illusion that the park is a complete world unto itself. Even before Disneyland was built, Walt Disney knew how effective a berm could be—he'd already constructed one around a section of Disney Studios in Burbank and another around the backyard of his house to shield his neighbors from his elaborate miniature railroad. While Disneyland's berm does restrict views to the neighborhoods beyond, it doesn't block them entirely. Here are eight ways guests have been able to look outside the berm from inside the park.

1. Astro-Orbitor: Flying above Tomorrowland, guests can see hotels to the east.

2. *Mark Twain* Riverboat: Circling Tom Sawyer Island, guests on the upper decks get a peek at a parking structure and backstage areas north of Frontierland.

3. Matterhorn Bobsleds: Quick glimpses from the moving bobsleds are of faraway Orange County buildings.

4. Monorail: From the Tomorrowland platform, guests can see hotels to the east; while it's circling Tomorrowland, the Monorail offers additional views of buildings beyond the berm. (The train actually leaves Disneyland, of course, and offers unobstructed views of Anaheim, Disney California Adventure, and Downtown Disney.)

5. Skyway: From 1956 to 1994, guests could drift almost six stories above Disneyland and get views of nearby Anaheim buildings.

6. Splash Mountain: As with the Matterhorn Bobsleds, the views from the top of Splash Mountain's plunge are glimpsed quickly, though here guests usually focus more on the drop than the Orange County vistas to the east.

7. Tarzan's Treehouse: Hotels to the west are visible from the platform seven stories up.

8. Town Square's train station: While waiting up on the platform for their trains, guests have always been able to look southward to vast areas outside Disneyland.

Counting the Steps of 36 Disneyland Stairways

For at least one of these stairways, you may have to remind yourself to "keep on moving, keep climbing . . . it's all about the climb," just like in *Hannah Montana: The Movie*. Here is the number of steps in 36 prominent Disneyland stairways.

1. Minnie's House = 2
2. Haunted Mansion = 3
3. Jolly Holiday Bakery Café = 3
4. Mickey's House = 3
5. Silhouette Studio's adjacent porch = 3
6. Blue Bayou's interior = 4
7. Casey Jr. Circus Train = 4
8. Gazebo in the center of Mickey's Toontown = 4
9. Golden Horseshoe's stage-level box at stage left (said to be Walt Disney's favorite) = 4

10. Plaza Inn = 4
11. Tomorrowland Terrace = 4
12. Enchanted Tiki Room = 5
13. Golden Horseshoe's stage = 5
14. Path behind Fowler's Inn = 5
15. Town Square's City Hall = 6
16. Hungry Bear Restaurant, down to the lower level = 8
17. New Orleans Square/Frontierland station = 8 (9 coming down)
18. House of the Future (extinct) exit down to ground level = 9
19. Sailing Ship *Columbia*, down to the Below-Decks Museum = 11
20. Treehouse outside Mike Fink's cabin on Tom Sawyer Island (rope ladder, inaccessible to guests) = 12
21. Chip 'n Dale Tree House = 16
22. Splash Mountain's uppermost queue area = 16
23. Golden Horseshoe's upper floor = 17
24. Jungle Cruise's queue area = 18
25. Space Mountain, disembarking up to the daylight exit = 18
26. Tom Sawyer Island's suspension bridge = 19
27. Disneyland Dream Suite (*above*) = 23
28. Skyway station in Fantasyland = 23
29. Tom Sawyer Island's Castle Rock = 23
30. New Orleans Square's Court des Anges staircase = 24
31. *Mark Twain*'s upper deck = 30

32. Monorail's Tomorrowland station, exit down to ground level = 30
33. Innoventions' interior route from first to second floor = 32
34. Sleeping Beauty Castle Walk-Through's highest point = 32
35. Indiana Jones Adventure exit = 47 (a combination of 22 up, 25 down)
36. Tarzan's Treehouse's highest point = 72

The 16 Tallest Structures in Disneyland History

Here's a list of the tallest structures in the park, including their debut years and heights in feet.

1. Matterhorn Mountain (1959; 147 feet)
2. Space Mountain (1977; 118)
3. Big Thunder Mountain (1979; 104)
4. Splash Mountain (1989; 87)
5. Rocket Jets tower (1967; 85)
6. Skyway tower (1956; 85)
7. Sailing Ship *Columbia* (1958; 84)
8. Pirate Ship Restaurant (*pages 34–35*) (1955; 80, estimated)
9. Sleeping Beauty Castle (1955; 77)
10. Original *Moonliner* rocket (1955; 76)
11. Cascade Peak (1960; 70, estimated)
12. Swiss Family Treehouse (1962; 70)
13. Flagpole in Town Square (1955; 65)
14. Astro-Orbitor (*page 95*) (1998; 64)
15. Christmas tree in Town Square (1955; 60)
16. New *Moonliner* rocket (1998; 53)

Disneyland's Hills

Most guests could list Disneyland's current mountains (Big Thunder, Matterhorn, Space, Splash). They may even remember Lookout Mountain (Sam McKim's large 1958 Fun Map placed this towards the southern end of Tom Sawyer Island) and the old Cascade Peak (formerly along the Rivers of America, demolished in 1998). But how many guests could list some Disneyland hills that have been given specific names?

1. **Boot Hill:** A target area inside the Frontierland Shooting Exposition.

2. **Chickapin Hill:** The top of Splash Mountain.

3. **Holiday Hill:** A twenty-foot, partially landscaped picnic area that preceded the Matterhorn.

4. **Indian Hill:** Site of Tom & Huck's Treehouse on Tom Sawyer Island, as marked on the 1957 island maps drawn by Sam McKim.

5. **Snow Hill:** Early plans for the Matterhorn site included a toboggan ride on a hill with man-made snow.

Speaking of hills . . .

6. **Billy Hill and the Hillbillies:** Acclaimed performers in Frontierland and Critter Country from 1987 to 2014.

7. **Hills Bros. Coffee House and Coffee Garden:** A Town Square café from 1958 to 1976.

7 Trains and Their Approximate Track Lengths

Walt Disney loved trains, so he put them throughout his park. These seven are listed by length from longest track to shortest track; parentheses show the years that the attraction operated.

1. **Monorail** (1959–ongoing): 2.3 miles from Tomorrowland to the Downtown Disney station and back

2. **Santa Fe & Disneyland Railroad** (1955–ongoing): 1.3 miles around the park (not including Mickey's Toontown, which is beyond the train tracks)

3. **PeopleMover** (1967–1995): .75 mile through Tomorrowland

4. **Viewliner** (1957–1958): .75 mile through Tomorrowland and Fantasyland

5. **Big Thunder Mountain Railroad** (1979–ongoing): .5 mile in Frontierland

6. **Casey Jr. Circus Train** (1955–ongoing): .3 mile in Fantasyland

7. **Mine Train** (1956–1977): .3 mile in Frontierland

A Dozen Distinctive Sights
Spotted from the Disneyland Railroad

Besides the panoramic park vistas, the Disneyland Railroad offers close-ups of some specific sights along its 1.3-mile circle tour.

1. A look at the population sign mounted at Town Square's train station (raised to 650 million in March 2013, elevation 138 feet).

2. Four train stations with four different designs: New Orleans Square/ Frontierland (elevation 144 feet), Mickey's Toontown (playful design), Tomorrowland (spartan), and Main Street (iconic).

3. Before the New Orleans Square/Frontierland station: Ninety seconds of lush foliage leading to the Mardi Gras Supply Company's display of giant Mardi Gras heads.

4. Interiors of five tunnels: Before New Orleans Square (eight seconds of tunnel); leading into Critter Country (thirty seconds); immediately after Critter Country (five seconds); before Mickey's Toontown (ten seconds), and before Main Street (three minutes of tunnel through the Grand Canyon and Primeval World dioramas).

5. Critter Country: An elevated side view of Splash Mountain's musical finale.

6. Frontierland: A reverse view of the Native American chief and wildlife normally observed from the Rivers of America.

7. Frontierland: Wooden stables behind the Big Thunder Ranch.

8. Fantasyland: Behind the hedge-filled It's a Small World façade.

9. Fantasyland: A backstage road and the beautiful Agrifuture billboard.

10. Fantasyland: Close-ups of the Monorail beam positioned about six feet off the ground.

11. Tomorrowland: Scenes from the Autopia's back roads.

12. Tomorrowland: A clear view of a two-story backstage building painted green.

9 Relocations Within Disneyland

All of these moved from one Disneyland location to another.

1. Bandstand: From a space near Sleeping Beauty Castle to a spot by the Rivers of America (and eventually out of Disneyland).

2. Disney Gallery: Above Pirates of the Caribbean from 1987 to 2007, now in Town Square.

3. Disneyana: On Main Street's west side from 1976 to May 1986; on Main Street's east side until the spring of 2013; reopened mid-2013 in Town Square.

4. Dumbo the Flying Elephant: In Fantasyland's western corner 1955–1982; reopened in its more central current location in 1983.

5. Indian Village: Tribal ceremonies in western Frontierland started in 1955, but shifted farther north until leaving in 1971.

6. King Arthur Carrousel: This 1955 attraction moved about twenty yards northward in 1983.

7. Le Bat en Rouge: Today's New Orleans Square shop was just a cart outside the Haunted Mansion in 2001; a year later, it became a shop near the Royal Street Veranda; in 2006, it relocated near the Blue Bayou.

8. Mad Hatter's Mad Tea Party: In 1955, the teacups were closer to the King Arthur Carrousel; in 1983, the party moved eastward near Alice in Wonderland.

9. Names Unraveled: A Fantasyland cart in the mid-1990s; a shop inside Sleeping Beauty Castle's walkway a few years later; a shop by Pinocchio's Daring Journey until circa 2005.

11 Serene Disneyland Hideaways

As crowded and noisy as Disneyland often is (some would say "usually is"), it's still possible to find some serenity. In 2014, these were relatively quiet, often shaded places slightly off the beaten path. Not listed is New Orleans Square's lovely Court des Anges, closed to the public in 2013. See Annie Fox's list on page 221 for a referral to this list of serene hideaways.

Critter Country

1. The Hungry Bear Restaurant's lower deck along the Rivers of America

Fantasyland

2. The shaded 150-foot path paralleling the parade route south of It's a Small World

Frontierland

3. Benches near Frontierland's entrance

4. Big Thunder Trail between Frontierland and Fantasyland

5. Tom Sawyer Island's east-facing docks

6. The winding walkway behind Fowler's Harbor

Hub

7. First Aid's garden

8. Snow White Wishing Well and Grotto

Main Street

9. The China Closet's porch (*right*).

Mickey's Toontown

10. Toon Park

New Orleans Square

11. Magnolia Park, the fountain area south of The Haunted Mansion

2 Dozen Disneyland Locations with Cemeteries, Skulls, and Skeletons

Now that you're feeling all serene from visiting the locations on the previous list, welcome to the dark side. Considering that it's "The Happiest Place on Earth," Disneyland sure has lots of reminders of death, including a smiling, axe-wielding, serial-killing bride inside the Haunted Mansion. Here are twenty-four additional examples, alphabetized by location.

Adventureland

1. Skulls: Mounted in front of the Enchanted Tiki Room.

2. Skulls and skeletons: In the Indiana Jones Adventure queue; thousands more fill entire rooms within the attraction.

3. Skulls: Displayed along the Jungle Cruise (*right*).

4. Skeleton: Standing in the base camp of Tarzan's Treehouse (*opposite, left*).

Fantasyland

5. Skull: On a Heraldry Shoppe shelf.

6. Skull: In the dungeon display of the Snow White's Scary Adventures queue area.

7. Skeletons: In the creepy dungeon scene halfway through Snow White's Scary Adventures.

8. Cemetery: At the church in Alice's miniature village, viewed from the Storybook Land Canal Boats.

Frontierland

9. Dinosaur skeleton: Protruding from rocks at the Big Thunder Mountain Railroad.

10. Disney characters as skeletons: Halloween Time at Big Thunder Ranch.

11. Cemetery: Boot Hill tombstones inside the Frontierland Shooting Exposition (hit the moving shovel here to coax a skeleton from his grave; hit the coffin to make skeletal hands lift the lid).

12. "Burial Ground": Formerly near the Indian Village in Frontierland's northwest corner, shown on the 1958 poster-size Fun Map (today's Indian Village north of Tom Sawyer Island includes displays of animal skulls).

13. Sun-bleached dinosaur bones: Formerly displayed along the old Mine Train's route.

14. Cemetery: Behind Tom Sawyer Island's Fort Wilderness.

15. Skulls and skeletons: Exhibited throughout Dead Man's Grotto on Tom Sawyer Island.

16. Skeleton: Tenaciously clutching the treasure chest that guests crank out of the water, near Tom Sawyer Island's pontoon bridge.

New Orleans Square

17. Pet cemetery: In front of the Haunted Mansion (*above right*); a hidden pet cemetery spreads behind the building.

18. Wall of humorous tombs: Lining the back of the Haunted Mansion's queue area.

19. Skeletons: Inside the Haunted Mansion—hanging above guests when lightning flashes early in the attraction; one of the paintings in the walk-through corridor changes to show a horse's and rider's skeletons; a skeleton tries to lift his coffin lid.

20. Cemetery: The elaborate scene near the end of the trip through the Haunted Mansion.

21. Skull: Displayed on the balcony behind the Mint Julep Bar.

22. Skulls and skeletons: Inside Pirates of the Caribbean.

Tomorrowland

23. Dinosaur skulls and skeletons: In the Disneyland Railroad's Primeval World scenes.

24. "Graveyard of Lost Ships": The 1958 Fun Map showed this in the Tomorrowland lagoon.

A Dozen Dazzling Disneyland Views

While almost any view inside Disneyland is potentially dazzling, these twelve alphabetical locations add elevation to the panorama.

1. Disney Gallery: Back when it was above Pirates of the Caribbean (1987–2007), the Disney Gallery had second-story balcony views overlooking Adventureland and New Orleans Square.

2. Disneyland Railroad: The famous twenty-five-minute scenic tour atop the berm.

3. Fort Wilderness: Today's closed fort used to offer guests second-story views from Tom Sawyer Island.

4. Innoventions: Second-story views across Tomorrowland.

5. Main Street Omnibus: Second-story views of the Town Square/Main Street/Hub area.

6. *Mark Twain*: Scenic Rivers of America views from the upper decks.

7. Matterhorn Bobsleds: Quick, high-altitude glimpses of areas inside and outside Disneyland.

8. Monorail: The long circuit includes Tomorrowland, Fantasyland, and the resort area.

9. PeopleMover: From 1967 to 1995, this beloved attraction gave leisurely sixteen-minute tours above Tomorrowland and through some of the buildings.

10. Skyway: Until 1994, this was a breathtaking open-air flight above half the park.

11. Swiss Family Treehouse/Tarzan's Treehouse: Views from almost seventy feet up.

12. Town Square's train station: The second-story look at Town Square and Main Street is especially spectacular during the fireworks.

A Dozen Disneyland Night Sights

As impressive as the next twelve locations are by day, they really shine at night. This alphabetical list doesn't include Fantasmic!, Disneyland's amazing fireworks, or the spectacular holiday lights that cover the park every winter.

1. Astro-Orbitor: The spinning lights and brilliant metal of this moving sculpture draw guests into Tomorrowland (*right*).

2. Big Thunder Mountain Railroad: Though Space Mountain's exterior looks cool at night, inside it's always dark, no matter the time of day. Big Thunder Mountain Railroad, however, becomes a different experience with radiant views after sunset.

3. Entrance: The shining train station and bright Mickey parterre offer one last beautiful sight to departing guests.

4. Fantasy Faire: The village's Tangled Tower sparkles to life at night.

5. The Haunted Mansion: It's imposing during the day, but nighttime is the right time to appreciate the building's eerie splendor.

6. It's a Small World: At night, this attraction's fascinating façade becomes a glittering jewel box.

7. King Arthur Carrousel: There's always been plenty to admire in Fantasyland at night (remember Skull Rock's green eyes?), but the gorgeous carousel has stayed perpetually magical.

8. Mad Hatter's Mad Tea Party: Glowing lanterns above the teacups create a lively party scene.

9. Main Street: For many guests, Main Street at twilight is Disneyland's loveliest sight.

10. Sleeping Beauty Castle: The majestic castle shimmers with color and light.

11. Storybook Land Canal Boats: Pretty by day, wondrous at night when tiny lights bring the structures to life.

12. Tomorrowland Lagoon: Nighttime's illuminated turquoise lagoon is even more spectacular than it is during daytime.

17 Facts About Disneyland's Flowers and Trees

Many guests love Disneyland's landscaping and ornamental flower gardens almost as much as they love its attractions. Culled from Morgan Evans's *Walt Disney Disneyland World of Flowers* and other Disney-authorized sources, here are seventeen factoids about Disneyland's foliage.

1. Over 12,000 orange trees were removed from the original 160-acre property.

2. The eucalyptus trees behind City Hall were on the property before Disneyland was built. They've been retained to serve as windbreaks.

3. The park's landscape architects were two brothers, Morgan "Bill" Evans and Jack Evans, who owned a business that supplied rare plants to Hollywood celebrities. The brothers landscaped Walt Disney's private home in 1952.

4. The Evans brothers' budget to transform the bulldozed orange groves into a verdant, beautifully manicured park: about $500,000.

5. The Evans brothers chose plants for many different uses: to provide shade in sunny areas; to screen off walls and areas not meant to be seen; to define borders and paths; to create entire environments (as seen on the Jungle Cruise and Storybook Land Canal Boats); to add thematic colors and patterns (as seen in the gardens at It's a Small World); to create recognizable shapes (as in the Mickey parterre at the entrance); and to add year-round beauty throughout Disneyland.

6. Only five percent of the flowers and trees the Evans brothers planted in Disneyland were native to California.

7. Among the thousands of plants and flowers brought in were some mature trees Bill Evans rescued after they were uprooted by construction on local freeways and in downtown Los Angeles.

8. About 10,000 flowers (replanted six times a year) form the Mickey face and surrounding decorations at the entrance.

9. Over 700 trees and over forty different kinds of plants (representing six continents) are planted along the Jungle Cruise.

10. Some trees were intentionally planted upside-down along the riverbanks of the Jungle Cruise so that their twisted, exotic-looking roots would spread above ground.

11. Bob Thomas's biography *Walt Disney: An American Original* recounts the last frantic days before the opening, when the brothers were running out of time, money, and plants. With some of Fantasyland's berm still bare, Walt Disney requested little signs with long Latin names to be placed among the native plants to disguise the weeds as desirable specimens.

12. The "Dominguez Palm" is the nickname for the tall palm tree near the entrance to the Jungle Cruise; this tree pre-dates Disneyland and is named for a family that lived here before Walt Disney bought the property.

13. Many of the miniature trees and flowers along the Storybook Land Canal Boats have been planted in their original containers to stunt their growth.

14. The name "Alice" is spelled out in plants near the Mad Hatter's Mad Tea Party (on the corner that juts towards the Storybook Land Canal Boats).

15. The park's official rose—the pink *Disneyland floribunda*—grows near Dumbo the Flying Elephant.

16. The name created for the seven-story artificial tree that holds Tarzan's Treehouse: *Disneyodendron semperflorens grandis* ("big ever-blooming Disney tree").

17. When we expand the definition of "treehouse" to include those built into the base or the stump of a tree, not just those built up in the limbs, we count ten current treehouses in Disneyland. (We aren't including the little elevated house outside Goofy's Playhouse, because the support there is more "signpost" than "tree.")

    1) Adventureland: Tarzan's immense estate.

    2) Critter Country: Owl's stylish six-square-footer up in a tree outside Many Adventures of Winnie the Pooh.

    3) Critter Country: Pooh's home (*right*), built at ground level into a tree outside Many Adventures of Winnie the Pooh.

    4) Critter Country: The small house built into a desiccated tree just past Splash Mountain's "Slippin' Falls" (look to the right).

    5) Fantasyland: The "Mole End" home built into the base of a tree, as seen from the Storybook Land Canal Boats.

    6) Frontierland: The open platform outside Mike Fink's cabin on Tom Sawyer Island.

    7) Frontierland: Tom and Huck's closed perch on Tom Sawyer Island.

    8) Hub: The sign outside Pixie Hollow is a treehouse with small homes.

    9) Mickey's Toontown: Chip 'n Dale's play structure.

    10) Tomorrowland: Innoventions' broad, futuristic two-story "Treehouse of Tech" with silhouetted inhabitants.

The Geography of Disneyland's Trash Cans

Just as Disneyland's restrooms are themed to the area where they are located (see page 169), so too are the park's approximately 1,250 trash cans given creative decorations that identify them with specific lands. Can you match the lands (listed alphabetically below) with the twelve trash cans shown here?

1. Adventureland	**7.** Indiana Jones Adventure
2. Entrance	**8.** It's a Small World
3. Fantasyland	**9.** Main Street
4. Frontierland	**10.** New Orleans Square
5. Haunted Mansion	**11.** Tomorrowland
6. Hub	**12.** Mickey's Toontown

Answers: 1–g; 2–b; 3–k; 4–d; 5–h; 6–f; 7–a; 8–c; 9–i; 10–j; 11–e; 12–l

19 Real People Whose Names Were Used for Disneyland Locations

Walt Disney's name appears throughout Disneyland, of course, but so do the names of a few other recognizable people, listed here alphabetically.

1. Marie Antoinette, eighteenth-century French queen: Mlle. Antoinette's Parfumerie, New Orleans Square (1967–1997, 2011–ongoing)

2. Arthur, King of the Britons (some scholars claim that Arthur was an actual sixth-century British king, according to nineteenth- and tenth-century texts describing his exploits): King Arthur Carrousel (1955–ongoing)

3. Davy Crockett, American frontier hero: Davy Crockett Arcade, Fron-

tierland (1955–1985); Davy Crockett Frontier Museum (July–October 1955); Davy Crockett's Explorer Canoes (replaced Frontierland's Indian War Canoes, 1971–ongoing); Davy Crockett's Pioneer Mercantile (1987–ongoing)

4. Don DeFore, TV/film actor: Don DeFore's Silver Banjo Barbecue, Frontierland (1955–1961)

5. Étienne de Silhouette, eighteenth-century French Controller-General of Finances: Silhouette Studio, Main Street (1956–ongoing)

6. Mike Fink, pre-Civil War keel boat brawler: Mike Fink Keel Boats, Frontierland (1995–1997)

7. Joe Fowler, U.S. Navy admiral and Disney Legend: Fowler's Harbor, Frontierland (1958–ongoing)

8. Charles Dana Gibson, American illustrator who drew early twentieth-century "pin-up" girls: Gibson Girls Ice Cream Parlor, Main Street (1997–ongoing)

9. Gibson Brothers, four Victorian Scottish printers: Gibson Greeting Cards, Main Street (1955–1959)

10. George Keller, twentieth-century circus entertainer: Keller's Jungle Killers, Fantasyland (February–September 1956)

11. Jean Laffite, nineteenth-century pirate: Laffite's Landing, Pirates of the Caribbean (1967–ongoing); Laffite's Silver Shop, New Orleans Square (1966–1988); Lafitte's [*sic*] Tavern (as of 2007, the new name for Harper's Mill on Tom Sawyer Island)

12. Abraham Lincoln, sixteenth U.S. president: Great Moments with Mr. Lincoln, Town Square (1965–1973; 1975–2005; 2009–ongoing)

13. Dr. Albert Schweitzer, recipient of the 1952 Nobel Peace Prize: The Jungle Cruise's Schweitzer Falls (1955–ongoing)

14. Jimmy Starr, movie publicist: Jimmy Starr's Show Business Souvenirs, Town Square (1956–1959)

15. Mark Twain, American author: *Mark Twain* Riverboat, Frontierland (1955–ongoing)

16. Dr. William Upjohn, nineteenth-century founder of a pharmaceutical company: Upjohn Pharmacy, Main Street (1955–1970)

17. Franz Rudolph Wurlitzer, nineteenth-century importer and manufacturer of musical instruments: Wurlitzer Music Hall, Main Street (1955–1968)

18.–19. Linus Yale and Henry Towne, nineteenth-century inventors and lock manufacturers: Yale & Towne Lock Shop, Main Street (1955–1964)

35 Disneyland Locations with Names of Real Places

While many things at Disneyland are magical and fantasy-based, the park does invoke real places. The following locations all include real places in their names. We're not counting events, like America on Parade, for this list, nor are we including Columbia (from the Sailing Ship *Columbia*), since that name refers to a female symbol for America, not to a city. The years given reflect the periods when the attractions had these names.

1. American Dairy Association Exhibit, Tomorrowland (1956–1958)
2. American Egg House, Town Square (1978–1983)
3. American Rifle Exhibit, Frontierland (1956–ca. 1986)
4. American Space Experience, Tomorrowland (1998–2003)
5. America Sings, Tomorrowland (1974–1988)
6. Bank of America, Town Square (1955–1983)
7. Casa Mexicana, Frontierland (1982–2001)
8. Cristal d'Orleans, New Orleans Square (1966–ongoing)
9. Delta Banjo, Frontierland (1974–ca. 1990)
10. Flight to the Moon, Tomorrowland (1967–1975)
11. French Market, New Orleans Square (1966–ongoing)
12. Grand Canyon Diorama, Tomorrowland section of the Disneyland Railroad (1958–ongoing)
13. Guatemalan Weavers, Adventureland (1956–1986)
14. Indiana Jones Adventure, Adventureland (1995–ongoing)
15. Indiana Jones Adventure Outpost, Adventureland (1995–ongoing)
16. Jewel of Orléans, New Orleans Square (1997–2011)
17. La Mascarade d'Orléans, New Orleans Square (ca. 1985–ongoing)
18. Matterhorn Mountain (Matterhorn Bobsleds), Tomorrowland/Fantasyland (1959–ongoing)

19. Mexican Village, Frontierland (ca. 1956–ca. 1969)

20. Mission to Mars, Tomorrowland (1975–1992)

21. New York World's Fair Exhibit, Tomorrowland (1963–1964)

22. New Orleans Square (1966–ongoing)

23. New Orleans Street, Frontierland (1955–1966)

24. Orleans Street, New Orleans Square (1966–ongoing)

25. Painted Desert, Frontierland (1955–1959)

26. Pirates of the Caribbean, New Orleans Square (1967–ongoing)

27. Port d'Orleans, New Orleans Square (ca. 1995–2002)

28. Port Royal, New Orleans Square (2006–ongoing)

29. Rivers of America, Frontierland (1955–ongoing)

30. Rocket to the Moon, Tomorrowland (1955–1966)

31. Santa Fe & Disneyland Railroad, Town Square (1955–1974)

32. Satellite View of America, Tomorrowland (1957–1960)

33. South Seas Traders, Adventureland (1984–ongoing)

34. Swiss Family Treehouse, Adventureland (1962–1999)

35. Tahitian Terrace, Adventureland (1962–1993)

11 Disneyland Locations Named After Royalty

As with the list above, the focus here is on places, not on vehicles like the Jungle Cruise boat named *Congo Queen*, or on events like Three Kings Day, or on characters like Princess Leia. By the way, one of the most obscure royal references we could find (but didn't include) is in the cabin on the top deck of the *Mark Twain*, where a Currier and Ives illustration called *"Wooding Up" on the Mississippi* shows a riverboat called *Princess*.

1. King Arthur Carrousel, Fantasyland (1955–ongoing)

2. King Triton Gardens, Fantasyland (1996–2008)

3. Mlle. Antoinette's Parfumerie, New Orleans Square (1967–1997, 2011–ongoing)

4. Once Upon a Time . . . The Disney Princess Shoppe, Fantasyland (2002–2009)

5. Princess Boutique, Fantasyland (ca. 1997–2005)

6. Princess Fantasy Faire, Fantasyland (2006–2013)

7. Royal Courtyard, between Port Royal and Pieces of Eight, New Orleans Square (1966–ongoing)

8. Royal Street, New Orleans Square (1966–ongoing)

9. Royal Street Sweets, New Orleans Square (1995–ongoing)

10. Royal Street Veranda, New Orleans Square (ca. 1966–ongoing)

11. Royal Theatre in Fantasy Faire, Hub (2013–ongoing)

3 Disneyland Locations Named After Songs

We didn't include Fantasyland's Sanctuary of Quasimodo (1996–1997), since the connection between the shop and the song "Sanctuary" from the 1996 Disney movie *The Hunchback of Notre Dame* seems tenuous at best. Nor did we include the Enchanted Chamber, because there's clearly no relationship between that Fantasyland shop (2008–ongoing) and "Into the Enchanted Chamber" by the Swedish metal band Timeless Miracle. And "Blue Bayou," Roy Orbison's hit song in 1963? Probably not the inspiration for the Blue Bayou, Disneyland's hit restaurant in 1967. But there's no doubting the links between the following locations and the Disney songs (all from Disney movies) that preceded them.

1. Bibbidi Bobbidi Boutique, Fantasyland (2009–ongoing): "Bibbidi-Bobbidi-Boo" (*Cinderella*, 1950)

2. Fortuosity Shop, Main Street (2008–ongoing): "Fortuosity" (*The Happiest Millionaire*, 1967)

3. Jolly Holiday Bakery Café, Hub (2012–ongoing): "Jolly Holiday" (*Mary Poppins*, 1964)

A Dozen Disneyland Locations with Magical or Supernatural Names

Phantoms, fairies, enchantment—it really *is* the Magic Kingdom, after all, as evidenced by these paranormal names for twelve Disneyland locations.

1. Enchanted Chamber, Fantasyland (2008–ongoing)

2. Enchanted Cottage Sweets & Treats, Fantasyland (2004–2009)

3. Enchanted Tiki Room and Enchanted Tiki Garden, Adventureland (1963–ongoing)

4. Ghost Galaxy at Space Mountain (2009–ongoing, seasonal)

5. The Haunted Mansion, New Orleans Square (1969–ongoing)

6. L'Ornement Magique, New Orleans Square (1998–2013)

7. Magic Eye Theater, Tomorrowland (1986–ongoing)

8. Main Street Magic Shop, Main Street (1957–ongoing)

9. Merlin's Magic Shop, Fantasyland (1955–1983)

10. Phantom Boats, Tomorrowland (1955–1956)

11. Three Fairies Magic Crystals, Fantasyland (2006–2008)

12. Witches' Cauldron inside Rainbow Caverns, Frontierland (1956–1977)

14 Disneyland Locations and Events Named After Mickey Mouse

There are more things named after Disneyland's "official host" than anybody else not named Walt Disney. These fourteen are listed alphabetically.

1. *Mickey and the Magical Map* (live Fantasyland show; 2013–ongoing)

2. Mickey at the Movies Parade (1960–1964)

3. Mickey Mouse Club Circus (Fantasyland attraction; 1955–1956)

4. Mickey Mouse Club Circus Parade (1955)

5. Mickey Mouse Club Headquarters (Town Square shop; 1963–1964)

6. Mickey Mouse Club Theater (Fantasyland building; 1955–1981)

7. Mickey's Christmas Chalet (Fantasyland shop; 1983–1987)

8. *Mickey's Detective School* (live Fantasyland show; 2001–2002)

9. Mickey's House (Mickey's Toontown building; 1993–ongoing)

10. Mickey's Magic Kingdom Celebration (parade; 2005)

11. *Mickey's Nutcracker* (live Fantasyland show; holiday seasons in 1991 and 1992)

12. Mickey's Shining Star Cavalcade (parade; 2005)

13. Mickey's Soundsational Parade (*right*) (2011–ongoing)

14. Mickey's Toontown (1993–ongoing)

15 Disneyland Maps

Disneyland has always used maps, either to help guests navigate the park's geography or to help elucidate stories. Here's a sampling of maps used for all different purposes.

1. Adventureland Map: In August 2014, a treasure map of Adventureland debuted to assist players in a new *Adventure Trading Company* interactive game.

2. Braille Map: Since about 2010, a large Braille map of Disneyland has spread out near City Hall in Town Square.

3. Coin-Press Machines: City Hall provides maps to show where Disneyland's many coin-press machines can be found.

4. Dial Guide: Sold in the 1970s and 1980s, these big, bright maps have a numbered index on the back and a built-in wheel that spins to point out locations.

5. Disneyland Railroad: A large park map inside Town Square's train station shows where the trains stop.

6. Emporium Directory: With the Emporium's 2011 remodel came new permanent maps at the doorways that identified the different retail spaces within this large store.

7. Frontierland Map: Large maps were mounted outside Bonanza Outfitters and the Golden Horseshoe, and near the Big Thunder Mountain Railroad's entrance to assist players in the *Legends of Frontierland* role-playing game that ran from July to September 2014.

8. Frontierland Map: A rustic Frontierland map is mounted crookedly in the shaded seating area north of the dock for the *Mark Twain*.

9. Fun Maps: Since 1958, these visually rich, poster-size park maps have been among the most evocative Disneyland collectibles, recreating fond memories and building eager expectations for future visits.

10. Guide Maps: Given away at the turnstiles, these small handy maps provide an overview of the park and identify over a hundred specific locations, everything from restrooms and restaurants to pay phones and smoking areas. INA (the Insurance Companies of North America) provided similar free Disneyland maps when it sponsored Main Street's Carefree Corner from the mid-1950s to the mid-1970s.

11. It's a Small World: The record album of this beloved attraction includes a two-page "picturegram" map that shows cartoony renditions of areas seen during the cruise.

12. Jungle Cruise: Available upon request at the dock, this free map (*opposite*) depicts the sights along the famed attraction.

13. *Mickey and the Magical Map*: Debuting in 2013, this Fantasyland show incorporates a huge interactive map of fanciful locations.

14. Pictorial Souvenir Books: In the 1950s and 1960s, these softcover photo books sold in Disneyland included a colorful two-page map in the center (see page 254 for more on these nostalgic collectibles).

15. Tom Sawyer Island: Two different island maps have been given away here—a green one drawn by Disney Legend Sam McKim in 1957 (shown on page 212) and a brown one created when Pirate's Lair at Tom Sawyer Island opened in 2007 (shown on page 125); also, at the southeastern tip a small wooden map points out the nearby dock.

ATTRACTIONS
Rides, Glides, Zooms, and Flumes

A Dozen Disneyland Attractions Commonly Shortened to One Word

These alphabetized attractions have long, formal names (shown in parentheses), but guests commonly identify them with just one word ("Teacups!").

1. "Autopia" (originally Tomorrowland Autopia, later Autopia, Presented by Chevron)
2. "Bobsleds" or "Matterhorn" (Matterhorn Bobsleds)
3. "Canoes" (originally Indian War Canoes, later Davy Crockett's Explorer Canoes)
4. "Carrousel" (King Arthur Carrousel)
5. *"Columbia"* (Sailing Ship *Columbia*)
6. "Dumbo" (Dumbo the Flying Elephant)
7. "Monorail" (originally Disneyland-Alweg Monorail, later Disneyland Monorail)
8. "Pirates" (Pirates of the Caribbean)
9. "Skyway" (listed in ticket books as Skyway to Fantasyland, Skyway to Tomorrowland)
10. "Submarines" (originally Submarine Voyage, later Finding Nemo Submarine Voyage)
11. "Teacups" (Mad Hatter's Mad Tea Party)
12. "Treehouse" (originally Swiss Family Treehouse, later Tarzan's Treehouse)

19 Disneyland Attractions with the Longest Names

Guests usually identify Disneyland destinations with just one or two words: "Tiki Room!" But if guests *did* use the long, formal names of locations, these are the longest ones they would have to utter. The number of characters is in parentheses.

1. The Disneyland Story Presenting Great Moments with Mr. Lincoln (54)
2. The Walt Disney Story Featuring Great Moments with Mr. Lincoln (53)
3. Western Mine Train Through Nature's Wonderland (41)
4. Pack Mules Through Nature's Wonderland (34)
5. Frontierland Shooting Exposition (30)
6. Many Adventures of Winnie the Pooh (29)

7. Pirate's Lair on Tom Sawyer Island (29)
8. Walt Disney's Enchanted Tiki Room (29)
9. Davy Crockett's Explorer Canoes (28)
10. Rainbow Mountain Stage Coaches (27)
11. Autopia, Presented by Chevron (26)
12. Big Thunder Mountain Railroad (26)
13. Buzz Lightyear Astro Blasters (26)
14. Davy Crockett Frontier Arcade (26)
15. Finding Nemo Submarine Voyage (26)
16. Motor Boat Cruise to Gummi Glen (26)
17. Santa Fe & Disneyland Railroad (26)
18. Snow White's Scary Adventures (26)
19. World Premiere Circle-Vision (26)

14 Imports from Walt Disney World

All of these park features were successes in Florida before they were introduced in California. The years of their Disneyland debuts are in parentheses.

1. Astro-Orbitor: Tomorrowland attraction (1998)
2. Buzz Lightyear Astro Blasters: Tomorrowland attraction (2005)
3. *Captain EO*: Tomorrowland film (1986)
4. Country Bear Jamboree: Bear Country attraction (1972)
5. FASTPASS: ticketing system (1999)
6. *Honey, I Shrunk the Audience*: Tomorrowland film (1998)
7. Innoventions: Tomorrowland attraction (1998)
8. *Magic Journeys*: Tomorrowland film (1984)
9. Many Adventures of Winnie the Pooh: Critter Country attraction (2003)
10. Mile Long Bar: Bear Country restaurant (1972)
11. PhotoPass: Disney photographers take guests' pictures (ca. 2000)
12. Pirates League: a seasonal New Orleans Square/Frontierland attraction (2012)
13. Space Mountain: Tomorrowland attraction (1977)
14. *Wonders of China*: Tomorrowland film (1984)

10 Disneyland Attractions
Not Found at Walt Disney World

We could devote several pages to all the things Walt Disney World has that Disneyland doesn't. We could also identify plenty of overlap between the two magnificent parks: both have a Haunted Mansion, Pirates of the Caribbean, Splash Mountain, etc. But there are still a few attractions Disneyland has that Walt Disney World doesn't, as shown by these ten examples, listed alphabetically.

1. Alice in Wonderland, Fantasyland
2. Casey Jr. Circus Train, Fantasyland
3. Castle Walk-Through, Fantasyland
4. Indiana Jones Adventure, Adventureland
5. Matterhorn Mountain/Matterhorn Bobsleds, Fantasyland
6. Mr. Toad's Wild Ride, Fantasyland
7. Pinocchio's Daring Journey, Fantasyland
8. Roger Rabbit's Car Toon Spin, Mickey's Toontown
9. Sailing Ship *Columbia*, Frontierland
10. Storybook Land Canal Boats, Fantasyland

10 Disneyland Attractions
Not Based on Films or Books

Many Disneyland attractions are based on films (the long list includes Pinocchio's Daring Journey and Star Tours, just to name two). A few attractions are also based on books (Tom Sawyer Island, for example). A couple of others were created for the 1964–1965 New York World's Fair before they were brought to Disneyland (including the Carousel of Progress and It's a Small World). But some attractions, including the ten listed alphabetically below with their locations and years of operation, are Disneyland originals, created just for the park (though they may have evolved into movies later).

1. Adventure Thru Inner Space: Tomorrowland, 1967–1985
2. Autopia: Tomorrowland, 1955–ongoing
3. Big Thunder Mountain Railroad: Frontierland, 1979–ongoing
4. Enchanted Tiki Room: Adventureland, 1963–ongoing
5. The Haunted Mansion: New Orleans Square, 1969–ongoing
6. Mine Train: Frontierland, 1956–1977

7. Monorail: Tomorrowland, 1959–ongoing
8. Pirates of the Caribbean: New Orleans Square, 1969–ongoing
9. Skyway: Fantasyland and Tomorrowland, 1956–1994
10. Submarine Voyage: Tomorrowland, 1959–1998

8 Attractions That Were Dramatically Different in the Planning Stages

These attractions had very different features on the drawing board.

1. Alice in Wonderland was originally meant to be a walk-through attraction, with pedestrians strolling past Wonderland scenes.
2. Casey Jr. Circus Train almost became Disneyland's first roller coaster, but it was toned down into a gentle journey instead.
3. The Enchanted Tiki Room was originally planned as a restaurant with mechanical birds, but Imagineers realized that diners mesmerized by the show would be slow to finish.
4. The Haunted Mansion was meant to be a walk-through past spooky scenes and a "Museum of the Weird," but Imagineers added the Doom Buggies for efficiency and better control of the guests' experience.
5. The hundreds of international dolls in It's a Small World were originally going to sing separate national anthems; to avoid the cacophony, the Sherman Brothers composed a hummable theme song instead.
6. Pirates of the Caribbean was planned as a walk-through wax museum of pirate scenes, but this idea was scuttled in favor of the bateaux.
7. Sketches from the mid-1960s by Disney Legend John Hench depict Space Mountain as a cone-shaped structure with tracks looping conspicuously around the exterior.
8. Before Tom Sawyer Island became a ludic paradise for unstructured play, the island was conceived as a showcase for replications of historic buildings.

Approximate Ride Times of Disneyland Attractions

1 Minute or Less
Gadget's Go Coaster; Rafts to Tom Sawyer Island.

90 Seconds–Under 3 Minutes
Jolly Trolley; King Arthur Carrousel; Mad Hatter's Mad Tea Party; Matterhorn

Bobsleds; Monorail; Mr. Toad's Wild Ride; Peter Pan's Flight; Snow White's Scary Adventures.

3–5 Minutes
Alice in Wonderland; Big Thunder Mountain Railroad; Buzz Lightyear Astro Blasters; Casey Jr. Circus Train; Indiana Jones Adventure; Many Adventures of Winnie the Pooh; Pinocchio's Daring Journey; Rocket Rods; Roger Rabbit's Car Toon Spin; Space Mountain; Space Station X-1; Star Tours.

6–9 Minutes
Adventure Thru Inner Space; Autopia; the Haunted Mansion; Jungle Cruise; Skyway (round-trip); Splash Mountain; Storybook Land Canal Boats; Submarine Voyage; Mine Train.

10–15 Minutes
Country Bear Jamboree; Great Moments with Mr. Lincoln; Indian War/ Davy Crockett's Explorer Canoes; Finding Nemo Submarine Voyage; It's a Small World; *Mark Twain* Riverboat; Mike Fink Keel Boats; Mission to Mars; Mule Pack; Rocket/Flight to the Moon; Sailing Ship *Columbia*; *A Tour of the West* film.

16–20 Minutes
America the Beautiful film; *Captain EO* film; Enchanted Tiki Room; *Honey, I Shrunk the Audience* film; *Magic Journeys* film; PeopleMover; Pirates of the Caribbean.

21+ Minutes
American Journeys film; America Sings; Fantasmic!; Santa Fe & Disneyland Railroad.

A Dozen Disneyland Attractions with Relatively Short Wait-Times

An alphabetical list based on decades of our own experience.

1. Astro-Orbitor (Tomorrowland)
2. Casey Jr. Circus Train (Fantasyland)
3. The Disneyland Story Presenting Great Moments With Mr. Lincoln (Town Square)
4. Donald's Boat (*right*) (Mickey's Toontown)
5. Frontierland Shooting Exposition (Frontierland)
6. Goofy's Playhouse (Mickey's Toontown)

7. Innoventions (Tomorrowland)

8. King Arthur Carrousel (Fantasyland)

9. Main Street Vehicles (Main Street)

10. Many Adventures of Winnie the Pooh (Critter Country)

11. Rafts to Tom Sawyer Island/Pirate's Lair on Tom Sawyer Island (Frontierland)

12. Tarzan's Treehouse (Adventureland)

You Must Be at Least 40" Tall to Read This List: Height Requirements for 9 Disneyland Attractions

Over 35 Inches

1. Gadget's Go Coaster (*right*)

Over 40 Inches

2. Big Thunder Mountain Railroad

3. Space Mountain

4. Splash Mountain

5. Star Tours

Over 42 Inches

6. Matterhorn Bobsleds

Over 46 Inches

7. Indiana Jones Adventure

Over 54 Inches

8. Autopia (to drive solo)

Under 52 Inches

9. Goofy's Playhouse

Approximate Speeds of 15 Disneyland Attractions

It's amazing how some of these attractions seem much faster than they actually are. (Space Mountain only goes about 30 mph? Really?)

40 mph   1. Splash Mountain: The awesome 47-degree plunge reaches 40 mph.

25–35 mph 2. Big Thunder Mountain Railroad: The ride feels faster, thanks to tight turns and scenery in close proximity to the train.

3. **Monorail:** This great train is capable of freeway speeds.

4. **Rocket Rods:** This short-lived attraction (1998–2000) lurched up to almost 35 mph before coming to quick, uncomfortable stops.

5. **Space Mountain:** Thanks to the darkness inside the attraction and the unseen dips and curves along its 3,500-foot track, guests think they're going twice as fast as they actually are.

6. **Viewliner:** Before there was a Monorail, from 1957 to 1958 this odd-looking train had stations in Tomorrowland and Fantasyland.

20 mph

7. **Gadget's Go Coaster:** Nice speeds for a minute-long trip that covers about 700 feet.

8. **Matterhorn Bobsleds:** For decades, park guests have debated which track (the Tomorrowland side or Fantasyland side) is fastest.

7–10 mph

9. **Autopia:** The cars in this attraction go a little faster than average jogging speeds.

4–6 mph

10. **King Arthur Carrousel:** Beautiful style over speed.

11. **Main Street Vehicles:** The cars reach brisk walking speeds.

12. **Skyway:** The slow, four-mph drift between Fantasyland and Tomorrowland approximated the pedestrians' speed below.

1–3 mph

13. **Main Street Electrical Parade:** Like most parades, this 1972–1996 extravaganza was slow and punctuated with pauses.

14. **PeopleMover:** Slow speeds were welcome for this attraction, since the focus was on relaxed observation rather than hurried transportation.

15. **Submarine Voyage/Finding Nemo Submarine Voyage:** Pedestrians cruising the lagoon's perimeter outpace the stately subs.

Disneyland's Watercraft

These sixteen boats ride on underwater rails, float freely, or remain anchored in one spot.

Attached to Rails:

1. Canal Boats of the World/Storybook Land Canal Boats, Fantasyland (1955; 1956–ongoing)
2. Jungle Cruise, Adventureland (1955–ongoing)
3. *Mark Twain* Riverboat, Frontierland (1955–ongoing)
4. Motor Boat Cruise, Fantasyland (1957–1993)
5. Sailing Ship *Columbia*, Frontierland (1958–ongoing)
6. Submarine Voyage/Finding Nemo Submarine Voyage, Tomorrowland (1959–1998; 2007–ongoing)

Free-Floating:

7. Indian War Canoes/Davy Crockett's Explorer Canoes, Frontierland (1956–ongoing)
8. It's a Small World, Fantasyland (1966–ongoing)
9. Mike Fink Keel Boats, Frontierland (1955–1997)
10. Phantom Boats, Tomorrowland (1955–1956)
11. Pirates of the Caribbean, New Orleans Square (1967–ongoing)
12. Rafts to Tom Sawyer Island, Frontierland (1956–ongoing)
13. Splash Mountain, Critter Country (1989–ongoing)

Stationary:

14. Donald's Boat, aka *Miss Daisy*, Mickey's Toontown (1993–ongoing)
15. Pirate Ship Restaurant, Fantasyland (1955–1982)
16. *Wicked Wench* (the pirate ship attacking the fort inside Pirates of the Caribbean), New Orleans Square (1967–ongoing)

The Names of the 8 Canal Boats of the World

Canal Boats of the World was one of Disneyland's shortest-lived attractions. The "Canal" was a winding river dug into one acre in the back of Fantasyland; "the World" referred to tiny, detailed international buildings that were to line the landscaped riverbanks. Disappointingly, the view from the eight boats as they toured the narrow canal was basically of desolate dirt banks (although guests could watch the Casey Jr. Circus Train, which circled the same area). What's more, the primitive motors on the boats were so loud that they overpowered the skippers' narration. Two months after opening, the original Canal Boats cruise sank into history. Here are the names of the attraction's eight boats.

1. *Annie Oakley*
2. *Bold Lochinvar*
3. *Gretel*
4. *Lady Guinivere* [sic]
5. *Lady Katrina*
6. *Lady of the Lake*
7. *Lady of Shallot*
8. *Nellie Bly*

The Names of the
15 Storybook Land Canal Boats

Nine months after the disappointing Canal Boats of the World attraction was removed, the wonderfully remodeled Storybook Land Canal Boats attraction opened, bringing with it the kind of delightful miniatures Walt Disney had originally desired, lavish landscaping, and quieter boats with new names.

1. *Alice*
2. *Ariel*
3. *Aurora*
4. *Belle*
5. *Cinderella*
6. *Daisy*
7. *Faline*
8. *Fauna*
9. *Flora*
10. *Flower*
11. *Katrina*
12. *Merryweather*
13. *Snow White*
14. *Tinker Bell*
15. *Wendy*

14 Miniature Scenes Viewed
from the Storybook Land Canal Boats

The landscaped setting of this lovely cruise includes these scenes, listed in order of appearance.

1. Monstro, the whale from *Pinocchio*.
2. Pigs' homes from *The Three Little Pigs*.
3. Village from *Alice in Wonderland*.
4. London Park from *Peter Pan*.
5. Sultan's palace from *Aladdin*.
6. Cave of Wonders from *Aladdin*.
7. Woodland cottage from *Snow White and the Seven Dwarfs*.
8. Village (*right*) and castle from *Cinderella*.
9. Patchwork quilt and gardens inspired by the 1933 cartoon *Lullaby Land*.
10. Mr. Mole's house and Toad Hall from *The Adventures of Ichabod and Mr. Toad*.
11. Village and mountains from *Frozen*

(late in 2014, this new tableau replaced the long-standing display of windmills from the 1937 cartoon *The Old Mill*).

12. Village and Geppetto's workshop from *Pinocchio*.

13. Prince Eric's ship and waterfront castle from *The Little Mermaid*.

14. King Triton's underwater grotto from *The Little Mermaid*.

The Evolving Names of Disneyland's 8 Submarines

There have been three sets of names for the submarines in the Submarine Voyage. In 1959, the original gray subs were named after nuclear vessels in America's naval fleet; the 1985 versions got some less-militaristic names to match the new yellow color and "explorer" theme of the attraction; and in 2007, half the names were replaced to suit the Finding Nemo Submarine Voyage update.

1959			
	1. *Ethan Allen*	4. *Patrick Henry*	7. *Skipjack*
	2. *George Washington*	5. *Seawolf*	8. *Triton*
	3. *Nautilus*	6. *Skate*	
1985			
	1. *Argonaut*	4. *Neptune*	7. *Seeker*
	2. *Explorer*	5. *Sea Star*	8. *Triton*
	3. *Nautilus*	6. *Seawolf*	
2007			
	1. *Argonaut*	4. *Nautilus*	7. *Seafarer*
	2. *Explorer*	5. *Neptune*	8. *Voyager*
	3. *Mariner*	6. *Scout*	

The Names of the 14 Jungle Cruise Boats

Exotic names for an exotic attraction—this list would make a cool geography quiz. (The names of the true rivers and continents are in parentheses; asterisks indicate original 1955 boats.)

1. *Amazon Belle** (Amazon River, South America)

2. *Congo Queen** (Congo River, Africa)

3. *Ganges Gal** (Ganges River, Asia)

4. *Hondo Hattie* (Rio Hondo, Central America)

5. *Irrawaddi Woman** (Irrawaddy River, Asia)

6. *Kissimmee Kate* (Kissimmee River, North America)

7. *Magdalena Maiden* (Magdalena River, South America)

8. *Mekong Maiden** (Mekong River, Asia)

9. *Nile Princess** (Nile River, Africa)

10. *Orinoco Adventuress* (Orinoco River, South America)

11. *Suwanee Lady** (Suwannee River, North America)

12. *Ucayali Una* (Ucayali River, South America)

13. *Yangtze Lotus* (Yangtze River, Asia)

14. *Zambesi Miss* (Zambezi River, Africa)

The Names of the 12 Astro-Jets

Stellar names for a rocket-ship attraction. Names are listed in descending order of the stars' apparent magnitude (brightness); the names of the constellations where the stars are located are in parentheses.

1. *Sirius* (Canis Major)
2. *Canopus* (Carina)
3. *Arcturus* (Boötis)
4. *Vega* (Lyra)
5. *Capella* (Auriga)
6. *Rigel* (Orion)
7. *Procyon* (Canis Minor)
8. *Altair* (Aquila)
9. *Antares* (Scorpius)
10. *Spica* (Virgo)
11. *Regulus* (Leo)
12. *Castor* (Gemini)

The Names of the
7 Big Thunder Mountain Railroad Trains

In keeping with the playful spirit of this rollicking roller coaster, Big Thunder's seven trains (one was retired after an accident in 2003) were given light-hearted names, listed here alphabetically.

1. *I. B. Hearty*
2. *I. M. Brave* (retired)
3. *I. M. Fearless*
4. *I. M. Loco*
5. *U. B. Bold*
6. *U. R. Courageous*
7. *U. R. Daring*

The Names of the
11 Birds in the Enchanted Tiki Room

The famous Enchanted Tiki Room features singing flowers, drumming tiki statues, a magical fountain, a thunderstorm, and these alphabetically listed singing birds.

Barker Bird

1. Juan (cousin of José, posted out front in the 1960s to attract guests)

Main Stars

2. Fritz (the German bird)
3. José (the Latin bird)
4. Michael (the Irish bird)
5. Pierre (the French bird)

Female Backup Singers

6. Colette
7. Fifi
8. Gigi
9. Josephine
10. Mimi
11. Susette

A Dozen Disneyland "Dark Ride" Vehicles

"Dark rides"—indoor attractions that feature moving vehicles—have existed for about as long as amusement parks have. The vehicles in Disneyland's traditional dark rides have their own personalities (and in some cases, their own names) that match the theme of each attraction.

1. Adventure Thru Inner Space: Capable of leaning back and turning to face displays, the Omnimover system's blue Atomobiles were revolutionary ride vehicles (1967–1985).

2. Alice in Wonderland: The pastel caterpillar vehicles are styled after the hookah-smoking movie character.

3. Buzz Lightyear Astro Blasters: Guests ride in brightly colored, toy-like space pods called XP-40 Space Cruisers.

4. The Haunted Mansion: These are black Omnimover vehicles (*above*) similar to the blue Atomobiles inside Adventure Thru Inner Space, but here they're called Doom Buggies.

5. Indiana Jones Adventure: Guests bounce through the ride in expensive and rugged jungle jeeps.

6. Many Adventures of Winnie the Pooh: Cute "hunny" pots known as "beehicles" are named after characters in the book.

7. Mr. Toad's Wild Ride: These small turn-of-the-century motor cars are named after characters from the story.

8. Peter Pan's Flight: Guests ride in ornate pirate galleons hanging from rails along the ceiling.

9. Pinocchio's Daring Journey: The ride's "woodcarver's carts" include character images.

10. Roger Rabbit's Car Toon Spin: The taxis are based on the movie's Bennie the Cab.

11. Snow White's Scary Adventures: The traditional mine cars are named after the seven dwarfs.

12. Space Mountain: Six-seat "shuttles" blast guests into space.

15 Unique Horses on the King Arthur Carrousel

Disneyland's classic carousel is fitted with sixty-eight leaping white horses, all of them with individual names and distinctive decorations. Here are fifteen unique steeds with their identifying ornamentation.

1. "Arabian Night" wears armor and carries two large scimitars.

2. "Baby" is decorated on one side with a large golden baby and a prominent "D" on its chest.

3. "Bink" has a large pink tongue flopping from its mouth.

4. "Champion" is decorated with colorful championship ribbons.

5. "Crusader"—whose likeness was used on a Disneyland collectible pin—displays a cross on one side.

6. "Dante" flaunts a long, unruly mane and bright red and green colors.

7. "Doubloon" wears an orange, purple, blue, and gold bridle; its gold tooth supposedly marks it as the favorite of Walt Disney's wife, Lillian.

8. "Eagle Scout" is decorated in patriotic red, white, and blue, with a circle of stars around its neck.

9. "Galaxy" is bedecked in purple and decorated with a sun and jeweled stars.

10. "Jester" has a large jester's face painted on its flank.

11. "Nipper," the only mule on the carousel, wears orange and dark blue colors.

12. "Jingles," Disneyland's most famous carousel horse, wears jingle bells, jeweled Hidden Mickeys, and an umbrella illustration in tribute to Julie Andrews and *Mary Poppins*.

13. "King" sports a braided mane and a large fleur-de-lis below its saddle.

14. "Pegasus" wears sky-blue colors and a golden wing on its shoulder.

15. "Unice" wears a yellow blanket adorned with a black unicorn.

A Dozen Geographic Locations Represented in It's a Small World

"The happiest cruise that ever sailed 'round the world" passes by representations of these geographic areas, listed in order of appearance.

1. Polar regions
2. Scandinavia
3. British Isles
4. Western Europe
5. Eastern Europe
6. Middle East
7. Asia
8. Africa
9. Central America
10. South America
11. South Seas
12. United States

A Dozen Views from the PeopleMover

"Tomorrow's transportation . . . today!" the PeopleMover's attraction poster once declared. From 1967 to 1995, that optimistic description seemed prophetic. The PeopleMover's small blue, red, green, and yellow cars slid at a leisurely two mph along a winding, elevated track for a sixteen-minute tour of Tomorrowland's buildings. Here are scenes along the way that made an appearance in the early 1990s.

1. The painted mural on Star Tours' exterior
2. The queue area inside Star Tours
3. The interior of the Star Trader store
4. The second floor inside the Starcade
5. Through Space Mountain's interior
6. A Superspeed Tunnel with *Tron* effects
7. Autopia's roadways
8. The Submarine Voyage
9. The Monorail's loading area
10. The pre-show area inside World Premiere Circle-Vision
11. Tomorrowland's entrance, with "the Plaza" (as it was called in the narration, known today as the Hub) to the west
12. Mary Blair's mosaic murals on World-Premiere Circle Vision's exterior

The 4 Theatrical Scenes on the Carousel of Progress

Long before Innoventions, there was the Carousel of Progress. From 1967 to 1973, this landmark attraction inside a distinctive Tomorrowland building featured a wheel of theater seats that slowly rotated around a core of stages.

Four main scenes showed how decades of advances in electricity were manifested inside the home (no surprise, since the sponsor was General Electric). Here are the scenes depicting how these advances affected a typical family (all Audio-Animatronic characters, including a pet dog) from "the good old days," according to the attraction poster, "to the possible present."

1. 1890s: Taking place before the Wright Brothers' flight, this scene includes devices like a cast-iron stove, an icebox, an early telephone, a gramophone, and gas lamps.

2. 1920s: In this Jazz Age scene, electricity powers the lights, iron, fan, stove, refrigerator, and radio.

3. 1940s: Automated "modern" conveniences in this scene include a combination refrigerator/freezer, automatic dishwasher, electric mixer, radio/phonograph console, black-and-white television, and hearing aids.

4. Late 1960s: Luxury living is enhanced in this scene by adjustable lighting, an all-electric range with a self-cleaning oven, kitchen appliances in matching colors, centralized hi-fi music that plays in any room, and a color TV with a "built-in video tape recorder" to record shows for later viewing.

15 Exciting Scenes Inside the Indiana Jones Adventure

Next time you hear the phrase "The Happiest Place on Earth," consider these fifteen gripping—and often treacherous—areas inside the Indiana Jones Adventure.

1. Chamber of Destiny
2. Hall of Promise
3. Tunnel of Torment
4. Gates of Doom
5. Cavern of Bubbling Death
6. Mummy Chamber
7. Bug Room
8. Bridge Over the Pit
9. Snake Temple
10. Mud Slide
11. Skull Room
12. Rat Cave
13. Dart Corridor
14. Rolling Boulder
15. Finale/Return to Base

8 Opportunities to Shoot Guns at Disneyland

Guests have watched pirates fire rifles and cannons on Pirates of the Caribbean, witnessed "shoot-outs" in Frontierland, and sat next to skippers firing pistols from aboard the Jungle Cruise, but they have also had their own chance to shoot guns in the park, at these eight attractions.

1. At Adventureland's Big Game Safari Shooting Gallery (1962–1982), guests paid cash to shoot "elephant guns" loaded with lead pellets.

2. Buzz Lightyear Astro Blasters (2005–ongoing) in Tomorrowland enables guests in spinnable spaceships to blast "laser cannons" at colorful targets with various point values.

3. The Davy Crockett Frontier Arcade (1955–1985) in Frontierland was a simple coin-operated, quick-draw shooting game.

4. The rootin' tootin' Frontierland Shooting Exposition (1957–ongoing) charges coins to shoot at frontier-themed targets. The original rifles fired lead pellets until new electronic rifles armed with infrared beams were installed in 1985.

5. Tomorrowland's Innoventions (1998–ongoing) allows guests to shoot various blasters at video game stations.

6. At the Main Street Shooting Gallery (1955–1962), the first and shortest-lived of Disneyland's three major shooting galleries, guests in the Penny Arcade area fired actual .22-caliber weapons.

7. Star Trader is one of at least six shops in Disneyland that currently sells rifles, pistols, or blasters (others include the Indiana Jones Adventure Outpost, Little Green Men Store Command, Mickey's Toontown Five & Dime, Pieces of Eight, and Pioneer Mercantile).

8. Tom Sawyer Island: From 1956 to 2001, guests could pull the trigger on realistic (but bulletless) rifles mounted in the lookout towers of the island's Fort Wilderness (demolished in 2007, rebuilt for cast members only).

13 Heart-Thumping Moments in Disneyland's Attractions

These thirteen unexpected moments have produced genuine surprise, shock, and scares in Disneyland's guests.

1. Autopia: Guests can no longer experience what may have been the scariest moments on any Disneyland attraction—the realization that they were about to be rammed by oncoming Autopia cars. This was a real possibility back when the Autopia's roadway had no center rail. Up until 1965, drivers could bash their cars into each other, run into the bushes, and even turn around and drive against traffic.

2. Finding Nemo Submarine Voyage: You're cruising along on this undersea adventure, enjoying the sights and looking at the pretty lights

floating through the darkness, when suddenly . . . AHHH! TEETH! YELLOW EYES! FANGS! FANGTEETH!

3. The Haunted Mansion: In the "stretching room" the narrator says, "Of course, there's always *my* way," before breaking into evil laughter as lightning flashes, guests are plunged into darkness, and a hanging corpse becomes visible above. The ensuing long scream sends chills down nearly every spine.

4. *Honey, I Shrunk the Audience*: Shown from 1998 to 2010, the 3-D film featured an immense snake that suddenly struck out at the "shrunken" audience. Some guests have yet to recover.

5. Indiana Jones Adventure: After surviving creepy crawlies in the dark, a giant boulder rolls toward guests in their stalled vehicles.

6. Matterhorn Bobsleds: During the ride, the Abominable Snowman makes several sudden attempts at "community outreach."

7. Mr. Toad's Wild Ride: An oncoming train arrives from out of the darkness after guests have experienced nearly a minute and a half of reckless driving.

8. Sleeping Beauty Castle Walk-Through: Near the end of the walk, Maleficent's shadow lurks down a creepy corridor. In the attraction's early years, this effect was taken out because scared kids wouldn't proceed down the hall, bottling up traffic behind them. The shadow has been reinstated since then.

9. Snow White's Scary Adventures: The evil queen/ugly witch transformation still affects first-timers.

10. Splash Mountain: Nearly everyone shrieks during the final forty-mph plunge into thorny briars.

11. Star Tours: In the first iteration of the ride, the chaotic journey climaxed with a long, frightening skid into the hangar.

12. Tarzan's Treehouse: Nobody expects the sudden roar that surges from Sabor when a hand gets too close to his jaws.

13. Pirate's Lair on Tom Sawyer Island: Halfway through the west-to-east walk through Dead Man's Grotto, a barred window on the left gives a sudden close-up of a skeletal pirate.

10 Factors That Make Tom Sawyer Island So Wonderfully Unique

For many guests, Tom Sawyer Island has remained one of Disneyland's most unique and entertaining locations, and not just because it offers an ideal place to relax on hot days under real trees near cool water. These ten factors make the island special.

1. In *Walt Disney: An American Original*, Bob Thomas writes that the island was the only early Disneyland attraction personally designed by Walt Disney. According to Thomas, Disney took the island's concept drawings home and worked on them "for hours in his red-barn workshop," returning them the next day with the instruction, "Now that's the way it should be." His design became the island that opened in 1956.

2. Guests must make a concerted effort (by taking the rafts) to reach the island; they can't stumble upon the island the way they might unexpectedly come across another attraction that happens to be on the way to something else.

3. Without any big stores or restaurants on the island, nothing distracts guests from fun or coaxes cash from wallets. In Disneyland, Tom Sawyer Island is about as far as guests can get from price tags.

4. Obviously, the island's environment is carefully designed and controlled, but it *feels* wild and untamed, unlike the safe, restrictive lands across the river.

5. Bordering three different lands (Frontierland, New Orleans Square, and Critter Country), the island offers grand views of such landmarks as the Golden Horseshoe, the Haunted Mansion, Splash Mountain, and the *Columbia*.

6. Unlike most of the other attractions, Tom Sawyer Island is not just a three-minute experience. Guests can stay all day if they want to; dusk is the only deadline.

7. While other attractions bring guests indoors, out of the California sunshine, this one encourages visitors to stay outside in an environment so low-tech that it's almost *no*-tech.

8. Guests invent the island experience themselves, with no "safety bar"

stifling imaginative impulses to explore hidden areas, secret passageways, and multiple trails.

9. Guests can no longer fish from the island as they once could, but they can still view the wildlife—and not just the realistic animal statues standing along the river banks (to the surprise of some guests, those wild ducks that drift across the waters are real).

10. In its early years, the island contained the highest point at Disneyland that guests could access (identified on free island maps as Tom & Huck's Treehouse).

A Half-Dozen Questions About Pirates of the Caribbean

When we asked ten Disneyland experts what their favorite attraction was, Pirates of the Caribbean was the most frequent answer (see page 318). Yet, as much as we love Pirates (we've been enjoying the ride since its first summer in 1967), there are still some questions about the attraction that we've never been able to answer.

1. Why are skeletons shown first and "live" pirates shown later? Is the cruise a flashback? If it is, does that make the wrecked ship we see in an early storm scene the same ship we later see attacking the fort?

2. Why do some of the skeletons move as if they're alive, while others remain motionless? The talking skull at the first waterfall moves, the skeleton steering a ship through a storm moves, but between them is a skeleton pinned to the wall by a sword, and he doesn't move. Shouldn't all the skeletons be *dead*, as in motionless? Or, conversely, shouldn't they all move?

3. The spooky voices that say, "Dead men tell no tales" and "Perhaps he knows too much"—which pirates speak those lines? Do we see them at some point during the attraction?

4. In the "Crew's Quarters" there's a painting called *A Portrait of Things to Come* that shows a voluptuous girl barely dressed in pirate's accessories. Is she the same curvy redhead who is later auctioned off?

5. As the bateaux slide up the waterfall at the end, why are there small, eerie eyes watching us from the darkness? Aren't these eyes better suited to the Haunted Mansion?

6. Does Captain Jack Sparrow's final triumph undermine this attraction's moral? Let's say that the first half of the cruise with the skeletons shows the outcome of "the pirate's life," and the second half shows pirates being pirates. If this is the case, the original finale that ended with reckless gunplay next to *explosivos* would lead us to expect that all the drunken sots on display were about to become skeletons themselves. (When the attraction was previewed in the January 21, 1968 episode of *Walt Disney's Wonderful World of Color*, a loud explosion behind guests as they rode back up the waterfall suggested that the pirates had blown themselves up.) Yet at the end of the ride, Captain Sparrow is shown surrounded by piles of treasure (obviously Sparrow is no ordinary pirate, but even in the movies he doesn't get away with all of this treasure). Doesn't Sparrow's triumph make the "curse" and all of the ride's skeletal foreshadowing irrelevant?

A Dozen Awesome Audio-Animatronic Characters

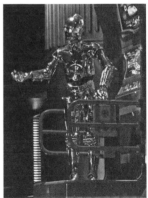

In 1963, the Enchanted Tiki Room introduced moving, talking birds that seemed realistic even when viewed up close. The word "Audio-Animatronic," a portmanteau word blending sound and animation, was coined to describe the new Disney technology that led to their development (which involved a primitive computer the size of a closet). Since then, there have been remarkable advances that have led to figures so lifelike that some guests swear they must be real people, not electro-mechanical robots. Here are a dozen of the best, listed chronologically.

1. 1965: Abraham Lincoln in Great Moments with Mr. Lincoln, the most ambitious Audio-Animatronic figure of its time.

2. 1966: Realistic dinosaurs in the Primeval World Diorama, still impressive and imposing.

3. 1967: Tom Morrow, a sophisticated scientist who directed activities in Flight to the Moon's pre-flight area.

4. 1967: Pirates of the Caribbean's pirate auctioneer, a marvel of subtle motion.

5. 1967: The personable time-traveling father in the Carousel of Progress.

6. 1972: Amiable bruins filled the Country Bear Jamboree, but Henry, the charismatic emcee, was the standout.

7. 1978: Seen only briefly, the Matterhorn's Abominable Snowman leaves a lasting impression.

8. 1987: Viewed in the Star Tours queue area, C-3PO jokes, frets, and moves just like the mechanical droid in the *Star Wars* films (*page 127*).

9. 1998: Tom Morrow (the second version), a wise-cracking Innoventions robot who had transparent skin and Nathan Lane's voice.

10. 2006: The Captain Sparrow character added throughout Pirates of the Caribbean in 2006 makes some guests believe they are actually seeing Johnny Depp.

11. 2010: Indiana Jones, introduced in the Indiana Jones Adventure in 1995 and updated fifteen years later, became one of the most realistic A-A machines ever.

12. 2013: The Figaro figure sitting on the Royal Hall's ledge is not a landmark development, but this playful cat is a charming addition to the Fantasy Faire area.

A Dozen Great Updates to Already-Existing Attractions

Attractions get updated all the time at Disneyland, but some updates are more comprehensive and impressive than others.

1. Alice in Wonderland: When it opened in 1958, this attraction's sets were made up of flat painted boards; a 1984 update brought major design improvements, a new "un-birthday" finale, and a minute of additional ride time.

2. Autopia: The cars and track have been undergoing modifications for decades, but in 2000 this attraction absorbed the nearby Fantasyland Autopia to offer a longer, more exciting, and more humorous driving experience that even includes a bouncy "off-road" section.

3. The Haunted Mansion: This 1969 classic got a whole new attic sequence in 2006 that introduced a murderous bride and her vanishing victims.

4. Jungle Cruise: There have been about a dozen updates to this classic attraction. Some of the most important changes came in the early 1960s. By 1964, there were playful elephants in a bathing pool and a "lost safari" (*opposite*) in the African Veldt, all described with humorous new patter from the skippers (in the Jungle Cruise's early years, the skippers delivered serious narration). In 1994, a new two-story queue area was made to look old and stuffed with period artifacts.

5. Mad Hatter's Mad Tea Party: In early 1982, Imagineers shut down the teacups for over a year and moved them 150 feet over by Alice in Wonderland. New party lights and other fun design elements add to the festive atmosphere.

6. Matterhorn Bobsleds: From 1959 to 1977, guests could clearly see the support beams inside the mountain. A terrific 1978 remodel added interior "ice cave" features and a scary Abominable Snowman.

7. Monorail: In 1961, the 0.8-mile track was dramatically extended outside the park by a mile and a half to a new Monorail station at the Disneyland Hotel. By delivering guests to and from the Tomorrowland station to another one outside the park (and even crossing over a public street), the Monorail became the mass-transit system Walt Disney had always intended it to be.

8. Mr. Toad's Wild Ride: A major renovation in 1983 introduced new scenes and gags to the interior and a stunning new mansion design to the exterior, making the multi-chimneyed Toad Hall one of Fantasyland's architectural highlights.

9. Sleeping Beauty Castle Walk-Through: Always a satisfying charmer with some of Fantasyland's best summer shade, this 1957 attraction quietly closed in 2001. It reopened in 2008, and fans rejoiced at the rejuvenated displays enhanced with beautiful new effects (and a new ground-floor viewing room for guests who couldn't negotiate the tight stairways).

10. Star Tours: The first iteration of this energetic flight-simulator lasted from 1987 to 2010. It reopened in 2011 as Star Tours: The Adventures Continue, an acclaimed re-imagining with a revised queue area, new film footage, multiple paths through the plot, and 3-D technology.

11. Submarine Voyage: After a nine-year closure and an upgrade rumored to cost over $70 million, the much-missed subs returned in 2007 as the Finding Nemo Submarine Voyage. The fleet now runs on electricity, not diesel fuel, and the new story involves little Nemo, Dory, Crush, new sea creatures and plants, a dazzling erupting volcano, a beautiful coral reef made of thirty tons of recycled glass, and an Australian narrator who mentions the old attraction's mermaids and sea serpent.

12. Tom Sawyer Island: Walt Disney himself designed the original island in 1956, so some purists resisted 2007's extensive new Pirate's Lair theme, which included a sunken pirate ship, hidden treasure, ghostly apparitions, and other modifications based on the *Pirates of the Caribbean* movies.

8 Surprising Scenes at Disneyland

Disneyland guests don't always see these surprising moments coming.

1. Autopia: It might have seemed like a good idea at the time, but now it's surprising that from 1955 to 1965, the Autopia in Tomorrowland had no center rail, giving drivers free reign to bash their cars together (or even turn around and drive against traffic).

2. Mr. Toad's Wild Ride: Not many first-time riders of this 1955 classic expect that their crazy, cartoony car trip is going to send them to a fiery, demon-populated hell.

3. Tom Sawyer Island: For decades, the burning cabin at the north end of the island (opened in 1956) had a dead settler sprawled in the dirt with an arrow sticking out of him; today, there's no body and the fire is out.

4. Holidayland: Despite Disneyland's "no public alcohol" policy, from 1957 to 1961 guests could buy picnic baskets with beer in Holidayland, the outdoor activity area west of Frontierland.

5. *40 Pounds of Trouble*: When Universal Pictures made this Tony Curtis film in 1962, it was allowed to film at Disneyland. The finished product includes about nineteen minutes of park footage, some of which distorts Disneyland's layout (the Monorail stops to let passengers out at Town Square, and several Fantasyland attractions seem to be connected so that one segues right into another).

6. Tomorrowland with no *Moonliner*: More icon than rocket, the statuesque seventy-six-foot-tall *Moonliner* was early Tomorrowland's most identifiable symbol; yet somehow it lasted only a decade, vanishing in 1966 and not returning until 1998 at just two-thirds the original size.

7. Pirates of the Caribbean: The humor and spirit of this 1967 attraction make it easier to accept some surprising scenes (such as the wench auction) that some viewers might otherwise object to.

8. State Fair: Walt Disney may have stated that prosaic carnival rides like the Ferris wheel had no place in Disneyland, but surprisingly (and disappointingly, to many guests) the 1987 State Fair promotion planted a Ferris wheel above the park's entrance tunnels.

A Dozen Innovative Disneyland Attractions

Every corner of Disneyland offers something to delight guests, but some attractions have been more than delightful—they've been truly innovative. Here are a dozen of the park's most inventive attractions, listed here in chronological order (debut years are in parentheses).

1. Jungle Cruise (1955): This landmark attraction introduced Disneyland's first realistic mechanical animals.

2. Peter Pan's Flight (1955): Ride vehicles with the track running along the ceiling, not on the ground, gave the illusion of flight.

3. House of the Future (1957): Guests got their first view of a microwave oven, picture phones, intercoms, and other futuristic devices.

4. Matterhorn Bobsleds (1959): This was the first coaster with tubular metal rails, allowing for quieter rides and sharper turns.

5. Bell Telephone Systems Phone Exhibits (1960): This exhibit featured the new wonders of long-distance dialing; later, the Chatterbox introduced the speakerphone experience.

6. Enchanted Tiki Room (1963): This attraction gave guests their first prolonged close-up look at Disney's revolutionary Audio-Animatronics technology.

7. Great Moments with Mr. Lincoln (1965): This patriotic favorite was an iconic milestone in the development of realistic Audio-Animatronics.

8. Pirates of the Caribbean (1967): A bayou beginning, subterranean cruise midpoint, and burning-town finale—one of the most ingenious and elaborate environments ever created for an attraction.

9. Adventure Thru Inner Space (1967): This was Disneyland's first implementation of the new Omnimover system, the cozy clam-shaped "pods" that turned and tilted so riders saw only what the designers wanted them to see.

10. The Haunted Mansion (1969): Guests still wonder how some of the effects are done.

11. Star Tours (1987): This is the most convincing flight simulator most guests will ever experience.

12. Indiana Jones Adventure (1995): Guests ride on Disneyland's most complex ride vehicles at this attraction, offering 160,000 variations of the Indy experience.

Ranking Disneyland's Thrill Rides

Disneyland has many famous attractions—Pirates of the Caribbean, the Haunted Mansion, the Jungle Cruise—but only a handful qualify as true "thrill rides." The park's high-speed attractions are ranked based on how much bang you get for your Disneyland buck.

1. Indiana Jones Adventure: A bumpy, unrelentingly intense experience so densely themed that you can barely catch all the sensory details.

2. Space Mountain: A lights-out thrill since 1977.

3. Star Tours: The speed is on the screen in this exhilarating flight simulator.

4. Matterhorn Bobsleds: Debuting in 1959, Disneyland's first major thrill ride is historically vital and still fun.

5. Splash Mountain: There's just one major thrill on this pleasant ten-minute journey—the heart-stopping plunge near the end—but it's a whopper.

6. Big Thunder Mountain: This moderately exciting roller coaster has impressive theming.

7. Gadget's Go Coaster: A charming roller coaster for children that lasts barely a minute.

10 Disneyland Attractions That We Wish Were Longer

Disneyland attractions are generally so flawless that it's almost heretical to suggest some could be better. But we think a few would be improved just by extending or enhancing what they already do. We acknowledge that there are probably cost, space, or safety issues that would be prohibitive. As Walt Disney said in 1966 regarding the implementation of his EPCOT ideas, "We don't presume to know all the answers."

1. Alice in Wonderland: We've always liked the forty-five-second Wonderland journey that brings the caterpillar vehicles outside and lowers them from the second story to the ground floor along the tops of oversized plants (still true, even after a 2014 refurbishment that slightly altered the experience). However, with the Matterhorn, Monorail, and some of Fantasyland in view during the ride, it's a nice little trip we'd happily double in length if we could.

2. Golden Horseshoe: The acts here are uniformly terrific, but for years there's been only one performing group per twenty-five-minute show; the original forty-five-minute *Golden Horseshoe Revue* (1955–1986) included various performers (a comedian, a singer, dancers, etc.) in every show, a classic variety format we'd like to see occasionally revived again.

3. The Haunted Mansion: Leaving the "stretching room" elevator, guests enter a sixty-foot-long hallway with intaglio busts at the far end and changing portraits lining the hallway's right-hand wall. The left-hand wall, however, feels underused, dominated by some furniture and ornately decorated windows that flash with lightning. Though the pedestrian traffic here might slow down a bit as a result, we wish this wall displayed additional only-in-Disneyland effects.

4. Peter Pan's Flight: The brief tours above London and Neverland are so enchanting that the whole flight could be more of the same without any characters or drama.

5. Pinocchio's Daring Journey: About two and a half minutes into the journey, the Blue Fairy appears and magically transforms Pinocchio into a boy, but her appearance is so quick and hard to see that some guests can't recall it even happening.

6. Pirates of the Caribbean: Everything that happens after you pass the talking skull and then glide down the two waterfalls is legendary, of course, but the first part of the cruise—the gentle drift through the serene bayou environment with clouds drifting above—is so lovely that it could go on and on with additional scenes.

7. Sleeping Beauty Castle Walk-Through: A wonderful castle experience that only begs for more—how cool would it be if guests could walk an exterior balcony, or at least look out a window? (Actually, one of the early Castle Walk-Through plans included a route that took guests outside to a second-floor balcony, where they would have looked out upon sleeping guards still under Maleficent's spell.)

8. Splash Mountain: If you embarked on the ride for the dramatic final plunge, you'll wish the five-second, high-speed moment stretched out even longer.

9. Tarzan's Treehouse: After the long climb up, guests reach a small area at the very top offering what Walt Disney called a "wonderful view" (in 1965's "Disneyland's Tenth Anniversary" episode of *Walt Disney's Wonderful World of Color*). While it is wonderful, it could be even more wonderful if it weren't so narrow. Imagine a wide, open platform at this high perch where guests could linger and scan the whole park, rather than just small slices of it. Guests would invent new adjectives to describe the breathtaking panorama.

10. Pirate's Lair on Tom Sawyer Island: Dead Man's Grotto (formerly Injun Joe's Cave) is terrific, but it basically goes in one crooked line for 120 feet, west to east across the island. Wouldn't this spelunking adventure be even cooler if it branched off in the middle to offer some north–south options?

18 Secrets in the Haunted Mansion

One of Disneyland's most eagerly awaited debuts was the opening of the Haunted Mansion on August 9, 1969. When it finally opened at the height of the summer tourist season, the exciting new attraction drew some of Disneyland's largest crowds ever. Fans have been teasing secrets out of the building ever since.

1. Before Disneyland opened in 1955, there were already tentative plans for some kind of haunted house (a 1951 concept drawing depicted a haunted mansion on a hill, and a 1953 illustration placed a rickety haunted house at the end of Main Street).

2. By 1957, there was a basic design and backstory for the mansion. The plot included a murderous sea captain who hanged himself (most of this plot was abandoned in the end, but some individual elements endured, such as the hanging corpse seen early in the attraction).

3. The maritime weathervane atop the Haunted Mansion refers to the original storyline about the murderous mariner.

4. Walt Disney quickly rejected any design that portrayed a dilapidated mansion reminiscent of the creepy haunted houses in films. Disneyland structures, he decreed, would not look run-down and neglected.

5. In 1961, the Haunted Mansion was slated for a 1963 debut. In fact, a tantalizing three-story mansion with four stately columns was built on time. Work then stopped so that Walt Disney and his designers could focus on creating four new attractions for the 1964–1965 New York World's Fair. Mansion construction resumed in 1967.

6. Before it debuted, the Haunted Mansion underwent two major revisions: transformation from a seriously scary attraction into a "happy haunt" with "frightfully funny" ghosts, and the introduction of the efficient Omnimover system (Doom Buggies) to convey thousands of riders through the attraction every hour.

7. Once inside the building and past the foyer, guests enter a "stretching room" that lowers them fifteen feet down into a subterranean walkway. This clever "portrait gallery" leads guests under Disneyland's railroad tracks to a one-acre "show building" next door, where the Doom Buggies await.

8. The elegantly dressed cast members at this attraction are actually encouraged *not* to smile.

9. Merchandise generated by the Haunted Mansion includes a jigsaw puzzle, board game, dinner plate, and soundtrack album.

10. Contrasting the colorful flowers elsewhere in Disneyland, many plants around the mansion are dark and foreboding.

11. A black cat and a raven were considered as guides inside the building before an unseen "Ghost Host," the character performed by Paul Frees, was invented (early on there was discussion about having Walt Disney record narration for the host's voice).

12. The Madame Leota floating-head illusion shows the face of Leota Toombs, a Disney Imagineer. Her voice was provided by veteran actress Eleanor Audley, who also voiced roles in the films *Cinderella* and *Sleeping Beauty*.

13. The ballroom's organ is from the film 20,000 *Leagues Under the Sea*.

14. In addition to the main pet cemetery in the queue area, there's also a hidden cemetery behind and to the right of the building.

15. The singing busts have names—Cousin Algernon, Ned Nub, Phineas P. Pock, Uncle Theodore, and Rollo Rumkin (Walt Disney's visage is not on a broken bust, as rumored; that's actually singer Thurl Ravenscroft).

16. The hitchhiking ghosts at the end of the Doom Buggy ride also have names: Phineas (carrying a bag), Ezra (lifting his hat), and Gus (holding a ball and chain).

17. The cake on the banquet table has thirteen candles.

18. At one time, a live cast member in a suit of armor would jump out to enliven the experience for repeat visitors.

A Dozen Quotes from the Haunted Mansion

As good as the effects are, the Haunted Mansion wouldn't be the same without its famous narration by the invisible "Ghost Host."

1. In the foyer: "When hinges creak in doorless chambers, and strange and frightening sounds echo through the halls; whenever candle lights flicker where the air is deathly still; that is the time when ghosts are present, practicing their terror with ghoulish delight!"

2. Pre-stretched portrait gallery: "Welcome, foolish mortals, to the Haunted Mansion! I am your host—your Ghost Host. Kindly step all the way in please and make room for everyone. There's no turning back now."

3. Pre-stretched portrait gallery: "Our tour begins here in this gallery where you see paintings of some of our guests as they appeared in their corruptible, mortal state."

4. Post-stretched portrait gallery: "And consider this dismaying observation: this chamber has no windows, and no doors. Which offers you this chilling challenge: to find a way out! Of course, there's always *my* way!"

5. Portrait hallway: "Now, as they say, look alive, and we'll continue our little tour. And let's all stay together, please . . . we have 999 happy haunts here, but there's room for a thousand. Any volunteers? If you insist on lagging behind, you may not need to volunteer!"

6. Inside the Doom Buggies: "Do not pull down on the safety bar, please; I will lower it for you."

7. Inside the Doom Buggies: "We find it delightfully unlivable here in this ghostly retreat. Every room has wall-to-wall creeps, and hot and cold running chills."

8. Madame Leota: "Creepies and crawlies, toads in a pond; let there be music, from regions beyond! Wizards and witches, wherever you dwell; give us a hint, by ringing a bell!"

9. Overlooking the Grand Ballroom: "The happy haunts have received your sympathetic vibrations and are beginning to materialize. They're assembling for a swinging wake."

10. Mirror at the exit: "Ah, there you are, and just in time. There's a little 1matter I forgot to mention. Beware of hitchhiking ghosts!"

11. Little Leota: "Hurry back! Hurry back! Be sure to bring your death certificate."

12. Song: "When the crypt doors creak and the tombstones quake, spooks come out for a swinging wake! Happy haunts materialize, and begin to vocalize. Grim grinning ghosts come out to socialize!"

A Dozen Quotes from Pirates of the Caribbean

In addition to its awesome engineering, environment, and robotics, this classic attraction's spoken script helps make it even more memorable.

1. Pirate skull: "Avast there! It be too late to alter course, mateys, and there be plundering pirates lurking in every cove, waitin' to board."

2. Pirate skull: "Mark well me words, mateys—dead men tell no tales! Ye come seekin' adventure and salty ol' pirates, eh? Sure ye come to the proper place."

3. Skeleton pirate with treasure: "Aye, blood money and cursed it be."

4. Narrator: "No fear have ye of evil curses, says you? Properly warned ye be, says I."

5. Ghostly pirate voice: "Perhaps he knows too much—he's seen the cursed treasure."

6. Captain of the *Wicked Wench*: "They need persuadin', mates! Fire at will! ... Give it to 'em again, lads!"

7. Pirate in town: "Wake up, you bilge rats! Where be the treasure?"

8. Auctioneer: "Shift yer cargo, dearie, show 'em yer larboard side."

9. Auctioneer: "Do I hear six? Who'll make it six?" Pirate: "Six it be. Six bottles of rum!"

10. Auctioneer: "Strike yer colors, ye brazen wench. No need to expose yer superstructure!"

11. Jailed pirates: "Mangy mutt! Hit him with a soup bone!"

12. Song: "Yo ho, yo ho, a pirate's life for me! We pillage, we plunder, we rifle and loot, drink up, me hearties, yo ho! We kidnap and ravage and don't give a hoot, drink up, me hearties, yo ho!"

10 Classic Jokes from the Mine Train

From 1956 to 1977, the Mine Train took guests on a long, relaxed tour of Frontierland wilderness. After the extensively re-landscaped Nature's Wonderland area opened in 1960, a steady stream of amiable recorded narration noted scenic highlights during the train's nearly ten-minute journey. Here are ten of our favorite jokes heard along the way.

1. "Please stay seated at all times and keep yer hands and arms inside the train—the animals get mighty hungry."

2. "As we come outta this first tunnel, we'll be enterin' Beaver Valley. Looks like the beavers are buildin' another dam. Yessir, they're really busy as a ... well, busy as a beaver."

3. "We're comin' up on Big Thunder, the biggest falls in all these here parts. Ya don't hafta worry though. Unless the wind changes."

4. "We're comin' into Bear Country now, folks, and while we're crossin' the old trestle ya gotta sit real still. No tellin' how long she's gonna last."

5. "Y'know, bears are one of the most playful animals there is. Lazy, too. All they wanna do is lay around an' scratch an' fish an' swim—that is, when they ain't sleepin'."

6. "Look on that bank across Bear Creek there. Now there's a real struggle fer survival: two stags are battlin' fer them cow elk. Maybe you folks can

tell me, though—does gettin' two women-folk mean yer the winner or the loser? Never could figure that one out."

7. "Now ahead of us, folks, is a giant saguaro cactus forest. The desert heat sometimes gets to ya an' makes these here cactus take on strange shapes—like animals, an' sometimes even people!"

8. "Them wild pigs has caught up with ol' Mr. Bobcat. He's in kind of a sticky situation."

9. "This is geyser country. . . . We never know when she's gonna go off. That's why we call her Ol' Unfaithful."

10. "Now to find the exit, folks, just head right fer the front of the train. And if ya got a mountain lion sittin' next to ya, don't feed him. Just tell him to hop out an' hightail it back to his own stompin' ground!"

30 Classic Jokes from the Jungle Cruise

These are just a few of the many variations of old and new gags we've heard on this laugh-a-minute jokefest—uh, perilous journey—down exotic rivers (and on the dock).

1. "No picture-taking in line. They're nailed to the wall for a reason, people."

2. "Bye, everybody! See you in three weeks! Just kidding, you'll never make it back."

3. "Welcome aboard the world-famous Jungle Cruise. I'll be your skipper for as far as we get."

4. "I'm your skipper, Les Capable."

5. "Turn around and wave goodbye to the folks back on the dock. You might never see them again."

6. "In case of a water landing, children can be used as flotation devices."

7. "Please don't worry about this gun. Each bullet is just like my mind. Blank."

8. "That building over there is something we call Indiana Jones and the Temple of the Three-Hour Line."

9. "This broken temple was Disneyland's first attempt at building the Monorail."

10. "Be careful of the crocodiles. They're always looking for a handout."

11. "Look at all the elephants! If you want to take pictures, go ahead, because they all have their trunks on."

12. "That's native art over on that dugout canoe. It's called a skull-pture."

13. "As we approach the gorillas, if you're wearing yellow, please don't make any noises like a banana. It drives them ape. They might find you very appealing."

14. "The owner of that upside-down Jeep should call TripleApe."

15. "We're in an area filled with rare tropical plants. I'll take a moment to point some out to you. There's one. There's another one."

16. "Now there's something on the right you don't see every day. But I do."

17. "We're now approaching beautiful Schweitzer Falls, named after the famous African explorer, Dr. Albert Falls."

18. "Here we are on the African Veldt. Don't worry, that zebra is just sleeping. Those lions are his friends. They're enjoying their favorite dish: zebra on the rocks."

19. "There's the lost safari. They're obviously involved in some kind of native uprising. That rhino seems to be getting his point across, and I'm sure the guy on the bottom will get the point in the end."

20. "If you get hit by a spear, throw it back. You can't keep souvenirs. We wouldn't want you to get stuck with one."

21. "Beautiful Schweitzer Falls once again. There it is, the backside of water! The chemical name is O2H."

22. "On the right are some fascinating rock formations. I point them out to people all the time, but they just take them for granite."

23. "See that snake? Know what kind it is? Plastic."

24. "There's old Trader Sam, head salesman in this area. Business has been shrinking lately, so Sam's offering a two-for-one special: two of his for one of yours."

25. "And now, the most dangerous part of our journey: the return to civilization."

26. "As we approach, please notice that there's a dock on the left, and a dock on the right. It's a paradox."

27. "The Jungle Cruise has been brought to you today by the Hippo Farmers of America. Hippo: the other-other white meat."

28. "I hope you all enjoyed your trip around the jungle. I had such a good time, I'm going to go again . . . and again . . . and again. Stay in school, kids. Seriously, stay in school."

29. "Please exit the boat the same way you entered—pushing and shoving."

30. "I'm going to tell you something my father told me when I turned eighteen. The free ride is over. Get out."

10 Announcements and Inside Jokes from Star Tours

The long Star Tours script has included references to scenes in the *Star Wars* movies, inside jokes about George Lucas (numbers two and six below), and even a mention of a figure who was found elsewhere in Tomorrowland (number seven).

1. Announcer: "Star Tours introduces the perfect getaway vacation with exclusive tour packages to Hoth. Now you can ski the most incredible slopes in the galaxy. Or, if you prefer, explore beautiful and mysterious ice caverns and the famed Echo Base of the Rebellion forces. And while you're there, be sure to enjoy an exhilarating ride on a Tauntaun. It's all on Hoth, and it all begins soon, only from Star Tours."

2. Announcer: "Will the owner of a red and black landspeeder, vehicle ID THX-1138, please return to your craft? You are parked in a no-hover area."

3. C-3PO: "I do wish I could go with you to Endor. On second thought, I just remembered how much I hate space travel. You have a nice trip though, Artoo."

4. Announcer: "Star Tours is now offering convenient daily departures to the exotic Moon of Endor. Come spend an afternoon or the entire day with the lovable Ewoks in their charming tribal villages. It's a fun-filled visit that you and your family will remember forever! Just ask for the Endor Express. Available only from Star Tours. Nonstop flights leave every few minutes, so don't delay. Visit Endor today!" C-3PO: "Things have certainly changed since we were last there. I thought we were doomed for sure."

5. Announcer: "Star Tours is proud to introduce the StarSpeeder 3000, the most advanced transport of its kind in existence. With high-speed warp drive and a travel range of over one billion light years, the 3000 makes touring the galaxy safe and comfortable. And all our StarSpeeders are piloted by the newest, most reliable RX droids, so you can sit back, relax, and enjoy the sights. Whenever your plans call for intergalactic travel, call on the best—Star Tours!" C-3PO: "If this transport is 'the best,' then why are we always repairing it?"

6. Announcer: "Departing Endor passenger Sacul, Mr. Egroeg Sacul, please see the Star Tours agent at gate number three."

7. Announcer: "Mr. Morrow, Mr. Tom Morrow, please check with the Star Tours agent at gate number four."

8. Maintenance droid: "Now was I supposed to weld that logic module positive to positive, or negative to negative? No, no, I'm positive it was

negative to positive, absolutely positive."

9. Maintenance droid: "What are you all staring at? Oh, me! Well, you got cameras, why don't you take a picture? It'll last longer!"

10. Captain Rex: "Welcome aboard! This is Captain Rex from the cockpit. I know this is probably your first flight, and it's mine, too!"

A Dozen Quotes from Other Disneyland Attractions

Veteran riders will recognize all these familiar phrases.

1. Adventure Thru Inner Space: "For centuries, man had but his own two eyes to explore the wonders of his world. Then he invented the microscope—a mighty eye—and discovered the fantastic universe beyond the limits of his own meager sight. Now your adventure through inner space has begun. Through Monsanto's Mighty Microscope, you will travel into the incredible universe found within a tiny fragment of a snowflake. I am the first person to make this fabulous journey. Suspended in the timelessness of inner space are the thought waves of my first impressions. They will be our only source of contact once you have passed beyond the limits of normal magnification-magnification-magnification."

2. Big Thunder Mountain Railroad: "This here's the wildest ride in the wilderness!"

3. Country Bear Jamboree: "Howdy folks! Welcome to the one and only o-riginal Country Bear Jamboree, featuring a bit of Americana, our musical heritage of the past. But enough of this chit-chat, yak-yak, and flimflam. Just refrain from hibernatin', and we'll all enjoy the show!"

4. Disneyland Railroad: "Ladies and Gentlemen, welcome aboard the Santa Fe & Disneyland Railroad. We're now embarking on a grand circle trip around Disneyland. Throughout our journey, we ask that you keep your hands and arms inside the train, remain seated at all times, and no smoking, please."

5. Fantasmic!: "Some imagination, huh?"

6. Indiana Jones Adventure: "Tourists! Why did it have to be tourists!"

7. Main Street Electrical Parade: "Ladies and gentlemen, boys and girls, Disneyland proudly presents our spectacular festival pageant of nighttime magic and imagination in thousands of sparkling lights and electro-synthe-magnetic musical sounds—the Main Street Electrical Parade!"

8. Mission to Mars: "Ladies and gentlemen, this is our McDonnell-Douglas Mission Control room at Disneyland Spaceport. The Director of

Operations has been expecting you, and while we're waiting for our flight to be called, he'll take a few minutes to describe what's going on. Excuse me, Mr. Johnson?"

9. Monorail: "We're now approaching the Tomorrowland Monorail Station, our final destination. Please remain seated until the Monorail comes to a complete stop. Then, collect your belongings, watch your head, and step carefully from the train. On behalf of all of our crew, thank you for traveling with us, and we hope you'll have a happy and memorable visit here at Disneyland. This is the Tomorrowland Monorail Station."

10. PeopleMover: "Welcome aboard the Goodyear PeopleMover, the first such transportation system anywhere in the world, and your front row seat for a grand circle tour of Tomorrowland."

11. Peter Pan's Flight: "Come on everybody, here we gooooooo!"

12. Space Mountain: "All personnel, clear launch platform."

5 Incongruities on Disneyland's Attractions

We're not complaining, because each of the following attractions is delightful in its own way. We're just pointing out some things we've noticed that seem like incongruities, none of which spoil the experiences but do start interesting conversations.

1. It's a Small World: This justifiably famous attraction can be interpreted as a celebration of youthful innocence, courtesy of its delightful scenes and memorable song that encourages global unity ("there's so much that we share"), optimism ("a world of hopes"), and affability ("a smile means friendship to everyone"). But a celebration of diversity? Not so much. True, the  adorable 300-plus dolls inside the attraction come in a variety of skin tones, hairstyles, and international costumes; however, except for a few Disney characters that were added in 2008, they're all basically the same shape and size, with the same basic facial features. Apparently, it's a clone world after all.

2. King Arthur Carrousel: Sure, the glittering carousel spins in the shadow of Sleeping Beauty Castle, but why were large images from the *Sleeping Beauty* movie added to the ride in 2003? Shouldn't the prominently displayed images around the carousel's core come from *The Sword in the*

Stone, in keeping with the King Arthur theme? Although the images are undeniably beautiful, and undoubtedly (for some viewers) connect the carousel with the castle, the *Sleeping Beauty* scenes still seem out of place, considering that royal crowns, shields from the Knights of the Round Table, and a horse named after Arthur's most famous knight are also part of this classic attraction.

3. Mr. Toad's Wild Ride: After a rollicking romp through London's streets, Toad's frantic escapade delivers him (and guests) to hell—literally, a blazing, demon-populated hell. No other Disneyland attraction veers so far from the movie that inspired it (the film ends with Toad giddily soaring off in a flying machine). Perhaps the finale is a warning—drive recklessly like Toad, and you'll suffer dire consequences—but the sudden prospect of eternal burning and jabbing by pitchfork-wielding demons is such a wonderfully absurd non sequitur that it seems more comedic than cautious.

4. Pixie Hollow: When did Tinker Bell get so tiny? In the movie *Peter Pan*, she flies up to Peter and is as tall as his whole face, a height of maybe seven inches. She also barely fits inside Hook's lantern, again suggesting she's six to eight inches tall. But in Disneyland's Pixie Hollow, she and the guests touring this adorable area are dwarfed by blades of grass, reducing everybody to, what—a half-inch tall? This dinky scale should be called Adventure Thru Tinker Space.

5. Snow White's Scary Adventures: After surviving a harrowing adventure, guests finally burst into the daylight, where they see a mural that reads, "And they lived happily ever after." On the mural is the handsome prince, finally making his first appearance. Where has he been all this time? He wasn't around to romance Snow White at the beginning of the attraction (as he was in the movie), and the dwarfs were the ones who eventually chased down the old hag, so what exactly did the prince do to earn Snow White's "ever after"?

11 Disneyland Attractions with Excellent Endings

After a few minutes of fun, some attractions (the King Arthur Carrousel and the Astro-Orbitor, for instance) simply slow down and stop. But others—including those listed here alphabetically—build to fun, fascinating, and even fabulous finales.

1. Adventure Thru Inner Space (1967–1985): This legendary Tomorrowland trip inside the atom sprung a clever final joke when it revealed the moving blue eye of the scientist who was watching with his microscope.

2. Alice in Wonderland (1958–ongoing): Not so much a big finish as a wonderful way to descend from the building's second story, this attraction's ending takes guests outside and glides them down onto the tops of giant plants, making this the only Fantasyland dark ride that takes riders out into the open air.

3. Big Thunder Mountain Railroad (1979–ongoing): A splashdown at the dinosaur bones brings this thrilling ride to a dramatic close.

4. The Haunted Mansion (1969–ongoing): Just when you think the hitch-hiking ghosts have ended this classic attraction with a memorable illusion, there's Little Leota watching you ride up the escalator and beckoning you to "hurry baaaaaack."

5. It's a Small World (1966–ongoing): You've made all these new friends, and at the end you get all these nice goodbyes from them.

6. Matterhorn Bobsleds (1959–ongoing): Disneyland's original splashdown is an effective and exciting way to slow down the speeding vehicles.

7. Mine Train (1956–1977): The climax of this seven-minute trip was resplendent Rainbow Caverns, where black lights illuminated neon-colored waterfalls and glowing pools of luminescent water. Choral mood music accompanied the complex visual effects.

8. Mr. Toad's Wild Ride: Not many first-time riders expect to end their fun and funny escapade in hell; the last scene before the exit adds a fantastic flourish to the wild ride.

9. Primeval World Diorama (1966–ongoing): The displays of realistic dinosaurs climax with a towering Tyrannosaurus rex and a sturdy stegosaurus in a stunning fight scene borrowed from *Fantasia*.

10. Splash Mountain (1989–ongoing): After the fearsome plummet at the end of the ride, the mountain gives riders a chance to catch their breath with a rousing musical finale that puts a happy spin on the preceding drama.

11. Star Tours (1987–ongoing): In its first iteration, the chaotic space flight culminated with a heart-stopping careen toward a fuel-laden vehicle.

A Half-Dozen Ways to Experience Disneyland's Attractions

Ready to hit some attractions? Everyone knows the standard advice: get to the popular rides early before the big crowds arrive, consult the Hub's information board for wait times, and take advantage of FASTPASS (duh). But here are six additional strategies that offer different ways of experiencing the attractions.

1. Visit the attractions in the chronological order they were built—oldest first—to witness the evolution of ride technology. This approach may mean occasionally skipping a nearby attraction in favor of one that is farther away.

2. Only go on the attractions that Walt Disney himself could have experienced. Since Disney died in 1966, this approach eliminates many of the most popular rides (including 1967's Pirates of the Caribbean). Still, sacrificing the newer attractions means that you get to experience the park as Walt Disney himself saw it, with a full day's worth of attractions (most of Fantasyland, the Jungle Cruise, the Matterhorn Bobsleds, the Monorail, and the *Mark Twain*, to name just a few).

3. Visit the attractions in reverse geographical order, starting with the farthest first. Most people enter Disneyland from the south and head northward, so they probably visit Adventureland, Fantasyland, Frontierland, or Tomorrowland first. Instead, take the Disneyland Railroad to Mickey's Toontown, visit Toontown, and then make your way southward—the opposite direction of the crowds. (Keep in mind that this won't work first thing in the morning, since Toontown usually opens later than the rest of Disneyland).

4. Build up to the scary attractions. This strategy might appeal to families with young kids, because they would get to enjoy the gentlest attractions (the Storybook Land Canal Boats, for instance) as they work up to rides like Snow White's Scary Adventures, the Haunted Mansion, and the rollicking roller coasters.

5. In summer, beat the heat by bunching attractions into three groups—outdoors/indoors/outdoors—and visit them in that order. This puts all the air-conditioned indoor attractions (Innoventions, Pirates of the Caribbean, etc.) together in the middle of a scorching day.

6. Skip the attractions altogether. (Are we crazy? Disneyland with no attractions, after paying that steep admission price? Just hear us out.) Before Disneyland started requiring guests to buy Passports for unlimited rides in 1982, guests could pay one very low admission price and choose not to pay extra for the attractions. As strange as this might seem, it was a delightful option. The attractionless park is still bursting with amazing architecture and beautiful landscaping, free shows and live music, lavish parades and fabulous fireworks, fascinating exhibits and famous characters, terrific shopping and varied dining. Consider also that an attractionless park won't require long waits in hot lines, there will be no stressful sprints to the next FASTPASS machine or worries about FASTPASS return times, and you won't get nauseous from a spinning teacup or soaked by the Splash Mountain splashdown.

DISNEYLAND BY DESIGN

Imagination Brought to Life

Ray Bradbury's Summary
of Key Disneyland Design Features

In 2005, famed author Ray Bradbury published an essay collection called *Bradbury Speaks*. One of these essays, "Disneyland, or Disney's Demon for Happiness," briefly analyzes three key design features that Walt Disney insisted on having at Disneyland. According to Bradbury, Walt Disney "based his feelings on three things that he felt were lacking, which he wanted to supply."

1. "He wanted an environment of trees. Thousands of trees and bushes were not necessary, but he placed them in Disneyland anyway."

2. "What about fountains? Who needed them? But he stationed them in Disneyland anyway."

3. "Was there a real need for extra benches where people could sit and people-watch? He placed those things strategically."

7 Double-Sided Structures in Disneyland

These buildings are designed with two lands in mind.

1. Adventureland Bazaar (1955–ongoing): The exterior walkway passes by both Adventureland's colored stone walls and Frontierland's rough-hewn logs. The two styles meet abruptly at the restrooms.

2. Chicken Plantation (1955–1962): This two-story building on the western edge of Frontierland looked like a distinguished white mansion when viewed from the east; from the west, however, it had a rough-timber construction themed to the wilderness.

3. Jolly Holiday Bakery Café (2012–ongoing): Because this lovely building spans the border between the Hub and Adventureland, two décor styles still meet outside on the roof. Depending on the angle, guests can see either cut shingles or tropical thatch.

4. Pirates of the Caribbean (1967–ongoing): View this building from the Tarzan's Treehouse exit to see Adventureland theming (green walls, Victorian wood trim) butting right up against New Orleans Square styles (pale peach tones, ironwork).

5. Rancho del Zocalo Restaurante (2001–ongoing): The building itself isn't double-sided, but the sixty-foot hallway leading to Fantasy Faire certainly is—two-thirds of the way through, it changes from Frontierland to Fantasyland theming.

6. River Belle Terrace (1971–ongoing): The corner location where Frontierland rounds into Adventureland dictates the styles of this venerable restaurant's two entrances (cream-colored on the Frontierland side, and

pale blue on the Adventureland side). The roof also has two separate themes that match each land.

7. Village Haus (1983–ongoing): The restrooms in this building are split between Fantasyland and Frontierland; the women's entrance is surrounded by smooth pastel Fantasyland rock, but the men's entrance closer to Frontierland has rougher, darker rock to anticipate the wilderness landscape along the adjacent Big Thunder Trail.

14 Hidden Mickeys in Disneyland

Hidden Mickeys are subtle design elements shaped like Mickey Mouse heads that are incorporated throughout the park. A true Hidden Mickey isn't part of an obvious design that all guests are meant to see, such as the giant floral Mickey face at the park's entrance or a Mickey-shaped lollipop. Instead, they are inconspicuous representations of the classic three-circle Mickey Mouse head. Here are fourteen examples, listed alphabetically. For hundreds more throughout the Disneyland Resort, see Steve Barrett's comprehensive *Disneyland's Hidden Mickeys.*

1. Autopia: A tiny Mickey is displayed on the small registration tags adorning each car's license plate (*below left*).

2. Entrance: The benches in the ticket area have recognizable end supports (*pages 146–147*); also note the brackets underneath the ticket-area shelves.

3. Golden Horseshoe: Up by the stage, there's a vent near the floor punched with holes, including a Hidden Mickey in the lower-right corner.

4. The Haunted Mansion: Observe the arrangement of dinner plates in the busy ballroom scene.

5. King Arthur Carrousel: Note the three-jewel pattern (*below right*) on the flank of Jingles, the popular horse with bells.

6. Main Street Cinema: Steps inside are lit by Hidden Mickeys.

7. Main Street Cinema: The doorway to the north is for the Disneyland Casting Agency; two Hidden Mickeys are worked into the decorative border of the glass panel.

8. Many Adventures of Winnie the Pooh: Prior to Pooh's birthday party scene, guests will see a wall on

the right-hand side with dozens of painted spheres, especially a Hidden Mickey trio at the bottom right (see also the three balloons at floor level, near the exit to the right).

9. Mickey's House: The red car parked outside has Hidden Mickeys on its silver hubcaps (inside the house, note the Mickey symbols stamped onto the player piano's sheet music).

10. Minnie's House: Find the red Hidden Mickey on the Cheese Relish inside Minnie's refrigerator (*above left*).

11. Pirates of the Caribbean: The hanging barrels near the end are grouped into a familiar pattern (*above right*).

12. Rivers of America: As seen from the *Mark Twain*, three rocks have been carefully arranged in the waters north of Tom Sawyer Island (*below left*).

13. Sleeping Beauty Castle: The safety railings added to the bridge across the moat in 2014 feature three-circle metalwork.

14. Tarzan's Treehouse: As Jane sketches Tarzan, a nearby chest on the floor features a Hidden Mickey keyhole (*far right*).

15 Cool Queues at Disneyland

Before Disneyland built its first line-management systems in the 1950s, queues in amusement parks usually stretched out in straight lines, blocking walkways and making people at the end feel as if the line went on forever. By contrast, Disneyland's queues snake back and forth with a series of ever-moving switchbacks, keeping everybody near the attraction's entrance and giving designers the chance to enliven the line with thematic elements. These fifteen alphabetically listed Disneyland attractions from the past and present have shown just how cool queues can be.

1. Adventure Thru Inner Space (extinct): Guests in line watched People-Mover trains move through the back of the queue area, a Mighty Microscope that seemed to shrink guests, and eight TV-sized terminals that

previewed the Inner Space journey ahead.

2. Autopia: Cute animations on a big queue-area screen were added when Chevron began sponsoring the attraction in 2000.

3. Big Thunder Mountain Railroad: Actual mining antiques and the miniature town of Rainbow Ridge reinforce the frontier experience.

4. Buzz Lightyear Astro Blasters: Bright murals and an Audio-Animatronic Buzz Lightyear precede the boarding area.

5. Circle-Vision 360 theater (extinct): Waiting guests could sit in a large room with phone exhibits and flag displays.

6. The Haunted Mansion: The line takes guests past a haunted hearse and a pet cemetery with humorous tombstones.

7. Indiana Jones Adventure: Disneyland's longest queue features short movies and interactive archaeological ruins. The queue area is so cool, it was open for guests to explore months before the actual attraction was ready.

8. It's a Small World: The elaborate façade, giant clock, and creative topiaries are so fascinating that some people come to see them without even going in the boats.

9. Jungle Cruise: The 1994 remodel added a two-story area with vintage adventure-themed displays.

10. Mickey's House: Before guests reach the main photo op with Mickey, they visit a theater where they can view various cartoons.

11. Roger Rabbit's Car Toon Spin: The comical garage interior is just right for this cartoony attraction.

12. Snow White's Scary Adventures: A shiny apple to touch and a creepy dungeon supplement the queue's colorful mural.

13. Space Mountain: An imposing spaceship dominates the main loading area.

14. Splash Mountain: Preceding the log ride are folksy themed interiors.

15. Star Tours: *Star Wars* imagery and lively Audio-Animatronic characters line the corridors as "official" announcements are made over loudspeakers, creating the experience of actually being in an intergalactic space port.

23 Castles in Disneyland

There's more than one castle in Disneyland—many more. Fantasyland is home to most of them, of course!

Fantasyland

1. Sleeping Beauty Castle is Disneyland's most iconic structure.

2. Some books and dioramas inside the Sleeping Beauty Castle Walk-Through show King Stefan's and Maleficent's castles.

3. Nearly two minutes into the Alice in Wonderland ride, the Queen of Hearts' castle can be seen in the background, behind a heart-shaped hedge.

4. Behind the counter of the Enchanted Chamber is a display that includes a two-foot-tall Sleeping Beauty Castle.

5. At least five castle shapes (turrets with crenellations) are discernible on the It's a Small World façade (*right*).

6. One of the twenty-five-foot-tall towers along Small World Way is topped with a castle shape.

7. A castle stands behind the guards in the England section of It's a Small World.

8. There's also a castle (this one with a bagpiper) in Small World's Scottish highlands.

9. A tall castle display with a dozen Disney princesses turns in the middle of the It's a Small World Toy Shop (smaller castles can also be seen in the ceiling décor).

10. Two purple castles, each about a foot high, are shown on the inner core of the King Arthur Carrousel.

11. One of the *Sleeping Beauty* panels at the center of the King Arthur Carrousel depicts a castle.

12. Castles, including one that looks just like Sleeping Beauty Castle, are shown in *Mickey and the Magical Map*.

13. The wicked queen's castle appears midway through Snow White's Scary Adventures (*right*).

14. The prince's castle appears at the end of Snow White's Scary Adventures.

15. Midway through the Storybook Land Canal Boats, the fifteen-foot castle on a hill belongs to Cinderella (note the pumpkin coach below it).

Frontierland

16. Identified on the free maps formerly handed out at Tom Sawyer

Island, the tall Castle Rock formation crowned the middle of the original island; beneath it was the Castle Dungeon.

Hub

17. A "Time Castle," adorned with a castle image and filled with "Disneyland memories, messages and milestones," was placed in front of Sleeping Beauty Castle on July 17, 1995.

Main Street

18. The Castle Bros. sign hangs outside the Disney Clothiers, Ltd. store on the east side of Main Street.

19. Disney Showcase has featured some charming wall displays, including at least one (in winter 2014) that included a beautiful castle illustration as a backdrop.

Mickey's Toontown

20. A large castle sits in the giant goldfish bowl near the Gadget's Go Coaster loading area.

Tomorrowland

21. A Starcade coin-press machine is in the shape of a castle.

Town Square

22. Occasionally, the Disneyland Band's big drum features a castle image.

23. The Disneyland Railroad's emblem includes a castle image.

21 Businesses in Rainbow Ridge

Since the 1950s, the miniature town of Rainbow Ridge (or Big Thunder, as the population sign used to call it) has been a delightful design element behind the loading areas of various Frontierland attractions, including the Mine Train and the Big Thunder Mountain Railroad. Here are twenty-one tiny businesses featured in those colorful little buildings over the years:

1. Assay Office	**4.** Big Thunder Saloon
2. Barber Shop	**5.** Comstock Block
3. Big Thunder *Epitaph*	**6.** Dentist

7. El Dorado Hotel
8. General Mercantile/ General Store Plain & Fancy Dry Goods
9. Gold Nugget Dance Hall
10. Leather Goods
11. Miner's Hardware
12. Mother Murphy Meals
13. Opera House
14. The Palace
15. Panhandle Hotel
16. Pat Casey's Last Chance Saloon
17. Pioneer Hotel
18. Rainbow Ridge *Clarion*
19. Rainbow Ridge Hotel
20. Sheriff's Office
21. U.S. Post Office

21 Locations with Authentic Antiques

Many things in Disneyland are made to look much older than they really are (Main Street's motorized vehicles, for example). However, there are also some objects that really *are* old. Here's a list of twenty-one locations that have (or had) antiques on view.

Adventureland

1. Jungle Cruise: Planted in 1896, the tall Canary Island palm near the FASTPASS machines originally grew in the area where the old parking lot was built. The plant was moved for Disneyland's 1955 opening.

Fantasyland

2. Dumbo the Flying Elephant: An authentic band organ built circa 1915 was added to this attraction in 1983 to pump out Disney classics.

3. King Arthur Carrousel: When Walt Disney bought the carousel in 1954, it had been operating in Canada since 1922. The original turntable dates back to 1875.

Frontierland

4. American Rifle Exhibit: A display of antique muskets, rifles, and pistols lasted from the 1950s to the 1980s (antique rifles can still be seen in many Frontierland shops).

5. Big Thunder Mountain Railroad: Genuine Old West mining equipment decorates the queue area.

6. Petrified Tree: Positioned near the Golden Horseshoe, Disneyland's oldest antique is 55–70 million years old, according to its nearby plaque.

7. Sailing Ship *Columbia*: The Below-Decks Museum displays many antiques, including locked-up antique rifles and a glass-encased wooden fish that once adorned a compass binnacle.

Hub

8. Plaza Inn: Some of the opulent furnishings and interior design details came from a Victorian mansion that once stood near downtown Los Angeles.

Main Street

9. Disney Clothiers, Ltd.: Many Main Street shops use antiques for their décor. The Disney Clothiers main room features antique shoes, hats, and other fashion accessories, while the Castle Bros. room has vintage typewriters, books, pennants, and sports equipment.

10. Main Street: The classic gas lamps were used in Baltimore in the mid-nineteenth century (*right*).

11. Main Street Photo Supply: Window displays include old photo equipment.

12. Penny Arcade: A still-working 1905 German Orchestron music maker sits in the back.

13. Refreshment Corner: Antique Coke bottles dating back to 1899 are displayed by the door.

14. Upjohn Pharmacy: From 1955 to 1970, vintage medicines and pharmaceutical equipment decorated this old-fashioned pharmacy.

New Orleans Square

15. Jewel of Orléans: From 1997 to 2010, this pretty shop sold antique estate jewelry, some worth thousands of dollars.

16. One-of-a-Kind Shop: From 1966 to 1996, Disneyland's most famous antique shop sold rare and unusual *objets d'art*.

Town Square

17. Fire Department: Numerous antiques, including old gauges and fire-fighting equipment, add authenticity to this interior.

18. Flagpole: Two genuine nineteenth-century French army cannons are positioned in corners forty feet from the flagpole.

19. Train station: The oldest of the five Disneyland Railroad engines is the *Fred G. Gurley*, built in Louisiana in 1894 (purchased in 1957 and restored, it went into Disneyland service in 1958).

20. Train station: Antiques, including clocks, phones, and luggage, are displayed inside the station.

21. Train station: The interior of the *Lilly Belle* caboose is adorned with antiques.

25 Morbid Gags
in the Haunted Mansion's Outdoor Cemetery

As guests wait outside the Haunted Mansion, they walk past a pet cemetery and a wall where departed loved ones are interred. Here are the names and comical messages on fourteen of those pets' tombstones, plus eleven that are on the wall.

Pet Tombstones Behind the Haunted Mansion

1. Cat: "In Memoriam Miss Kitty: After losing eight lives you still had no fear; you caught a snake in your ninth and that's why you're here."

2. Dog: "Big Jake: Here lies my good dog Jake; chased a toad down a well was his one mistake."

3. Frog: "R.I.P. Bully: You didn't drink; you didn't smoke; I just can't figure what made you croak."

4. Skunk: "In loving memory of our pet Stripey; you may be departed but your presence will always linger on."

Pets Tombstones in Front of the Haunted Mansion

5. Bat: "Freddie the Bat, 1847, We'll Miss You."

6. Dog: "Buddy, Our friend until the end."

7. Dog: "Sparky" (added in 2012 to celebrate the *Frankenweenie* movie).

8. Fish: "October 10, 1867."

9. Frog: "Old Flybait, He Croaked, August 9, 1869."

10. Pig: "Rosie: She was a poor little Pig but she bought the Farm, 1849."

11. Rat: "In Memory of My Rat Whom I Loved, Now He Resides in the Realms Up Above."

12. Skunk: "Beloved Lilac, Long on Curiosity . . . Short on Common Scents, 1847."

13. Snake: "Here lies my snake whose fatal mistake was frightening the gardener who carried a rake."

14. Spider: "Here lies Long Legged Jeb, Got tangled up in his very own Web."

Interred in the Wall

15. Dustin T. Dust

16. G. I. Missyou

17. I. L. Beback

18. I. M. Mortal

19. I. Trudy Departed

20. Levi Tation

21. M. T. Tomb

22. Ray N. Carnation

23. Rustin Peece

24. Theo Later

25. U. R. Gone

A Dozen Tombstones
in the Tom Sawyer Island Cemetery

Most of these twelve names and dates on the Tom Sawyer Island Cemetery tombstones are fictitious, but two names belong to real employees of the Disney Studios: Wally Feignoux, an overseas executive; and "Laurence Clemmings," a variation on longtime story supervisor Larry Clemmons's name. The cemetery also includes one other authentic name: Sacajawea, the Shoshone woman famous for helping the 1805 Lewis and Clark expedition. The cemetery is located behind Tom Sawyer Island's Fort Wilderness.

1. Thaddeus Walker 1812

2. Rufus Finley

3. Amos Wilson 1797–1862

4. Wing Lee 1811

5. W. Pierre Feignoux *j'y suis j'y reste* 1809

6. Lieut. Laurence Clemmings fell here defending the right

7. Jno. C. Sawyer 1813

8. Eliza Hodgkins died June 7, 1812, 27 years

9. Unknown Remains found 1808

10. Sacajawea Indian Scout

11. Ebinizer Browne 1812

12. Unknown Guest

The Evolution of
Tom Sawyer Island's Burning Cabin

One of Disneyland's most unusual design elements is the isolated cabin on the northern tip of Tom Sawyer Island. Inaccessible to guests, but sitting in plain view of river traffic, the cabin was called "perhaps the most altered attraction" in Disneyland by the *Los Angeles Times*. Here is a list of the cabin's various iterations.

1. Originally, a fire convincingly looked to be raging through the cabin, and a dead settler was sprawled in the dirt in front of it—"the victim of an Indian arrow."

2. With the gas crisis in full effect in the mid-1970s, the flames were extinguished, though the dead settler remained (apparently killed by river pirates).

3. In 1984, a simulated flame effect was introduced to the cabin, and the dead settler was replaced by a passed-out moonshiner whose exploding still had ignited the cabin.

4. In the 1990s, the cabin was re-themed as

an animal habitat that had been carelessly set on fire by a settler.

5. The fire was put out in 2007 and the cabin was restored so that it looked like animals and an unseen settler lived on the property.

6. In 2010, the cabin was remodeled to look like the home of river rogue Mike Fink (one of his famed keel boats is docked nearby).

Burning Down the Mouse: A Dozen Daily Fires at the Park

All kinds of (controlled) fires burn in Disneyland every day. Here are thirteen of them, not including Tom Sawyer Island's cabin, which no longer burns now that Mike Fink has moved in (see "The Evolution of Tom Sawyer Island's Burning Cabin" above).

1. Adventureland entrance: Live flames burn in the tiki torches along the walkway.

2. Enchanted Tiki Room: Live flames burn in tiki torches at the entrance (*right*) and (periodically) from the hat of Pele, one of the tiki statues in the Enchanted Tiki Garden.

3. Fantasmic!: Dramatic flames accompany the dragon's appearance.

4. Indiana Jones Adventure: Several large, prominent fires burn during the ride.

5. Indian Village: North of Tom Sawyer Island, smoke (but no flame) rises from two fire pits.

6. Main Street: Live flames flicker in the street's old-fashioned gas lamps.

7. Mickey's House: Two fireplaces glow with "fire."

8. Minnie's House: Minnie also has a "fire" in her living room fireplace.

9. Mr. Toad's Wild Ride: In the first ten seconds, the cars burst through a lit fireplace.

10. New Orleans Square: Open to all guests until 2013, the Court des Anges carried live flames in its gas lamps. Nearby, the rebuilt entrance to Club 33 opened in July 2014 with new gas lamps burning next to the doorway.

11. Pirates of the Caribbean: A faux fire burns down a Caribbean town.

12. Sleeping Beauty Castle Walk-Through: Three different displays show a spinning wheel bonfire, a dungeon fire with rising ghouls, and an inferno launched by the fire-breathing dragon.

A Mouse's Natural Predator: 14 Owls Throughout Disneyland

Owls hunt mice, right? But in the park where Mickey and Minnie live, owls have stood in almost every land.

Critter Country

1. In front of Many Adventures of Winnie the Pooh, Owl's house is mounted to a tree; Owl himself appears forty-five seconds into the attraction and again in the final party scene ("Owl" is also the name of one of the ride's vehicles).

2. The Owl character is one of the pins in the seven-piece Winnie the Pooh set sold at Pooh Corner.

3. Professor Barnaby Owl runs his Photographic Art Studio near Splash Mountain's exit (*right*).

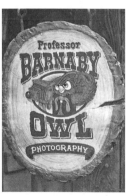

4. Two owls stand inside Splash Mountain, one on the left of the second upwards hill and another above and to the left near the end.

Fantasyland

5. In Alice in Wonderland, an owl watches Alice early in the attraction.

6. A big owl is part of the display behind the Enchanted Chamber's counter.

7. A golden-eyed owl observes from a post at Fantasy Faire (*below left*).

8. An owl holds the "Beware!" sign at the start of Snow White's Scary Adventure. Owls also decorate the interiors and backs of the mine carts.

Frontierland

9. Hooting owls are among the recorded bird sounds heard along the Big Thunder Trail.

10. An owl is perched in the main tree inside the Frontierland Shooting Exposition (*far right*).

Hub

11. Two small owl statues stand in front of Sleeping Beauty Castle (one on either side of the main walkway) (*right*).

Main Street

12. Displays during the Halloween season have featured owls—for instance, 2014 brought owls to a Disney Clothiers, Ltd. window and Disney Showcase wall displays.

Tomorrowland

13. Tomorrowland: An owl named Ollie was one of the main characters in America Sings (1975–1988).

Town Square

14. Beginning in 1973, an Audio-Animatronic owl narrated a pre-show presentation at the Walt Disney Story inside the Opera House.

18 Sound Effects You Can Hear Only by Standing in the Right Spot

Music can be heard almost everywhere in the park, and the sounds of distant attractions (the booming horn of the Monorail, the old-fashioned whistle of the *Mark Twain*) drift from one land to another. However, some creative sounds specifically themed to a particular place can be heard just by standing in the right spots.

1. Adventureland Bazaar (Adventureland): Every few minutes, Aladdin's Other Lamp in the back of the Bazaar cracks jokes and tries to coax coins out of guests.

2. Bear Country's entrance (Critter Country): Before this land became Critter Country, Rufus, a sleeping bear, loudly snored in his cave near the entrance.

3. Big Thunder Trail (Frontierland): Animal and bird sounds can be heard on the western side of the trail. In 2014, the sound of miners working in the northern tunnel near Fantasyland were also added.

4. Dentist's Office (Main Street): Some of the upstairs rooms at the end of East Center Street belong to a dentist, verified by the realistic sounds emanating from the second floor.

5. Donald's Boat (Mickey's Toontown): The giant speaker inside the boat projects various voices, even the pirates' "Yo Ho!" song, as sung by ducks.

6. Five & Dime (Mickey's Toontown): Stand above the manhole cover outside the store to pick up subterranean voices.

7. Hotel Marceline (Main Street): Stand in front of this East Center Street hotel to hear a "guest" gargling and shaving.

8. It's a Small World (Fantasyland): Stand in front of the attraction and listen for the tick-tock of its fanciful clock.

9. Jungle Cruise (Adventureland): Listen for exotic jungle birds in the general area around this attraction.

10. Lagoon (Tomorrowland): Pause alongside the water to listen to chatty seagulls.

11. Lost and Found (entrance): Outside of Disneyland, stand near the area west of the turnstiles to hear occasional gunshots as skippers fire their pistols in the hippo pool of the nearby Jungle Cruise.

12. The *Mark Twain* (Frontierland): As the passes Mike Fink's cabin on Tom Sawyer Island, listen for the sound of voices coming from the cabin.

13. Mint Julep Bar (New Orleans Square): Behind this establishment, listen for eerie moans and voodoo sounds drifting from upstairs windows.

14. New Orleans Square/Frontierland train station (Frontierland): Stand at this spot to hear a landline telegraph tapping out lines from Walt Disney's dedication speech on Disneyland's Opening Day (July 17, 1955).

15. Sleeping Beauty Castle Walk-Through (Fantasyland): Halfway through the attraction inside, there's a door on the left with a small window in it. Stand in front of it for a few seconds to hear rattling chains, followed by the sudden appearance of a malevolent guard. (There used to be another sound effect in the Walk-Through that's no longer heard—guests' voices were picked up by a hidden microphone and echoed through a bottomless chamber.)

16. Snow White Wishing Well (Fantasyland): Stand at the well to hear a soft rendition of "Some Day My Prince Will Come."

17. Tom Sawyer Island (Frontierland): One version of the island featured ominous moans emanating from the Bottomless Pit inside Injun Joe's Cave. Today, Dead Man's Grotto rewards explorers with a cave full of voices and sounds.

18. Wishing well at Minnie's House (Mickey's Toontown): Stand beside the well to hear Minnie's cooing voice.

Please *Do* Touch: 20 Touchable Objects That Generate Unexpected Actions and/or Sound Effects

Interactivity is a major part of Disneyland's magic—and it's especially fun when it produces unexpected results! Visit these locations and touch away for surprising rewards.

1. Disneyana/Villain's Lair/Le Bat en Rouge: Beginning in 1976, guests inside Main Street's Disneyana shop encountered a creepy, two-foot-tall Audio-Animatronic figure in a cage. The figure was the old hag from *Snow White and the Seven Dwarfs*, who would come alive when her cage was touched and cajole guests into releasing her. Imported from Walt Disney World, this display moved to Villain's Lair (Fantasyland) and then Le Bat en Rouge (New Orleans Square) before it was finally retired.

2. Indiana Jones Adventure: While in the queue, pull the rope marked "Do Not Pull Rope!" to hear a voice yelling.

3. Indiana Jones Adventure: In the queue, guests used to be able to shake the pole in the "spike room" for the effects of the collapsing ceiling.

4. Market House: Pick up the old-fashioned phone on the wall to listen in on conversations.

5. Mickey's Toontown: The Dog Pound in Mickey's Toontown has bendable bars.

6. Mickey's Toontown: Drink from the water fountain at Goofy's Gas Station to hear gurgling and voices.

7. Mickey's Toontown: Open the mailbox near Roger Rabbit's Car Toon Spin to hear it talk.

8. Mickey's Toontown: Pull the Power House's doorknob for noisy results.

9. Mickey's Toontown: Push the Camera Shop's doorbell to set off a photo flash.

10. Mickey's Toontown: Push the Dog Pound's doorbell to hear cats.

11. Mickey's Toontown: Push the Fire Department's doorbell to make a puppy emerge from the window above.

12. Mickey's Toontown: Push the Fireworks Factory's plunger to hear explosions.

13. Mickey's Toontown: Push the Insurance doorbell to hear breaking glass.

14. Mickey's Toontown: Twist the Post Office's six mailbox knobs to hear the famous voices of the mail recipients.

15. Pirate's Lair on Tom Sawyer Island: Touch the Dead Man's Chest inside

Dead Man's Grotto to see special lighting effects, hear warnings, and feel
Davy Jones's heartbeat (*right*).

16. Pirate's Lair on Tom Sawyer Island:
    Touch (or reach toward) four different
    windows inside Dead Man's Grotto
    to make treasure vanish and cursed
    pirates materialize.

17. Sailing Ship *Columbia*: In the Below-Decks Museum, pump the bellows
    to intensify the blacksmith's fire.

18. Snow White's Scary Adventures: Touch the bronze apple out front to
    hear thunder and cackling.

19. Tarzan's Treehouse: Pull on the anchored rope outside the Treehouse to
    hear animal sounds.

20. Tarzan's Treehouse: In the base camp, pump the bellows with your foot
    to light the stove and make the pots boil.

Laying Down the Law:
15 Examples of "Police Presence" in Disneyland

You might feel safer knowing that there are "jails" and "law enforcement
officers" throughout "The Happiest Place on Earth."

1. Fantasyland: On Mr. Toad's Wild Ride, "bobbies" and a jail are depicted
   in the mural out front; inside, policemen try to stop the runaway cars,
   and the buildings include a Constabulary and Prison.

2. Fantasyland: A Canadian Mountie waves his arms inside It's a Small
   World.

3. Frontierland: From July 1955 to July 1956, a Marshal's Office stood approximately where today's Rancho del Zocalo Restaurante is located.

4. Frontierland: Back in the 1950s, Sheriff Lucky was a costumed character
   who had "shootouts" with Black Bart near the Golden Horseshoe.

5. Frontierland: Near the Big Thunder Mountain Railroad's loading area is
   the miniature town of Rainbow Ridge; one of this town's buildings has
   been a Sheriff's Office.

6. Frontierland: One of the buildings in the background of the Frontierland Shooting Exposition is labeled "Jail."

7. Frontierland: *Legends of Frontierland*, an interactive live-action game
   played in Frontierland during 2014's summer months, added a Sheriff's
   Office and a jail cell outside the Golden Horseshoe.

8. Main Street: Decades ago, a musical group called the Keystone Cops dressed in old-time police uniforms and played along Main Street.

9. Main Street: During 1956's Antique Automobile Parade, an old-fashioned traffic cop used a stop sign to pause vehicles and wave pedestrians through.

10. Mickey's Toontown: By the Power House, there's a "police phone" offering humorous crime reports.

11. New Orleans Square: In Pirates of the Caribbean, three jailed pirates beg a dog for the key to the cell door (*right*).

12. Tomorrowland: America Sings played in Tomorrowland's Carousel Theater from 1974 to 1988; its "Gay '90s" scene included a dog wearing an old-fashioned police uniform and carrying a baton.

13. Tomorrowland: In 1955, two of the Autopia vehicles were black-and-white police cars that could go twice as fast as the others.

14. Town Square: The Police Station was the brick building just south of City Hall (no police were actually in the building; the building's sign changed to Guided Tours and then disappeared altogether).

15. Town Square: On some of the poster-size Fun Maps sold in the park, an old-fashioned policeman waves his baton in Town Square.

22 Books in City Hall's Bookcase

Books and bookshelves and bookcases are sprinkled all throughout Disneyland. One of the first collections to be displayed at the park is inside Town Square's City Hall. Here are twenty-two titles of books in the short bookcase next to the City Hall doorway (listed alphabetically, with "authors" in parentheses).

1. *Aladdin* (Abu)

2. *Alice in Wonderland* (The Hatter)

3. *Beauty and the Beast* (Cogsworth & Lumiere)

4. *Cinderella* (Drusilla/Anastasia)

5. *Hercules* (Megara)

6. *Hunchback of Notre Dame* (Quasimodo)

7. *Jungle Book* (Mancub)

8. *Lambert the Sheepish Lion* (Peet, Wright, Banta)

9. *Lillybelle* (W. E. Disney)

10. *Mary Poppins* (The Banks)

11. *Mickey Mouse* (Disney)

12. *Mulan* (Mulan)

13. *101 Dalmatians* (DeVille)

14. *Peter Pan* (The Lost Boys)

15. *Pinocchio* (J. Cricket)

16. *Pollyanna* (Polly Harrington)

17. *The Real Little Mermaid* (Scuttle)

18. *The Sign Painting Course* (Matthews)

19. *Sleeping Beauty* (Flora, Fauna, Merryweather)

20. *Snow White* (Seven Authors)

21. *Walt and You* (Sidejas, Kimbrell)

22. *Wonderful World of Color* (no author)

31 Books on Mr. Toad's Shelves

The humor of Mr. Toad's Wild Ride begins even before guests climb into the motorcars. Here are thirty-one titles out of the hundreds of books on his shelves.

1. *Aquatic Life Vol. 1–3*

2. *Armitage*

3. *Everything You Wanted to Know About Toads But Were Afraid to Ask*

4. *Famous Frogs*

5. *Famous Lakes and Ponds*

6. *For Whom the Toads Croak*

7. *Frogean Psychology*

8. *Frogs I Have Loved*

9. *Horace Tadpole's Essays*

10. *I, Toadius*

11. *Ivantoad*

12. *Job-Hopping: A Guide*

13. *Lady Froggy's Lover*

14. *Model A Toadsters*

15. *Mother Toad*

16. *Pond Life in Our Time*

17. *Pond Politics*

18. *The Ribbit Heard Round the World*

19. *Robin Toad*

20. *Rumple Toadskin*

21. *Sky Above, Toad Below*

22. *A Tadpole Grows in Brooklyn*

23. *Teenage Tadpole*

24. *Toad Atlas*

25. *Toadenomics*

26. *Toadman of Alcatraz*
27. *The Travels of a Toad*
28. *12 Angry Toads*
29. *Twice Toad Tales*
30. *Wart N Peace*
31. *Wyatt Toad*

11 Books and Magazines in Minnie's House

Minnie is quite the reader. Here are eleven examples of the reading material in her bookshelves and beside her comfy chair.

1. *Ben Fur*
2. *Cat on a Hot Toon Roof*
3. *Cheese Louise*
4. *Cheese and Remembrance*
5. *Cosmousepolitan Magazine,* Spring Issue
6. *A Doll's Mouse*
7. *Five Cheesy Pieces*
8. *From Ear to Eternity*
9. Jessica's Secret catalog, Spring Collection
10. *Little Mouse on the Prairie*
11. *Volume 1*

Minnie's Shopping List

One of the lists actually on display in Disneyland is in Mickey's Toontown. Stuck to the refrigerator inside Minnie's House is this handwritten shopping list (spellings and capitalizations are hers).

Don't forget the . . .

Sharp Cheddar	Brie	Cheeze Cake
Grated Parmesan	Colby	Cheeze Danish
Bleu	Lite Mozzarella	Cheeze Crackers
Shredded Provolone	Edam	Welsh Rarebit
Gorgonzola	Smoked Gouda	Cottage Danish
Swiss	Cheeze Puffs	Broccoli with Cheeze sause
Muenster	Cheeze Bread	
Gruyere	Cheeze Pizza	

13 License Plates in Roger Rabbit's Car Toon Spin

The imaginative queue area for this Mickey's Toontown attraction includes a wall of license plates, listed here alphabetically and spelled out in parentheses.

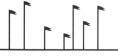
1. BB WOLF (Big Bad Wolf)
2. CAP 10 HK (Captain Hook)
3. FAN T C (Fantasy)
4. IM L8 (I'm late)
5. L MERM8 (Little Mermaid)
6. MR TOAD (Mr. Toad)
7. 1D N PTR (Wendy and Peter)

8. 1DRLND (Wonderland)
9. 101 DLMN (101 Dalmatians)
10. RS2CAT (Aristocat)
11. 3 LIL PIGS (Three Little Pigs)
12. 2N TOWN (Toontown)
13. ZPD2DA (Zip a dee doo dah)

7 Fantasyland Attractions Topped with Charming Spires and Weathervanes

When in Fantasyland, look upward to catch some of these delightful details.

1. Edelweiss Snacks: A spire with compass points.
2. King Arthur Carrousel: A golden crown.
3. Peter Pan's Flight: A crocodile (*right*), a galleon, and a star.
4. Pinocchio's Daring Journey: A school of eight fish, a stork with a baby, and a whale.
5. Motor Boat Cruise dock: A compass.
6. Mr. Toad's Wild Ride: Toad riding in a car.
7. Village Haus: A rooster.

15 Fine Fountains in Disneyland

Take a moment to pause and admire these fifteen beautiful fountains scattered throughout the park.

1. Adventureland: A "magic fountain" rises up inside the Enchanted Tiki Room.
2. Critter Country: Halfway through Splash Mountain's cruise, a fountain bubbles up among oversized mushrooms.
3. Fantasyland: The core of Dumbo the Flying Elephant sits in a low, circular fountain.
4. Fantasyland: The display at Snow White's Wishing Well and Grotto includes fish and frogs that spray water into their pond.
5. Fantasyland: Inside Mr. Toad's Wild Ride is a Toad-topped fountain rimmed with spouting fish.

6. Frontierland: A lovely fountain crowned with a bird sculpture sits inside Rancho del Zocalo Restaurante.

7. Hub: The garden pool in front of Pixie Hollow includes a fountain that's beautifully lit at night.

8. Mickey's Toontown: Mickey Mouse's fountain is, fittingly, near Mickey's House.

9. Mickey's Toontown: Roger Rabbit's fountain is located close by Roger Rabbit's Car Toon Spin.

10. New Orleans Square: Hidden from most guests, a simple but lovely fountain with a bench is built into a back wall of the exclusive Court des Anges.

11. New Orleans Square: Between the French Market and the Haunted Mansion, a majestic fountain stands in Magnolia Park.

12. New Orleans Square: A small fountain is built into a tiled wall of Pirates of the Caribbean's outdoor queue area.

13. Tomorrowland: Along the Autopia route, two cars standing on end lean together to form a unique fountain (*right*).

14. Tomorrowland: Painted on an inside wall of Innoventions is a futuristic cityscape that depicts a butterfly flying over an outdoor fountain.

15. Tomorrowland: The climax of Adventure Thru Inner Space (1967–1985) was the spectacular floor-to-ceiling Fountain of Fashion dripping thousands of oil beads down thin threads (the "fashion" was inside the structure, where mannequins displayed the latest synthetic fabrics).

A Dozen Delightful Drinking Fountains in Disneyland

Of the many drinking fountains in Disneyland, we've picked twelve favorites.

1. Alice in Wonderland: The shaded double fountain at the exit comes with its own mural (*opposite, second from left*).

2. First Aid: This simple metal drinking fountain delivers cold, filtered water and has a registered nurse on hand should anything go horribly awry.

3. The Haunted Mansion: The triple fountain out front has a distinctive black base and brass fittings.

4. Indiana Jones Adventure: In the queue area, a drinking fountain is built into the temple wall and includes a graphic above it.

5. Jungle Cruise: Built into the rocks outside is a shaded double fountain.

6. Main Street: On East Center Street, a classic single fountain is attached to the old, oddly patterned brick wall next to Main Street Lockers & Storage.

7. New Orleans Square: A beautiful fountain featuring tile and a mural is outside Mlle. Antoinette's Parfumerie (*above, second from right*).

8. Pirates of the Caribbean: The drinking fountain in the outdoor queue is a welcome respite while waiting in line.

9. Sleeping Beauty Castle courtyard: Probably the most photographed drinking fountain in the park, this elegant structure in the castle courtyard features a statue of the Sleeping Beauty couple (*above, far left*).

10. Tom Sawyer Island: Near the dock is a shaded triple fountain.

11. Town Square: On either side of the central area in Town Square, these triple fountains come with long views down Main Street.

12. Village Haus: Our personal favorite is the drinking fountain inside this restaurant, built in a wood cabinet with old-fashioned toys on top and decorative tile placed around it (*above, far right*).

16 Splendid Disneyland Restrooms

Not included: Club 33's legendary gilded restroom, which is off-limits to nearly all guests. Some splendid door signs are shown on the next page.

1. Adventureland: At the entrance is a restroom of above-average size, themed outside with rocks and tiki murals.

2. Aladdin's Oasis: This inconspicuous "companion restroom" is spacious and private.

3. Alice in Wonderland: Back toward the Matterhorn, the "Kings" restroom

(*above, second from left*) is spacious, tiled, and features playing cards on the stall doors. It also has a triple drinking fountain outside.

4. Autopia Winner's Circle: This enormous restroom has the busiest tile floor ever.

5. Big Thunder Ranch: By the barn is a good-sized restroom with a frontier theme and a mural.

6. Blue Bayou: Wallpaper, wainscoting, and wood trim make this a stylish private restroom inside the restaurant.

7. Carnation Café: At the back of this outdoor eatery is an average-size bathroom with stained glass above the door and tile and artwork inside.

8. Fantasyland Theatre: Another spacious and tiled restroom.

9. Fort Wilderness on Tom Sawyer Island: A decently sized restroom with a frontier theme.

10. Hungry Bear Restaurant: Designed to match the Critter Country theme and displaying a mural at its entrance, "Gomer's Gentlemen's Lair" on the lower level of the restaurant is one of Disneyland's biggest restrooms.

11. New Orleans Square Train Station: Left of the steps is a spacious restroom with drinking fountains outside.

12. Plaza Inn: Left of the main entrance is a restroom with attractive décor and a mural in the doorway.

13. Rancho del Zocalo: Within this building are spacious, handsomely tiled restrooms.

14. Service Animal Relief Areas: About a half-dozen inconspicuous service animal "restrooms" in the fresh air are marked on Disneyland's free maps, and there's small signage at the actual spots (which include Big Thunder Ranch and the fenced lawn near the French Market).

15. Space Mountain: Located near Spaceport Document Control, this huge modern restroom offers bench seats and a drinking fountain outside. It gets our vote for Best of the Rest(rooms).

16. Village Haus: The restroom outside the restaurant is spacious, nicely tiled, and comes with a drinking fountain and mural.

4 Wise Disneyland Machines

Slip a coin into these machines to hear advice or have your fortune told.

1. Aladdin's Other Lamp (Adventureland's Adventureland Bazaar)
2. Esmeralda (Main Street's Penny Arcade)
3. Fortune Red (New Orleans Square's Pieces of Eight)
4. Shrunken Ned (Adventureland's Adventureland Bazaar)

10 Foreign Languages Used as Design Elements

Foreign languages appear on informational signs throughout Disneyland, but they're also used as design elements to add atmosphere and interest.

1. "Alien": Space Mountain (exit and Spaceport Document

Control) and Star Tours (boarding info, on the doors) both feature a mysterious alien language (*above*).

2. Arabic: A wall near the Jungle Cruise docks reads "Fine Food, Fine Dining, Fine Entertainment" (as translated in Dave Smith's *Disney Trivia from the Vault*); the Tropical Imports building displays similar writing (*right*).

3. Chinese: In January and February, banners offer Happy Lunar New Year wishes.

4. French: An alpine sign at the entrance to the Matterhorn Bobsleds reads *"Liberte et Patrie,"* which means "Freedom and Fatherland"; posters mounted outside La Mascarade d'Orléans and on construction walls in New Orleans Square advertise *"Beignets Delicieux"*; the names for over a dozen establishments in New Orleans Square are French (Le Chapeau, Le Forgeron, etc.); a sign at Rainbow Ridge's General Mercantile in Frontierland advertises *Le Flor de Erb* cigars; posters in the Jungle Cruise queue also feature French terms.

5. German: After a redesign, Fantasyland's Village Inn was renamed the Village Haus, reinforcing the Bavarian theme.

6. Greek: Astrological symbols appear on Fantasyland's Skyway station and on Tomorrowland's Astro-Orbitor jets; *"eo"* (as in Captain EO) is Greek for "dawn."

7. Hawaiian: Foreign languages are displayed throughout It's a Small World

(particularly at the "farewell" finale); *"Aloha"* welcomes guests into the Hawaii section.

8. Latin: Above the entrance to Mr. Toad's Wild Ride is the line *"Toadi Acceleratio Semper Absurda,"* usually translated as "Speeding with Toad Is Always Absurd"); the tombstones in the graveyard scene near the end of the Haunted Mansion feature Latin phrases; the flower pots at the base camp of Tarzan's Treehouse display Latin words; on Opening Day, weeds were given invented Latin names to add to their significance, and so was the artificial tree holding the Swiss Family Treehouse/Tarzan's Treehouse (*Disneyodendron eximius*, or "out-of-the-ordinary Disney tree," according to the August 1963 issue of *National Geographic*, and *Disneyodendron semperflorens grandis*, "big ever-blooming Disney tree," according to Randy Bright's *Disneyland: Inside Story*, 1987); and Roman numerals mark the time on certain clocks throughout the park, including those above Town Square's train station, in the Sleeping Beauty Castle walkway, on the Bibbidi Bobbidi Boutique tower, and on the Village Haus spire.

9. Maraglyphics: These invented hieroglyphics can be found inside Indiana Jones Adventure.

10. Spanish: A sign at Frontierland's Rancho del Zocalo Restaurante reads *"mi casa es su casa,"* meaning "my house is your house"; buildings near the end of the Pirates of the Caribbean cruise read *"Costurera"* for the dressmaker and *"Mercado"* for the market; and a sign just before the Big Thunder Mountain Railroad's mine explosion warns *"Peligro! Explosiones!"*

2 Dozen Outdoor Murals in Disneyland

Beautiful murals are a great example of the "added value" guests can expect on a trip to Disneyland. Other than covering what might otherwise be a big blank wall, there's often no reason for the murals (usually they're not advertising current attractions or new merchandise, for instance), and by themselves they're not generating any revenue (if anything, the murals cost money to create and maintain). What they're generating is good will, visual interest, and thematic elements that help unify the areas where they're located. Without including all the murals in front of and inside the attractions (in the queue area for Peter Pan's Flight, for example), and without including the lovely artwork on the walls of restaurants and stores (Little Green Men Store Command is a prime example), here are twenty-four outdoor murals worth seeking out.

Critter Country

1. A small mural for "Quilted Northern" tissue is painted outside the men's

restroom on the Hungry Bear Restaurant's lower floor (*near right*).

2. On the side of the Harbour Galley, a pleasing maritime mural invites guests to "Come Ashore For Dockside Dining" (*above right*).

Fantasyland

3. Viewed from the Disneyland Railroad as it circles behind Fantasyland, a wide "Agrifuture" billboard shows off healthy farm products and the rural couple from Grant Wood's *American Gothic*.

4. Sleeping Beauty Castle's main walkway is adorned with two memorable scenes from the 1959 movie *Sleeping Beauty* (*right*).

5. Grapes are painted on the tower outside the Bibbidi Bobbidi Boutique.

6. At the Village Haus's outdoor restrooms, there's a pretty floral mural behind the drinking fountain.

Frontierland

7. Outside the restroom in the Big Thunder Ranch area is a large mural for Northern Bath Tissue ("soft and 100% splinter free").

8. On the side of the Big Thunder Barbecue is a vertical mural for "the happiest horses on Earth."

9. Not really a mural, but it's atmospheric—seen from the Disneyland Railroad, the wooden stables behind the Big Thunder Ranch have the words "Livery Hay & Grain Feed" painted on them.

10. A mural in the Big Thunder Trail's smoking area attempts to recruit horse soldiers with dramatic imagery and words: "Join the Cavalry and have a courageous friend" and "The Horse Is Man's Noblest Companion" (*right*).

11. Another display adding atmosphere but no imagery—decorating the exterior of Fowler's Inn in Frontierland is text announcing two businesses, "Chandlery, Joseph Barrell, Proprietor," and "Christopher Alton's Bait & Tackle."

12. Near the dock for the *Mark Twain* is a small wood structure with a beautiful mural behind it advertising "River Excursions" (and also showing a small Hidden Mickey on the boat's lower deck).

13. At the entrance to Rancho del Zocalo Restaurante is a large, colorful mural that includes Zorro on his horse.

14. On a wooden wall facing the Rivers of America is a stylish mural advertising the fireworks of the Laod Bhang & Co. Rocket Factory (*right*).

15. Along the Rivers of America, an informational mural advises guests that if they want "To Book Passage, Contact the Frontierland River Packet & Steam Navigation Co."

16. In the Frontierland Shooting Exposition, a mural on the side of Shorty's Hotel says to "Drink Mousehead Beer."

Hub

17. A mural advertising the Royal Theatre is next to Clopin's Music Box in Fantasy Faire.

New Orleans Square

18. A small mural outside La Mascarade d'Orleans honors Marché aux Fleurs, Sacs et Mode, a shop that left this location in the 1980s.

19. A small atmospheric mural is painted above the pay phones behind the Mint Julep Bar.

Tomorrowland

20. The two curving buildings that house today's Buzz Lightyear Astro Blasters and Star Tours display thrilling murals of galactic action (formerly this area was the Corridor of Murals, decorated with two huge tile mosaics created by Mary Blair).

21. The Innoventions building displays artwork with a futuristic theme.

22. Technically, this may not qualify as an outdoor mural, but guests who sit in Tomorrowland Terrace's patio area can look up at a stunning ceiling painted with strong colors and astronomical shapes.

Town Square

23. Guests who enter Disneyland through the right-hand (eastern) tunnel will approach what was once the bank; appropriately, there's a Bank of Main Street mural here that declares, "a penny saved is a penny earned."

24. Next to the Fire Department is a nostalgic mural that encourages viewers to "Discover the Joy of Motoring" with images of antique cars.

7 Pirate Murals Inside Pirates of the Caribbean

Before boarding their bateaux, guests walk by seven murals featuring pirates both fictional and nonfictional.

1. Anne Bonny/Mary Read (Irish, 1702–1782; English, 1685–1721)

2. Captain Barbossa (fictional)

3. Captain Jack Sparrow (fictional)

4. Ned Low (English, 1690–1724)

5. Captain Charles Gibbs (American, 1798–1831)

6. Sir Henry Mainwaring (English, 1587–1653)

7. Sir Francis Verney (English, 1584–1615)

11 Plaques in Disneyland

There are hundreds of signs throughout the park announcing locations, directions, safety guidelines, and more. But there are also a few prominently placed plaques, often made of metal and cast with important quotes or historical information. (Decorative plaques with few or no words are also found in the park; see various New Orleans Square walls or the Mr. Toad's Wild Ride queue for examples.)

1. Entrance, above the tunnels leading to Town Square: "Here you leave today and enter the world of yesterday, tomorrow and fantasy."

2. Fantasyland, in front of It's a Small World: Roy E. Disney's 1989 quote honoring the silver anniversary of the attraction's first voyage on April 22, 1964.

3. Frontierland, at the Flagpole: Text by the American Humane Association lauds Walt Disney's humanitarian efforts.

4. Frontierland, at Silver Spur Supplies' Halloween Tree during Halloween Time: This plaque identifies the "stately oak" as Ray Bradbury's "symbol for the holiday."

5. Hub, at the base of the *Partners* statue: "I think most of all what I want

Disneyland to be is a happy place . . . where parents and children can have fun, together." —Walt Disney

6. Hub, in front of Sleeping Beauty Castle: This plaque describes the "Disneyland 40th Anniversary Time Castle" buried beneath this spot in 1995.

7. New Orleans Square, along the walkway of Rivers of America: Historical "facts" about the anchor have been placed here.

8. New Orleans Square, in the Pirates of the Caribbean queue: The plaque displays a rousing thirtieth anniversary tribute to the "Buccaneer Crew" that designed and built this milestone attraction.

9. Tomorrowland, at the entrance: Walt Disney's Tomorrowland dedication, delivered on July 17, 1955, is on this plaque.

10. Tomorrowland, in the Monorail's loading area: The American Society of Mechanical Engineers' put their detailed designation of the "Disneyland Monorail System" as a "Historical Mechanical Engineering Landmark" on this plaque (*right*).

11. Town Square, at the base of the flagpole: Walt Disney's famous welcome speech, delivered to a national TV audience on July 17, 1955, is stamped on this plaque.

"I'm Late! I'm Late!" 2 Dozen Disneyland Clocks That Tell the *Wrong* Time

Clocks can be found throughout Disneyland, but not all of them keep accurate time. Do not rely on the twenty-four clocks listed below!

1. Emporium windows: In 2014's *Ratatouille* display, the clock was fixed at 2:53.

2. Emporium interior: A 2014 wall display contained about two dozen non-working antique clocks.

3. Emporium interior: In the north-end Storybook Store, an incorrect clock stands near the ceiling.

4. Fire Department: The interior wall clock is fixed at 2:31.

5. The Haunted Mansion exterior: Displayed over the doorway at Halloween Time, this clock quickly spins past months, not hours.

6. The Haunted Mansion interior: The hallway grandfather clock is marked for only one hour—13:00.

7. Innoventions' two-sided sign: Both sides spin quickly, one forward and

the other backward, to give different times.

8. It's a Small World interior: Early on, a polar clock is fixed at 12:00.

9. It's a Small World interior: The clock painted on the wall behind the German scene forever reads 11:58.

10. Market House interior: Two clocks at either end of the Book Rest are fixed at 4:52 and 3:43.

11. Mickey's House interior: The cuckoo clock is fixed at 5:05.

12. Mickey's House interior: The alarm clock is fixed at 2:50.

13. Mickey's Toontown City Hall: This clock spins quickly.

14. Mickey's Toontown Clock Repair: The two-sided alarm clock on the shop's sign shows two different times, both incorrect.

15. Peter Pan's Flight interior: Big Ben, on the entrance mural and standing inside, shows 7:15, while a tiny Ben on an exit sign shows 11:48.

16. Pinocchio's Daring Journey interior: The final scene displays non-working cuckoo clocks.

17. Port Royal: Displays inside this New Orleans Square shop include many non-working clocks.

18. Sleeping Beauty Castle walkway, north end: This clock doesn't keep time, but the hands are occasionally repositioned manually.

19. Snow White's Scary Adventures interior: The cuckoo clock at the dwarfs' cottage doesn't function.

20. Storybook Land Canal Boats, on the main tower of Cinderella's castle: The hands of this clock are fixed at 12:00.

21. Tarzan's Treehouse interior: In Kala's room, the clock is fixed at 9:00.

22. Village Haus interior: A side-room cuckoo clock is fixed at 4:59, with a nearby mural showing a clock at 3:00.

23. White Rabbit statue in the Hub: The Rabbit's oversized pocket watch is fixed at 5:05 (*right*).

24. White Rabbit figure inside Alice in Wonderland: His oversized pocket watch spins wildly.

2 Dozen Disneyland Clocks That Tell the *Right* Time

Here are the locations of twenty-four functioning clocks inside the park.

1. Autopia entrance
2. Bibbidi Bobbidi Boutique tower (*right*)
3. Big Thunder Mountain Railroad entrance
4. Big Thunder Ranch stage
5. Disney Gallery (back room)
6. Emporium (indoors, at the exit)
7. Festival Arena (two stage clocks, both working)
8. Fortuosity Shop (a round "pocket watch" hangs outside)

9. The Haunted Mansion entrance
10. Indiana Jones Adventure entrance
11. It's a Small World (the giant clock activates every fifteen minutes to display the time)
12. Jolly Holiday Bakery Café interior
13. Main Street Magic Shop (correct, but spins backward)
14. Many Adventures of Winnie the Pooh entrance
15. *Mark Twain* dock
16. Mickey's House interior (on the mantel above the fireplace)
17. Peter Pan's Flight tower
18. Silhouette Studio (a tall, old-fashioned clock stands outside)
19. Space Mountain entrance
20. Star Tours entrance
21. Splash Mountain entrance
22. Town Square's train station, exterior tower
23. Town Square's train station, interior hallway
24. Village Haus tower

2 Dozen Displays of Alluring Women in Disneyland

Despite Disneyland's reputation for wholesome family fun, at times it has showcased rather enticing-looking females. This alphabetical list of locations doesn't include the many princesses who appear in the park, the "Wizard of Bras" displays inside Main Street's Intimate Apparel (1955–1956), or the one thing literally called the *Wicked Wench* (the ship attacking the fort

inside Pirates of the Caribbean).

1. **Disneyana:** There's a small statue of Fortuna, the lovely Goddess of Good Fortune, on a stand near the ceiling of the back room (*above left*).

2. **Flash Mountain:** Splash Mountain's nickname, bestowed in the 1990s when women began lifting their tops for the photos taken on the climactic plunge.

3. **Gibson Girl Ice Cream Parlor:** Portraits on the walls have featured pretty turn-of-the-century models.

4. **Golden Horseshoe:** Live can-can dancers once appeared here throughout the day; an illustration of a dancer is on an old-time advertisement posted outside (*above right*).

5. **Golden Horseshoe:** Above the bar is a painting of a reclining woman, semi-clad in lacey white fabric.

6. **Golden Horseshoe:** Eight scantily clad bas-relief beauties adorn the tall planters near the entrance.

7. **The Haunted Mansion:** A "reclining catwoman" portrait hangs in the walk-through corridor just before the Doom Buggies (*above middle*).

8. **Main Street Cinema:** *Fatima's Dance*, a short silent film about a risqué dancer, is no longer shown.

9. **Minnie's House:** One of the catalogs inside is titled "Jessica's Secret"—a play on Victoria's Secret—with Jessica Rabbit as the cover girl.

10. **Mr. Toad's Wild Ride:** A poster of a dancing girl is inside Winky's Pub.

11. **Penny Arcade:** *A Wee Bit o' Scotch*, a 1919 film shown on one of the viewing machines, presented a pretty girl taking a sip of the spirit.

12. **Penny Arcade:** The beautiful Esmeralda dispenses fortunes (and enticing winks) from her Main Street booth.

13. **Peter Pan's Flight:** A glamorous mermaid trio graces the queue's mural and the lagoon scene two minutes into the flight.

14. **Pirate Ship Restaurant:** The figurehead on the prow of this long-gone

Fantasyland ship was a fabulous blonde mermaid wearing a skin-tight, off-the-shoulder outfit.

15. Pirate's Lair on Tom Sawyer Island: The upper half of a woman is carved into a statue on the side of Lafitte's Tavern.

16. Pirates of the Caribbean: A mural depicts two attractive pirates in the queue (*above, far left*); in the "Crew's Quarters," a voluptuous, barely dressed redhead is shown in Marc Davis's painting *A Portrait of Things to Come*.

17. Pirates of the Caribbean: At the auction, drunken pirates bid on a desirable, well-dressed redhead (possibly the same woman in the painting mentioned above).

18. Pixie Hollow: According to an urban legend, Tinker Bell's (*above, second from right*) look was inspired by Marilyn Monroe (Disney names actress Margaret Kerry as the actual model).

19. Roger Rabbit's Car Toon Spin: Jessica Rabbit, perhaps the sexiest character in the entire Disney canon, is a sensual silhouette in this attraction's queue and a weasel-bashing heroine (*above, second from left*) on the attraction (also check out her sign at the Goofy's Gas Station restroom).

20. Roger Rabbit's Car Toon Spin: "Miss August" is a fetching blonde pin-up girl on a queue calendar.

21. Sailing Ship *Columbia*: The figurehead on the prow is a confident, curvy long-haired blonde in blue and white (*above, far right*).

22. Submarine Voyage: Live "mermaids" swam in and lounged around Tomorrowland's lagoon in the mid-1960s, and tethered (and seemingly topless) submerged mermaid mannequins were viewed from the old Submarine Voyage.

23. Tomorrowland: From the mid-1950s to the mid-1960s, Space Girl roamed Tomorrowland wearing futuristic clothes that sometimes included a short white dress, stylish boots, and a cape.

24. Village Haus: Four high-kicking dancers decorate the "actor's life for me" mural inside this Fantasyland restaurant.

Drink Up Me Hearties, Yo Ho: 16 Liquor Sightings in Disneyland

Club 33 may be the only place in Disneyland where guests can buy alcohol, but evidence of liquor has been on display in many other locations.

Bear Country

1. Jugs of moonshine adorned the old Country Bear Jamboree stage; one of the bears played an empty jug.

Fantasyland

2. Someone must've spiked the tea at Alice in Wonderland's climactic party, because the dormouse in the teapot sure looks tipsy (just as he is in the movie).

3. Inside Mr. Toad's Wild Ride, Winky the smiling bartender tosses mugs of beer into the air as the cars enter his pub. Outside, a sign advertises a "Publicke House" called the Green Dragon.

Frontierland

4. In the Frontierland Shooting Exposition, the first of two tombstones reads, "1801–1855 He loved to dance, he drank his fill, he drinks no more but dances still." A second tombstone reads, "One last drink was his demand, he died a reaching Red Eye Dan, Dec. 21." Liquor bottles are nearby.

5. In the Frontierland Shooting Exposition, painted on the side of Shorty's Hotel is an ad that reads, "Drink Mousehead Beer" (fortunately, Thumbelina's Cantina is nearby).

6. The Golden Horseshoe never sold alcohol, but there have been two other saloons in the area that looked like they did: Pat Casey's Last Chance Saloon and the Big Thunder Saloon. However, both were inaccessible because they were in Rainbow Ridge, the miniature town near the loading areas of the old Mine Train and today's Big Thunder Mountain Railroad. Also, painted on the Gold Nugget Dance Hall here is the slogan, "We Serve the Finest Corn Whiskey."

7. Moonshine jugs are on display inside Pioneer Mercantile.

8. In the 1980s and early 1990s, the burning cabin at the north end of Tom Sawyer Island featured a passed-out moonshiner (the fire was attributed to his exploded still).

9. Goblets, bottles, kegs of ale, and casks of grog are displayed throughout Tom Sawyer Island.

New Orleans Square

10. Empty wine bottles stand in the window displays at Café Orleans.

11. In the Haunted Mansion's ballroom scene, those are probably water goblets on the banquet table, but the ghosts reveling up in the chandelier wave red champagne glasses. Later, in the cemetery scene, an elderly couple and a skeletal arm all hold those same red glasses.

12. Bottles clearly marked "Rum" have been exhibited on the shelves of Pieces of Eight.

13. Bottles and drunken pirates are conspicuous in many scenes throughout Pirates of the Caribbean, as is a La Cantina sign behind the wench auction.

Tomorrowland

14. When the geese sang "I've Been Working on the Railroad" in America Sings (1974–1988), they were in a bar with bottles behind them (one of the geese held a bottle). Later, in a "Gay '90s" scene, the geese clutched beer mugs as they warbled a medley (a police dog even escorted an inebriated goose).

15. Occasionally standing on a kitchen countertop inside the House of the Future (1957–1967) were what looked like wine bottles, ready for the wine glasses set on the dining room table.

16. The former Innoventions Dream Home once included a Siemens Vinothek built-in wine cooler with sixteen wine bottles inside.

Rolly Crump's 5 Toughest Assignments

Disney Legend Roland Crump began his artistic career at the Disney Studios working on animated films such as *Peter Pan* and *Sleeping Beauty*. Moving on to Disneyland in the 1960s, he was a leader on projects all throughout the park, designing buildings, elaborate parade floats, inventive trash cans, and outdoor lighting displays. Before giving us the list of his five toughest Disneyland assignments below, Rolly told us: "Just about everything we did back then was a challenge because it had never been done before. Walt didn't just create Disneyland, he created the beginning of a new industry—theme parks."

1. **Enchanted Tiki Room**
   "I had never sculpted before, but I was asked to create the tiki sculptures outside the Tiki Room. Converting my research on tiki gods into three-dimensional shapes, I sculpted various statues while being true to

the overall look and color of the adjacent building. Inside, I had to transform the metal framework of the 'bird mobile' (as Walt called it) into what would look like a wooden chandelier."

2. **Adventureland Bazaar**

"I was given only six weeks to design, build, and install this big Adventureland shopping area. We built it from scratch using nothing but items from Disneyland's 'bone yard' and our imagination."

3. **Toys Inside It's a Small World**

"I had to design and build the Small World toys (the Swiss bell ringers, the bicycle riders, the penguins, etc.), originally for the 1964–1965 New York World's Fair. Using styrofoam, which we used in the model shop and I knew was easy to work with, I discovered the toys would look like they were made from papier-mâché."

4. **It's a Small World Façade**

"I had to keep in mind Walt's concern about the size and scale of the façade at Disneyland. He actually said he didn't want it to look like Las Vegas. I wanted to be true to Mary Blair's style and sketches while converting them into a three-dimensional architectural sculpture. I did a full scale mock-up in the Imagineering parking lot to show Walt, which he approved with no changes."

5. **The Haunted Mansion**

"Walt asked Yale Gracey and me to come up with spooky ideas that could be used in the Mansion. We did a lot of research, reading all we could and seeing as many ghost movies as possible. I came up with the seance room and the organ player; Yale came up with the head in the crystal ball and the ballroom sequence modeled after the Pepper's Ghost illusion."

SHOPS AND RESTAURANTS

You Can Buy!
You Can Buy!
You Can Buy!

A Dozen Attractions That Lead
Guests to a Similarly Themed Store

Maybe Disneyland didn't invent the concept of merging attraction exits with store entrances, but the park sure perfected it. So many attractions end where the gift shops begin that Banksy even used this idea as the title for his 2010 film, *Exit Through the Gift Shop.* (Actually, some Disneyland attractions put the gift shop at the entrance, as with the Autopia Winner's Circle, which stands in the walkway that leads to Tomorrowland's Autopia.) At the following twelve locations, guests have been able to demonstrate at cash registers their enthusiasm for the attractions nearby.

1. Buzz Lightyear Astro Blasters: Next to the Astro Blasters' exit is Little Green Men Store Command (the store's name playing on Buzz's Star Command), where pins, toys, and clothes celebrate the galactic hero.

2. Indian Village: In 1955, Frontierland's Indian Village started presenting authentic Native American dances; seven years later, this area added the Indian Trading Post, where guests could shop for turquoise jewelry, clothing, and pottery.

3. It's a Small World: Cashing in on the high volume of pedestrian traffic emerging from the cheerful cruise, the It's a Small World Toy Shop opened in the path of departing guests. When Mattel was the sponsor, the shelves were lined with Hot Wheels cars and Barbie dolls, but today they display Disney dolls and toys for tots.

4. King Arthur Carrousel: Before the carousel was moved farther north in 1983, the thematically related Merlin's Magic Shop was just a few steps away. Today's guests can walk to a nearby medieval cart called Carrousel Candies.

5. Mad Hatter's Mad Tea Party: Dizzy from the teacups, guests might wander into the Mad Hatter of Fantasyland next door to splurge on elaborate headgear.

6. Many Adventures of Winnie the Pooh: Across from this attraction's exit is Pooh Corner, Disneyland's Winnie the Pooh headquarters for all the candy, plush toys, and gift merchandise any Pooh fan could want.

7. Peter Pan's Flight: From 1957 to 2002, guests could look across the courtyard from Pan's exit and see the Tinker Bell Toy Shoppe with its enchanting gifts.

8. Pinocchio's Daring Journey: Guests exiting Pinocchio's attraction between 1983 and 2004 passed the gift shop run by Pinocchio's father.

Geppetto's Arts & Crafts (selling music boxes, marionettes, and old-fashioned cuckoo clocks) was renamed Geppetto's Toys & Gifts in the 1990s. Until late 2014, a *Frozen* meet-and-greet filled the little cottage, but the *Pinocchio*-related Stromboli's Wagon is still just around the corner by the Casey Jr. Circus Train.

9. Pirates of the Caribbean: Since the 1980s, exhilarated guests still humming "Yo Ho (A Pirate's Life for Me)" have been able to walk out of Pirates of the Caribbean and into Pieces of Eight, a well-themed shop filled with pirate treasure (hats, shirts, toys, gifts).

10. Pixie Hollow: From 2008 to 2011, anyone primed to buy sparkly fairy merchandise found the Pixie Hollow Gift Cart parked at Pixie Hollow's exit. The creatively decorated cart and its adjacent display stands sold dolls, wings, wands, wigs, and gifts, all inspired by Tink and her fairy friends.

11. Sleeping Beauty Castle Walk-Through: From 2006 to 2008, Three Fairies Magic Crystals, named for the magical fairy trio in *Sleeping Beauty*, was around the corner from the Walk-Through's exit.

12. Star Tours: Welcoming Star Tours' departing passengers is Star Trader, which opened in 1986 before the attraction did. One of Disneyland's biggest retail stores, Star Trader has the Force in full force with a galaxy of *Star Wars* and Star Tours merchandise.

Ooh La La: 14 New Orleans Square Establishments with French Names

New Orleans was named after French royalty (Philippe II, Duke of Orléans) and was once a French colony; consequently, many of New Orleans Square's businesses have either had French names or been named after famous French figures.

1. Cristal d'Orleans: A beautiful crystal shop still in the heart of New Orleans Square (1966–ongoing).

2. La Boutique de Noël: A Christmas shop formerly where Le Bat en Rouge is now (1998–2006).

3. La Boutique d'Or: Glittering jewelry and gifts (ca. 1974–ca. 1980).

4. Laffite's Silver Shop: Silver items ready for engraving in a shop named for the early nineteenth-century privateer (1966–1988).

5. La Mascarade d'Orléans: A fanciful Parisian confection formerly specializing in Mardi Gras masks, now offering regal jewelry (1985–ongoing).

6. La Petite Patisserie: "The little pastry shop" was a hidden jewel across from Jewel of Orléans (1988–ca. 2004).

7. Le Bat en Rouge: This playful take on Baton Rouge offers humorously scary wares (2002–ongoing).

8. Le Chapeau: Disneyland has never lacked hat shops; this one behind the French Market may have been the classiest (1966–ca. 1974).

9. Le Forgeron: French for "blacksmith," this Royal Street shop offered old-fashioned metal and leaded-glass objects for the home (1966–ca. 1974).

10. Le Gourmet: Fine kitchen accessories in a large space near the Blue Bayou (1966–ca. 2002).

11. L'Ornement Magique: A charming location for elaborate handcrafted ornaments (1998–2013).

12. Marché aux Fleurs, Sacs et Mode: "Flower Market, Stylish Bags" sold fancy handbags, accessories, and hats behind the French Market (1975–ca. 1985).

13. Mlle. Antoinette's Parfumerie: An elegant perfume shop that closed and later reopened (1967–1997; 2011–ongoing).

14. Port d'Orléans: A cooking-related shop at the back of New Orleans Square (ca. 1995–2002).

15 Unique But Extinct Disneyland Shops

Gone but not forgotten, these stores offered unique and memorable items, rather than the usual generic souvenirs.

1. Art Corner: Art, art supplies, and actual Disney artists drawing pictures, in Tomorrowland (1955–1966).

2. Candle Shop: From the 1950s to the 1970s, this colorful Main Street shop sold beautiful and imaginative candles.

3. Cole of California Swimsuits: Formerly a silent-movie actor, Fred Cole sold fashionable swimwear at Main Street's northern end (1956–1957).

4. Disney Villains: Next to Sleeping Beauty Castle, this themed shop was filled with sinister merchandise (1991–1996; reopened as Villains Lair 1998–2004).

5. Fine Tobacco: The wooden Indian on today's Main Street indicates where this store sold international brands of cigarettes (1955–1990).

6. Flower Mart, aka Flower Market: For about forty years, guests could buy beautiful artificial flowers, "the world's finest natural flowers not grown by nature," from a gathering of open-air carts on Main Street (briefly reopened for display in 2013).

7. Guatemalan Weavers: Adventureland's fabric-and-fashions shop sold colorful products from Central and South America (1956–1986).

8. Hobbyland: Models and hobby kits at an outdoor site near today's Star Trader (1955–1966).

9. Hurricane Lamp Shop: Halfway down Main Street, the Hurricane Lamp Shop sold Victorian hurricane lamps with glass chimneys and oil-burning wicks (1972–1975).

10. Intimate Apparel: The famed "corset shop" on Main Street was run by "the Wizard of Bras" (1955–1956).

11. Jimmy Starr's Show Business Souvenirs: A Town Square spot for movie props, photos, and collectibles (1956–1959).

12. Le Forgeron: In the 1960s and 1970s, this New Orleans Square "blacksmith" shop offered old-fashioned metal and leaded-glass objects.

13. One-of-a-Kind Shop: New Orleans Square's legendary antiques shop, inspired by Mrs. Disney (1966–1996).

14. Pendleton Woolen Mills Dry Goods Store: Today's Bonanza Outfitters was yesterday's frontier store filled with durable Pendleton clothes (1955–1990).

15. Pen Shop: In the late 1950s, a small business selling writing instruments, displaying historical documents, and analyzing handwriting operated near Main Street's Market House.

A Dozen Shops with Actual Artists at Work

It may seem like most Disneyland stores sell the same Disney merchandise, but a few specialty shops have had actual artists on view creating customized works for guests.

1. Art Corner (1955–1966): This art shop near today's Tomorrowland Terrace had Disney animators on hand to draw quick portraits for only $1.50.

2. Bibbidi Bobbidi Boutique (2009–ongoing): Formerly the site of the Tinker Bell Toy Shoppe, this salon's stylists provide fairytale makeovers for young princesses and princes.

3. Fortuosity Shop (2008–ongoing): Skilled cast members used to hand-paint Disney-themed watch faces here as Main Street guests watched; as of 2013, they now assemble watches.

4. Glass blower (1955–1966): Main Street's Crystal Arcade leased space to a glass blower who created delicate glass figurines in full view of guests;

a similar artist worked in a room in the Sleeping Beauty Castle walkway into the 1970s.

5. Main Street Magic Shop (1957–ongoing): Sleight-of-hand magicians demonstrate tricks.

6. Merlin's Magic Shop (1955–1983): The first of Disneyland's two magic shops, Merlin's was next to Fantasyland's Peter Pan attraction and offered disguises, toys, gag gifts, and trick-demonstrating cast members.

7. Mlle. Antoinette's Parfumerie (1967–1997; 2011–ongoing): Until 1997, this elegant New Orleans Square shop was staffed by trained perfumers who expertly blended customized fragrances. It reopened in 2011 without the perfumers but with dozens of brand-name perfumes for sale.

8. Parasol Cart (1990–ongoing): Parked near the French Market is this pretty cart with artists who will hand-paint designs, patterns, and names onto the parasols (*right*).

9. Portrait Artists (ca. 1986–ongoing): Portrait artists have graced Town Square's Opera House, Tomorrowland's Art Corner, and the Main Street area's Center Street. Today, the artists do realistic portraits and caricatures in New Orleans Square.

10. Silhouette Studio (1956–ongoing): These artists hand-cut accurate paper silhouettes of guests' profiles in under a minute.

11. New Century Watches & Clocks (1972–2008): In 1972, New Century replaced Main Street's Upjohn Pharmacy and put an artist in the window who hand-painted Disney-themed watch faces.

12. Disneyana (2013–ongoing): When Disneyana moved from Main Street to Town Square in 2013, it introduced a new Ink & Paint Cel area that occasionally features artists creating animation cels and character sketches.

13 Disneyland Shops and Their Most Expensive Items

Inquiries inside various Disneyland shops identified their most expensive items, listed below (the dollar figures are rounded up, and tax isn't included).

1. Le Bat en Rouge (New Orleans Square): Betsey Johnson purse = $129

2. Star Trader (Tomorrowland): Darth Vader Force FX collectible light saber = $170

3. Bibbidi Bobbidi Boutique (Fantasyland): Castle Package princess make-over with gown = starts at $190

4. Heraldry Shoppe (Fantasyland): Lord of the Rings Anduril sword with sheath = $225

5. Pioneer Mercantile (Frontierland): American West three-compartment leather tote bag = $258

6. Mlle. Antoinette's Parfumerie (New Orleans Square): 125 ml. of Guer-lain's Mon Precieux Nectar = $270

7. Mickey's Toontown Five & Dime: Collectible Ingersoll Mickey Mouse watch = $270 (shouldn't the most expensive item in this store be only ten cents?)

8. Disney Showcase (Main Street): Dooney & Bourke vinyl bag with leather trim = $395

9. Fortuosity Shop (Main Street): Wristwatch with color art and separate painting = $590

10. Main Street Magic Shop: Authentic key owned by Harry Houdini = $875

11. Cristal d'Orleans (New Orleans Square): Small crystal castle = $6,800

12. Disneyana (Town Square): *Tropical Hide-away*, Shag's original acrylic on panel showing the Enchanted Tiki Room = $18,000

13. Crystal Arts (Main Street): Large crystal castle (*right*) – $37,500

8 Reasons Why Main Street's Emporium Is Disneyland's Best Store

Just as a small American town's main street probably contains a sizeable de-partment store, so too does Disneyland's Main Street have its own Empori-um. It's the park's best store, because it offers . . .

1. Size. It's Disneyland's biggest store (the most square footage in 1955, and it's only gotten bigger over the decades, swelling to over 4,000 square feet and engulfing smaller shops to the north and west).

2. A perfect location. For guests walking along Main Street's west side, the Emporium is the first and last major store they'll encounter upon enter-ing and leaving Disneyland.

3. Convenience. It usually stays open at night, even after the rest of Disneyland has closed (offering guests one last chance to stock up).

4. Style. It has one of Main Street's most beautiful exteriors, especially at night. It's decorated on the outside with charming dioramas in its windows—Disneyland's best "window shopping."

5. Did we mention style? It's decorated on the inside with rich wood walls and beautiful light fixtures (especially after a 2011 remodel), as well as humorous turn-of-the-century tableaux up by the ceiling (*above*).

6. Functionality. It's easier than ever to navigate after a 2011 remodel pushed the cash registers to the perimeter.

7. Variety. It's stocked with a wide selection of merchandise (unlike many other Disneyland stores that specialize in one type of item—crystal, hats, candy, etc.).

8. Efficiency. It's a handy shortcut when everyone else is clogging up the Main Street sidewalk during parades.

A Dozen Stores and Eateries with Puns and Jokes in Their Names

Disney's Imagineers love a good joke. Here are twelve puns they've worked into the titles of various Disneyland establishments.

1. Bibbidi Bobbidi Boutique: A play on the title of the Fairy Godmother's song in *Cinderella.*

2. Brer Bar: A good name for an eatery in Critter Country, where guests will see a statue of Br'er Bear.

3. Chester Drawer's: This little Main Street space sells "togs for toddlers."

4. Chicken of the Sea Pirate Ship and Restaurant, aka Captain Hook's Galley: Some consider "chicken of the sea" a joke on the cowardly Captain Hook (the slogan also applied to Starkist, long-time sponsor of this Fantasyland location that closed in 1982).

5. Le Bat en Rouge: A play on Baton Rouge, the Louisiana capital within 100 miles of New Orleans and thus a suitable identity for this New Orleans Square shop.

6. Little Green Men Store Command: A takeoff on Buzz Lightyear's Star Command.

7. Lunching Pad: This little eatery was located underneath the loading areas of the old Rocket Jets and PeopleMover; it opened the same year as nearby Space Mountain, so "launching" was an appropriate theme here.

8. Mod Hatter: In 1967, the Mad Hatter of Tomorrowland got a new location and a psychedelic new name—Mod Hatter—that was suitable for the times. In the 1980s, the name went less mod and more space-y when it became Hatmosphere.

9. Pluto's Dog House: A Mickey's Toontown snack counter that serves (what else?) hot dogs.

10. Space Bar: This Tomorrowland restaurant (1955–1966) had a name alluding to computer keyboards and outer space—two components of space age living.

11. Sunkist, I Presume: The name of this Adventureland snack shack (1962–1992) came from Henry Stanley's famous 1871 meeting with David Livingstone in African jungles (Stanley's first words to the reclusive missionary were "Dr. Livingstone, I presume").

12. Tomorrowlanding: The "landing" could be the loading areas for the Rocket Jets and the PeopleMover, both of which were directly above this location before the small shop opened in 2006.

Disneyland's Bars, Inns, Taverns, and Saloons

Considering that it epitomizes the family-friendly theme park, Disneyland has sure had a lot of bars. And inns. And taverns. And saloons. Of course, only one establishment in the park has ever actually sold alcohol—Club 33. Here are sixteen Disneyland businesses with "bar," "inn," "tavern," or "saloon" in their names, as well as their locations and years of operation.

1. Big Thunder Saloon (an inaccessible display in Frontierland's miniature Rainbow Ridge, which has been on view since 1955)

2. Blue Whale Inn (inaccessible, seen in Geppetto's Village from Fantasyland's Storybook Land Canal Boats, 1956–-ongoing)

3. Brer Bar (Bear Country, 1989–2003)

4. Dairy Bar (Tomorrowland, 1956–1958)

5. Fowler's Inn (inaccessible, near Fowler's Harbor, Frontierland, 1958–ongoing)

6. Golden Horseshoe Saloon (Frontierland, 1955–ongoing)

7. Mile Long Bar (Bear Country, 1972–1989)

8. Mint Julep Bar (New Orleans Square, 1966–ongoing)
9. Oaks Tavern (Frontierland, 1956–1978)
10. Pat Casey's Last Chance Saloon (inaccessible, Rainbow Ridge)
11. Red Wagon Inn/Plaza Inn (Hub, 1955–ongoing)
12. Space Bar (Tomorrowland, 1955–1966)
13. Tiki Juice Bar (Adventureland, 1976–ongoing)
14. Troubadour Tavern (Fantasyland, 2009–ongoing)
15. Village Inn (renamed Village Haus, Fantasyland, 1983–ongoing)
16. Yacht Bar (Tomorrowland, 1957–1966)

A Dozen Iconic Disneyland Dishes and Sides

There's plenty of room for debate on this tasty topic, but this alphabetically listed group should whet your appetite.

1. Citrus Fire-Grilled Chicken (Rancho del Zocalo Restaurante)
2. Chowder, Gumbo, or Chili in a Bread Bowl (Café Orleans, Harbour Galley, Royal Street Veranda)
3. Corn Dog (Little Red Wagon)
4. Fried Green Tomato Sandwich (Hungry Bear Restaurant)
5. Fruit Salad (Tahitian Terrace, extinct)
6. "Jungle Skewers" (Bengal Barbecue)
7. Mickey Mouse Pancakes (River Belle Terrace)
8. Monte Cristo Sandwich (Blue Bayou)
9. Mozzarella Sticks (usually available upon request at Golden Horseshoe and Stage Door Café)
10. Oscar's Choice (Carnation Café)
11. Pommes Frites (French Market)
12. Turkey Leg (Edelweiss Snacks and other locations)

A Dozen Iconic Disneyland Desserts, Snacks, Candies, and Beverages

With an overwhelming abundance of choices, we had a tasty time narrowing the list to these twelve favorites.

1. Apple Fritters (Royal Street Veranda)
2. Candy Canes (handmade during the holiday season at the Candy Palace)

3. Chocolate Ganache Cake (Blue Bayou)

4. Churro (Churro Cart, various locations)

5. Coca-Cola (fired into the air at Tomorrowland's Spirit of Refreshment)

6. Dill pickle (Main Street Fruit Cart and other locations)

7. Jungle Julep (Sunkist, I Presume, extinct)

8. Mickey Pretzels (Refreshment Corner and other locations)

9. Mile-High Chocolate Cake (Golden Horseshoe)

10. Mint Julep (Mint Julep Bar)

11. Pineapple Dole Whip (Tiki Juice Bar)

12. Sundaes (Gibson Girl Ice Cream Parlor; the ice cream called Fantasia was a favorite flavor here and at Carnation Plaza Gardens, but it was discontinued)

7 Disneyland Locations with Popcorn Machine Mechanical Grinders

Another example of Disneyland's subtle charms are the tiny mechanical grinders working away in the park's popcorn machines. Spinning cylinders of popcorn inside colorful glass-walled carts, these small figures (nicknamed "Roastie-Toasties") can often be found in the following areas.

1. Fantasyland: Abominable Snowman (*above*), clown (orange-and-purple costume).

2. Frontierland: Dapper Dan (blue costume), explorer.

3. Hub: Clown (black-and-yellow costume), Santa Claus.

4. Mickey's Toontown: Conductor.

5. New Orleans Square: Ghoulish undertaker, Oogie Boogie.

6. Tomorrowland: Rocketeer

7. Town Square: Dapper Dan (red costume).

ATTENDANCE, TICKETS, AND OPERATIONS

The Business of Fun

20 Disneyland Attendance Milestones

These landmarks in Disneyland's attendance history are listed chronologically.

1. July 18, 1955: First admission ticket (#000001) purchased for $1 by Roy O. Disney
2. September 8, 1955: One-millionth guest arrives
3. October 4, 1956: Five-millionth guest
4. December 31, 1957: Ten-millionth guest
5. 1959: The first year annual attendance is over five-million guests
6. April 19, 1961: Twenty-five-millionth guest
7. August 12, 1965: Fifty-millionth guest
8. 1970: The first year annual attendance is over ten million guests
9. June 17, 1971: 100-millionth guest
10. July 4, 1979: First baby born in Disneyland
11. January 8, 1981: 200-millionth guest
12. August 24, 1985: 250-millionth guest
13. September 1, 1989: 300-millionth guest
14. 1996: The first year annual attendance is over fifteen million guests
15. July 5, 1997: 400-millionth guest
16. March 15, 2001: 450-millionth guest
17. January 8, 2004: 500-millionth guest
18. May 2, 2006: Two-billionth guest to attend any Disney Park arrives at Disneyland
19. May 28, 2009: Five-millionth Grad Nite guest since this all-night spring party debuted in 1961
20. 2011: The first year annual attendance is more than sixteen million guests (recent annual attendance hovers around this mark, which averages out to 6,000 people *more* than a full Fenway Park every day of the year, rain or shine)

Disneyland's Busiest Weeks of the Year

Based on our own informal observations, these chronologically listed weeks seem to draw Disneyland's biggest crowds.

1. February: The week surrounding President's Day
2. March: The two weeks corresponding to Spring Break for colleges

3. April: Easter week

4. May: The week of Memorial Day

5. June: The mid-month week when schools get out

6. July: The week of July 4 and the week surrounding the park's July 17 birthday (both weeks often feature special events)

7. August: Every week of the month

8. September: The week of Labor Day

9. November: The week of Thanksgiving

10. December: The two weeks surrounding Christmas Day (possibly the year's busiest weeks)

Disneyland's Least-Crowded Weeks of the Year

Conversely, these weeks seem to draw Disneyland's smallest crowds. For many of these weeks, huge crowds have recently left after some major holiday, and Disneyland hasn't yet begun decorating for the next holiday

1. January: The weeks between New Year's Day and Martin Luther King, Jr. Day

2. February: The weeks before Valentine's Day week

3. March: The weeks before Spring Break

4. April/May: The weeks between Easter and Memorial Day

5. September/October: The weeks between Labor Day and mid-October

6. November: The first two weeks

7. December: The first two weeks

Ticketed Attractions, 1955–1982

On October 11, 1955, Disneyland introduced its famous ticket books. Initially, these books offered a total of eight A, B, and C tickets for $2.50. With new Frontierland attractions opening nine months later, the books were expanded to include D tickets; simultaneously, several existing attractions that had previously cost a C ticket were reclassified as D-ticket attractions. The famous high-demand E ticket was added in 1959 to coincide with the Matterhorn Bobsleds, Monorail, and Submarine Voyage debuts. For the next twenty-three years, new attractions were steadily added to the A–E lineup, and some existing attractions continued to shift around in ticket value, sometimes going up in cost (Main Street Cinema, from A to B), sometimes going down (Sleeping Beauty Castle Walk-Through, C to B to A), and sometimes both (Snow White Adventures, C to D to C again). The following list gives the five ticket prices charged most frequently for attractions.

1. **A Ticket**

   King Arthur Carrousel; Main Street Vehicles; Satellite View of America; Sleeping Beauty Castle Walk-Through; Space Station X-1; 20,000 Leagues Under the Sea Exhibit.

2. **B Ticket**

   Alice in Wonderland; Art of Animation; Big Game Safari Shooting Gallery; Casey Jr. Circus Train; Conestoga Wagons; Main Street Cinema; Main Street Shooting Gallery; Mickey Mouse Club Theater; Midget Autopia; Motor Boat Cruise; Phantom Boats; Swiss Family Treehouse; Viewliner.

3. **C Ticket**

   Adventure Thru Inner Space; Astro-Jets; Dumbo the Flying Elephant; Fantasyland Autopia; Frontierland Shooting Gallery; Junior Autopia; Mad Hatter's Mad Tea Party; Mike Fink Keel Boats; Mr. Toad's Wild Ride; Peter Pan Flight; Rocket to the Moon; Snow White Adventures; Stage Coach; Tomorrowland Autopia.

4. **D Ticket**

   Flying Saucers; Indian War/ Davy Crockett's Explorer Canoes; *Mark Twain* Riverboat; Mission to Mars; PeopleMover; Flight to the Moon; Rafts to Tom Sawyer Island; Mine Train; Rainbow Ridge Pack Mules; Rocket Jets; Sailing  Ship *Columbia*; Santa Fe & Disneyland Railroad; Skyway (one way to Fantasyland or Tomorrowland); Storybook Land Canal Boats.

5. **E Ticket**

   America Sings; Big Thunder Mountain Railroad; Country Bear Jamboree; Enchanted Tiki Room; Great Moments with Mr. Lincoln; the Haunted Mansion; It's a Small World; Jungle Cruise; Matterhorn Bobsleds; Monorail; Pirates of the Caribbean; Pack Mules Through Nature's Wonderland; Space Mountain; Submarine Voyage.

Adult Admission Prices Since 1982

From Opening Day in 1955 until early 1982, the full Disneyland experience required guests to make at least two purchases. One was the low-priced park admission ($1 in 1955), and the other was for supplemental tickets for attractions. For most of this period, attraction tickets were sold in convenient ticket books filled with the famous A-B-C-D-E tickets. However, by the end of the 1970s, Disneyland began experimenting with an all-inclusive, unlimited-attraction admission policy patterned after a successful pricing program used at other parks. In 1981, Disneyland guests could skip the tickets books if they wanted to and instead pay a single price for unlimited rides: $10.25, with an after-7 PM option available in the summer for $8. A year later, ticket books were eliminated and all adult guests paid a mandatory single price—$12—for a one-day, unlimited-attraction Passport (the shooting galleries were not included for unlimited use; also, young children were free, as they are now). Since 1982, the price of a daily Passport has climbed steadily, sometimes jumping upwards twice in the same year. The following chronological list shows the various prices in nineteen different years.

1. 1982: $12
2. 1984: $14
3. 1986: $18
4. 1990: $25.50
5. 1994: $31
6. 2000: $41

7. 2002: $45
8. 2003: $47
9. 2005: $53
10. 2006: $63
11. 2007: $66
12. 2008: $69
13. 2009: $72

14. 2010: $76
15. 2011: $80
16. 2012: $87
17. 2013: $92
18. 2014: $96
19. 2015: $99

30 Years of Annual Passports

As Disneyland was selling daily Passports in the mid-1980s, the park introduced Annual Passports "for those of you who can never have too much fun!" Originally offered to members of the Magic Kingdom Club (a corporate discount program), the new Annual Passports gave unlimited admission and unlimited use of attractions all year long. Over the decades, the number and variety of Annual Passports have changed, as seen in this chronologically ordered sampling.

1. 1986: Low-priced seasonal options supplemented year-long Passports.

   Annual Passport = $114.95 (100 percent of the year)

   Three-Season Passport = $49.95 (good for only May, September, and January, "when crowds are down and special events and entertainment are still going strong")

   Summer Nights Passport = $49.95 (summer after 5 PM)

   Senior Fun Passport = $13.95 (Monday–Friday, September–June, must be sixty years old or over)

2. 1991: The seasonal option tripled in length (from three months to nine months), but only doubled (roughly) in price over the 1986 plan.

Annual Passport = $180 (100 percent of the year)

Seasonal Passport = $95 (September 1–May 31, excluding Saturdays and December 25–31)

Senior Fun Passport = $22 (Sunday–Friday, September–June, must be sixty years old or over)

3. 2000: No more short seasonal options; the $99 Passport approximates today's price for a single-day adult admission.

Three tiers of Annual Passports = $199 (100 percent of the year); $129 (92 percent); $99 (82 percent)

4. 2002: After Disney's California Adventure (now Disney California Adventure) opened in 2001, there were separate prices for Disneyland-only Annual Passports and Disneyland + DCA Annual Passports.

Two tiers of Disneyland-only Annual Passports = $199 (100 percent of the year); $139 (88 percent)

Two tiers of Disneyland + DCA Annual Passports = $299 (100 percent of the year); $199 (88 percent)

Southern California Disneyland-only Annual Passport for residents in specific zip codes = $89 (56 percent of the year)

Southern California Disneyland + DCA Annual Passport for residents in specific zip codes = $149 (56 percent of the year)

5. 2010: Annual Passports gave admission to both Disneyland and Disney California Adventure.

Two tiers of Annual Passports = $459 (100 percent of the year); $329 (86 percent)

Two tiers of Southern California Annual Passports for residents of specific zip codes = $239 (59 percent of the year); $189 (44 percent)

6. 2012: Annual Passports, annual price jumps.

Disney Premier Passport, including the entire Disneyland Resort and all the parks at the Walt Disney World Resort = $849 (100 percent of the year)

Two tiers of Annual Passports = $629 (100 percent of the year); $469 (87 percent)

Two tiers of Southern California Annual Passport for residents of specific zip codes = $329 (59 percent of the year); $269 (47 percent)

7. 2013: New year, new prices.

Disney Premier Passport, including the entire Disneyland Resort all the parks at the Walt Disney World Resort = $979 (100 percent of the year)

Two tiers of Annual Passports = $669 (100 percent of the year); $499 (87 percent)

Two tiers of Southern California Annual Passport for residents of specific zip codes = $359 (59 percent of the year); $279 (47 percent)

8. 2015: High ho, high ho!

Disney Premier Passport, including the entire Disneyland Resort and all the parks at the Walt Disney World Resort = $1,099 (100 percent of the year)

Two tiers of Annual Passports = $779 (100 percent of the year); $549 (86 percent)

Only one Southern California Annual Passport for residents of specific zip codes, the Southern California Select = $299 (47 percent of the year)

Original Investors in Disneyland, Inc.

The Walt Disney Company owns Disneyland, but it wasn't always that way. The company had to buy out Disneyland's original investors, which it gradually did as Disneyland profits rolled in (Walt Disney Productions bought out the last outside investor, ABC, in 1960). Listed in descending order, here are the Disneyland, Inc. investors at the park's 1955 opening, according to Leonard Mosley's *Disney's World* and Bob Thomas's *Walt Disney: An American Original.* One name not on the list is Bob Hope, who, according to Richard Zoglin's *Hope: Entertainer of the Century,* turned down Walt Disney's invitation to become an early investor because he was "convinced Disneyland would be a flop."

1. Walt Disney Productions = 34.48 percent

2. American Broadcasting Company = 34.48 percent

3. Walt Disney = 17.25 percent

4. Western Printing and Lithographing = 13.79 percent

22 Sponsors of Multiple Locations Within Disneyland

When it comes to sponsoring Disneyland locations, some companies, including those listed alphabetically below, have been more active than others.

1. Arribas Brothers: Castle Arts (Fantasyland); Cristal d'Orleans (New Orleans Square); Crystal Arts (Main Street).

2. Atchison, Topeka & Santa Fe Railway (aka Santa Fe Railway): Santa Fe & Disneyland Railroad; Viewliner (Tomorrowland).

3. Bank of America: Bank of America (Main Street); It's a Small World (Fantasyland).

4. Brawny: Big Thunder Barbecue, Big Thunder Ranch (Frontierland).

5. Carnation: Baby Station, Carnation Plaza Gardens (Hub); Carnation Café, Carnation Ice Cream Parlor (Main Street).

6. Coca-Cola: Refreshment Corner (Main Street); Spirit of Refreshment, Tomorrowland Terrace (Tomorrowland).

7. Del Monte: America Sings (Tomorrowland); Market House (Main Street).

8. Dole: Enchanted Tiki Room, Tiki Juice Bar (Adventureland).

9. Dreyer's: Gibson Girl Ice Cream Parlor, Main Street Cone Shop (Main Street).

10. General Electric: Carousel of Progress (Tomorrowland); Main Street Electrical Parade.

11. Gibson Art Co.: Gibson Greeting Cards, Card Corner (Main Street).

12. Hills Bros.: Hills Bros. Coffee House and Coffee Garden (Town Square); Market House (Main Street).

13. Kodak: Golden Horseshoe (Frontierland); Kodak Camera Center, Main Street Photo Supply Co. (Main Street); Magic Eye Theater (Tomorrowland).

14. McDonald's: Harbour Galley (Critter Country); Westward Ho Conestoga Wagon Fries (Frontierland).

15. McDonnell-Douglas: Flight to the Moon, Mission to Mars (Tomorrowland).

16. Monsanto: Adventure Thru Inner Space, Fashions and Fabrics Through the Ages, Hall of Chemistry, House of the Future (Tomorrowland).

17. Nestlé: Baby Care Center (Hub); Chocolate Collection (New Orleans Square); Blue Ribbon Bakery, Gibson Girl Ice Cream Parlor (Main Street); Enchanted Cottage Sweets & Treats, Princess Fantasy Faire (Fantasyland).

18. Pepsi-Cola: Country Bear Jamboree (Bear Country); Golden Horseshoe (Frontierland).

19. Stouffer's: French Market (New Orleans Square); Plaza Pavilion (Hub); Tahitian Terrace (Adventureland).

20. Sunkist: River Belle Terrace (Frontierland); Sunkist Citrus House (Main Street); Sunkist, I Presume (Adventureland).

21. Swift: Chicken Plantation (Frontierland); Market House (Main Street); Red Wagon Inn (Hub).

22. Trans World Airlines (TWA): *Moonliner*, Rocket to the Moon (Tomorrowland).

22 Official Products of Disneyland

Throughout Disneyland's history, various companies have signed agreements to call their products "The Official ___ of Disneyland." The following twenty-two alphabetically listed products have at one time or another been promoted as "official" products of Disneyland (followed by the companies that did the promoting).

1. Airline: PSA, TWA

2. Automobile: Honda

3. Bank: Bank of America, Bank One, Union Bank of California

4. Bread: Wonder Bread

5. Camera: Nikon

6. Car rental: Alamo

7. Coffee: Joffrey's, Nescafé

8. Credit card: American Express

9. Film: GAF

10. Fruit snack: Ocean Spray Craisins Dried Cranberries

11. Gasoline: Richfield

12. Hotel: Disneyland Hotel

13. Ketchup: Hunt's

14. Movers: Global Van Lines

15. "Musical instrument supplier": Yamaha

16. Orange soda: Nesbitt's

17. Pet food: Kal Kan

18. Piano: Wurlitzer

19. Popcorn: Orville Redenbacher's

20. Railroad: Atchison, Topeka & Santa Fe Railway

21. Sugar: C & H

22. Wireless provider: AT&T

25 Marketing Campaigns

Disneyland has often generated big marketing campaigns to celebrate special anniversaries (the silver and golden anniversaries, for instance). However, in recent years the park has sometimes built its promotions around creative gimmicks, not historical milestones. Listed chronologically are twenty-five campaigns through the decades.

1. 1965: The year-long Tencennial Celebration for Disneyland's tenth birthday kicked off with a special *Walt Disney's Wonderful World of Color* episode; debuts included Great Moments with Mr. Lincoln, a Tencennial Parade, and an anniversary march composed by the Sherman Brothers.

2. 1971: The Year of a Hundred Million Smiles offered special giveaways leading up to the arrival of the park's 100-millionth guest.

3. 1975: With Disneyland turning twenty, Mission to Mars debuting, and Mr. Lincoln returning after a two-year absence, a new ad campaign offered this reminder: "Disneyland, the happiest part of growing up. Come live it again."

4. 1980: For Disneyland's silver anniversary, former cast members were invited for a special night of entertainment called the Family Reunion. Meanwhile a Danny Kaye-hosted TV special, a new parade, and a twenty-five-hour party from July 17 to July 18 added to the year's festivities.

5. 1985–1986: When it turned thirty, Disneyland threw itself an all-night party in mid-July (with special $30 tickets). The entrance displayed a running tally of ticket sales in anticipation of the park's 250-millionth guest, and throughout the year, the Gift-Giver Extraordinaire Machine gave out thousands of prizes (for example, every thirtieth guest through the turnstiles won an instant prize, and every thirty-thousandth guest won a new car).

6. 1986–1988 (seasonal): To spur ticket sales during the slow season, Circus Fantasy filled Main Street and the Hub with real circus acts (elephants, a Main Street high-wire act, a motorcycle daredevil, and more) for the winters of 1986, 1987, and 1988.

7. 1987–1988 (seasonal): The State Fair, complete with traditional carnival games and a Ferris wheel, was a spirited simulation of the real thing held annually across the U.S. While some guests were amused by the midway booths and pig races, purists couldn't believe that such mundane attractions were being prominently showcased in a park famous for innovation.

8. 1987–ongoing: "I'm going to Disneyland" became a famous commercial catchphrase after Disney paid quarterback Phil Simms to say it

immediately after winning Super Bowl XXI. In most years since, Disney has recruited star players to say the line after winning various championships (in response to the question, "What are you going to do next?"). A variation on the response is, "I'm going to Disney World." In his book *Work in Progress*, Michael Eisner, Disney's former CEO, credits his wife with hearing the sentence in 1986 and suggesting it for an ad campaign (Eisner himself said it upon announcing his 1994 retirement, as quoted in *Newsweek*, September 20, 2004). On January 4, 2005, 72,000 spectators at Miami's Orange Bowl football game were coached to yell, "I'm going to Disneyland!" simultaneously upon receiving free tickets to any Disney park.

9. 1988–1989 (seasonal): With the 1950s making a comeback (*Happy Days*, *Grease*, and *Back to the Future* had been hits in the 1970s and 1980s), spring's spectacular Blast to the Past Celebration featured nostalgic bands, an enormous jukebox in the Hub, colorful costumes, themed parades, special events, and giveaways, all evoking the bygone days of poodle skirts and sock hops.

10. 1990: For its thirty-fifth birthday, Disneyland debuted the Dream Machine, giving guests a chance to pull a lever on a giant cake-like slot machine at the Hub to win prizes.

11. 1995: The park's fortieth birthday was celebrated with "40 Years of Adventure"—TV specials, merchandise, free Collector Series Cards commemorating Disneyland milestones, a "Time Castle" buried in front of Sleeping Beauty Castle, and the Indiana Jones Adventure debut.

12. 2001–2003: After Disney's California Adventure opened to disappointing crowd numbers, Disneyland reminded guests about the magnificent park next door with a "Where the Magic Began" promotion, featuring new banners, special merchandise, and "100 Years of Magic" festivities celebrating what would have been Walt Disney's 100th birthday on December 5.

13. 2005: To celebrate the 2005 reopening of Space Mountain, Honda launched its "Coolest Ride in the Galaxy" sweepstakes that gave away a new 2006 Honda Civic to a lucky guest every day in October.

14. 2005–2006: The Happiest Homecoming on Earth was a comprehensive tribute to Disneyland's fiftieth birthday with Julie Andrews as the official ambassador. The special events and shows included celebratory decorations and merchandise, a new daily parade, new nightly fireworks, and a new Opera House documentary starring Steve Martin.

15. 2006–2008: In the Year of a Million Dreams (*page 208, top*), randomly chosen guests received surprise gifts (pins, FASTPASS badges, free meals, trips, and more).

16. 2007–2008: During the Disney Dreams Give-away, randomly chosen guests received overnight stays in the New Orleans Square rooms formerly used for the Disney Gallery.

17. 2008: The Indiana Jones Summer of Hidden Mysteries tied in with the release of the new *Indiana Jones and the Kingdom of the Crystal Skull* movie. This summer-long promotional event included changes to the Jungle Cruise and live appearances by an Indy character.

18. 2009–2010: The rhetorical "What Will You Celebrate?" question got guests free admission on their birthdays.

19. 2010: A Give a Day, Get a Day promotion meant that community volunteers earned vouchers for free Disneyland admission. After ten weeks, a million people had received the vouchers and the promotion ended.

20. 2011–2013: To "Let the Memories Begin," guests could share their Disneyland photos and stories on Disney websites. Meanwhile, a new nighttime show called "The Magic, the Memories, and You!" splashed photos of guests across the It's a Small World façade.

21. 2013: Limited Time Magic was an inelegant name for an ambitious program of short-term events that were announced via social media. These events were usually timed with seasonal festivities (a New Orleans Bayou Bash for Mardi Gras, True Love Week for Valentine's Day, etc.). A simultaneous Year of the Ear promotion introduced new mouse hat designs.

22. 2013: The Monstrous Summer was timed with the release of the new *Monsters University* movie and kicked off with a Monstrous Summer All-Nighter on May 24, 2013.

23. 2013–2104: Show Your Disney Side was introduced in September 2013 with humorous commercials, but no major impact on Disneyland itself. Guests were invited to dress up as Disney characters during 2014's Rock Your Disney Side twenty-four-hour party on Memorial Day weekend (*opposite, bottom*); they were also encouraged to submit photos and videos to social networks.

24. 2014–2015: Starting in January 2014, signs announcing "Keeps Getting Happier" appeared throughout the Disneyland Resort with variations on a "happiness" theme.

25. 2015–ongoing: The Diamond Celebration offered a new parade, new fireworks, and new merchandise to promote Disneyland's sixtieth anniversary.

Jack Lindquist
Describes 5 Disneyland Promotions

Want to learn about Disneyland's most in-novative promotions? Ask Jack Lindquist—that's what we did. An official Disney Legend, Lindquist is designated as the park's "Honor-ary Mayor" and "Master of Fun" on his City Hall tribute window (there's also a Goofy's Playhouse pumpkin in his likeness). Before earning those titles, he was a child actor in the early 1930s. He started working for Disneyland in 1955 as the advertising manager and later headed the marketing department, eventually becoming Disneyland's first president in 1990. His acclaimed 2010 memoir, *In Service to the Mouse*, is a must-read for Disneyland fans. Below, in text he wrote exclusively for *The Disneyland Book of Lists*, Jack Lindquist goes behind the scenes of five exciting promotions he was intimately involved in during his thirty-eight-year Disneyland career.

1. **Expanding Disneyland's Reach, 1956**
   "In January and February, we made the first attempt to try to identify markets outside the L.A./Orange County area that could provide real-time data on the depth of the one-day drive market. We went to the prominent Green Frog Market in Bakersfield, California. This promotion included bringing Disneyland's Autopia cars to give free rides to children on a course set up in the parking lot. Plus, there were appearances by Annette [Funicello], Jimmie Dodd, Roy Williams (the big 'Mooseketeer'), and others from the *Mickey Mouse Club* TV show. The successful Green Frog experience gave us the rationalization and confidence to expand our marketing territorial boundaries to include

Las Vegas, Phoenix, Fresno, Santa Barbara, San Diego, and, of course, Bakersfield."

2. **First Advance-Sale Ticket Program, 1957**
"This was to support the first New Year's Eve party at Disneyland. Later the program was expanded to support Dixieland at Disneyland, Spring Fling, and other 'hard ticket' Disneyland events. What was a first in 1957 led to normal advance-sale ticketing for arenas, theaters, concerts, etc. Some mega-companies, through specialization and with new technology, have made advance-ticket sales an essential part of the entertainment landscape."

3. **Magic Kingdom Club, 1958**
"Milt Albright created this corporate discount club, and I enthusiastically supported it (I was Director of Marketing back then). The club had phenomenal growth and we eventually had Magic Kingdom Clubs at Tokyo Disneyland and Disneyland Paris. At its height, the MKC boasted over 5,500,000 members at more than 8,000 companies worldwide and was responsible for over $100 million dollars annually in revenue to Disney."

4. **Tencennial Newspaper Supplement, 1965**
"To celebrate Disneyland's tenth anniversary, Pete Clark, Marty Sklar, Phil Bauer, Charles Boyer, and I created, sold, and produced a twenty-four-page color supplement. At the time it was one of the largest newspaper supplements ever done, and it was also the biggest advertising broadside that Disneyland had ever launched. It went into all the Southern California newspapers, plus papers in San Francisco, Portland, Seattle, Las Vegas, Phoenix, Salt Lake City, Tucson, and even Chicago. Our supplement contributed immensely to the overall success, image, and identity of Disneyland's landmark Tencennial Celebration."

5. **Disney Dollars, 1987**
"I created the concept of 'official currency' at Disney theme parks and led its development. Two weeks after we introduced Disney Dollars, I received a call from a leading breakfast cereal company wanting to explore the possibility of including a Disney Dollar in every box of cereal for ninety days. I told them we were interested, so they sent a team of sales and marketing execs to meet with me at Disneyland. At the meeting, they explained the amount of advertising and promotion effort they would put behind the endeavor. They claimed they would sell a minimum of 1,500,000 boxes of cereal per month with a Disney Dollar in each box. I told them I was very impressed and would love to make a deal. They asked what Disney would charge them for each Disney Dollar. I told them $1. They were shocked! They said they were not prepared to pay more than ten cents for each Disney Dollar. I told them again our

price was one U.S. dollar for each Disney Dollar. They said I was being completely unreasonable. Okay, I said, I'll compromise: you come back and tell me how much the U.S. Treasury will discount their dollars for the same promotion, and I will match it—no more discussion, that is the deal. They picked up their briefcases, walked out of the office, and I never heard from them again. Remember, Disney Dollars were not some slick promotional gimmick—they were real 'coins of the Kingdom' at Disneyland, Walt Disney World, and beyond. In 1996, there was over $150 million in unredeemed Disney Dollars in circulation."

11 Disneyland Giveaways from the Past

As he's released from the lamp, the Genie in *Aladdin: A Musical Spectacular* yells, "Free at last! Free at last! Something at Disney is free at last!" While it sometimes seems like everything costs money at Disneyland, many free items have actually been handed out over the decades. Here are eleven from yesteryear.

1. Carefree Corner (1956–1985; 1988–1994): Insurance Companies of North America sponsored Main Street's hospitality center from the 1950s to the 1970s, giving away maps and brochures that are now collectors' items.

2. Enchanted Tiki Room (1963–ongoing): In 1963, free brochures described this new attraction (fans flocked to 2013's fiftieth anniversary celebration when free souvenir replicas of the old brochures became available).

3. Fine Tobacco (1955–1990): Disneyland's headquarters for cigarettes, cigars, and pipes handed out complimentary matchbooks with stylish designs.

4. Market House (1955–ongoing): Before Starbucks arrived in mid-2013, guests who bought coffee here could return with that day's receipt for free refills.

5. Rocket to the Moon (1955–1966): In this Tomorrowland attraction's early years, guests got a free commemorative certificate, signed by the fictitious Captain P. J. Collins.

6. Rafts to Tom Sawyer Island (1956–ongoing): For decades, racks here offered free island maps (*page 212*) drawn by Disney Legend Sam McKim.

7. Sleeping Beauty Castle Walk-Through (1957– 2001; 2008–ongoing): When this attraction opened in 1957, free color books telling the Sleeping Beauty story were available at the exit.

8. Splash Mountain (1989–ongoing): In mid-July 2014, Disneyland gave

special mini-versions of Splash Mountain's attraction poster "Celebrating 25 Zip-A-Dee-Doo-Dah Years!"

9. Tahitian Terrace (1962–1993): Guests attending this tropical Adventureland restaurant could get free leis.

10. Town Square Realty (1955–1960): To spur interest in land sales eighty miles away, this realtor handed out little pouches of authentic California dirt.

11. Upjohn Pharmacy (1955–1970): This Main Street exhibit area dispensed free jars of all-purpose vitamin pills.

Estimated Costs of 40 Disneyland Projects

Listed from most to least expensive, these hard-to-pin-down dollar figures represent the approximate costs when the projects opened (they have not been adjusted for inflation). Debut years are in parentheses. Sources include *Disneyland: The First Thirty Years*, Gordon and Mumford's *Disneyland: The Nickel Tour*, and Gennawey's *The Disneyland Story*.

1. $100–125 million: Indiana Jones Adventure (1995)

2. $75 million: Splash Mountain (1989)

3. $70 million: Finding Nemo Submarine Voyage (2007)

4. $55 million: "New Fantasyland" with Pinocchio's Daring Journey (1983)

5. $30 million: Star Tours (1987)

6. $30 million: Fantasmic! (1992)

7. $30 million: Many Adventures of Winnie the Pooh (2003)

8. $28 million: Pirate's Lair on Tom Sawyer Island (2007)

9. $25 million: Rocket Rods (1998)

10. $23 million: "New Tomorrowland" with PeopleMover (1967)

11. $20 million: Space Mountain (1977)

12. $20 million: Light Magic (1997)

13. $18 million: New Orleans Square (1966)

14. $17 million: Disneyland (1955)

15. $17 million: *Captain EO* (1986)

16. $16 million: Big Thunder Mountain Railroad (1979)

17. $15 million: Innoventions Dream Home (2008)

18. $15 million: Fantasy Faire (2013)

19. $8.4 million: Remodeling Carnation Café/Gibson Girl Ice Cream Parlor/ Candy Palace/Penny Arcade (2012)

20. $8 million: Carousel of Progress/Carousel Theater (1967)

21. $8 million: Pirates of the Caribbean (1967)

22. $8 million: Bear Country (1972)

23. $7 million: The Haunted Mansion (1969)

24. $6 million: America Sings (1974)

25. $4 million: Remodeling Big Thunder Mountain (2013–2014)

26. $3 million: Videopolis (1985)

27. $2.5 million: Submarine Voyage (1959)

28. $2.5 million: Nature's Wonderland (1960)

29. $1.9 million: Monorail extension to Disneyland Hotel (1961)

30. $1.8 million: Western Mine Train Through Nature's Wonderland (1960)

31. $1.5 million: Matterhorn Mountain (1959)

32. $1.4 million: Monorail (1959)

33. $500,000: Rainbow Caverns Mine Train (1956)

34. $400,000: Grand Canyon Diorama (1958)

35. $300,000: Skyway (1956)

36. $300,000: Sailing Ship *Columbia* (1958)

37. $250,000: Swiss Family Treehouse (1962)

38. $250,000: Tom Sawyer Island (1956)

39. $200,000: Astro-Jets (1956)

40. $200,000: Storybook Land Canal Boats (1956)

THE GUEST LIST

Disneyland Is Your Land

80 Celebrity Visitors Between 1955 and the 1980s

Celebrities quickly jumped on the Disneyland bandwagon in its earliest decades. Veteran stars recognized that being photographed at family-friendly Disneyland would burnish their wholesome reputations. The young park benefited from this as well, gaining attention and respect by hosting (and photographing) Hollywood royalty at play. Some celebrities, however, arrived quietly, bringing their kids and not their publicists (Dolores Hope once mentioned that she and her husband Bob had brought their kids and grandkids on separate trips, but there are no widely circulated publicity photos of any of these family visits). Below are eighty famous people who enjoyed Disneyland's fun and photo ops from the 1950s through the 1980s.

Actors/Actresses

1. Julie Andrews
2. Carroll Baker
3. Lucille Ball
4. Richard Burton
5. Carol Channing
6. Macauley Culkin
7. Bob Cummings
8. Irene Dunne
9. Buddy Ebsen
10. Annette Funicello
11. James Garner
12. Charlton Heston
13. Dustin Hoffman
14. Anjelica Huston
15. Betty Hutton
16. Alan Ladd
17. Dorothy Lamour
18. Elsa Lanchester
19. Charles Laughton
20. Sophia Loren
21. Fred MacMurray
22. Jayne Mansfield
23. Hayley Mills
24. John Mills
25. Audie Murphy
26. Ozzie and Harriet Nelson
27. Jack Nicholson
28. Leslie Nielsen
29. Donald O'Connor
30. Fess Parker
31. Mary Pickford
32. Walter Pidgeon
33. Vincent Price
34. Ronald Reagan
35. Buddy Rogers
36. James Stewart
37. Elizabeth Taylor
38. Shirley Temple
39. Jane Wyman
40. Alan Young

Athletes

41. Kareem Abdul-Jabbar
42. Muhammed Ali
43. Joe DiMaggio
44. Orel Hershiser
45. Sir Edmund Hillary
46. Jack Benny
47. Milton Berle
48. Joe E. Brown
49. Jerry Colonna
50. Bob Hope
51. Jerry Lewis
52. Bob Newhart
53. Martha Raye
54. Don Rickles
55. Red Skelton
56. Ed Wynn

Entertainers/Models/Musicians/Writers

57. Desi Arnaz
58. Pat Boone
59. Ray Bradbury
60. Dave Brubeck
61. Johnny Cash
62. Maurice Chevalier
63. Rosemary Clooney
64. Nat "King" Cole

65. Walter Cronkite
66. Sammy Davis, Jr.
67. Dale Evans
68. Eddie Fisher
69. Michael Jackson
70. Elton John
71. Danny Kaye
72. Art Linkletter
73. Ed McMahon
74. Tony Orlando
75. Dolly Parton
76. Roy Rogers
77. Bobby Sherman
78. Dinah Shore
79. Frank Sinatra
80. Twiggy

135 Celebrity Visitors Since January 2011

Grouped by profession, these modern celebrities have had their visits chronicled by E! Online, *Us Magazine,* and other media outlets.

Actors/Actresses

1. Ben Affleck
2. Jessica Alba
3. Kirstie Alley
4. Christian Bale
5. Drew Barrymore
6. Jason Bateman
7. Drake Bell
8. Halle Berry
9. Cate Blanchett
10. Sandra Bullock
11. Gerard Butler
12. Amanda Bynes
13. Nicolas Cage
14. Nick Cannon
15. Steve Carell
16. Miranda Cosgrove
17. Tom Cruise
18. Penelope Cruz
19. Miley Cyrus
20. Matt Damon
21. Geena Davis
22. Johnny Depp
23. Laura Dern
24. Hilary Duff
25. Zac Efron
26. Dakota Fanning
27. Megan Fox
28. Andrew Garfield
29. Jennifer Garner
30. Jennie Garth
31. Sarah Michelle Gellar
32. Ginnifer Goodwin
33. Ryan Gosling
34. Alyson Hannigan
35. Marcia Gay Harden
36. Mariska Hargitay
37. Teri Hatcher
38. Salma Hayek
39. Patricia Heaton
40. Katie Holmes
41. Olivia Holt
42. Vanessa Hudgens
43. Kate Hudson
44. Hugh Jackman
45. Milla Jovovich
46. Shia LaBeouf
47. Jessica Lange
48. Matt LeBlanc
49. Blake Lively
50. Eva Longoria
51. Mario Lopez
52. Kate Mara
53. Marlee Matlin
54. Rachel McAdams
55. Melissa McCarthy
56. Eva Mendes
57. Mandy Moore
58. Amanda Peet
59. Lou Diamond Phillips
60. Freddie Prinze, Jr.
61. Ryan Reynolds
62. Molly Ringwald
63. Emma Roberts
64. Emmy Rossum
65. Geoffrey Rush
66. Kurt Russell

67. Ashlee Simpson
68. Gary Sinise
69. David Spade
70. John Stamos
71. Emma Stone
72. Allison Sweeney
73. Tiffani Thiessen
74. Emma Thompson
75. Dick Van Dyke
76. Vince Vaughn
77. Sofia Vergara
78. Kerry Washington
79. Olivia Wilde
80. Bruce Willis
81. Reese Witherspoon

Athletes
82. David Beckham
83. Tom Brady
84. Kobe Bryant
85. Maria Sharapova

Comedians
86. George Lopez
87. Jason Sudeikis

Entertainers/ Models/Musicians
88. Christina Aguilera
89. Erin Andrews
90. Marc Anthony
91. Backstreet Boys
92. Tyra Banks
93. Victoria Beckham
94. Justin Bieber
95. Michael Buble
96. Gisele Bündchen
97. Mariah Carey
98. Sean Combs
99. Brooklyn Decker
100. Drake
101. Melissa Etheridge
102. Selena Gomez
103. Crystal Hefner
104. Hugh Hefner
105. Kris Jenner
106. Kevin Jonas
107. Kim Kardashian
108. Kourtney Kardashian
109. Larry King
110. Heidi Klum

111. Nick Lachey
112. Avril Lavigne
113. Jennifer Lopez
114. Demi Lovato
115. Holly Madison
116. John Mayer
117. Kate Moss
118. Jack Osbourne
119. Kelly Osbourne
120. Katy Perry
121. Keith Richards
122. Nicole Richie
123. LeAnn Rimes
124. Skrillex
125. Snoop Dogg
126. Britney Spears
127. Tori Spelling
128. Gwen Stefani
129. Courtney Stodden
130. Taylor Swift
131. Channing Tatum
132. Robin Thicke
133. Steven Tyler
134. Usher
135. Pete Wentz

15 Presidential Politicians Who Visited Disneyland

No president has visited Disneyland while he was in office, but many have visited before or after their terms. Disneyland's own souvenir books show photos of many of these presidential politicians. The following alphabetical list shows who visited when, and also includes men who ran for the presidency but lost.

1. **George H. W. Bush:** Forty-first president (1989–1993); visited in 1988 while he was President Reagan's vice president.

2. **Jimmy Carter:** Thirty-ninth president (1977–1981); out of office when he jogged through the park circa 1982.

3. **Dwight Eisenhower:** Thirty-fourth president (1953–1961); out of office when he and his wife Mamie visited in late 1961.

4. **Gerald Ford:** Thirty-eighth president (1974–1977); thought to have visited in 1964 while still a U.S. congressman.

5. **John Glenn:** Former astronaut, U.S. senator (1974–1999), and candidate for both vice president and president; visited alongside Bobby Kennedy in 1968.

6. **Hubert Humphrey:** Senator, LBJ's vice president, and presidential candidate in the 1960s; thought to have visited in 1972.

7. **John F. Kennedy:** Senator Kennedy had not yet been elected the thirty-fifth president when he visited in October 1959.

8. **Robert F. Kennedy:** A few days before he was assassinated, Senator (and presidential candidate) Kennedy visited in June 1968.

9. **Ted Kennedy:** The younger Kennedy brother, a long-time senator, and a presidential candidate in 1972; thought to have visited in 1960.

10. **Richard Nixon:** Before he was America's thirty-seventh president, Nixon made several visits to Disneyland in the 1950s and 1960s; he was Eisenhower's vice president when he helped dedicate the Monorail in 1959.

11. **Barack Obama:** While covering Obama's 2012 visit to Walt Disney World, the *Washington Post* website mentioned that he had visited Disneyland in the past, but no date was given.

12. **Ronald Reagan:** Fortieth president (1981–1989); made at least two visits to Disneyland, most famously when he helped host 1955's nationally televised Opening Day ceremonies. In *Life* magazine's August 1965 issue, he said he wished he could visit Disneyland "more often," but he admitted he couldn't "just wander around" because he was already "a tourist attraction" himself.

13. **Mitt Romney:** Two weeks after losing the 2012 presidential election, Romney and his family spent a much-photographed day at Disneyland.

14. **Harry Truman:** Thirty-third president (1945–1953); out of office when he and his wife Bess visited in 1957.

15. **George Wallace:** Alabama's former governor was a third-party presidential candidate when he and his family visited in August 1968.

7 Historic Moments for Disneyland's Guests

1. First paying guest: Dave MacPherson, a twenty-two-year-old college student who had lined up at 2 AM on July 18, 1955, the first day Disneyland opened to the public.

2. The first children: Five-year-old Kristine Vess and her cousin, seven-year-old Michael Schwartner, were the first children to enter the park on July 18, 1955 (Walt Disney greeted them personally).

3. Youngest guests: At least three guests have been zero years old, because they were born in Disneyland (the first was in 1979, near the Plaza Inn).

4. Oldest guest: Possibly a 108-year-old woman from New Mexico who visited with her great-granddaughter (both were photographed by the *Long Beach Press-Telegram* on December 31, 1965).

5. Most visits in one year: To make being unemployed more tolerable, two adults in their forties visited Disneyland every day of 2012 (they both extended their streaks for another year; one of them celebrated his one-thousandth consecutive visit in September 2014).

6. Most famous guest turned away from the park: Soviet Premier Nikita Khrushchev requested that he be taken to Disneyland during his 1959 visit to America, but government officials (not park officials) denied the request, saying they couldn't assure security. According to Peter Carlson in *K Blows Top*, the incident drew international attention when an irate Khrushchev threw a tantrum in front of journalists and celebrities and invented bizarre reasons ("cholera," "rocket-launching pads") for the denial. "I say, 'I would very much like to see Disneyland.' They say, 'We cannot guarantee your security.' Then what must I do, commit suicide?"

7. Most infamous episode of guests' behavior leading to Disneyland's closure: On August 6, 1970, the controversial Youth International Party staged a Disneyland "convention." Over 300 anti-establishment protesters intended to pull off numerous pranks and demonstrations on the twenty-fifth anniversary of the atomic bombing of Hiroshima, but basically what they did was vandalize, march, shout obscenities, and engage in shoving matches with security personnel. With "Yippie Day" ruining the park experience for thousands of other guests, Disneyland closed about six hours early and offered free return admission. The next day's newspapers reported up to twenty-three arrests and briefly gave the Yippies the media attention they craved.

Annie Fox Explains 5 Ways to Teach Kids to Be Good People at Disneyland

If you want to learn how to have fun with your kids at Disneyland while being a great parent, you turn to a parenting expert like Annie Fox, M.Ed. (*right*). An award-winning author, blogger, and host of the weekly podcast *Family Confidential*, Annie has been answering email from kids and parents around the world since 1997. Her books include *Teaching Kids to Be Good People* and *The Girls' Friendship Q&A Book*. Learn more at www.anniefox.com.

"At the Magic Kingdom with your family? Lucky you! You've got endless opportunities to enjoy the park and create wonderful memories. You'll also have tons of opportunities to reinforce your family values."

1. Be patient.

"Some kids (and adults) have trouble waiting. But hey, waiting is part of life. If you whine while waiting for food or an attraction, your kids will do the same. To teach patience, *model* patience yourself. And turn waiting into a game. ('How long can you balance on one foot? Time starts now!' 'I spy with my little eye, a girl wearing orange shoes.' 'Find three things that we never see at home.') Best places for families to practice patience: Mickey's House—once inside, there's a long lead-up to the eagerly awaited meeting with the mouse. Fortunately, there's lots to look at and investigate together while waiting. Nearby, try Goofy's Playhouse, since this house and its adjacent garden offer kids unstructured play areas (not rigidly controlled rides), creating lots of opportunities for making up simple games, taking turns, sharing, and respecting boundaries. Or go find a good spot to sit and wait for a daily parade to go by—your family can relax, people-watch, study the beautiful surroundings, and make up quiet activities."

2. Play as a team.

"It takes cooperation to navigate Disneyland while keeping everyone (and all of your stuff) together. Before you start your park visit, gather the troops and give the team a pep talk: 'We're here to have fun and to take good care of each other.' Assign each family member something or someone to be responsible for. Make sure you praise all teamwork. Remember, we're not looking for perfection, just progress. Best places for families to play as a team: Pirate's Lair on Tom Sawyer Island (see analysis of this fabled island's unique appeal in the list on page 125); Davy Crockett's Explorer Canoes (you all gotta row, or canoes don't go!)."

3. **Observe and learn from other families.**

"Being in the park is an amazing opportunity to experience how parents and children from around the world interact. Remind your children that other families will be observing *your* family, too. Tell your kids that they represent your family and your country. You want them to act in a way that makes you proud of them and makes them proud of themselves. Best place to observe other cultures: It's a Small World, which doesn't have signs identifying its countries—by looking at this attraction's clothes and traditions, can your kids identify the places they're seeing?" (Small World's areas are listed on page 121.)

4. **Sincerely apologize.**

"Siblings can push each other's buttons like nobody's business. Especially when they're spending more time together than usual. Teach your children that when they realize they've hurt someone's feelings, they need to apologize *sincerely*. (*Sorreee!* No bogus apologies allowed.) Then they need to make amends for what they've done. The other has to accept the apology and let go of the hurt. Best places to share a peace offering: Miss Chris' Cabin at Big Thunder Ranch, where kids can quietly draw and color together. At Frontierland's Leather Shop in Pioneer Mercantile, kids can buy (and customize) inexpensive leather bracelets for each other. And inside Main Street's Gibson Girls Ice Cream Parlor, one big scrumptious dessert, shared *fairly* by two kids, may do wonders to smooth away hurt feelings."

5. **Take a break.**

"One cranky child (or adult) can affect the whole family. When you notice someone's bad mood, hit the brakes. Take some slow deep breaths and teach your kids to do the same. (It will lower your heart rate, relax your body, and clear your brain.) Feeling calmer? Good! Now smile and say, 'I think we could *all* use a break.' (Do *not* name names. It just adds more stress.) Best places for families to take a chill break: Get away from the noise and crowds at any of the serene spots pinpointed in the list on page 91."

Adult Action:
8 Ways Disneyland Has Tried to Attract Adults

There's a reason that adults have usually outnumbered children in Disneyland by three- or four-to-one: the park has courted them, as shown in the following alphabetical list.

1. Date Nite: This pleasant summer tradition began in June 1957 as a way to draw in young couples. That first month, Disneyland stayed open on Fridays and Saturdays until midnight; in July and August, the hours ex-

tended until 1:00 AM; a year later, Date Nite became a nightly, not just a weekend, summertime event. The Hub's outdoor Plaza Gardens provided the dance location, and the Date Niters (the Elliot Bros. Orchestra) provided the dance music. Though the Date Nite concept was abandoned after a few years, evening entertainment would continue with such shows as the Cavalcade of Bands in the 1960s, Big Bands at Disneyland in the 1980s, and the Jump, Jive, Boogie Swing Party in the 2000s.

2. Disneyland After Dark: In the early 1960s, Disneyland inaugurated special programs that ran until midnight. "The greatest show in town," put on every summer evening, included bands, dancing, "special entertainment," and more (all showcased on a 1962 episode of *Walt Disney's Wonderful World of Color*, with Louis Armstrong announcing, "We're gonna rock this ol' *Mark Twain* right on down to New Orleans!").

3. Dixieland at Disneyland: Adults loved this exuberant concert series, held each fall from 1960 to 1970. Special tickets included admission, unlimited attractions, and live performances by world-renowned jazz musicians such as Louis Armstrong and Al Hirt, plus Disneyland's own Firehouse Five Plus Two and the Strawhatters. For the first five years, the shows were held evenings at the Rivers of America in Frontierland and featured fireworks and the *Mark Twain* paddlewheeling past the cheering audience while the musicians and a 200-person choir performed "When the Saints Go Marchin' In." For the last half of the 1960s, the show moved to Main Street, where bands performed on wagons and paraded through Disneyland.

4. Fireworks: Episodes of 1954's *Disneyland* TV series began with an animation of fireworks, but Disneyland didn't actually have pyrotechnics until mid-1957. New state-of-the-art "Fantasy in the Sky" fireworks were the brainstorm of entertainment director Tommy Walker, who hoped adults would stay for dinner.

5. Intimate Apparel: The "corset shop" for ladies' undergarments (1955–1956) represents just one of the sophisticated stores intended for adults (two others, both extinct, would be Main Street's Fine Tobacco and New Orleans Square's kitchen-oriented Le Forgeron).

6. Landscaping: Kids might not notice or appreciate the beautiful flowerbeds and trees in the park, but their parents probably do. Disneyland's landscaping is high-maintenance, expensive, and all-year, all-weather spectacular.

7. New Orleans Square: Focusing on architecture and ambience, this sophisticated area is appreciated more by adults than their fast-moving kids. French-themed shops and cafés are adorned with authentic design details such as hanging plants, French doors, cozy verandas, and lacy

wrought-iron railings. Appropriately, New Orleans Square doesn't include huge stores or towering mountains, and its only two attractions,
Pirates of the Caribbean and the Haunted Mansion, are sophisticated
and slow, not noisy and whirling.

8. Red Wagon Inn/Plaza Inn: One of the ways Walt Disney separated his sophisticated Disneyland from juvenile amusement parks was by offering
dining options better than the typical hot dogs, popcorn, and sodas. In
the 1950s, the Hub's Red Wagon Inn (later the Plaza Inn) was the park's
glitziest restaurant, presenting full-service, full-course adult meals in
rooms lit by crystal chandeliers. In 1967, the Blue Bayou brought its
unique elegance to New Orleans Square, followed four years later by
Frontierland's stately River Belle Terrace.

Teen Scene: 10 Ways Disneyland Has Tried to Attract Teenagers

So it wouldn't be classified as a family park only for children, Disneyland has
tailored some of its events and attractions for teenagers. This effort was especially noticeable in the 1970s, when Magic Mountain (only an hour away)
drew big crowds with thrilling new roller coasters at a time when Disneyland had only one true "thrill ride," the venerable Matterhorn Bobsleds that
dated back to 1959. The following chronological list shows how Disneyland
has tried to keep up with the teen scene over the years.

1. Grad Nite: What started as a single spring night in 1961 was soon drawing tens of thousands of well-dressed teens from all over the country to
all-night parties held several times each year.

2. Tomorrowland Stage: Filling a big corner of Tomorrowland, 1967's Tomorrowland Stage (later renamed the Space Stage) was the park's venue
for teen-themed concerts featuring acts like Herman's Hermits, Linda
Ronstadt, and Disneyland's own Kids of the Kingdom.

3. Tomorrowland Terrace: Opened in July 1967 and still in place, this
small futuristic stage hosted nighttime dance concerts featuring 1960s
hit-makers like Paul Revere and the Raiders. Disneyland's souvenir
books of the early 1970s showcased Tomorrowland Terrace's youth appeal with energetic photos.

4. Adventure Thru Inner Space: Teens quickly discovered this ground-
breaking Tomorrowland attraction that opened in August 1967—revolutionary semi-enclosed Omnimover pods and darkness made this one of
Disneyland's best make-out locations. Amorous activity and vandalism
became so problematic that closed-circuit cameras were installed and
the pods were speeded up to get everyone through faster.

5. Space Mountain: To contend with the dynamic new roller coasters luring teens to other Southern California parks, Disneyland opened this new thrill ride in 1977. Space Mountain was instantly popular because it did what other coasters didn't—it turned off the lights.

6. Starcade: Opening alongside Space Mountain in 1977, this complex once spread over two stories and housed multitudes of teen-ready games (a smaller version now occupies the first floor).

7. Big Thunder Mountain Railroad: Two years after Space Mountain's 1977 debut, Disneyland replaced the pokey Mine Train with Big Thunder, a rollicking mountain roller coaster well-themed for Frontierland.

8. Videopolis: With the indoor Magic Eye Theater about to replace the outdoor Space Stage, Disneyland needed a venue for large open-air concerts. *Voilà* Videopolis, a dazzling concert and dance area that opened in 1985 where the Fantasyland Theatre is now.

9. *Captain EO*: Debuting in Tomorrowland's Magic Eye Theater in 1986 and running into the twenty-first century, this George Lucas/Francis Ford Coppola 3D sci-fi spectacular starred Michael Jackson, the world's biggest pop star at the time.

10. Splash Mountain: With Bear Country becoming Bore Country for many guests, in 1989 Disneyland opened its dramatic Splash Mountain, a teen magnet touted as "the world's steepest, highest, scariest, wildest adventure."

10 Disneyland "Extras" Guests Can Request

Disneyland's special experiences can be even more special if you get a little extra *something*. Politely make these ten requests of a cast member; if the timing is right, wishes could come true.

1. City Hall: Tell the cast members here that you're celebrating an anniversary, graduation, or some other special event, and they'll give you a colorful button to wear—cast members throughout the park will then congratulate you all day long.

2. Disneyland Railroad: It's sometimes possible to sit on the "tender seat" (a small bench right behind the engineer). This opportunity is only available at Town Square's train station.

3. The Haunted Mansion: To visit the hidden pet cemetery, ask cast members to escort you to the small path to the right of the main doorway.

4. Jungle Cruise: Ask a dockside cast member for a Jungle Cruise map (you may be asked to "make the sound of any jungle animal" before you get it).

5. Main Street: Ask to pet the horses pulling the big streetcars.

6. *Mark Twain* Riverboat: It's possible to visit this magnificent boat's wheelhouse. Once there, you might get to turn the wheel, toot the whistle, and ring the bell.

7. *Mark Twain* Riverboat: Ask any cast member here for a pilot's certificate, a small document signed by Commodore Walt Disney.

8. Monorail: Ask to ride in front for a wide panoramic view of approaching scenery (as opposed to the standard view of scenery passing by the side windows).

9. Pin trading: Cast members can make trades, your pin for one of theirs, so if you see a pin you like, ask to swap.

10. Splash Mountain: On most attractions involving boats (Pirates of the Caribbean, It's a Small World, etc.) you can ask to sit up front. Do this on Pirates and Small World for clearer views and more leg room; do it on Splash Mountain for more splash.

10 Free Celebratory Buttons Guests Can Get at City Hall

As noted in the previous list, City Hall distributes free celebratory buttons. These ten are usually available; wear one to get special greetings from cast members throughout the park.

1. Family Reunion
2. 1st Visit!
3. . . . Happily Ever After!
4. Happy Anniversary!
5. Happy Birthday

6. Honorary Citizen of Disneyland
7. I'm Celebrating!
8. Just Engaged!
9. Just Graduated!
10. Just Married!

15 Affectionate Quotes About Disneyland's Guests

1. "To all who come to this happy place: welcome. Disneyland is your land." (Walt Disney; Sklar, *Walt Disney's Disneyland*)

2. "We hope that you'll find here a place of knowledge and happiness." (Walt Disney; *Disneyland* TV series)

3. "We love to entertain kings and queens, but at Disneyland everyone is a VIP." (Walt Disney; Disneyland's 1968 pictorial souvenir book)

4. "I stand here in the park and talk to people. It's a most gratifying thing. All I've got from the public is thank-yous." (Walt Disney; Bright, *Disneyland: Inside Story*)

5. "They aren't customers, we call them paying guests." (Walt Disney; *Look* magazine)

6. "When guests come here they're coming because of an integrity we've established over the years. They drive hundreds of miles. I feel a responsibility to the public." (Walt Disney; France, *Window on Main Street*)

7. "You're dead if you aim only for the kids. Adults are only kids grown up, anyway." (Walt Disney; Smith, *Walt Disney Famous Quotes*)

8. "It's four adults to one child. That is, we're counting the teenagers as adults.... In the winter time, you can go out there during the week and you won't see any children. You'll see all the oldsters out there riding all these rides and having fun and everything." (Walt Disney; Jackson, *Walt Disney Conversations*)

9. "[At Grad Nite] there are over 50,000 young kids—the boys in coat-and-tie, the girls all in party dresses, the park is theirs. Beautiful! And of them all, there are only fifty or a hundred characters that we have to take care of." (Walt Disney; Jackson, *Walt Disney Conversations*)

10. "Look at them! . . . Did you ever see so many happy people? So many people just enjoying themselves?" (Walt Disney; Thomas, *Walt Disney: An American Original*)

11. "When Walt built Disneyland, he was striving to make people feel better about themselves. I think he had discovered what people were looking for—the feeling of being alive and in love with life." (John Hench, artist/Disney Legend; Green and Green, *Remembering Walt*)

12. "[Disneyland] liberates men to their better selves.... [to be] truly happy. ... [It] causes you to care all over again. You feel it is that first day in the spring of that special year when you discovered you were really alive." (Ray Bradbury; *Holiday* magazine)

13. "Walt kept emphasizing to us that he wanted the public to participate. He wanted them onstage." (Bill Evans, landscape architect/Disney Legend; Green and Green, *Remembering Walt*)

14. "What is the secret of Disneyland's success? . . . To pinpoint a single element, it would be imagination—not just imagination on the part of its impresarios, but their evocation of the imagination of cash customers. . . . The visitor indulges eagerly in that most ancient of games: let's pretend." (*New York Times*)

15. "What Disney seemed to know was that while there is very little grown-up in every child, there is a lot of child in every grown-up. To a child, this weary world is brand-new, gift-wrapped. Disney tried to keep it that way for adults." (CBS News commentator Eric Sevareid, eulogizing Walt Disney)

MEDIAPEDIA
Disneyland in Popular Culture

16 Fictionalized Disneylands in Popular Culture

Listed alphabetically are movies, TV shows, comic strips, and more that have all included a Disneyland-like park (but without the Disneyland name) to tell their stories.

1. *Beany and Cecil*: "Beanyland" is a 1959 *Beany and Cecil* cartoon that features the "Happiest Place Off Earth," a lunar theme park with "Day After Tomorrow Land," a central castle called "Slipping Beauty Castle," a mountain called the "Madhatter Horn," and Disneyland's same rounded-triangle shape.

2. *Duke Nukem 3D*: This 1996 shoot-'em-up video game has a level called Babe Land with a big dancing mouse and a Babes of the Caribbean ride.

3. *FoxTrot*: In Bill Amend's comic strip, the family goes to Fun-Fun Universe for summer vacation; near Souvenirland, they encounter the singing dolls of It's a Fun-Fun World.

4. "The Happiest Place": Gordon McAlpine's short story (published in the 2010 crime anthology *Orange County Noir*) is set at an unidentified Anaheim theme park that has variations on Disneyland's place names.

5. *L.A. Confidential*: Dream-a-Dreamland, a thinly disguised Disneyland, is a key setting in James Ellroy's 1990 novel (neither the park nor a Walt Disney-type villain appears in the movie).

6. *Li'l Abner*: Al Capp parodied Disneyland as Hal Yappland in a 1955 comic strip.

7. *Mad* magazine: "Dizzyland" is a 1956 parody that reduces Disneyland's various lands (Frontrearland, Fantasticland, etc.) to a single theme (Moneyland).

8. *National Lampoon's Vacation*: At the end of this 1983 film, Chevy Chase and his family finally reach Southern California's Walley World, run by Roy Walley. Scenes of "America's Favorite Family Fun Park" were shot at Magic Mountain, sixty miles north of Anaheim.

9. *The Rabbit Factory*: In Marshall Karp's 2006 comic thriller, two L.A. detectives investigate the murder of a costumed character at Familyland, a theme park run by a fictional animation house (Lamaar Studios) that has grown into a Disney-esque entertainment giant.

10. *The Simpsons*: The 1991 episode "Old Money" briefly shows Grampa in a theme park called Diz-Nee-Land, which declares it's "not affiliated with Disneyland, Disney World, or anything else from the Walt Disney Company."

11. *The Simpsons*: In 1993's "Selma's Choice" episode, Bart, Lisa, and Selma

spend time together in Duff Gardens, a theme park with Disneyland-like rides.

12. *The Simpsons*: In a classic 1994 episode called "Itchy and Scratchy Land," Homer takes the family to a theme park closely modeled on Disneyland but billed as "the violentest place on Earth."

13. *The Simpsons*: The first episode of 2015 begins in Dizzneeland, "The Happiest Hell on Earth," with Mr. Bug's Slow Crawl, Jabba the Tiki Hut, and a politically correct Pirates of the Caribbean among the rides.

14. *South Park*: The 2001 "Cartmanland" episode presents a theme park with many Disneyland elements.

15. *Still Foolin' 'Em*: In his 2013 memoirs, Billy Crystal invents Lenin Land, a "Disneyland-like park" in Russia that has "a tiny roller coaster" going "right through dead Lenin's head."

16. *Westworld*: Michael Crichton's 1973 movie is set in an adult theme park with obvious parallels to Disneyland (especially Frontierland).

23 Disney-Produced TV Programs Showcasing Disneyland

1. July 17, 1955: "Dateline: Disneyland"—the famous live presentation of Opening Day festivities with hosts Bob Cummings, Art Linkletter, and Ronald Reagan.

2. June 15, 1959: "Disneyland '59," aka "Kodak Presents Disneyland '59"— a live salute to new attractions.

3. April 10, 1974: "Sandy in Disneyland"—starred Sandy Duncan.

4. July 11, 1974: "Herbie Day at Disneyland"—Bob Crane, Helen Hayes, and Volkswagens promoted the film *Herbie Rides Again.*

5. April 3, 1976: "Monsanto Presents Walt Disney's America on Parade"— with Red Skelton.

6. December 6, 1976: "Christmas in Disneyland with Art Carney"— featured Sandy Duncan and Glen Campbell.

7. March 6, 1980: "Kraft Salutes Disneyland's Twenty-Fifth Anniversary"— with Danny Kaye.

8. June 28, 1984: "Big Bands at Disneyland"—the first of twelve Disney Channel music shows.

9. February 18, 1985: "Disneyland's 30th Anniversary Celebration"— starred Drew Barrymore and John Forsythe.

10. May 23, 1986: "Disneyland's Summer Vacation Party"—featured Jay Leno and Jerry Seinfeld.

11. September 20, 1986: "Disney's *Captain EO* Grand Opening"—with Patrick Duffy, Justine Bateman, and the Moody Blues.

12. February 12, 1988: "Disney's Magic in the Magic Kingdom"—with George Burns.

13. November 13, 1988: "Mickey's 60th Birthday"—with John Ritter and Carl Reiner.

14. December 11, 1988: "Disneyland's All-Star Comedy Circus"—featured circus stars.

15. May 20, 1989: "Disneyland Blast to the Past"—showcased the park's Blast to the Past Celebration.

16. February 4, 1990: "Disneyland's 35th Anniversary Celebration"—starred Tony Danza and the Muppets.

17. September 14, 1991: "Disney Afternoon Live! at Disneyland"—spotlighted Splash Mountain.

18. July 10, 1993: "Disneyland Presents: Tales of Toontown"—showed off the new Mickey's Toontown.

19. March 4, 1995: "40 Years of Adventure"—Wil Shriner and the new Indiana Jones Adventure attraction.

20. May 23, 1997: "Light Magic: A Spectacular Journey"—showed the short-lived street show.

21. December 12, 1998: "Holiday Greetings from Disneyland: The Merriest Place On Earth"—with Wil Shriner.

22. February 1, 2000: "Disneyland 2000: 45 Years of Magic"—with Ryan Seacrest.

23. October 14, 2003: "Disneyland Resort: Behind the Scenes"—aired on the Travel Channel.

15 Episodes of the *Disneyland* TV Show Featuring the Park Itself

Walt Disney launched his first regular prime-time show, *Disneyland*, in 1954's fall season on Wednesday nights. Like the park, this series had four main sections called Adventureland, Fantasyland, Frontierland, and Tomorrowland (he even advised viewers in the first episode that "Disneyland the place and Disneyland the TV show are all part of the same"). Throughout its long history and its many name changes, *Disneyland* frequently presented episodes that included lengthy segments devoted solely to the park.

1. October 27, 1954: "The Disneyland Story," aka "What Is Disneyland?"—the premiere episode introducing the park.

2. February 9, 1955: "A Progress Report/Nature's Half Acre"—an aerial tour seven months into park construction.

3. July 13, 1955: "A Pre-Opening Report from Disneyland," aka "A Further Report on Disneyland"—broadcast four days before Opening Day.

4. February 29, 1956: "A Trip Through Adventureland/Water Birds"—spotlighted the Jungle Cruise.

5. April 3, 1957: "Disneyland the Park/Pecos Bill"—an aerial tour of the park.

6. April 9, 1958: "An Adventure in the Magic Kingdom"—provided a guided tour by an animated Tinker Bell.

7. May 28, 1961: "Disneyland '61/Olympic Elk"—featured recent park additions.

8. April 15, 1962: "Disneyland After Dark"—showcased nighttime music and fireworks.

9. September 23, 1962: *Golden Horseshoe Revue*—celebrated the popular show's ten-thousandth performance.

10. December 23, 1962: "Holiday Time at Disneyland"—Walt Disney led a tour for the holidays.

11. May 17, 1964: "Disneyland Goes to the World's Fair"—previewed the 1964–1965 New York World's Fair.

12. January 3, 1965: "Disneyland's Tenth Anniversary"—Miss Disneyland (Julie Reihm) helped preview Pirates of the Caribbean and the Haunted Mansion.

13. December 18, 1966: "Disneyland Around the Seasons"—spotlighted New Orleans Square and It's a Small World.

14. January 21, 1968: "Disneyland—From the Pirates of the Caribbean to the World of Tomorrow"—previewed Tomorrowland changes.

15. March 22, 1970: "Disneyland Showtime"—the Osmond Brothers and Kurt Russell celebrated the new Haunted Mansion.

16 More Disneyland Appearances and Mentions on TV Shows

The following alphabetical list of TV shows does not include episodes of the long-running Disney TV series originally hosted by Walt Disney, which are presented in the previous list.

1. *The Bell Telephone Hour*: One 1961 episode of this music series, "The Sounds of America," spotlights Disneyland's Frontierland and Main Street.

2. *Blossom*: The February 1993 episode called "The Best Laid Plans of Mice and Men" takes place at Disneyland, where Blossom, riding the Skyway, sees her boyfriend with another girl.

3. *The Big Bang Theory*: Penny takes Sheldon to Disneyland in a 2010 episode called "The Spaghetti Catalyst." "The Contractual Obligation Implementation" episode from March 2013 includes a joke about racy Splash Mountain photos and sends Penny, Amy, and Bernadette to Disneyland for princess makeovers. In May 2013's "The Bon Voyage Reaction," Leonard admits he once got seasick on It's a Small World.

4. *Conan*: Promoting *Saving Mr. Banks* in December 2013, Tom Hanks talked about guests using "O tickets" to get on Disneyland's extinct Skyway in hopes of joining the "Mile-High Club."

5. *Dads*: This 2013 Fox sitcom joked about a dad who hoped to get free lunches with Goofy by shaving his son's head before a Disneyland trip.

6. *George Lopez*: In the April 2004 episode "George Goes to Disneyland," the comedian, deprived of going to Disneyland as a kid, finally attends the park as a grown-up. The show features a contest with viewers winning prizes for spotting Hidden Mickeys.

7. *Hard Time on Planet Earth*: This short-lived 1989 sci-fi comedy takes its hero to Disneyland in the "Losing Control" episode. When the robot sidekick short-circuits, a young guest takes it home.

8. *Law & Order: Special Victims Unit*: In 2009's "Ballerina" episode, a CSI tech proudly (but prematurely) announces a case's solution and then asks, "Are we all going to Disneyland?"

9. *Mad Men*: In 2009's "Wee Small Hours" episode, Conrad Hilton makes Don Draper laugh when he says, "Khruschev—you know what made him fall apart? He couldn't get into Disneyland!" A year later, "Tomorrowland," the season-four finale, sends Don, his kids, and his young secretary on a California trip that included a visit to Disneyland (not shown, but discussed and later referenced in June 2013). Season seven's opener in April 2014 includes an airline passenger mentioning how she scattered her husband's ashes on Disneyland's Tom Sawyer Island ("they were very vigilant, it took some doing").

10. *Meet Me at Disneyland*: On Saturday nights in the summer of 1962, KTTV, an independent L.A. TV station, aired this one-hour show shot live in Disneyland and hosted by actor Johnny Jacobs.

11. *The Middle*: The park gets a mention in the May 2014 season finale when the characters, holding Disneyland tickets, show up at Walt Disney World by mistake.

12. *Modern Family*: Most of "Disneyland," a May 2012 episode featuring the

choice of proper footwear for the park as a key plot element, was filmed at Disneyland.

13. *The Odd Couple*: "The Odd Holiday," a 1973 episode of this Emmy-winning sitcom, features Oscar complaining about his ex-wife: "For eight years, we never made it through one vacation. . . . We fought in front of Goofy at Disneyland!"

14. *Roseanne*: A 1993 episode called "The Jackie Thomas Show" sends the family to Hollywood; Roseanne jokes en route about "Darlene versus 'The Happiest Place on Earth.'"

15. *The Simpsons*: Several mentions of the actual Disneyland have been made on the show, such as 1992's "Lisa the Beauty Queen" episode, in which a banner for the Springfield Elementary School Carnival reads "The Happiest Place on Earth" (a Disney lawyer arrives and declares that Disneyland owns the phrase). In 1996's "You Only Move Twice" episode, a particular redwood tree has "enough sawdust to cover an entire day's worth of vomit at Disneyland." In 2004's "The Wandering Juvie" episode, a character named Gina Vendetti is in a juvenile correctional facility for having pushed Snow White from a Disneyland parapet.

16. *The Tonight Show*: Jay Leno interrupted a 1995 show for a ninety-second skit in which he drives to Disneyland and cuts the Splash Mountain line.

29 Additional Disneyland Appearances and Mentions on the Stage and Screen

Listed below are twenty-nine theatrically released movies, stage productions, videos, and more that have mentioned Disneyland or used it as a setting.

1. *The Boys*: Given a limited released in theaters, this 2009 documentary from Walt Disney Productions celebrates the Sherman Brothers' lives and music and includes three minutes of park footage.

2. *The Burn*: A 2012 episode of Jeff Ross's comedy show includes a short visit with John Stamos, who discusses the "D" letter he bought when Disneyland's old marquee was dismantled.

3. The Carpenters: The pop duo's video for their peppy version of "Please Mr. Postman" was filmed at Disneyland.

4. *Casino*: At the end of Martin Scorsese's 1995 film, Robert De Niro's character derides modern Las Vegas, saying, "The town will never be the same. . . . Today it looks like Disneyland [where] kids play cardboard pirates" (visuals include tourists, an outdoor pirate ship, and a castle-themed hotel).

5. *A Day at Disneyland*: Released on video in 1982, this forty-minute documentary features many Disney characters frolicking through Disneyland. A 1993 re-release added Mickey's Toontown and Fantasmic!

6. *Disneyland Dream*: Robbins Barstow, a Connecticut man whose family won a free Disneyland trip, shot this thirty-minute home movie in 1956. His amateur footage was admitted by the National Film Registry of the Library of Congress in 2008.

7. *Disneyland Fun: It's a Small World:* Released by the Walt Disney Company in 1990, this twenty-nine-minute children's entertainment video is part of the Disney Sing Along Songs series, so it features Disney characters playing and singing in Disneyland as lyrics show on the screen.

8. *Disneyland on Parade, It's a Small World*, and *Meet Me on Main Street*: Roy London's three plays about relationships, all with Disneyland settings, were performed in Los Angeles in 1983.

9. *Disney Parks: Disneyland Resort Behind the Scenes*: Lightship Entertainment's well-made 2010 documentary was shown on TV and is available as a DVD.

10. *Disneyland, U.S.A.*: This Disney featurette, released in theaters in 1956, has forty-two minutes of Disneyland footage.

11. *Escape from Tomorrow*: Released into theaters in 2013, this independent black-and-white horror film is set in Walt Disney World but includes Disneyland footage shot "guerrilla-style" without permission.

12. *Exit Through the Gift Shop*: Banksy's 2010 Oscar-nominated documentary includes six minutes of a Disneyland prank—he displays an inflatable doll for ninety minutes at Big Thunder Mountain, with interesting results.

13. *40 Pounds of Trouble*: Universal Pictures' 1962 feature film has about nineteen minutes of Disneyland scenes, most of them showing Tony Curtis in a comedic chase that ends in the parking lot.

14. *Gala Day at Disneyland*: Released into theaters in 1960, this Walt Disney Productions featurette has twenty-seven minutes of footage showing off Disneyland's newest attractions.

15. *Jurassic Park*: In Steven Spielberg's 1993 film, the beleaguered John Hammond, director of Jurassic Park, rationalizes his park's problems by saying, "When they opened Disneyland in 1956, nothing worked" (surprisingly, during the filming nobody corrected this error—Disneyland opened in 1955). Hammond's line draws a quick retort from mathematician Ian Malcolm, who explains that when Pirates of the Caribbean breaks down "the pirates don't eat the tourists."

16. Kinect Disneyland Adventures: Recreating Disneyland for players to explore, Microsoft Studios' 2011 family-friendly video game for the Xbox 360 presents mini-games to play and Disney characters to meet.

17. Kodak commercial: Ed Sullivan wears a business suit as he pretends to ride the Jungle Cruise while touting the 1958 Brownie camera and Disneyland—"Disneyland is really a world all its own, a wonderful place to have fun."

18. *The Magic of Disneyland*: Released in October 1969, this 16mm color documentary gives a general overview of Disneyland and shows climbers on the Matterhorn, various entertainers, and a live Tinker Bell in flight.

19. *The Magic of Disneyland at Christmas*: Available at Disneyland in 1992, Disney's VHS cassette presents holiday activities.

20. *Missing in the Mansion:* A 2012 Internet hit, this short video of "found footage" explores fictional disappearances at the Haunted Mansion.

21. Pepsi-Cola commercial: The 1965 Pepsi Generation celebrates the "come alive" theme in this fast-paced, attraction-filled commercial.

22. *The Perfect American*: Peter Stephan Jungk's "fictional biography" includes a memorable scene where Walt Disney visits Disneyland after-hours and confronts his Audio-Animatronic Mr. Lincoln. Later, dying in the hospital, a boy says his "happiest moment" was a day at Disneyland. This controversial book is the basis for the 2013 opera by Philip Glass.

23. *A Public Reading of an Unproduced Screenplay About the Death of Walt Disney*: Lucas Hnath's new play was introduced by Manhattan's SoHo Rep contemporary theater company in spring 2013. It presents a dying Disney (Larry Pine) and his family members, who together read a screenplay Disney supposedly has written that includes several references to Disneyland.

24. *Saving Mr. Banks*: In this 2013 feature by Walt Disney Studios, Tom Hanks plays Walt Disney, and modern Disneyland plays 1960s Disneyland.

25. T-shirt: A tee produced by L.A. Imprints, called "Layman's Glossary of Computer Terms," includes Disneyland as the definition for "Mousepad."

26. *That Thing You Do!*: Tom Hanks's Oscar-nominated feature film, distributed by 20th Century Fox in 1996, includes fifteen seconds of Disneyland scenes in which a character runs off for a whirlwind day at the park.

27. *The View*: This talk show did live broadcasts from Disneyland November 18–22, 2013.

28. *Walt Disney Treasures*: Walt Disney Video's acclaimed series of DVDs includes two that are packed with historical footage and fascinating

documentaries—*Disneyland U.S.A.* (2001) and *Disneyland Secrets, Stories & Magic* (2007). The *Tomorrow Land* DVD (2004) also includes some Disneyland discussion and footage.

29. *Working for the Mouse*: Trevor Allen's entertaining one-man stage show about working at Disneyland won awards in 1996 and returned for a long run in San Francisco in 2011.

A Half-Dozen DVDs with Disneyland Footage in Their Special Features

The following DVDs (all feature-length movies from Walt Disney Pictures) include special features set in Disneyland. Titles are listed alphabetically and release dates are for the DVDs, not the theatrical films.

1. *The Haunted Mansion* (2004): Snippets of Disneyland's Haunted Mansion appear in a special feature about the making of the Eddie Murphy movie; the "enhanced computer features" that are no longer accessible included a history of the attraction.

2. *The Love Bug* (2003): As fascinating for the groovy 1960s fashions as it is for the colorful cars and festive parade, the twelve minutes of historical scenes focus on Disneyland's first Love Bug Day, held on March 23, 1969, to celebrate *The Love Bug*.

3. *Oz the Great and Powerful* (2013): The aborted Oz project planned for Fantasyland is discussed along with thirty seconds of footage in a documentary called "Walt Disney and the Road to Oz."

4. *Pirates of the Caribbean: The Curse of the Black Pearl* (2003): The documentary "An Epic At Sea" includes two minutes and fifteen seconds of the movie's world premiere, held at Disneyland on June 28, 2003. Additionally, "Disneyland from the Pirates of the Caribbean to the World of Tomorrow," a January 21, 1968 episode from *Walt Disney's Wonderful World of Color*, has eighteen minutes of behind-the-scenes footage of Disneyland's attraction and its grand opening. The "enhanced computer features" that are no longer accessible included an image gallery.

5. *Sleeping Beauty* (2008): Three documentaries present about thirty minutes of behind-the-scenes looks at Disneyland's Sleeping Beauty Castle Walk-Through attraction, including a detailed virtual tour of the original 1957 attraction and analyses of the terrific special effects.

6. *Swiss Family Robinson* (2002): Hayley Mills narrates three minutes and forty seconds of color footage showing Walt Disney at the 1962 opening of Disneyland's Swiss Family Treehouse.

45 Movies That Inspired Disneyland's Attractions, Buildings, and Exhibits

These movies, some made by Disney and some made by other studios, have been a rich source of ideas and material for Disneyland. Here's an alphabetical list of film titles and the attractions, buildings, and exhibits they inspired.

1. *The African Queen*: Jungle Cruise
2. *Aladdin*: Aladdin's Oasis
3. *Alice in Wonderland*: Alice in Wonderland; Mad Hatter's Mad Tea Party; Mad Hatter hat shops
4. *Babes in Toyland*: Babes in Toyland Exhibit
5. *Brave*: Brave: Meet Merida
6. *Calamity Jane*: Golden Horseshoe
7. *Captain America*: Innoventions exhibit called Captain America: The Living Legend and Symbol of Courage
8. *Davy Crockett: King of the Wild Frontier*: Davy Crockett Arcade; Davy Crockett Frontier Museum; Davy Crockett's Explorer Canoes; Mike Fink Keel Boats
9. *Dumbo*: Casey Jr. Circus Train, Dumbo the Flying Elephant
10. *Fantasia*: Fantasia Gardens; Primeval World Diorama
11. *Finding Nemo*: Finding Nemo Submarine Voyage
12. *Frozen*: Frozen Royal Reception
13. *Home on the Range*: Little Patch of Heaven at Big Thunder Ranch
14. *Honey, I Shrunk the Kids*: *Honey, I Shrunk the Audience*
15. *The Hunchback of Notre Dame*: Festival of Fools; Festival of Foods; Quasimodo's Attic
16. *Indiana Jones* trilogy: Indiana Jones Adventure; Indiana Jones Adventure Outpost; Indy Fruit Cart
17. *Iron Man 3*: Innoventions exhibit called Iron Man Tech Presented by Stark Industries
18. *The Jungle Book*: Baloo's Dressing Room
19. *The Little Mermaid*: King Triton Gardens
20. *The Many Adventures of Winnie the Pooh*: Many Adventures of Winnie the Pooh; Pooh Corner
21. *Mary Poppins*: Jolly Holiday Bakery Café
22. *One Hundred and One Dalmatians*: Dalmatian Celebration
23. *Peter Pan*: Peter Pan Flight; Tinker Bell & Friends; Tinker Bell Toy Shoppe

24. *Pinocchio*: Geppetto's Arts & Crafts; Geppetto's Candy Shoppe; Pinocchio's Daring Journey; Stromboli's Wagon

25. *Pirates of the Caribbean*: Port Royal; Pirate's Lair on Tom Sawyer Island

26. *Sleeping Beauty*: Art of Animation; Sleeping Beauty Castle; Sleeping Beauty Castle Walk-Through; Three Fairies Magic Crystals

27. *Snow White and the Seven Dwarfs*: Snow White Adventures, Snow White Wishing Well and Grotto

28. *So Dear to My Heart*: Frontierland train station

29. *Song of the South*: Briar Patch; Splash Mountain

30. *Star Wars* trilogy: Star Tours; Star Trader

31. *Swiss Family Robinson*: Swiss Family Treehouse

32. *Switzerland*: Matterhorn Bobsleds; Matterhorn Mountain

33. *Sword in the Stone*: Merlin's Magic Shop; Sword in the Stone Ceremony

34. *Tangled*: Tangled

35. *Tarzan*: Tarzan's Treehouse

36. *Third Man on the Mountain*: Matterhorn Bobsleds; Matterhorn Mountain

37. *Thor: The Dark World*: Innoventions exhibit called Thor: Treasures of Asgard

38. *Tinker Bell*: Pixie Hollow; Pixie Hollow Gift Cart

39. *Toy Story*: Buzz Lightyear Astro Blasters; Club Buzz; Little Green Men Store Command; Toy Story Funhouse

40. *Tron*: A 1982 update to the PeopleMover's Superspeed Tunnel

41. *True-Life Adventure* documentaries: Grand Canyon Diorama; Jungle Cruise; Living Desert; Nature's Wonderland

42. *20,000 Leagues Under the Sea*: 20,000 Leagues Under the Sea Exhibit

43. *Who Framed Roger Rabbit*: Mickey's Toontown; Roger Rabbit's Car Toon Spin

44. *The Wind in the Willows*: Mr. Toad's Wild Ride

45. *Wreck-It Ralph*: Wreck-It Ralph meet-and-greet area in Tomorrowland

13 Movies Inspired by Disneyland's Attractions

Movies have inspired many Disneyland attractions (Fantasyland offers several examples). In the twenty-first century, this trend has occasionally been reversed—attractions have inspired movies instead, as shown in this chronological list of titles from Walt Disney Pictures.

1. *The Country Bears* (2002): The Country Bear Band reunites in this comedy.

2. *The Haunted Mansion* (2003): Eddie Murphy and his family confront ghosts.

3. *Pirates of the Caribbean: Curse of the Black Pearl* (2003): Johnny Depp's first Oscar nomination.

4. *Pirates of the Caribbean: Dead Man's Chest* (2006): The Davy Jones character was incorporated into Disneyland's Pirates of the Caribbean attraction.

5. *Pirates of the Caribbean: At World's End* (2007): Keith Richards as Jack Sparrow's father (Richards had inspired Depp's performance in the first *Pirates* movie).

6. *Pirates of the Caribbean: On Stranger Tides* (2011): Featuring Penelope Cruz and the Fountain of Youth.

7. *Tomorrowland* (2015): George Clooney, 1950s sci-fi, and an enticing title that suggests a Disneyland connection.

8. *Pirates of the Caribbean: Dead Men Tell No Tales* (2017): You can't keep a billion-dollar franchise down.

9. *The Haunted Mansion* (in development): A long-gestating film from Guillermo *"Hellboy"* del Toro.

10. *The Hill* (in development): Based on Disneyland's Matterhorn.

11. *Magic Kingdom* (in development): Supposedly the park's attractions will come alive at night.

12. *Mr. Toad's Wild Ride* (in development): What do you think—will this movie be true to Disney's animated movie or the Disneyland attraction?

13. *It's a Small World* (in development): To be directed by Jon *"National Treasure"* Turteltaub.

15 Movies Shown in Disneyland

Movies have always been a memorable part of the Disneyland experience. Not included in this alphabetical list are short cartoons like Mission to Mars's *Mad Mars Myths*, the Main Street Cinema's lineup, the Mickey Mouse Club Theater's cartoons, the Penny Arcade's brief silents, and Star Tours.

1. *All Because Man Wanted to Fly*: Eight-minute documentary shown in Tomorrowland's World Premiere Circle-Vision building starting in 1984.

2. *America the Beautiful*: Sixteen-minute documentary shown in Tomorrowland's Circarama building starting in 1960; revised in 1967 and 1996.

3. *American Journeys*: Twenty-one-minute documentary shown in Tomorrowland's World Premiere Circle-Vision building starting in 1984.

4. *Captain EO/Captain EO* Tribute: Seventeen-minute 3-D film shown in Tomorrowland's Magic Eye Theater starting in 1986; closed in 1997 and revived in 2010.

5. *Disneyland: The First 50 Magical Years*: Seventeen-minute documentary narrated by Steve Martin, first shown on the big screen in the Opera House in 2005 and then on a small screen in the lobby.

6. *Guardians of the Galaxy*: An "exclusive sneak peek" in 3-D played in Tomorrowland's Magic Eye Theater from July to September 2014. In October and November, the theater presented a *Big Hero 6* preview.

7. *Honey, I Shrunk the Audience*: Eighteen-minute 3-D film shown in Tomorrowland's Magic Eye Theater starting in 1998.

8. *Lady and the Tramp*: 1955 feature film, shown on Valentine's Day in 2013 as one of the Disney classics presented in the Opera House during that year's Limited Time Magic program of special events.

9. *Magic Journeys*: Sixteen-minute 3-D fantasy shown at Tomorrowland's Space Stage in 1984 and in the Magic Eye Theater two years later.

10. *Pirates of the Caribbean: The Curse of the Black Pearl*: Full-length, one-night-only premiere shown outdoors at Tom Sawyer Island in 2003.

11. *Pirates of the Caribbean: Dead Men's Chest*: Full-length, one-night-only premiere shown outdoors at Tom Sawyer Island in 2006.

12. *Pirates of the Caribbean: On Stranger Tides*: Full-length, one-night-only premiere shown outdoors at the Festival Arena in 2011.

13. *Star Wars*: Excerpts showing light saber duels have run inside Tomorrowland's Star Trader store.

14. *A Tour of the West*: Twelve-minute documentary shown in Tomorrowland's Circarama building in 1955.

15. *Wonders of China*: Nineteen-minute documentary shown in the World Premiere Circle-Vision building starting in 1984.

A Dozen Disneyland Locations with Movie Props on Display

Makes sense—with Hollywood nearby, many leftover movie props have found a new home at Disneyland. Here are some places where guests have been able to see authentic props in Disneyland.

1. Babes in Toyland Exhibit (1961–1963): Sets and props from Disney's live-action musical.

2. Big Thunder Mountain Railroad: Still displayed in the queue area and at the exit are antique-looking train props from 1978's *Hot Lead and Cold Feet*.

3. Club 33: Few guests get to see the props in this exclusive club, including a side table from *Mary Poppins*.

4. The Haunted Mansion: The ballroom scene's organ appeared in the 1954 Disney film 20,000 *Leagues Under the Sea*.

5. Indiana Jones Adventure: The battered truck near the entrance is from Paramount Pictures' film *Raiders of the Lost Ark*.

6. Indian Village (1955–1971): Some of the teepees and camp items appeared in the 1956 Disney film *Westward Ho, the Wagons!*

7. Jimmy Starr's Show Business Souvenirs (1956–1959): Guests did more than just look at the movie props, photos, and collectibles in this Town Square shop—they had the opportunity to buy them, too.

8. Mike Fink Keel Boats (1955–1997): Until 1958, two keel boats from the old Davy Crockett episodes on the *Disneyland* TV series were used for Frontierland's Mike Fink Keel Boats attraction; sturdy fiberglass replicas then replaced the wooden originals. One of these replicas, the *Gullywhumper*, has been seen moored in different places along the Rivers of America since 2003.

9. One-of-a-Kind Shop (1966–1996): This legendary New Orleans Square shop offered some actual movie props for sale, including a display case from the *Nautilus* in 20,000 *Leagues Under the Sea*.

10. Swiss Family Treehouse (1962–1999): Disney's 1960 movie provided some of the props for Adventureland's treehouse.

11. 20,000 Leagues Under the Sea Exhibit (1956–1966): Guests got up-close to movie sets and props from this Oscar-winning Disney movie.

12. The Walt Disney Story (1973–2005): This long-running biographical exhibit inside the Opera House included original art from Disney's animated films and props from his TV series.

Long-Running Programs at the Main Street Cinema

The small but stylish Main Street Cinema has played old movies and cartoons to standing-room-only audiences since 1955. (The years the films debuted are in parentheses.)

6 Silent Films

1. *A Dash Through the Clouds*: Mack Sennett's drama about biplanes (1912)
2. *Dealing for Daisy*: A William S. Hart Western (1915)
3. *Fatima's Dance*: Fatima's risqué belly dance (year uncertain)
4. *Gertie the Dinosaur*: Winsor McCay's cartoon, one of the first ever made (1915)
5. *The Noise of Bombs*: A Keystone Kops comedy (1914)
6. *Shifting Sands*: A Gloria Swanson melodrama (1918)

5 Silents, 1 Talkie

1. *All Jazzed Up*: A country couple go to the big city (1920)
2. *The Great Train Robbery*: Edison's landmark film (1903)
3. *Spring Fever*: A Harold Lloyd comedy (1919)
4. *Steamboat Willie*: The classic Disney cartoon with synchronized sound (1928)
5. *Tumbleweeds*: A William S. Hart Western (1925)
6. 20,000 *Leagues Under the Sea*: Underwater footage and a mysterious island (1916)

6 Disney Cartoons

1. *The Dognapper*: Starring Mickey and Donald (1934)
2. *Mickey's Polo Team*: Starring Mickey, Donald, and Goofy (1936)
3. *The Moose Hunt*: Starring Mickey and Pluto (1931)
4. *Plane Crazy*: Starring Mickey and Minnie (1928)
5. *Steamboat Willie*: Starring Mickey and Minnie (1928)
6. *Traffic Troubles*: Starring Mickey and Minnie (1931)

10 Disneyland-Related Inaccuracies in *Saving Mr. Banks*

The main characters in 2013's *Saving Mr. Banks* spend five minutes in Disneyland. The movie is set in 1961, but filming at Disneyland took place in November 2012. While clever camera angles and soft focus hide many of the post-1961 structures (Space Mountain, for instance), there are still some on-screen anachronisms and inaccuracies (most, it should be noted, are viewed fleetingly, and none detract from the pleasure of watching the movie). Here are ten of those movie miscues.

1. Walt Disney never took P. L. Travers on a tour around Disneyland (a

studio employee did).

2. In the film, the row of turnstiles at the entrance curves away from the train station, but in 1961, the row curved toward the station. Also, it's hard to tell, but modern computer screens appear to be mounted at the turnstiles.

3. At the entrance, the walkway in front of the Mickey flowerbed is covered with paver stones, not 1961's smooth red concrete. Also, attraction posters are shown mounted on top of a brick wall, but in 1961, those posters would have been partially in front of the wall—which, by the way, was made of beige cement, not red brick.

4. A big red sign announcing 1965's Great Moments with Mr. Lincoln is shown on the front of the Opera House (the text is illegible, but the sign, which wasn't there in 1961, is conspicuous).

5. The 20th Century Music Company can be identified in a long shot by the gramophone on the store's exterior, and then in a closer shot when the two stars walk by a partially obscured "New Sounds for a New Century" sign. In 1961, Fine Tobacco, not the Music Company, occupied this space.

6. The "Disney family crest" and animal-shaped downspouts can be seen on the front of the castle, but none of these were there in 1961.

7. In 1961, Fantasyland's buildings had their original "medieval tournament" exteriors, not the cohesive "European village" architecture that debuted in 1983 and makes an appearance in the film. As Tom Hanks waves from the King Arthur Carrousel, Toad Hall and signage for Pinocchio's Daring Journey, both added in 1983, are visible.

8. The King Arthur Carrousel is in the wrong place; in 1961, it was about sixty feet closer to Sleeping Beauty Castle (it was moved away from the castle in 1983 to ease congestion).

9. The King Arthur Carrousel's roof had vertical stripes in 1961, not the abstract shapes shown in the movie.

10. The ten panels on the interior of the King Arthur Carrousel that show scenes from *Sleeping Beauty* were added in 2003.

25 Disneyland-Themed Record Albums

In the 1950s, back before everyone knew what Disneyland was, vinyl records helped promote and clarify the newly built park with narration, sound effects, and music. Some of the later albums spotlighted specific, more elaborate attractions (the Haunted Mansion, for instance). More recent CD collections have anthologized Disneyland's musical history.

1. *Music from Disneyland* (1955)

2. *A Visit to Disneyland* (1955)

3. *Walt Disney Takes You to Disneyland* (1956, with 7″ records devoted to each land—*Walt Disney Takes You to Adventureland, Walt Disney Takes You to Frontierland*, etc.)

4. *A Day at Disneyland with Walt Disney and Jiminy Cricket* (1957)

5. *Echoes of Disneyland* (1957)

6. *Meet Me Down on Main Street* (1957)

7. *Slue-Foot Sue's Golden Horseshoe Revue* (1957)

8. *A Christmas Adventure in Disneyland* (1958)

9. *Date Nite at Disneyland* (1958)

10. *The Dukes at Disneyland, Volume 1* (1962)

11. *Firehouse Five Plus Two at Disneyland* (1962)

12. *Walt Disney presents It's a Small World* (1964)

13. *Walt Disney's Pirates of the Caribbean: The Sound Track of the Fabulous Adventure* (1966)

14. *Walt Disney's The Enchanted Tiki Room* (1968)

15. *The Story and Song from the Haunted Mansion* (1969)

16. *Walt Disney presents The Haunted Mansion* (1970)

17. *Disneyland's Main Street Electrical Parade* (1973)

18. *America Sings: The Original Soundtrack of the Disneyland Attraction* (1974)

19. *A Musical Souvenir of America on Parade* (1975)

20. *The Official Album of Disneyland/Walt Disney World* (1981)

21. *Big Bands at Disneyland* (1984)

22. *Disney's Happiest Celebration on Earth* (2005)

23. *A Musical History of Disneyland* (2005)

24. *Disneyland Sing-A-Long* (2008)

25. *Disneyland Resort Official Album* (2013)

14 Disneyland Attraction Theme Songs

Music is a vital part of Disneyland attractions (imagine Pirates of the Caribbean without its rousing "yo ho" chorus). Some of the alphabetically listed songs that follow were composed for their specific attractions, while others came from movies. Parentheses indicate which are originals, which come from other sources, and who the composers are.

1. Adventure Thru Inner Space: "Miracles from Molecules" (original, Sherman Brothers)

2. Carousel of Progress: "There's a Great Big Beautiful Tomorrow" (original, Sherman Brothers)

3. Casey Jr. Circus Train: "Casey Junior" (*Dumbo* movie, Frank Churchill/ Ned Washington)

4. Enchanted Tiki Room: "The Tiki, Tiki, Tiki Room" (original, Sherman Brothers)

5. Grand Canyon Diorama: "On the Trail" (excerpt from the *Grand Canyon Suite*, Ferde Grofé)

6. It's a Small World: "It's a Small World" (original, Sherman Brothers)

7. The Haunted Mansion: "Grim Grinning Ghosts" (original, Buddy Baker/X. Atencio)

8. Mad Hatter's Mad Tea Party: "A Very Merry Un-Birthday (to You)" (*Alice in Wonderland* movie, Mack David/Al Hoffman/Jerry Livingston)

9. Monorail: "The Monorail Song" (original, Sherman Brothers)

10. Peter Pan Flight: "You Can Fly! You Can Fly! You Can Fly!" (*Peter Pan* movie, Sammy Cahn/Sammy Fain)

11. Pirates of the Caribbean: "Yo Ho (A Pirate's Life for Me)" (original, George Bruns/X. Atencio)

12. Mine Train: "All Aboard the Mine Train (The Mine Train Song)" (original, Sherman Brothers)

13. Rocket Rods: "Magic Highways of Tomorrow" (original, Sherman Brothers)

14. Swiss Family Treehouse: "Swisskapolka" (*Swiss Family Robinson* movie, Buddy Baker)

16 Non-Disney Songs About Disneyland

Some of these alphabetically listed songs incorporate affectionate references to the park, some are more oblique, and some are downright scary, but they all make allusions to Disneyland (or a "park" that we can safely assume is Disneyland). Songs that briefly mention Disneyland a single time—such as Billy Joel's "We Didn't Start the Fire"—are not listed.

1. "Calico Train" by Steve Martin: In the liner notes to his Grammy-winning album *The Crow*, Martin dedicates this joyful song to the old Mine

Train (which he misidentifies): "The Calico Mine Ride was an attraction at Disneyland when I worked there as a teenager, and I gave this song the title in tribute to the memories of those days."

2. "Death at Disneyland" by Rasputina: A nightmare about death and the afterlife at Disneyland.

3. "Death at Disneyland" by the Smugglers: A litany of the park's "fatal attractions."

4. "Disneyland" by Five for Fighting: Balladeer John Ondrasik's dream about "a nice day" in Disneyland.

5. "Disneyland" by Frankie Goes to Hollywood: The English New Wavers produce lots of chanting and mostly unintelligible words.

6. "Disneyland" from the musical *Smile*: Jodi Benson sang this in the 1986 Broadcast show.

7. "The Disneyland Song" by Joule Thief: Search YouTube to find this witty music video, shot in Disneyland, about two friends getting separated in the park.

8. "Disneyland Was Made for You and Me" by Timbuk 3: These hit-makers once sang "the future's so bright I gotta wear shades," but in this song, life isn't so sunny.

9. "Dizz Knee Land" by Dada: A criminal on the run heads to Disneyland.

10. "Madman" by Ugly Kid Joe: A savage killer is on the loose at Disneyland.

11. "Mickey Mouse" by Sparks: The quirky pop-rock brothers sing about Mickey, Minnie, and their "place in Disneyland, California."

12. "Pirate's Life" by the Vandals: Pirates of the Caribbean and LSD don't mix.

13. "Skipper Dan" by Weird Al Yankovic: "Workin' on the Jungle Cruise ride" is not all it's cracked up to be, according to Weird Al.

14. "Splendid Isolation" by Warren Zevon: One verse depicts Michael Jackson alone in Disneyland.

15. "Stukas Over Disneyland" by the Dickies: A punk anthem about a Nazi invasion.

16. "Tragic Kingdom" by No Doubt: An ultra-cynical view that includes a frozen Walt Disney.

32 Disneyland Appearances in Print and Paint

Listed alphabetically are thirty-two novels, stories, poems, and artworks that use the actual park (not a fictionalized version) to help tell their tales.

1. **"All I Thought About Was Disneyland"**: In Alicia Alarcón's powerful short story, Disneyland is the "magical paradise" for two girls from El Salvador who are being smuggled into the U.S.

2. **"Bob the Dinosaur Goes to Disneyland"**: From horror writer Joe Lansdale comes this weird 1989 short story about an inflatable talking T. rex that carries a Disney lunchbox, wears mouse ears, and visits Disneyland.

3. *The Book of Daniel*: Award-winning author E. L. Doctorow spends seven cynical pages of this novel having his narrator analyze Disneyland during the holidays. He compliments the "impressively real," "technologically perfect" machinery and the efficient line management, but disparages the visitors, the distortion of history, "the many junk shops," the "macrocephalic" costumed characters, and even Anaheim, "a town somewhere between Buchenwald and Belsen."

4. *Chez Chance*: A paraplegic man checks into a seedy Anaheim motel, spends a tiring day at Disneyland, and encounters some unusual locals in this humorous, sad, and ultimately affecting novel by Jay Gummerman.

5. *Dan Gets a Minivan*: Popular columnist Dan Zevin offers lighthearted advice about raising a family; the humorous "Directions for Enjoying Disneyland" chapter reads like an FAQ.

6. **"disneyland"**: A salesman takes his son's girlfriend to Disneyland several times in Rick DeMarinis's R-rated short story.

7. **"Disneyland"**: Poet H. C. Kim goes to Disneyland "to find something" that turns out to be "deep happiness."

8. **"Disneyland"**: Set in 1960, Barbara Gowdy's dark short story tells of a father who promises his family a long trip to Disneyland, but instead makes everyone live in a backyard bomb shelter for two weeks.

9. **"Disneyland"**: Michele Richmond's brief short story uses the park for the title, the final image, and the last word.

10. *Disneyland Hostage*: A kids' mystery by Eric Wilson about young detective Liz Austen investigating a Disneyland Hotel disappearance.

11. *Disneyland, Please*: A Canadian football player dreams of Disneyland in Clive Doucet's 1978 novel.

12. *Ellray Jakes is NOT a chicken!*: In this acclaimed kids' novel by Sally Warner, Ellray's dad dangles Disneyland as the reward if Ellray can stay out of trouble, but the trip has an unexpected twist.

13. *Holidays in Heck*: *Holidays in Hell* was P. J. O'Rourke's 1988 collection of travel essays; *Holidays in Heck* is a sequel of sorts and includes a chapter in which the former *National Lampoon* humorist takes his family to Disneyland.

14. *Iceberg*: The violent climax of Clive Cussler's adventure novel is a long, vicious fight inside Disneyland's Pirates of the Caribbean.

15. *Larry Gets Lost in Los Angeles:* In this children's picture book by Michael Mullin and John Skewes, a dog gets separated from his owners on a family trip to Disneyland and searches for them in real locations throughout Los Angeles.

16. *Life After Murder*: A paroled killer takes his family to Disneyland in this nonfiction work by award-winning journalist Nancy Mullane.

17. *Lost Boy*: A wild child of the 1960s becomes the senior pastor of a mega-church and rents Disneyland for an evangelical Harvest Crusade, an event described in this spiritual memoir by Greg Laurie.

18. *Minn and Jake's Almost Terrible Summer*: The kids in this whimsical free-verse novel by Janet S. Wong have various summer adventures, one of which is a day at Disneyland.

19. "Mocha in Disneyland": There's "an affirmative action" at the heart of Gary D. Keller's humorous short story—a professor and his young son hide out overnight in Disneyland.

20. *Moonbeam*: Maureen Garth's twenty-four gentle meditations help children relax; one chapter, "Disneyland," floats listeners into the park.

21. *One Crazy Summer*: In Rita Williams-Garcia's children's story set in 1968, kids get sent to California for summer vacation and hope for a Disneyland trip (it comes up several times); instead, they get a tumultuous visit to Oakland.

22. Postage stamp: In 1968, the United States Postal Service issued a commemorative six-cent postage stamp depicting Walt Disney, what looked to be Sleeping Beauty Castle, and children resembling It's a Small World dolls.

23. *Protesters at Disneyland*: A poem about park guests written by Samuel Maio, first published in *The Chariton Review.*

24. Shag: Many artists have painted Disneyland scenes, but one of the most popular is Shag (Josh Agle), whose large serigraphs for the park's fiftieth anniversary present "1950s cool" renditions of Main Street and the four original lands, plus a stylized park map. See Shag's list on page 319.

25. "Splash Mountain": James Franco's 2014 poetry collection includes this eighteen-line poem that recounts some of his Disneyland memories. It begins with "New Orleans Square is my favorite part of Disneyland."

26. Thomas Struth: This noted German photographer's 2014 exhibition in Manhattan's Marian Goodman Gallery included a half-dozen brightly colored Disneyland landscapes, some covering seventy-seven square feet.

27. "Tomorrowland": California State University, Northridge presented this 2012 exhibition inspired by Tomorrowland. The paintings by eight artists displayed a somewhat more pessimistic vision of the future than Disneyland's.

28. *The Turtle Street Trading Co.*: To raise Disneyland's $9 admission price (this is an old book), four kids start a toy-trading business in this breezy children's story by Jill R. Klevin.

29. *What We Could Have Done with the Money*: Writer Rob Simpson's thought-provoking, outrageous, and sometimes even humorous suggestions for spending the trillion dollars that went to the war in Iraq. Chapter 35 explains how everyone in America could have gotten four all-expenses-paid vacations to Disneyland.

30. *Wishing on a Star*: This rare 1983 postcard (as discussed in Paul Krassner's *Who's to Say What's Obscene*) shows a nuclear bomb destroying Disneyland; artist Carl Chaplin intended to distribute it for free, but Disney compelled him to turn over all the postcards.

31. *Word Smart*: Adam Robinson's best-selling vocabulary builder uses the park to exemplify the word "bemused" ("confused, bewildered")—"The two stood *bemused* in the middle of the parking lot at Disneyland, trying to remember where they had parked their car."

32. *World Wide Loss*: Published in Spokane's *Spokesman-Review* newspaper right after Walt Disney's death, Shaw McCutcheon's editorial cartoon shows the entire world as Disneyland while Pluto sobs in front of Sleeping Beauty Castle.

10 Dell Comic Books Spotlighting Disneyland

In the 1950s, Dell Comics was probably the world's largest publisher of comic books, and Dell's Disney-licensed comics were probably its most successful line (Disney comics were the top-sellers on newsstands in 1953, for instance, ahead of every other well-known national magazine). Once Disneyland opened in 1955, the Disney comics included some that put the characters right in the park. Here are ten from Disneyland's first five years, listed chronologically with cover images in parentheses.

1. *Walt Disney's Donald Duck in Disneyland*, September 1955 (Donald on a flying carpet over Town Square)

2. *Walt Disney's Mickey Mouse in Frontierland*, May 1956 (Disney characters in a stagecoach)

3. *Walt Disney's Mickey Mouse in Fantasyland*, May 1957 (Disney characters on the Casey Jr. Circus Train)

4. *Walt Disney's Uncle Scrooge Goes to Disneyland*, August 1957 (Uncle Scrooge in the Hub)

5. *Walt Disney's Christmas in Disneyland*, December 1957 (Disney characters, a Christmas tree, and Sleeping Beauty Castle)

6. *Walt Disney's Donald and Mickey in Disneyland*, May 1958 (Donald, Mickey, and a Tom Sawyer Island raft)

7. *Walt Disney's Vacation in Disneyland*, August 1958 (Disney characters on the Skyway)

8. *Walt Disney's Disneyland Birthday Party*, October 1958 (Disney characters on the Teacups)

9. *Walt Disney's Vacation in Disneyland*, August 1959 (Donald, Mickey, and the Astro-Jets)

10. *Walt Disney's Disneyland U.S.A.*, August 1960 (Disney characters in Tomorrowland)

61 Disneyland Attraction Posters

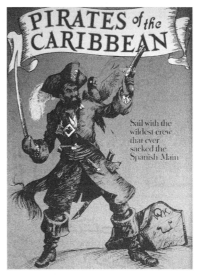

Beautiful attraction posters have adorned Disneyland since 1956. So ubiquitous, recognizable, and important are these posters that they've been analyzed in books, sold as valuable framed artwork, and incorporated into films such as *Up* and *Monsters, Inc.* Today's guests are familiar with the sixteen posters hung inside the two main tunnels leading into Town Square, but the posters haven't always been there. In the 1950s and 1960s, they were placed in front of the entrance's Mickey Mouse flower bed; posters have also appeared along the Avenue of the Flags, at the Plaza Gardens, on Monorail pylons, inside Redd Rockett's Pizza Port, and in the Penny Arcade.

The posters' large size—three feet wide by four and a half feet tall—means they can be seen from a distance, and the simple designs make them perspicuous for anyone unfamiliar with the subject being illustrated. While the majority of the posters have spotlighted major attractions, sometimes with multiple posters, they have also promoted exhibits, restaurants, and businesses (even the Disneyland Hotel). Below is an alphabetical list of sixty-one subjects on Disneyland's posters.

Adventureland

1. Enchanted Tiki Room
2. Indiana Jones Adventure
3. Jungle River/Jungle Cruise/ Jingle Cruise
4. Swiss Family Treehouse
5. Tarzan's Treehouse

Critter Country

6. Country Bear Jamboree
7. Many Adventures of Winnie the Pooh
8. Splash Mountain

Fantasyland

9. Alice in Wonderland
10. Dumbo the Flying Elephant
11. It's a Small World
12. Mad Hatter's Mad Tea Party
13. Magical Fireworks
14. Matterhorn Bobsleds
15. Mickey Mouse Club 3-D Theater
16. Mr. Toad's Wild Ride
17. Peter Pan's Flight
18. Pinocchio's Daring Journey
19. Remember . . . Dreams Come True Fireworks
20. Snow White's Scary Adventures
21. Storybook Land Canal Boats

Frontierland

22. Big Thunder Mountain Railroad
23. Casa de Fritos
24. *Golden Horseshoe Revue*
25. *Mark Twain* Riverboat

26. Nature's Wonderland/Rainbow Caverns
27. Pirate's Lair on Tom Sawyer Island
28. Sailing Ship *Columbia*
29. Stage Coach/Mine Train/Mule Pack
30. Tom Sawyer Island

Hub, Main Street, Town Square

31. Great Moments with Mr. Lincoln
32. Primeval World
33. Red Wagon Inn
34. Santa Fe & Disneyland Railroad

New Orleans Square

35. The Haunted Mansion
36. Pirates of the Caribbean

Tomorrowland

37. Adventure Thru Inner Space

38. *American Journeys*

39. *America the Beautiful*

40. Art Corner

41. Art of Animation

42. Astro-Jets

43. Autopia

44. *Captain EO* Tribute

45. Carousel of Progress

46. Finding Nemo Submarine Voyage

47. Flight to the Moon

48. Flying Saucers

49. *Guardians of the Galaxy*

50. *Magic Journeys*

51. Monorail

52. PeopleMover

53. Rocket Jets

54. Rocket to the Moon

55. Skyway

56. Space Mountain

57. Space Station X-1

58. Star Tours

59. Submarine Voyage

60. 20,000 Leagues Under the Sea Exhibit

61. *Wonders of China*

Disneyland's Pictorial Souvenir Books

Official publications of the Walt Disney Company, Disneyland's pictorial souvenirs (as they're usually called) have been sold since 1955. In early years, the books cost only a quarter, a price so low that the profit on each sale was a single penny. They have soft covers, twenty-eight to thirty-eight photo-filled pages, and chapters dedicated to each of the park's lands.

For Disney, these books have served several purposes. The books welcome first-time visitors with warm words from an avuncular Walt Disney, introduce Disneyland's novel hub-and-spoke layout, and describe the thrills to expect from each major attraction. In addition, the books serve as beautiful keepsakes to help guests remember their park visits and describe them to other potential guests. Supplementing the lovely photos are imaginative drawings and evocative text that help capture Disneyland's diverse environments. For the first two decades, the books also included illustrated maps and lists of attractions, stores, and restaurants to help navigate the park's unique geography. Often the books have devoted a few tantalizing pages to coming attractions or other Disney developments around the world.

Occasionally the softcover books have been supplemented with special hardcover editions that commemorate park anniversaries while re-telling Disneyland's long history (these longer books are included in another list called "A Dozen Picture Books for Every Disneyland Fan's Bookshelf"—see page 256). Meanwhile, here are twenty pictorial souvenir books in chronological order, with details about their formats and front covers.

1. 1955: A small horizontal booklet (8.75" wide by 6" tall); Walt Disney stands in front of Peter Ellenshaw's large concept painting of Disneyland.

2. 1956: A vertical book (8.25" wide by 11.5" tall) with a cover photo of guests streaming in and out of Sleeping Beauty Castle on a sunny afternoon.

3. 1957: Vertical, same cover as 1956, though the year "1957" is noted in the upper-right corner.

4. 1958: The first classic horizontal book (11.5" wide by 8" tall) shows a smiling Walt Disney and a Tinker Bell illustration against a background of Sleeping Beauty Castle on an overcast day.

5. 1959: Horizontal; same cover as 1958.

6. 1960: Horizontal; Walt Disney has eight smaller photos of Disneyland scenes behind him; this book also had a wrap-around cover spotlighting the new Nature's Wonderland area.

7. 1961: Horizontal; Walt Disney has a montage of Disneyland illustrations behind him.

8. 1962: Horizontal; Walt Disney has a different montage of Disneyland illustrations in the foreground.

9. 1963: Horizontal; same cover as the 1962 book, with a red color scheme.

10. 1964: Horizontal; Walt Disney is in the right corner and blue and green stripes across the page carry Disneyland illustrations.

11. 1965: A 10.5" by 10.5" square with Walt Disney in front of a background painting of Mickey Mouse and Sleeping Beauty Castle.

12. 1968: The classic horizontal format with Walt Disney signing autographs on Main Street (this Thomas Nebbia photo first ran in the August 1963 issue of *National Geographic*).

13. 1971: Horizontal; the sunny Sleeping Beauty Castle in front of the Matterhorn.

14. 1976: Horizontal; a new castle photo taken from the east side.

15. 1986: Horizontal; a smaller castle photo (shot from the west) surrounded by a metallic design.

16. 1989: Horizontal; a new sunny castle photo taken from the Hub and surrounded by cartoons of Disney characters.

17. 1993: Horizontal; a new sunny castle photo.

18. 1999: A smaller, almost square book, 8.5" wide by 9" tall; across the center is an illustration of the castle and many Disney characters, with stars spelling out "45" in the background (2000 would be Disneyland's forty-fifth anniversary).

19. 2005: Horizontal; cover includes Disney's California Adventure (as it was called then).

20. In 2010, *Disneyland: From Once Upon a Time to Happily Ever After* replaced the traditional pictorial souvenir books with a fascinating tour of park history and side-by-side photos comparing nostalgic scenes with their modern counterparts.

A Dozen Picture Books
for Every Disneyland Fan's Bookshelf

These volumes contain historic Disneyland art and photos (books are listed alphabetically).

1. *The Art of Disneyland* (Jeff Kurtti and Bruce Gordon): Beautiful artwork by famous Disney artists.

2. *Behind the Magic: 50 Years of Disneyland* (Karal Ann Marling and Donna R. Braden): An image-rich companion to a popular museum exhibition.

3. *Disneyland: A Pictorial Souvenir* (Walt Disney Productions): Sold since 1955, these helpful softcover books (detailed in the previous list) are official Walt Disney Company publications, often with photos and text carried over from year to year.

4. *Disneyland: From Once Upon a Time to Happily Ever After* (Jeff Kurtti): Side-by-side comparisons of historic and modern photographs.

5. *Disneyland: Inside Story* (Randy Bright): A comprehensive, photo-laden history written by a Disneyland insider.

6. *Disneyland … The Beginning* (Carlene Thie): One of several collections of historic photos taken by photojournalist Mell Kilpatrick.

7. *Disneyland: The First Quarter Century* (Walt Disney Productions): Produced for Disneyland's silver anniversary; followed by *Disneyland: The First Thirty Years* in 1985.

8. *Disneyland: The Nickel Tour* (Bruce Gordon and David Mumford): Old postcards illustrate a detailed history of Disneyland.

9. *Disneyland Through the Decades: A Photographic Celebration* (Jeff Kurtti): Photos and art tell the Disneyland story.

10. *Disneyland: Then, Now, and Forever* (Bruce Gordon and Tim O'Day): Published for Disneyland's golden anniversary, this glossy book presents the park's history by subject ("Traditions," "Music," "Secrets," etc.).

11. *The Magic of Disneyland and Walt Disney World* (Valerie Childs): A professional photographer tours the parks.

12. *Walt Disney's Disneyland* (Martin A. Sklar): The first hardcover souvenir book telling the park's story was published in 1964 and written by a future Disney Legend; an updated edition followed five years later.

A Dozen Famous Photographs of Disneyland

Billions of pictures have been taken at Disneyland, one of the most-photographed locations on Earth. A few of those photos are more famous than the rest; here are a dozen that most fans have probably seen, listed chronologically.

1. 1954: Walt Disney smiles and points at Peter Ellenshaw's four-by-eight-foot painting of the park, as viewed from 2,000 feet up. This color photo was on the cover of Disneyland's first pictorial souvenir book (*page 254*).

2. 1955: A familiar black-and-white photo taken on Opening Day shows Walt Disney at the microphone in Town Square.

3. Ca. 1957: Walt Disney walks in front of Sleeping Beauty Castle, holding hands with a young girl and a boy in a Cub Scout uniform. From 1958 to 1964, this color photo was the first one shown inside Disneyland's pictorial souvenir books.

4. Ca. 1957: Walt Disney, wearing a red neckerchief and engineer's hat, waves from the engine of the Santa Fe & Disneyland Railroad. This color photo (like others of Walt Disney driving an Autopia car, wearing a Native American headdress, wearing a skipper's cap at the helm of a Jungle Cruise boat, and waving from a Peter Pan's Flight galleon) was shown in pictorial souvenir books for decades.

5. 1959: A staged black-and-white publicity photo positions Walt Disney outside the new Monorail while Vice President Richard Nixon and his family sit inside the front cabin and Art Linkletter pops up in the bubble canopy.

6. 1962: Steve Martin says he was present when legendary photographer Diane Arbus shot *A Castle in California*, her memorable black-and-white photo of Sleeping Beauty Castle at night.

7. 1963: For the August 1963 issue of *National Geographic*, Thomas Nebbia took the photo of a smiling Walt Disney signing autographs on a busy Main Street. This shot appeared on the cover of Disneyland's 1968 pictorial souvenir book.

8. 1963: Nebbia also took the shot of Walt Disney, Lillian Disney, and their three grandchildren inside their Town Square apartment for the August 1963 issue of *National Geographic*. This photo gave the world its first glimpse of Disney's "supersecret hideaway," which up until then had "never before been photographed," according to the caption.

9. 1964: Renie Bardeau, who later became Disneyland's chief photographer, took the famous black-and-white shot of Walt Disney walking alone through Sleeping Beauty Castle.

10. 1964: In another popular photo, Walt Disney looks down Main Street while standing under the tribute window to his father, Elias. Disney wears the same casual clothes that he wore in the castle photo listed above, so this is most likely another Renie Bardeau image taken on the same day.

11. 1966: Renie Bardeau took the last official photos of Walt Disney in Disneyland, including one of him with Mickey Mouse in a fire engine with Sleeping Beauty Castle behind them. This iconic photo was turned into a familiar collage (*right*) that was prominently displayed inside the Opera House.

12. 2012: Since 2007, celebrity photographer Annie Leibovitz has been shooting the Disney Dream Portraits, a series of lavish Disney Park ads that run in *Vanity Fair* and other prominent magazines. Some of these clearly show Disneyland locations, such as the 2012 image of actors Jack Black, Will Ferrell, and Jason Segal as hitchhiking ghosts in front of the Haunted Mansion (the tag line reads: "Where you can go on the ride of your afterlife").

17 Magazines Featuring Disneyland on Their Covers

Considering how world-famous and well-photographed Disneyland is, it's been on surprisingly few magazine covers. One that Disneyland almost landed was *Life* magazine; according to Martin Sklar's *Dream It!, Do It!*, Disneyland's Grad Nite was bumped from a 1961 *Life* cover by sudden developments at the Berlin Wall (presumably the August 25, 1961 issue). The following periodicals are listed alphabetically, with dates and cover subjects in parentheses. We haven't included Disney-owned free promotional magazines (*Disneyland Holiday* from 1957–1958 and the subsequent *Vacationland*, for instance), which regularly showed Disneyland covers.

1. *The American Weekly* (March 27, 1960; Sleeping Beauty Castle)

2. *Business Week* (July 9, 1955; Walt Disney and Sleeping Beauty Castle)

3. *California* ("Official State Visitor's Guide," 2005; Sleeping Beauty Castle)

4. *Fence Industry* (January 1981; Town Square's train station)

5. *Hudson Family Magazine* (1955, vol. 1, #3; Walt Disney with a painting of attractions)

6. *Jack and Jill* (December 1961; a painting of "Santa's Parade at Disneyland")

7. *Kodak Movie News* (Summer 1961; Mine Train)

8. *Meccano Magazine* (for hobbyists, November 1968; Monorail)

9. *Nash Airflyte Magazine* (July 1956; Sleeping Beauty Castle)

10. *National Geographic* (August 1963; Mad Hatter's Mad Tea Party)

11. *Newsweek* (December 31, 1962; Walt Disney and castle model)

12. *Parade* (April 7, 1957; Tom Nabbe, the Tom Sawyer character on Tom Sawyer Island)

13. *Parade* (March 26, 1961; tour guides)

14. *Radio & TV News* (June 1958; *Mark Twain* Riverboat)

15. *Santa Fe Magazine* (August 1955; Walt Disney and the *E.P. Ripley* locomotive)

16. *Santa Fe Magazine* (June 1958; Walt Disney at the tunnel entrance to the Grand Canyon Diorama)

17. *Storyboard* (March/April 1990; Sleeping Beauty Castle)

IMAGINEERS, CAST MEMBERS, AND PERFORMERS

Making the Dream a Reality

89 Names on the Main Street Tribute Windows

Walt Disney once said that "it takes people to make a dream a reality." Many of those people who made his Disneyland dream come true are honored on Main Street's windows. Typically, the windows identify a "proprietor" and then briefly describe a fictional business supposedly operating behind the window. That descriptive text is usually a clue as to what the person did at Disneyland. For instance, the window for Wally Boag, the Golden Horseshoe's long-time comedian, states that his business is "Golden Vaudeville Routines." Some tribute windows are not located on Main Street at all; actor Fess Parker and designer Harper Goff are honored in Frontierland and Adventureland, respectively, and Walt Disney's window is in Mickey's Toontown. Listed below are eighty-nine tribute windows with the actual Disneyland-related occupations of the recipients.

1. Milt Albright, accountant/manager
2. Charles Alexander, construction supervisor
3. W. F. Allen, executive at Upjohn Pharmacy, an early sponsor
4. Hideo Amemiya, Disneyland Hotel executive
5. American Broadcasting Company, TV network
6. Ken Anderson, artist
7. X. Atencio, artist/writer
8. Renie Bardeau, official park photographer
9. H. Draegart Barnard, Walt Disney's doctor
10. Tony Baxter, designer
11. Wally Boag, comedian
12. Chuck Boyajian, custodial superintendent
13. Charles Boyer, artist
14. C. Randy Bright, writer/executive
15. Roger Broggie, engineer
16. Harriet Burns, model maker
17. Bruce Bushman, artist
18. Cast members (honoring the long history of park employees)
19. John Louis Catone, communications services
20. Royal Clark, treasurer
21. Claude Coats, artist
22. Renie Conley, costume designer
23. Ray Conway, construction

24. Jim Cora, executive
25. W. Dennis Cottrell, planner/designer
26. Roland F. Crump, artist
27. Don DaGradi, writer
28. Alice Davis, costume designer
29. Marc Davis, artist
30. Marvin Davis, architect/designer
31. Elias Disney, father of Walt Disney
32. Walt Disney (in Mickey's Toontown)
33. Ron Dominguez, executive
34. Don Edgren, engineer
35. Peter Ellenshaw, artist
36. Greg A. Emmer, executive

37. Morgan "Bill" Evans, landscape architect
38. Orlando Ferrante, executive
39. Van Arsdale France, guest services
40. Blaine Gibson, sculptor
41. Donald S. Gilmore, chairman of Upjohn Pharmacy, an early sponsor
42. Harper Goff, architect/designer (in Adventureland)
43. Bob Gurr, engineer
44. Jacob Samuel Hamel, engineer
45. John Hench, artist
46. Glenn Hicks, executive (in Frontierland)
47. Alexander Irvine, doctor
48. Richard Irvine, art director/designer
49. Robert F. Jani, entertainment planner
50. Fred Joerger, model maker
51. Bill Justice, artist/engineer
52. Emile Kuri, decorator
53. Fred Leopold, lawyer
54. Gunther R. Lessing, lawyer
55. Jack Lindquist, marketing/executive
56. Mary Anne Mang, community relations
57. Bill Martin, art director/designer

58. Ivan Martin, prop builder
59. Sam McKim, artist
60. Edward T. Meck, publicist
61. Christopher D. Miller, Walt Disney's grandson
62. George Mills, carpenter
63. Seb Morey, taxidermist
64. Dick Nunis, executive
65. Fess Parker, actor (in Frontierland)
66. George Patrick, art director
67. C. V. Patterson, executive at Upjohn Pharmacy, an early sponsor

68. Bob Penfield, cast member from Opening Day to mid-1997
69. Harrison "Buzz" Price, consultant
70. Cicely Rigdon, supervisor of Guest Relations
71. Wathel Rogers, model maker/engineer
72. Jack Rorex, construction
73. L. H. Roth, construction
74. Wade B. Rubottom, art director
75. Herb Ryman, artist
76. Gabriel Scognamillo, art director
77. Richard Sherman and Robert Sherman, composers
78. Doc Sherwood M.D., Walt Disney's boyhood neighbor
79. Cash Shockey, painter
80. Martin Sklar, writer/executive
81. E. G. Upjohn, president of Upjohn Pharmacy, an early sponsor
82. Ray Van De Warker, attractions/management
83. Robert Washo, supervisor of plaster department
84. Frank Wells, executive
85. William T. Wheeler, engineer
86. George Whitney, designer/manager
87. Ed Winger, supervisor of paint department
88. John Wise, engineer
89. Gordon Youngman, lawyer

A Dozen Tributes to Imagineers
and Employees on Disneyland Attractions

Main Street's windows show dozens of tributes to significant people from Disneyland's history, but there are other places to look for subtle tributes.

1. Julie Andrews: This Disney Legend's initials are on the saddle of "Jingles" at the King Arthur Carrousel.

2. Tony Baxter: The "Baxter Boring Co." crate that used to be conspicuous in the Big Thunder Mountain Railroad queue area acknowledged this attraction's lead Imagineer.

3. Mary Blair: Standing on the Eiffel Tower inside It's a Small World is a doll holding a balloon, representing the artist behind this attraction's look.

4. Wally Boag/Fulton Burley/Betty Taylor: These three entertainment legends are identified inside the Golden Horseshoe, where they performed for decades. All three are depicted in a Frontierland Hall of Fame portrait, identified as the "best entertainment in the West." During shows by the Laughing Stock Company, their names also appear on the backdrop—"Boag's Beans," "Fulton's Steel Cut Oats," and "Slue Foot Sue's Finishing School, Miss Taylor Head Mistress."

5. Pat Burke: The "Burke Assay Office" crate visible during the trip on the Big Thunder Mountain Railroad acknowledges one of this attraction's key Imagineers.

6. Joe Fowler: Fowler's Inn (at Fowler's Harbor in Frontierland) and a Fowler's Cellar sign (inside Splash Mountain) honor this Disney Legend, who was in charge of Disneyland's construction (*right*).

7. John Hench: In the interior halls of Space Mountain's queue is a Command Module sign in Bay 12 that names "Capt. J. Hench," a nod to one of the chief designers (*below right*).

8. Imagineers: The letters on the license plates of the Autopia cars are believed to be those of this attraction's various designers.

9. Jack Lindquist: Disneyland's first president (and its Honorary Mayor) is celebrated at Goofy's Playhouse, where a pumpkin carved in his likeness sits in the garden.

10. George Lucas: At Star Tours, listen for the page asking for "departing Endor passenger Sacul, Mr. Egroeg Sacul" ("George Lucas" spelled backward).

11. Leota Toombs: In the Haunted Mansion, "Madame Leota" is the name of the character inside the floating crystal ball. Toombs was a Disney artist whose image was used for the disembodied head.

12. Frank Wells: The display of "Frank Wells Expedition" equipment glimpsed from speeding Matterhorn Bobsleds commemorates this top Disney executive who was killed in a 1994 helicopter accident.

30 Profiles of Legendary Imagineers

In July 1954, the first volume of *The Lord of the Rings* trilogy, "The Fellowship of the Ring," was published in the United Kingdom. That same month, Disneyland construction began.

Like Gandalf, the wizard Walt Disney assembled around him his own "fellowship of the park," the vital allies who together would complete the mission he set for them.

Primarily, Disney drew on the amazing talent pool right in his own company—his Disney Studio animators, set decorators, and special effects innovators. Consequently, many of the thirty names that follow walked straight out of movie history and into Disneyland history. Collectively they became known as Imagineers, a hybrid term that merges imagination with engineering (Martin Sklar's *Dream It! Do It!* credits Harrison Price, listed below, with inventing the term, which Sklar defines as "the blending of creative imagination with technical know-how"). Most of these Imagineers are "Disney Legends," an honorary title the Walt Disney Company has been using since 1987 to recognize key contributors to the Disney legacy. The following summaries of their Disneyland accomplishments only scratch the surface of their far-ranging contributions. For more info, search the Disney Legends Web pages (www.d23.com/disney-legends) and see Kurtti's *Walt Disney's Imagineering Legends and the Genesis of the Disney Theme Park*. Three additional legendary Imagineers—Rolly Crump, Bob Gurr, and Jack Lindquist—are profiled on pages 182, 74, and 209, respectively.

As for Walt Disney himself, he knew what he was good at: "Of all the things I've done," he said in 1954, "the most vital is coordinating the talents of those who work for us and pointing them at a certain goal."

1. Ken Anderson (1909–1993): Anderson worked on Disney's animated films and then helped try to develop a nine-inch-tall "dancing man"—the earliest attempt at Audio-Animatronics. In the early 1950s, he joined the core Disneyland designers and laid out scenes for many Fantasyland attractions.

2. **Francis Xavier "X." Atencio (1920–):** After working as a Disney animator, Atencio started on Disneyland projects in the 1960s. He's best remembered for writing the scripts and song lyrics for Pirates of the Caribbean and the Haunted Mansion. Known by many as "X." (which is how he's identified on his Main Street Tribute Window), he even performed the sinister voice for the talking pirate skull at Pirates' first waterfall.

3. **Tony Baxter (1947–):** One of the most important Imagineers in recent decades, Baxter got a job as a teen scooping ice cream at Disneyland. In 1971, he began his Imagineering career building models and soon invented one of Disneyland's most exciting attractions, the Big Thunder Mountain Railroad. Before retiring in 2013, he spearheaded important new developments that energized every corner of the park: Star Tours, Splash Mountain, the Indiana Jones Adventure, and more. Fans recognize him as an articulate spokesperson on numerous Disney documentaries.

4. **Mary Blair (1911–1978):** One of Disneyland's most iconic attractions was given color and style by the prolific artist Mary Blair. She began working in the Disney Studios animation department in 1940, but two decades later Walt Disney himself invited her to design It's a Small World. In 1967, the main buildings in Tomorrowland were decorated with huge, beautiful tile mosaics of Blair's joyous art.

5. **Chuck Boyajian (1917–2004):** Walt Disney made immaculate cleanliness a key part of his Disneyland dream. Chuck Boyajian was in charge of the park's spotless reputation. Boyajian worked at Disneyland from its opening until 1981 as the manager of custodial operations, creating procedures, setting standards, and training cast members to keep Disneyland radiantly clean, even on its busiest days.

6. **Roger Broggie (1908–1991):** Renowned at the Disney Studios as a mechanical genius, Broggie developed special cameras and ran the machine shop. He was then instrumental in the creation of such varied attractions as Disneyland's original railroad, Great Moments with Mr. Lincoln, and the futuristic Monorail.

7. **Harriet Burns (1928–2008):** The first female Imagineer, Harriet Burns helped design Las Vegas hotels before joining Disney Studios in 1955. Switching to park projects, she was one of Disneyland's original model makers and thus was a key contributor to Sleeping Beauty Castle, New Orleans Square, and the Jungle Cruise, among many others. Her versatile artistry extended to pirate hair, mermaid costumes, and Tiki Room

plumage. She was, according to Martin Sklar's *Dream It! Do It!*, "Walt Disney's favorite Imagineer."

8. Claude Coats (1913–1992): Coats was one of the company's busiest and most gifted artists, known especially for his sublime background paintings in classic animated films like *Pinocchio* and *Fantasia*. At Disneyland he painted the displays and backgrounds on many Fantasyland attractions, created the Rainbow Caverns interiors for Frontierland's Mine Train, and added interior designs to Adventure Thru Inner Space, the Haunted Mansion, and Pirates of the Caribbean.

9. Bill Cottrell (1906–1995): A member of the Disney family (he was married to the sister of Walt Disney's wife), Cottrell was the first Disney employee to be recognized for fifty years of service. Writing and directing at Disney Studios, he made major contributions to *Snow White and the Seven Dwarfs* and *Pinocchio*, among others. At Disneyland, Cottrell was considered Walt Disney's "right-hand man"; in addition to planning and overseeing many park projects, he wrote scripts for attractions, added many important details, and was later promoted to president of the design and development department (today's Imagineers).

10. Marc Davis (1913–2000): One of Disney Studios' legendary "nine old men," Marc Davis created memorable characters (Tinker Bell, Cruella De Vil) for classic animated films. He became an Imagineer in 1961, and his creative contributions have been seen and heard all over Disneyland—jokes for the Enchanted Tiki Room, comic scenes for the Jungle Cruise and It's a Small World, musical characters for the Country Bear Jamboree and America Sings, humorous portraits in the Haunted Mansion, and entertaining scenes in Pirates of the Caribbean. His wife, Alice (another Disney Legend), was a costume designer who created hundreds of costumes for Disneyland attractions, among them It's a Small World, Pirates of the Caribbean, and the Carousel of Progress.

11. Marvin Davis (1910–1998): When it came to creating Disneyland's layout and overall design, Davis probably worked as closely with Walt Disney as anyone. Davis planned many specific areas and attractions, came up with over 100 variations of the main entrance, and helped create New Orleans Square. He also directed Disney movies and TV shows, winning an Emmy in 1962.

12. Roy O. Disney (1893–1971): Without the advice and efforts of his older brother, Roy, Walt Disney never would have been able to make his Disneyland dream a reality. Their roles were generally the same throughout their careers—Roy the financial leader (technically, he wasn't an Imagineer like the designers and artists) supported Walt the creative genius. Fiercely loyal to Walt and for over forty years the CEO of their company, Roy found and won over the investors who would back Disneyland's

construction. After Walt's death in 1966, Roy assumed leadership of the impending Walt Disney World and guided the immensely complex project to its 1971 opening.

13. Don Edgren (1923–2006): Whatever the Imagineers dreamed up, Don Edgren, leader of Disneyland's engineers, got it built. His team figured out how bobsleds would wind through Matterhorn Mountain and rockets would streak through Space Mountain. Their biggest challenge may have been Pirates of the Caribbean—what was originally designed as a walk-through exhibit became a subterranean boat ride requiring elaborate waterways and a new "show building" beyond the park's perimeter berm.

14. Morgan Evans (1910–2002): Guests who love Disneyland's landscaping can thank Morgan "Bill" Evans and his brother, Jack, the men who first planted Disneyland's flora. Hired to landscape the grounds of Walt Disney's private home, they then became Disneyland's chief landscape architects. They created a verdant, beautifully manicured park filled with lush environments (as on the Jungle Cruise) and elaborate floral patterns (as in the Mickey parterre at the entrance) that are impressive all year round.

15. Joe Fowler (1894–1993): The man in charge of building Disneyland was a naval architect who headed two dozen shipyards in the 1940s. After retiring as a rear admiral, Fowler oversaw Disneyland construction and had it built within a year. He then supervised operations into the next decade and spearheaded several complex developments—the Matterhorn, Submarine Voyage, Monorail, New Orleans Square, Haunted Mansion, Pirates of the Caribbean, and 1967's "new Tomorrowland." In Frontierland, Fowler's Harbor is named after him.

16. Van Arsdale France (1912–1999): One of Disneyland's hallmarks is its extraordinary customer service. Van Arsdale France instructed employees in their conduct, creating along the way many of the training techniques still used throughout corporate America. A labor relations expert in the 1940s, France was hired to make Disneyland cast members the most efficient and congenial employees anywhere, which he did by establishing the "Disney University" to teach Disneyland philosophy first and specific job skills second.

17. Blaine Gibson (1918–): Gibson's childhood sculpting hobby became his sculpting career. Though he worked in the Disney Studios animation department, Gibson started making models for Disneyland in the 1950s. For the next three decades, the works he and his sculpture department created were transformed into characters in such diverse attractions as the Enchanted Tiki Room, Great Moments with Mr. Lincoln, and the Haunted Mansion. Gibson's fair maiden graces the bow of the

Sailing Ship *Columbia*, and his famous *Partners* statue stands in Disneyland's Hub.

18. Harper Goff (1911–1993): After drawing illustrations for *Esquire* and other popular magazines in the 1930s, Goff started working at Disney Studios in the 1940s and later helped make 20,000 *Leagues Under the Sea* an Oscar-winning classic. Then, as one of Disneyland's first designers, he researched other parks and drew up early concept art. Goff oversaw Jungle Cruise construction and created the Golden Horseshoe's interior. Several of the Disneyland buildings he designed, including City Hall, were based on actual buildings in his hometown of Fort Collins, Colorado.

19. Yale Gracey (1910–1983): It's no coincidence that one of the characters in the 2003 film *The Haunted Mansion* is named Master Gracey; in fact, the whole eerie building carries the Gracey name, because Yale Gracey created many of the memorable special effects in Disneyland's Haunted Mansion. Born in China, Gracey was a Disney Studios animator when Walt Disney saw some of the homemade gadgets he had built. Disney then invited him to add special effects to Disneyland attractions, which included the ingenious "fire" that burns through the town in Pirates of the Caribbean.

20. John Hench (1908–2004): Many historians have concluded that no person—other than the man Disneyland was named after—had more influence on Disney theme parks, or understood them better, than John Hench. After fifteen years at Disney Studios as an artist and story editor, in 1954 Hench started shaping Disneyland's aesthetics, which meant that everything from attraction layout to garden landscaping to color schemes was within his purview. Hench was one of the chief designers of the *Moonliner*, New Orleans Square, the Carousel of Progress, Tomorrowland, and many Main Street buildings. Also, as Mickey Mouse's official portrait artist, he created new commemorative paintings for the star's birthdays.

21. Richard Irvine (1910–1976): Most Imagineers have led the way to new Disneyland attractions; but Richard Irvine led the Imagineers themselves. An Oscar-nominated art director, he contributed to such notable films as *Miracle on 34th Street* and Disney's *The Three Caballeros*. Joining the early Disneyland planning team, Irvine headed the group that created the attractions. After Walt Disney died in 1966, Irvine became Walt Disney World's master planner (an old-fashioned steamboat there is now named after him). His daughter-in-law, Kim Irvine, is an acclaimed Disneyland art director who has worked on everything from Rivers of America to the Disney Gallery.

22. Robert Jani (1934–1989): Disneyland's longtime entertainment specialist

invented imaginative productions that redefined the parade concept. In 1955, Jani was the first person to head Guest Relations, Disneyland's information and problem-solving department. In 1967, he became the entertainment director and later created two famous street shows, the patriotic America on Parade spectacular and the legendary Main Street Electrical Parade.

23. Fred Joerger (1913–2005): This craftsman turned drawings into intricate three-dimensional models. After starting out at Warner Bros. Studios, Joerger joined Disneyland's model-making team in 1953 and constructed elaborate miniatures of the *Mark Twain* Riverboat, the Jungle Cruise, Sleeping Beauty Castle, and Main Street buildings, all before they were built. (Not wanting to be misled by a "pretty picture," Walt Disney relied on models as his "secret weapon" for designing attractions, according to *Walt Disney Imagineering: A Behind the Dreams Look at Making MORE Magic Real*.) Joerger's 3-D Matterhorn rendering led to Disneyland's tallest structure, and his Haunted Mansion model preceded one of Disneyland's most famous attractions. Joerger also sculpted the faux rocks that add realistic atmosphere to Tom Sawyer Island and Pirates of the Caribbean.

24. Bill Justice (1914–2011): Animator, programmer, artist—Bill Justice wore many hats as a key Disney employee for over four decades. He began as an animator on early classics such as *Bambi* (Thumper was his creation) and then became a director of animated sequences for Disney movies and TV shows. In 1965, Justice switched to Disneyland attractions, particularly those involving sophisticated Audio-Animatronic figures (such as Great Moments with Mr. Lincoln and Pirates of the Caribbean). He also designed costumes for Disneyland's walk-around characters, devised floats for the parades, and painted murals for some of Fantasyland's attractions.

25. Bill Martin (1917–2010): Martin was a set designer recruited from 20th Century Fox. After joining Disneyland's planning team in 1953, he had a hand in nearly everything at the park—creating the look and layout of the original Fantasyland, helping to design many of the attractions, working on the big Nature's Wonderland area, and laying out the Monorail's long path. In the 1960s, Martin was a key architect of New Orleans Square, and helped design Walt Disney's New Orleans Square apartment. He became vice president of design in 1971.

26. Sam McKim (1924–2004): One of Disneyland' best souvenirs is a beautifully illustrated Fun Map. McKim drew the first of these, as well as the free Tom Sawyer Island maps. A child actor in numerous Westerns, McKim later became an artist for 20th Century Fox until a layoff eventually brought him to Disneyland, where he sketched new attractions

and worked closely with Walt Disney. His detailed concept drawings of Frontierland, the Golden Horseshoe, Main Street, the Monorail, New Orleans Square, and more still inspire modern Imagineers.

27. Harrison Price (1921–2010): While he wasn't a creative Imagineer who drew and designed, Price holds an esteemed place in Disneyland history—he's the man who found Anaheim for Walt Disney. "Buzz" Price was at the Stanford Research Institute consulting on key Disneyland decisions, especially its location (see page 24 for details about Price's input on Disneyland's location). With Disneyland a stunning success, Price formed his own consulting company and continued advising on Disney projects, including the location for Walt Disney World.

28. Wathel Rogers (1919–2000): A Disney employee for forty-eight years, Rogers started out as a film animator on such classics as *Pinocchio* and *Bambi*. Later, he made Disneyland models and worked on realistic Audio-Animatronic figures for the Enchanted Tiki Room, Pirates of the Caribbean, and Great Moments with Mr. Lincoln.

29. Herb Ryman (1910–1989): Few Disneyland artists have been as important as Ryman. On September 26–27, 1953, he drew a detailed aerial view of the unbuilt park as Walt Disney described it to him; that landmark sketch (*page 39*) was a key component of Roy Disney's successful presentations to potential investors. Ryman then helped design Sleeping Beauty Castle, the Jungle Cruise, Main Street buildings, and New Orleans Square. His Disneyland creations were the crowning achievements of a long art career that included stints as an illustrator at MGM, Disney Studios, and 20th Century Fox.

30. Sherman Brothers (Robert and Richard, 1925–2012 and 1928–): The two men behind many famous Disney songs were sons of a Tin Pan Alley composer. After writing hit songs for Annette Funicello, in 1960 the Shermans became Disney Studios' staff songwriters, crafting popular songs and soundtracks for *The Parent Trap*, *Mary Poppins*, and more (they also wrote a notable non-Disney hit, Johnny Burnette's "You're Sixteen"). For Disneyland, they wrote familiar theme songs for many attractions, most famously It's a Small World. The Sherman Brothers have received several Oscars and Grammy Awards, had blockbuster shows on Broadway, and been inducted into the Songwriters Hall of Fame.

10 Rules and Regulations for Cast Members

A wholesome, clean-cut image is a standard requirement to work at Disneyland, though the definition of "the Disney look" has gradually evolved. Here are few of the many clothing and grooming requirements paraphrased from past employee manuals. For more about cast members, refer to David Koenig's *Mouse Tales* books.

Men and Women

1. No visible tattoos (this rule is still in effect).

2. Prescription eyewear must be conservative (still in effect).

Men

3. No mustaches (this rule loosened up in 2000—fully grown-in mustaches can be the width of the mouth, though they can extend down past the corners of the mouth if they're meeting short beards; mustaches can't be grown over the upper lip).

4. No beards (short beards and goatees one-fourth of an inch long have been permitted since 2012; men with no facial hair must be clean-shaven).

5. Shirts must be tucked in (untucked shirts are now allowed).

Women

6. No earrings in pierced ears (one earring per pierced ear is now permitted, but still no nose rings or tongue piercings).

7. When wearing skirts, stockings are required (as per 2010 and 2013 updates, hosiery is now optional for most employment positions; if nylons are worn, they must be sheer, opaque, or subdued).

8. No eyeshadow, eyeliner, or fake eyelashes allowed (conservative, "natural-looking" mascara, blush, and lipstick are allowed).

9. Neutral is the only nail polish color allowed (this rule is still in effect; no decals are allowed, and nails may not extend more than one-fourth of an inch beyond the fingertip).

10. Hair color, even if it's artificial, must be "natural-looking"—no extreme colors or styles allowed (still in effect).

22 Terms and Nicknames Used by Cast Members

"Cast member" is what Disneyland calls an employee. The term indicates how visiting Disneyland is supposed to be like attending a theatrical show—employees aren't merely workers, they are costumed performers. Here are more terms in the unique vernacular that Disney Legend Martin Sklar calls the "Disneyland Dictionary," plus some insider nicknames.

1. "Attraction": A Disneyland ride.

2. "Backstage": A behind-the-scenes area (kitchen, office, etc.) hidden from guests.

3. "Bertha": The employees' nickname for the Jungle Cruise elephant that sprays water.

4. "Blood Alley": Disney Legend Van France's *Window on Main Street* claims this was the old nickname for the Autopia.

5. "Bucky": Nickname for the Fantasmic! dragon.

6. "Casting Center": Disney's employment office.

7. "Christine": A Main Street driver told us that this nickname was given to Main Street's red horseless carriage after it ran over a cast member's foot (the nickname comes from the killer car in Stephen King's novel *Christine*).

8. "CM": Cast member.

9. "Costume": An employee's uniform.

10. "Food Host/Hostess": Waiter/waitress.

11. "Fuzzies": Walk-around characters with full face-concealing costumes.

12. "Guest": Customer.

13. "Harold": Nickname for the Matterhorn's Abominable Snowman.

14. "I'll find out": The preferred alternative to any question that would lead to a "no" or "I don't know" answer.

15. "Murphy": When the updated Fantasmic! dragon was breaking down frequently in 2009, cast members gave it this nickname (as in Murphy's Law).

16. "Old Smiley": Nickname for the Jungle Cruise's open-mouthed crocodile.

17. "Onstage": An area intended to be seen by guests.

18. "Pixie dust": John Van Maanen, a noted ethnographer and MIT professor who was fired from his job as a Disneyland ride operator in the 1960s, says in his lecture video *Cultural Collisions* that cast members spread this on #19 (*below*) before cleaning it up.

19. "Protein spill" (also "Code V"): Euphemism for vomit.

20. "Quick-service restaurant": Fast-food counter.

21. "Screamers and dreamers": According to Van Maanen, these are cast members' terms for roller coasters and slow, "drifting Small World kind of rides."

22. "Todayland": According to Bright in his book *Disneyland: Inside Story*, this is what a frustrated Walt Disney nicknamed Tomorrowland.

69 Famous People Who Worked or Performed at Disneyland

Here are the greats and the near-greats, listed alphabetically with performances in parentheses.

1. Louis Armstrong, jazz legend (performed live, 1960s)
2. Frankie Avalon, 1950s pop singer (appeared in a 1996 parade)
3. Backstreet Boys, 1990s/2000s pop group (2012 TV special)
4. Drew Barrymore, actress (1985 TV special)
5. Tony Baxter, future Imagineer (worked at the Carnation Plaza Gardens, 1960s)
6. Chuck Berry, 1950s rock legend (performed live, 1970s)
7. Mary J. Blige, pop singer (2013 TV special)
8. Pat Boone, 1950s pop singer (performed live, 1960s)
9. Les Brown, jazz legend (performed live, 1960s)
10. George Burns, comedian (1988 TV special)
11. Cab Calloway, jazz legend (performed live, 1960s)
12. Glen Campbell, 1970s country singer (1976 TV special)
13. Nick Cannon, actor (2013 TV special)
14. Richard Carpenter, one-half of the Carpenters (performed live at Coke Corner, 1967)
15. Chubby Checker, 1960s pop star (performed live, 1980s)
16. Roy Clark, 1970s country singer (1985 TV special)
17. Kevin Costner, actor/director (Michael Eisner's memoir *Work in Progress* states that Costner "met his future wife, Cyndi, when they both appeared as characters in the daily parade along Main Street")
18. Count Basie, jazz legend (performed live, 1960s)
19. The Cowsills, 1960s rock group (performed live, 1970s)
20. Tony Danza, actor (1990 TV special)
21. Jackie DeShannon, 1960s pop singer (performed live, 1970s)
22. Sandy Duncan, actress (1974 and 1976 TV specials)
23. Buddy Ebsen, actor (performed on Opening Day)
24. Duke Ellington, jazz legend (performed live, 1960s)
25. Annette Funicello, actress (performed on Opening Day and in 1960s *Walt Disney's Wonderful World of Color* episodes)
26. Teri Garr, actress (performed in Tomorrowland's *Show Me America*, 1970)

27. Gary Lewis and the Playboys, 1960s pop group (performed live, 1960s)

28. Bobbie Gentry, 1970s country singer (performed live, 1970s)

29. Benny Goodman, jazz legend (performed live, 1960s)

30. Al Green, 1970s soul singer (performed live, 1972)

31. Lionel Hampton, jazz legend (performed live, 1960s)

32. Helen Hayes, actress (1974 TV special)

33. Woody Herman, jazz legend (performed live, 1960s)

34. Herman's Hermits, 1960s pop group (performed live, 1980s)

35. Harry James, jazz legend (performed live, 1960s)

36. Jay and the Americans, 1960s pop group (performed live, 1960s)

37. Danny Kaye, actor (1980 TV special)

38. Evelyn "Champagne" King, 1970s disco star (performed live, 1980s)

39. Gene Krupa, jazz legend (performed live, 1960s)

40. Lady Antebellum, 2000s country group (performed live, 2013)

41. John Lasseter, director/Pixar's chief creative officer (Tomorrowland sweeper, Jungle Cruise skipper, 1970s)

42. Jay Leno, comedian (1986 TV special)

43. Kenny Loggins, 1970s pop star (performed live, 2000)

44. Demi Lovato, 2000s pop singer (2013 TV special)

45. Lovin' Spoonful, 1960s rock group (performed live, 1960s)

46. Steve Martin, comedian/actor/author (sold souvenir guidebooks and worked in the two magic shops, 1950s–1960s)

47. Moody Blues, 1960s rock group (1986 TV special)

48. Osmond Brothers, 1960s pop group (performed live, 1960s)

49. Patti Page, 1950s pop singer (performed live, 1960s)

50. Fess Parker, actor (performed on Opening Day)

51. Paul Revere and the Raiders, 1960s pop group (performed live, 1980s)

52. Peaches and Herb, 1970s disco group (performed live, 1970s)

53. Michelle Pfeiffer, actress (costumed as "Alice" in parades, 1970s)

54. Carl Reiner, comedian (1988 TV special)

55. The Righteous Brothers, 1960s pop group (performed live, 1960s)

56. John Ritter, actor (1988 TV special)

57. Linda Ronstadt, 1970s pop singer (performed live, 1971)

58. Kurt Russell, actor (1970 and 2013 TV specials)

59. Ryan Seacrest, entertainer (2000 TV special)

60. Jerry Seinfeld, comedian (1986 TV special)

61. Smokey Robinson and the Miracles, 1960s soul group (performed live, 1971)

62. John Stamos, actor (performed live with the Instant Replay Band, 2008)

63. The Turtles, 1960s pop group (performed live, 1980s)

64. Dick Van Dyke, actor (performed live with the Dapper Dans, 1999)

65. Debra Winger, actress (costumed character, 1972)

66. Stevie Wonder, soul legend (2009 TV special)

67. Trisha Yearwood, 2000s country singer (2014 TV special)

68. The Young Rascals, 1960s pop group (performed live, 1960s)

69. Ron Ziegler, Nixon's press secretary (Jungle Cruise skipper, 1960s)

Donny Osmond
Remembers His Disneyland Childhood

The Osmond Brothers began their careers singing barbershop, and in 1962 debuted at Disneyland on Main Street, U.S.A. Donny Osmond joined his brothers onstage when he was only five years old, debuting on *The Andy Williams Show*. Shortly thereafter, the singing family began appearing regularly on televisions throughout the world. By the 1970s, Donny was a teen idol sensation, and would ultimately become a versatile entertainment legend. In the following list, he answers eight questions about his Disneyland childhood in this exclusive interview.

1. **The Disneyland crowds that watched the Osmond Brothers in the early 1960s had probably never seen the Osmonds sing live before. How did they react as you performed?**
   "By the time I joined my brothers onstage, most people had started to recognize the Osmond name. I've always recalled receiving a favorable response from Disneyland crowds. Besides, Disneyland is 'The Happiest Place on Earth'; no one is going to throw tomatoes there, or even 'One Bad Apple'!"

2. **You performed in several Disneyland locations—which one was your favorite? Did you have a favorite song?**
   "I remember performing on the Tomorrowland Stage—it stood where the Captain EO Tribute attraction is today. My brothers and I performed

there a few times, but I especially recall one instance when Kurt Russell introduced us. Alan, Wayne, Merrill, Jay, and I performed 'Golden Rainbow,' 'Aquarius,' and 'Let the Sunshine In.'"

3. Do you have a favorite memory relating to your Disneyland performances?

"My favorite memories of Disneyland are of the Haunted Mansion (it sounds funny to say, but it's true!). There were rooms on the upper floors of that building where I remember doing my schoolwork as a boy. Because my brothers and I were constantly on the road, attending a regular school to earn an education wasn't possible; instead, we had tutors and our mother. Whenever we had breaks from our performances, we would go back to the Haunted Mansion and work on algebra or English lessons. Quite literally, the Haunted Mansion was my schoolhouse. So, for all those kids out there who think school is a scary place, try learning with ghosts and witches haunting your classroom!"

4. Did you have a favorite attraction back then?

"I loved, and still do love, Autopia. I've probably ridden that ride hundreds of times throughout my life. As a young parent, I remember taking my children on the ride; now as a grandparent, I've taken my grandchildren on it as well."

5. Did you have any favorite foods or treats at Disneyland back then?

"Nope. But I am sure I raided just about every ice cream cart in the park. Okay, now that I think about it . . . ice cream sandwiches . . . and popcorn . . . and a Mickey ice cream bar. I guess I did have a few favorites."

6. What was your favorite place to visit at Disneyland?

"I've always been enthralled with innovation and technology. My favorite place to visit at Disneyland is Tomorrowland. As a child I remember going through the attractions there and looking at displays of upcoming innovation. I always thought it was a cool place to visit. I can still sing the song, 'It's a great big beautiful tomorrow. . .'"

7. As you made visits in later years, what became your favorite attraction?

"I love big thrill rides. Although, now what I love most is taking my children and grandchildren to Disneyland, and watching their reactions as they experience the attractions for themselves. But I always go back to the Haunted Mansion for old times' sake. Plus, it's fun to hear the voices of Candy Candido and Paul Frees—good friends of mine who did many of the voices on the attraction."

8. If you could bring back one thing that's no longer at Disneyland, what would it be?

"The PeopleMover. I remember riding it throughout the years. I really hope Disney is able to reinstate that ride, or use the track somehow. It seems a shame to see an abandoned elevated track in Tomorrowland."

40 Long-Lasting Park Performers

These groups enjoyed long runs performing at Disneyland.

Adventureland

1. Alturas
2. Royal Tahitians
3. Trinidad & Tobago Showboat Steel Orchestra

Fantasyland

4. Make Believe Brass
5. Pearly Band
6. Royal Jesters

Frontierland

7. Big Thunder Breakdown Boys
8. Billy Hill and the Hillbillies
9. Firehouse Five Plus Two
10. Gonzalez Trio
11. Laughing Stock Company
12. Strawhatters

Hub/Main Street/Town Square

13. All-American College Band
14. Charles Dickens Carolers, aka Holiday Carolers
15. Coke Corner Pianist
16. Dapper Dans
17. Date Niters
18. Hook and Ladder Company
19. Keystone Cops
20. Main Street Maniacs
21. Sax Quintet

New Orleans Square

22. Bayou Brass Band
23. Bilge Rats & Bootstrappers
24. Delta Ramblers
25. Gloryland Brass Band
26. Jambalaya Jazz Band
27. Jazz Minors
28. Jolly Roger
29. New Orleans Traditional Jazz Band
30. Orleans Street Band
31. River Rascals
32. Royal Street Bachelors
33. Side Street Strutters
34. Young Men from New Orleans

Tomorrowland

35. Kids of the Kingdom
36. Krash
37. Mustangs
38. Papa Doo Run Run
39. Pizzazz
40. Trash Can Trio

22 Celebrities Who Narrated the Holiday Candlelight Procession

The Candlelight Procession is one of the inspirational highlights of the holiday season. First performed in 1958, the Candlelight Procession sends legions of carolers and candles down a garlanded Main Street toward Town Square and culminates with a dramatic retelling of the traditional Christmas story. Celebrities usually serve as the event's narrator. Here are twenty-two of them, listed alphabetically. (These narrators are different from the celebrities who have presided over "the official lighting of Disneyland Park," a holiday tradition started in 1999 by Bob Hope.)

1. Beau Bridges
2. Henry Fonda
3. Cary Grant
4. Marcia Gay Harden
5. Patricia Heaton
6. Charlton Heston
7. Rock Hudson
8. Dean Jones
9. James Earl Jones
10. Dennis Morgan
11. Gregory Peck
12. Lou Diamond Phillips
13. Molly Ringwald
14. Mickey Rooney
15. Kurt Russell
16. Jane Seymour
17. Gary Sinise
18. John Stamos
19. Blair Underwood
20. Dick Van Dyke
21. Jon Voight
22. John Wayne

A Dozen Unique Characters No Longer Seen in Disneyland

Unlike the many Disney characters who walk around Disneyland in full costume with headgear that conceals their faces, most of the people in the following list were "face characters" whose faces were exposed (such as today's Disney princes and princesses).

1. Aunt Jemima: From 1955 to 1970, Aunt Jemima's Pancake House in Frontierland featured an Aunt Jemima character who greeted guests.

2. Black Bart: A classic Western villain who participated in mock Frontierland shootouts with Sheriff Lucky (also no longer seen) in the 1950s.

3. Indiana Jones: An Indy character appeared at 1995's "40 Years of Adventure" celebration. In the summer of 2008, when *Indiana Jones and the Kingdom of the Crystal Skull* brought the famed archaeologist back to movie theaters, Indy put on live shows involving a chase in Adventureland.

4. Juggler: In the early 1960s, a costumed character juggled, performed magic tricks, and occasionally rode a unicycle in Fantasyland.

5. Knight: Inside the Haunted Mansion was a cast member in knight's armor who would periodically lunge at guests to frighten them.

6. Mr. Hyde/Phantom of the Opera: When the silent films *Dr. Jekyll and Mr. Hyde* and *The Phantom of the Opera* were on the Main Street Cinema's marquee in the mid-1960s, these creepy ghouls (who wore formal clothing and appeared to be the same character) stood outside the theater.

7. Organ Grinder: In the 1950s, this old-fashioned character had an actual monkey with him on Main Street.

8. Rocket Man: A white-suited character jetpacked over Tomorrowland during 1965's winter holidays.

9. Shoeshine Boys: For most of the 1960s, two colorfully costumed youths shined shoes and danced, first in Town Square and later in New Orleans Square.

10. Space Girl/Space Man: This futuristic couple used to walk around Tomorrowland in unrealistic "astronaut" costumes (Space Girl had a cape).

11. Tom Sawyer: In the 1950s and 1960s, a freckle-faced teen named Tom Nabbe played the barefoot boy out on Tom Sawyer Island, where he fished and showed guests around.

12. Zorro: From 1958 to 1960, five weekends of Zorro Days brought out the dashing sword-wielding hero to promote Disney's TV show.

A Mermaid's Memories

When the new Submarine Voyage launched in mid-1959, eight costumed mermaids splashed around in Tomorrowland's lagoon as part of the celebratory festivities. Six years later, Disneyland brought back a new group of mermaids for three consecutive summers. Though the mermaids were popular, extensive exposure to the lagoon's chlorine eventually became a concern, and park officials finally whistled everyone out of the pool in 1967.

One of 1959's mermaids was an eighteen-year-old brunette named Susan Musfelt (now Susan Hoose). After her summer frolicking as a mermaid, Susan (*page 281, seated*) attended Arizona State University, where she met her future husband. Back in California, they raised four children (her marriage and her kids, she says, are her proudest accomplishments). Now living in Scottsdale, Arizona, Susan took time out from her busy real estate career to recall her Disneyland experience with this list of six mermaid-related topics.

1. Tryouts

"In early 1959, I responded to a newspaper ad that was a cattle call for 'potential mermaids' at Disneyland. Hundreds of girls showed up at the Disneyland Hotel. As I recall, the age requirements were eighteen to twenty-four, and you had to have long hair and swimming experience. Fortunately I'd had four years of experience swimming aqua ballet in high school, and I would turn eighteen before the submarines opened. I came directly from softball practice still wearing my shirt and shorts— being the only girl not in a bikini, I must have stood out. We were told to line up in rows of fifteen or twenty, and a man and a woman walked through the rows checking us out. I certainly didn't know what they were looking for. Those of us who were tapped were asked to go sit down near the side of the pool."

2. Swimming

"About forty girls made it to the swimming part of the tryouts, but at least half dropped out before they even got into the water, once they realized what was expected. As our names were called, we were asked to stand at the deep end of the hotel's pool. Our ankles and wrists were tied with a soft cloth, and we were instructed to dive in and then 'porpoise' swim the length of the pool underwater as lifeguards watched over us. I had seen a couple girls succeed before my name was called, so I knew it was possible. When I dove in, I found myself sinking clear to the bottom. My stomach grazed the bottom of the pool before I felt myself gradually rising. The porpoise movement propelled me to the shallow end, where lifeguards helped me untie and climb out of the pool. I was instructed to leave my name and phone number, I was handed a book of ride tickets, and I was thanked for coming. I had no idea whether I had succeeded or not. My family was excited that I had tried out and even more excited when, that same week, my father got a call from a Disney executive informing him that I had been selected. I was thrilled—my first real job, and I was going to be making $45 a week as a Disneyland mermaid!"

3. Practice

"Training was rigorous, and it was difficult to juggle swimming, school, finals, and graduation. For months prior to the grand opening, the mermaids met each afternoon at the Disneyland Hotel's pool. Hour after hour, we practiced synchronized routines. We weren't wearing the fins yet because they were still being built. The first time we swam in the Tomorrowland lagoon was only a few weeks before the June 14 grand opening. Construction was ongoing around us; I remember seeing scaffolding and workmen up on the Matterhorn, and work continued up until the last minute. I didn't meet Walt Disney personally, but we were introduced to him as a group just prior to the grand opening."

4. Submarines

"Once the Submarine Voyage began running that summer, I took the opportunity to ride in a sub to get a better perspective of how the mermaids were viewed. From the small portholes in front of their seats, passengers could see the mermaids as we swam past while music and a running commentary were piped into the sub. For the mermaids, the view was limited. We could not see any faces inside the sub—the windows appeared blank underwater. I smiled, waved, and did flips and turns with my fins. We never surfaced until the sub had passed. The water was only fifty-five degrees and felt freezing cold, so between the subs we sat on the rocks, warming in the sun [*page 327*]."

5. Costumes

"We wore halter tops and matching tails. The tails were heavy rubber and came in different colors; I wore green. We slipped our feet into the fins and then flipped over to our stomachs to be zipped into the tails by two young men. Holding our hands, they then lowered us into the water. This process was reversed whenever we needed to get out of the water. Years later I thought I recognized the fins we wore when I saw Daryl Hannah in the movie *Splash*."

6. The Public

"We entered the water from a dock behind the scenes, so the public's first view of us came when we were already swimming. We'd swim on and off for about two hours and then get a forty-five-minute break. There was no verbal interaction between the mermaids and the public. In fact, we were instructed to remain in the middle of the lagoon, which put us too far from the public to interact verbally (although we could hear them call out to us). One afternoon, some boys jumped into the water to swim out to us, but they were intercepted by Disney personnel and never reached the rocks where we were sitting. Ultimately, being a mermaid and having the opportunity to work for Walt Disney was fantastic, and I treasure those memories."

LIVE SHOWS, EXHIBITS, AND SPECIAL EVENTS

A New Concept in Entertainment

10 Times of the Year When Disneyland Dresses Up for the Holidays

Kids of all ages love to play dress-up; so does Disneyland, which gets decked out with special décor for special events. In fact, these days Disneyland spends so many weeks embellished with celebratory décor that it's rare to find the park in "normal" mode!

1. Valentine's Day: Two weeks of hearts and flowers.

2. Mardi Gras: Music, beads, and special foods turn New Orleans Square into party central for several winter weeks.

3. Easter: The Easter Bunny, pastel colors, parades, and even interactive bunny hops down Main Street have been featured during this week.

4. Mother's Day: Free flowers, displays, and a few special menus.

5. Memorial Day: Bunting, flags, and red, white, and blue flowers throughout Town Square and Main Street constitute a patriotic tribute.

6. Fourth of July: Disneyland is packed with guests who come for lots of red, white, and blue and a week of special fireworks.

7. Dia de los Muertos: Though this event overlaps with Halloween, the skeletons (*right*) and colorful exhibits in Frontierland's El Zocalo Park make it clear that the two celebrations are separate.

8. Halloween: Since 2006, Halloween Time has been a major event celebrated for over a month, featuring themed food, merchandise, fireworks, new décor on Space Mountain and the Haunted Mansion, a sixteen-foot-tall jack-o'-lantern on Main Street, and hundreds of smaller carved pumpkins throughout Disneyland.

9. Thanksgiving: In years past, the presidentially pardoned turkey was on display during this holiday. Nowadays, Disneyland is filled with holiday decorations and seasonal foods.

10. Christmas: December has been an important (and lucrative) month for Disneyland, when special parades and fireworks, holiday-themed foods and merchandise, Santa and live reindeer, elaborate winter decorations (which start appearing in early fall), and even snow have combined to make this the year's most festive season.

47 Disneyland Parades

Extravagant parades have been a daily Disney-land ritual since Opening Day. Typically (but not always), they begin deep in Fantasyland and travel south to Town Square, lasting about a half hour and often culminating with an appearance by Mickey Mouse. Parades might include vehicles, horses, circus acts, elaborate floats, Disney characters, live music, street performers who interact with the crowd, celebrities, and anything else the Imagineers can dream up. The Main Street Electrical Parade, which is featured on a Main Street Tribute Window, is probably Disneyland's most famous parade; the Candlelight Procession, which debuted in 1958 and still runs every holiday season, is the longest-lasting. Here are forty-seven park parades and "street spectaculars," listed in chronological order.

1. 1955: Opening Day Parade
2. 1955: Mickey Mouse Club Circus Parade
3. 1955: Christmas Show Parade
4. 1956: Antique Automobile Parade (aka Old Fashioned Automobile Parade)
5. 1957–1960; 1962–1964: Christmas in Many Lands Parade
6. 1958–ongoing: Candlelight Procession
7. 1958–1959: Zorro Days Parade
8. 1960–1964: Mickey at the Movies Parade
9. 1961–1962: Parade of All Nations
10. 1961–1962: Parade of Toys
11. 1965–1976; 1980–1985: Fantasy on Parade
12. 1965: Tencennial Parade
13. 1967: Easter Parade
14. 1968: Valentine's Day Party
15. 1968: St. Patrick's Day Parade
16. 1968: Cinco de Mayo Fiesta
17. 1969; 1974: Love Bug Day Parade
18. 1972–1975; 1977–1983; 1985–1996: Main Street Electrical Parade
19. 1974: Viva Mexico Parade

20. 1975–1976: America on Parade
21. 1977–1979; 1987–1994: Very Merry Christmas Parade
22. 1980–1981: Family Reunion Parade
23. 1983: Flights of Fantasy Parade
24. 1984: Donald Duck's 50th Birthday Parade
25. 1985: Disneyland 30th Anniversary Parade
26. 1986: Totally Minnie Parade
27. 1986–1988: Circus on Parade
28. 1987: *Snow White and the Seven Dwarfs* Golden Anniversary Celebration Parade
29. 1987–1988: Come to the Fair Parade
30. 1990: Party Gras Parade
31. 1991: Celebration USA Parade
32. 1992: World According to Goofy Parade
33. 1993–1994: Aladdin's Royal Caravan Parade
34. 1994–1997: Lion King Celebration
35. 1994–ongoing: Christmas Fantasy Parade
36. 1997–1998: Hercules Victory Parade
37. 1997: Light Magic
38. 1998–1999: Mulan Parade
39. 2000–2005: 45 Years of Magic Parade
40. 2000–2005: Parade of the Stars
41. 2005: Mickey's Shining Star Cavalcade
42. 2005: Sleeping Beauty's Royal Celebration
43. 2005: Mickey's Magic Kingdom Celebration
44. 2005–2008: Walt Disney's Parade of Dreams
45. 2009–2010: Celebrate! A Street Party
46. 2011–2015: Mickey's Soundsational Parade
47. 2015–ongoing: Paint the Night

Ooh . . . Ahh . . .
9 of Disneyland's Dazzling Fireworks Shows

Disneyland is known for its spectacular fireworks shows. Besides the famous fireworks that began launching above Fantasyland in mid-1957, the park also features the Fireworks Factory in Mickey's Toontown and the Laod Bhang & Co. Rocket Factory, colorfully advertised on a Frontierland wall. Here are nine fireworks shows in the park (listed chronologically with their debut years in parentheses).

1. Fantasy in the Sky (1957)

2. Believe . . . There's Magic in the Stars (2000)

3. Believe . . . In Holiday Magic (2000)

4. Imagine . . . A Fantasy in the Sky (2004)

5. Remember . . . Dreams Come True (2005)

6. Disney's Celebrate America! A 4th of July Concert in the Sky (2008)

7. Halloween Screams: A Villainous Surprise in the Skies (2009)

8. Magical: Disney's New Nighttime Spectacular of Magical Celebrations (2009)

9. Disneyland Forever (2015)

Disneyland at the Tournament of Roses Parade

When it comes to theme parks and bowl games, Disneyland and the Rose Bowl could both be called "the granddaddy of them all." In 1960, Disneyland began hosting the two teams playing in the Rose Bowl on New Year's Day. Additionally, Walt Disney and Disneyland have made several appearances at Pasadena's famous Tournament of Roses Parade, held in early January since 1890 and televised since 1947 (the 1954 parade, televised one year before Disneyland was first represented with a float, was the first-ever national TV broadcast of a color program). Appearances by movie characters (as in the 1938, 1971, and 1973 parades), and the Disney California Adventure floats of 2004 and 2013, are not included in this chronological list. For an extensive examination of all things connecting Disney with the Tournament of Roses, see Jim Korkis's "A Brief History of Disney and the Rose Parade" articles on www.mouseplanet.com.

1. 1955: Six months before Opening Day, Disneyland's first float in the Tournament of Roses Parade featured Mickey Mouse and representations of the castle and the upcoming Dumbo attraction. Though simple by today's standards, this float won an award.

2. 1966: Four months before the Fantasyland attraction opened, It's a Small World was the theme of the 77th Rose Parade; Walt Disney rode in a

big white convertible as Grand Marshal.

3. 1990: The unique, forty-foot-long Mouseorail—a vehicle shaped like Disneyland's Monorail—drove through the parade before heading out on a national tour to promote Disneyland's thirty-fifth anniversary.

4. 2000: Roy E. Disney, Walt Disney's nephew, was Grand Marshal of the 111th Rose Parade (making Disney the only family represented by two Grand Marshals).

5. 2005: With Mickey Mouse as Grand Marshal, Disneyland touted its fiftieth birthday with a beautiful castle-themed float called "The Happiest Celebration on Earth."

6. 2006: Audiences were again reminded of Disneyland's fiftieth with "The Most Magical Celebration on Earth," a spectacular castle-themed float that was, at 150 feet long, about the same length as the five-car Disneyland Monorail.

7. 2007: The City of Anaheim celebrated its 150th birthday with an "Always Fresh & Never Grows Old" float featuring local landmarks, one of which was a monorail.

11 Live Stage Shows at the Fantasyland Theatre

Videopolis was a $3-million, state-of-the-art concert area that opened in Fantasyland in 1985. Catering to teenagers for its first decade, Videopolis was billed as "a musical kaleidoscope of sight and sound" and offered boisterous nighttime concerts. As teens gradually lost interest, the theater was eventually repurposed for live family-oriented stage shows. The results were so successful that in 1995, Videopolis received a more traditional theater name—Fantasyland Theatre. These shows usually lasted one or two years and became increasingly spectacular: *Snow White: An Enchanting Musical* boasted a performance by actor Patrick Stewart, elaborate sets, and a Broadway production team. In 2006, the space was reinvented as a new themed area called the Princess Fantasy Faire, but the Fantasyland Theatre name returned in 2013 with *Mickey and the Magical Map*. Here are eleven shows that have appeared on the Fantasyland Theatre stage since 1989.

1. 1989–1990: *One Man's Dream* (based on Walt Disney's life)

2. 1990: *Dick Tracy Starring in Diamond Double-Cross* (based on the 1990 movie)

3. 1991: *Plane Crazy* (starring Baloo)

4. Winter season, 1991; winter season, 1992: *Mickey's Nutcracker*

5. 1992–1995: *Beauty and the Beast* (based on the 1991 movie)

6. 1995–1997: *The Spirit of Pocahontas* (based on the 1995 movie)

7. 1998–2001: *Animazement: The Musical* (a tribute to Disney animation)

8. 2001–2002: *Mickey's Detective School* (Disney characters search for Pluto)

9. Winter season, 2001; winter season, 2002: *Minnie's Christmas Party*

10. 2004–2006: *Snow White—An Enchanting Musical* (based on the 1937 movie)

11. 2013–ongoing: *Mickey and the Magical Map* (incorporating new high-tech effects)

13 Educational Exhibits

Disneyland has enthusiastically hosted many educational exhibits that have sought to inform, not sell. These exhibits have fulfilled one of Walt Disney's stated goals for even building Disneyland in the first place; a year before the park opened, Disney told *Look* magazine that he wanted Disneyland to be a place "for teachers and pupils to discover greater ways of understanding and education." These thirteen chronologically listed exhibits have made education a priority.

1. **Davy Crockett Frontier Museum: July 1955–October 1955**
   Capitalizing on the success of TV's Davy Crockett episodes, Imagineers installed Davy Crockett displays inside the big Frontierland building that is today's Pioneer Mercantile. The highlight was a detailed, life-size re-creation of a meeting between Crockett (resembling actor Fess Parker, who portrayed Crockett on the show), his sidekick George Russel (with one "l," and a Buddy Ebsen lookalike), and Andrew Jackson (a dead ringer for Andrew Jackson) inside Jackson's headquarters.

2. **World Beneath Us Exhibit: 1955–1959**
   In 1955, Richfield Oil sponsored two different Tomorrowland locations. One—the Autopia—used gas, while the other—the World Beneath Us Exhibit—promoted it, in the building where Little Green Men Store Command is today. The exhibit featured a cartoon that had prehistoric cavemen teaching modern audiences about oil formation. Afterward, a diorama and L.A. map spotlighted oil fields along the coast.

3. **Hall of Chemistry: 1955–1966**
   Today's Star Tours building was adorned in 1955 with atoms and the red Monsanto logo. Inside was a free walk-through exhibit that celebrated chemical engineering with oversized test tubes and electrified wall displays.

4. **Upjohn Pharmacy: 1955–1970**
   The Upjohn Company (now part of Pfizer) was a huge pharmaceutical manufacturer that recreated a turn-of-the-century apothecary on Main

Street where today's Fortuosity Shop sits. Old-fashioned medicines and antique equipment lined the shelves and counters, but it was a display of leeches that riveted guests' attention. While nothing was for sale, jars of all-purpose vitamin pills were freely dispensed. A side room displayed the latest in 1955 pharmaceutical technology.

5. **Indian Village: 1955–1971**
   In 1955, the realistic Indian Village opened along Frontierland's western border. For the first few months, the area consisted of a few teepees and simple wooden structures that recreated the dwellings of various nineteenth-century Plains Indians, with actual Native Americans demonstrating their customs and ceremonial dances. Unlike most of Disneyland, the village had dusty dirt paths winding through it instead of paved sidewalks. Within a year, the Indian Village was relocated farther north to a larger space with an ornate dance circle, additional teepees, lodges, and a burial ground. Demonstrations of archery and displays of arts and crafts added to the fun. Despite a 1962 remodel, dwindling interest and mounting labor problems led to the village's end in 1971 so that Bear Country could move in.

6. **Hall of Aluminum Fame: 1955–1960**
   In Disneyland's first year, Walt Disney needed some Tomorrowland sponsors who could provide their own exhibits, thus freeing him to concentrate his time and money elsewhere. Late in 1955, the Kaiser Aluminum & Chemical Company debuted its shiny Hall of Aluminum Fame in the building that would eventually house Star Tours. Guests walked through the base of a giant telescope and entered a room lined with displays showing the history and uses of aluminum.

7. **Bathroom of Tomorrow: 1956–1960**
   This unusual exhibit was born nine months after Opening Day in today's Star Tours building. The Crane Plumbing Company installed a twenty-foot-wide bathroom display that guests could examine (but not use). Flush with enthusiasm, Crane added to the excitement with separate laundry facilities and a kids' play area called Fun with Water (a colorful mobile, plus guest-controlled fountains and spigots). While it's easy to joke about an archaic exhibit with a posture-enhancing toilet seat, the Bathroom of Tomorrow was a serious attempt to show technology impacting the modern world.

8. **American Rifle Exhibit and Frontier Gun Shop: 1956–ca. 1986**
   The glass cases in this Frontierland exhibit displayed antique weapons from American history, including various muskets, Kentucky rifles, and Colt pistols (a nearby Gun Shop sold replicas). In 1987, the building was transformed into Pioneer Mercantile, which still displays some antique guns on its walls.

9. **House of the Future: 1957–1967**

The House of the Future was a free walk-through exhibit located outside Tomorrowland's entrance. Some 20 million guests (more than the entire population of California back then) walked through this tract home designed by MIT and Monsanto engineers to show off advances in plastics technology. The house stood on a platform surrounded by contemporary gardens and a winding pool that collectively covered about a quarter of an acre (the pool was part of the building's cooling system). From above, the 1,280-square-foot, three-bedroom, two-bath home was shaped like a graceful plus sign. Its four compartmentalized modules were each eight feet tall and sixteen feet long and extended from a central core outwards over open air. Pre-recorded narration proclaimed that nearly everything on view was artificial and adjustable. Some of these features included push-button bathroom fixtures, cabinet shelves that could be raised or lowered, and a climate-controlled air system that could be instantly warmed, cooled, purified, or scented. The futuristic communications included an intercom, picture phones, and a sound system in the shower. Highlights in the "step saver" kitchen included an "ultrasonic dishwasher" and a microwave oven. Eventually, the two-week demolition had to be done by hand with crowbars and saws because the wrecking ball merely bounced off the house's resilient sides.

10. **Fashions and Fabrics Through the Ages: 1965**

In 1965, Monsanto installed a fashion exhibit near Tomorrowland's entrance. Wall displays and mannequins showed the evolution of women's garments, beginning with ragged animal skins worn by cavewomen and culminating with synthetic spacewear.

11. **Great Moments with Mr. Lincoln: 1965–1973; 1975–2005; 2009–ongoing**

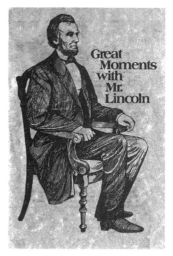

A decade of advances in Audio-Animatronic technology culminated in 1964 with the creation of a mechanical Abraham Lincoln for the 1964–1965 New York World's Fair. The life-size electronic effigy incorporated everything Disney designers had learned from the mechanical animals made for Disneyland's Enchanted Tiki Room and other attractions. Lincoln, however, was by far the most ambitious Audio-Animatronic project yet, capable of rising from a chair and displaying a range of motions. Soon an even more sophisticated Lincoln opened in Disneyland's Opera House for the 1965 Tencennial Celebration. Presented by Lincoln Savings and Loan, the thirteen-minute show began with a short biographical film and featured a dramatic monologue that blended excerpts from four speeches. Mr. Lincoln briefly "retired" in 1973 and 2005, but he kept coming back with updates in 1984, 2001, and 2009 that enhanced the presentation with new effects and better sound.

12. Legacy of Walt Disney: 1970–1973
Four years after Walt Disney's death, a new educational exhibit celebrating the life and achievements of the man behind the mouse opened on the Main Street corner where Disney Showcase is today. The Legacy exhibit offered biographical information and displays of some of his awards, tributes, and honors. After three years, the displays were moved to the Opera House for a new presentation called the Walt Disney Story.

13. American Space Experience: 1998–2003
The Tomorrowland Stage presented a live broadcast of the historic Apollo 11 moonwalk on July 20, 1969 (for many viewers, it was the first time they'd seen a large-scale TV broadcast); twenty-nine years later, NASA's achievements in outer space were celebrated with an educational walkthrough exhibit in the large Tomorrowland building where Little Green Men Store Command is now. The American Space Experience displays included an actual moon rock, an Apollo spacesuit, a scale revealing weights on other planets, and aerogel, a bizarre ultralight material that is 99.8 percent air.

10 Disneyland Displays at the Walt Disney Family Museum

Open since 2009, the acclaimed Walt Disney Family Museum houses ten permanent galleries and hundreds of artifacts that showcase Walt Disney's life and accomplishments. They included these Disneyland displays seen on recent visits.

1. An Autopia car from 1955.

2. An original Circarama camera with a cluster of eleven 16mm cameras pointing outwards to film a 360-degree movie.

3. A Griffith Park bench where Walt Disney sat and thought about building Disneyland as his daughters rode the nearby carousel.

4. The original 1953 model of Sleeping Beauty Castle.

5. *The Disneyland News*—"The official publication of Disneyland California"—vol. 1, issue 1 from July 1955, headlined "50,000 Attend Gala Park Opening."

6. "The Disneyland of Walt's Imagination," a remarkably detailed twelve-foot-diameter model, shows Walt Disney's ever-evolving vision of Disneyland.

7. Furniture from Walt Disney's private apartment above the Fire Department.

8. The miniature *Lilly Belle* train that Walt Disney built and ran in his Holmby Hills backyard (this train was a precursor to the Disneyland Railroad).

9. An area with an It's a Small World theme, complete with artist Mary Blair's desk.

10. Attraction posters for Rocket to the Moon, Adventure Thru Inner Space, and more.

A Dozen Famous Faces in the Fifth Freedom Mural

In 1941, President Franklin Delano Roosevelt identified the four freedoms America would defend: freedom of speech, freedom of worship, freedom from want, and freedom from fear. A fifth freedom—freedom of free enterprise—was celebrated at Disneyland with a huge 300-square-foot painted mural that opened in Town Square's Opera House in 1965 (most of it has been covered up in the last decade). Here are twelve famous faces depicted in the mural, listed alphabetically with their occupations in parentheses.

1. Bell, Alexander Graham (inventor)

2. Buck, Pearl S. (Nobel Prize-winning novelist)

3. Carnegie, Andrew (industrialist)

4. Carver, George Washington (chemist and educator)

5. Disney, Walt

6. Edison, Thomas (inventor)

7. Einstein, Albert (physicist)

8. Ford, Henry (industrialist)

9. Goddard, Robert (rocket scientist)

10. Sarnoff, David (telecommunications pioneer)

11. Wright, Orville (aviation pioneer)

12. Wright, Wilbur (aviation pioneer)

A Dozen Spirits of America Inside the Opera House

Near the model of the U.S. Capitol inside the Opera House is a display of small figures that represent the Spirits of America. They "symbolize many diverse people working together in unity to fulfill the hopes and dreams of our country's pioneers." They are the spirits of . . .

1. Heritage
2. Self-Reliance
3. Tomorrow
4. Innovation
5. Independence
6. Freedom
7. Discovery
8. Compassion
9. Pioneering
10. Adventure
11. Knowledge
12. Individualism

26 Special Events at Disneyland You May Not Have Heard Of

Besides the prominent anniversaries, much-publicized grand openings, and televised celebrations, there have been hundreds of smaller, lesser-known events held at Disneyland, including some that only took place once. Here are twenty-six of them, listed chronologically.

1. Spring 1957–spring 1964 (seasonal): The California State Pancake Races supported Quaker Oats, sponsors of Aunt Jemima's Pancake House in Frontierland. Hoping to win $100 and prizes, two dozen women sprinted from the Hub to Town Square while flipping pancakes over ribbons draped across Main Street.

2. March 28, 1958–ca. 1965 (seasonal): This one-day Kids Amateur Dog Show fetched guests every spring with a parade of dogs on Main Street and contests that awarded new bikes to the pet owners.

3. April 14, 1962–spring 1972 (seasonal): To generate some off-season excitement, Disneyland presented the Spring Fling one weekend night each spring. Special tickets brought dancing, free prizes, and unlimited use of all the attractions ("unlimited use" was an appealing concept back then). The Spring Fling name was revived in March 2013 for a week of activities featuring the Easter Bunny and an interactive "bunny hop" show.

4. April 22, 1962: To celebrate Easter Sunday, the giant hot-air balloon from the 1956 film *Around the World in 80 Days* lifted off from Disneyland's Hub and rose thousands of feet into the air before landing miles away.

5. July–September 1963: Co-sponsored by the Mexican Tourist Council,

the Salute to Mexico festival brought decorations and crafts from south of the border to Main Street.

6. December 2, 1967: McDonnell-Douglas Night was a special event for the dedication of Tomorrowland's Flight to the Moon, featuring balloons, fireworks, and both executives and thousands of employees from the new sponsor.

7. Ca. 1968–ca. 1973: For about five years, Disneyland offered a unique double-header—Angels-Disneyland Fun Day, which offered same-day admission to both Disneyland and a California Angels' game at nearby Anaheim Stadium.

8. March 23, 1969 and June 30, 1974: Love Bug Day in 1969 celebrated the box office triumph of *The Love Bug*. A VW Beetle-decorating contest in the parking lot preceded a parade of all the wildly embellished cars, culminating with a new VW given to the winner by the movie's star, Dean Jones. Five years later, with *Herbie Rides Again* in theaters, a second Love Bug Day was celebrated with a contest, parade, and TV special.

9. February 21–22, 1970: Boys' Club Days was a two-day event for Boys' Club members, families, and leaders, offering a few morning hours of "free play" when no A–E tickets were required.

10. January 30–31, 1971: Alice in Wonderland Days featured special parades and photo ops with *Alice in Wonderland* characters.

11. February 27–28, 1971: Donald Duck Days included special parades and photo ops with Disney characters.

12. 1972 and 1976: Two elaborate Pooh for President campaigns coincided with the presidential elections of 1972 and 1976 (the bear had informally entered the 1968 election). Eeyore and Tigger helped with the special parades, shows, and merchandise.

13. February 28–March 1, 1981: America Sings Weekend gave guests free admission to America Sings and offered photo ops and special live performances.

14. March 24, 1984: Olympic Night Disneyland celebrated the 1984 Olympics in L.A. and raised $600,000 for the U.S. team. At the event, Olympic athletes signed autographs and posed for pictures with guests.

15. November 14, 1991: In honor of the Bill of Rights' 200th anniversary, 251 people were sworn in as new U.S. citizens at Town Square.

16. February 27, 1992: Celebrating her sixtieth birthday, Hollywood legend Elizabeth Taylor held a private after-hours party at Disneyland with about 1,000 guests (Barry Manilow led a rendition of the "Happy Birthday" song).

17. October 31, 1994: Disneyland's first official in-park Halloween event was a party co-sponsored by radio station KIIS-FM that gave free admission to costumed guests arriving before 8:30 AM.

18. March 26, 1995: Various distance races (half marathons, 10Ks, etc.) currently start and end at Disneyland, but there was only one full-length Disneyland Marathon held at the park. However, during the marathon, all the runners veered off-course through Anaheim and spontaneously created a shortcut (race organizers quickly tacked on extra distance at the end to make it an official marathon). This major goof landed the 1995 race in *Running Times* magazine, which included the event in a November 1, 1999 article called "Running's Greatest Bloopers."

19. October 25 and 26, 2000: On October 25, a small group of fans paid $2,000 each for a Disney hotel room, lunch at Club 33, and a special Haunted Mansion dinner. The following night's Villains Enchanted Evening offered another feast and limited-edition merchandise for $150 per person.

20. December 5, 2001: Honoring what would have been Walt Disney's 100th birthday, a mid-morning Hub ceremony featured speeches and an appearance by composer Richard Sherman.

21. November 11, 2003–March 31, 2004: "Disney's Wildfire Heroes Salute" offered complimentary three-day admission to firefighters, law enforcement officers, and rescue personnel. The event recurred in 2007 and 2008.

22. October 5, 2004: "Disney's Swim with the Stars" national tour included three Olympic medalists swimming down a three-lane, 165-foot-long pool constructed on Main Street.

23. October 6, 2008: Celebrating her sixteenth birthday a month early, Miley Cyrus held a private after-hours party at the park with about 5,000 guests.

24. July 17, 2010: Disneyland's modest fifty-fifth birthday celebration included a re-dedication ceremony, special dining options, and commemorative merchandise.

25. September 10, 2013: With Disneyland closed to the public, television personality Holly Madison (*The Girls Next Door*) got married in New Orleans Square.

26. July 14, 2014: On this day, local TV station KTLA launched an online contest, asking the public to "tell us how your family dealt with a scary situation." The winning family got to spend the night in Disneyland's Haunted Mansion.

Fantasmic! by the Numbers

"Some imagination, huh?" So concludes Mickey Mouse at the end of Fantasmic!, and it's doubtful any viewers could disagree. Fantasmic! is a twenty-two-minute, state-of-the-art outdoor music and pyrotechnic show that almost defies definition. Just as the Main Street Electrical Parade reinvented nighttime entertainment in the 1970s, Fantasmic! reinvented it in the 1990s. Here are ten Fantasmic! factoids.

1. First public show: May 13, 1992
2. Cast members: Over fifty (most taking on multiple roles)
3. Dimensions of the water screens: Thirty feet tall by fifty feet wide by four inches thick
4. Special effects: About 125, some generating six-foot flames
5. Floating watercraft: Eleven
6. Height of the spotlight towers: Thirty feet
7. Length of Kaa the snake: 100 feet
8. Dimensions of the crocodile: Twenty-five feet wide by seventeen feet tall
9. Height of Ursula from *The Little Mermaid*: Twenty feet
10. Height of the nine-ton, fire-breathing mechanical dragon: Forty-five feet

3 Disneyland Requirements for Linda Ronstadt's 1971 Performances

In *Simple Dreams*, Linda Ronstadt's 2013 memoir, the singer recalls her 1971 performances at Disneyland's Grad Nite. Also on the bill were Smokey Robinson and the Miracles and the Staples Singers, and Ronstadt's "official backup band" was the newly formed Eagles. In her book, she names several of the "particular requirements" spelled out in her Disneyland contract, which we've quoted here.

1. She was "required to wear a bra."
2. Her "skirt had to be a certain number of inches from the ground" when she kneeled.
3. She and the other performers "weren't allowed to wander through the park in between shows." (The bands played multiple shows a night, into

the early morning hours; Ronstadt writes that she spent most of her backstage time trying to attract Smokey Robinson's attention, but he and the Eagles were too busy playing poker.)

A Dozen Rules for Grad Nite

The long-running party known as Grad Nite was first held on June 15, 1961 for over 8,000 local high school students. Students got dressed up, paid $6 each (including unlimited use of attractions), were admitted between 11 PM and 1 AM, and stayed until 5 AM. Within a few years, tens of thousands of students were coming from all over the country to party at Grad Nite. In the 1990s, over 150,000 grads were spread over seven or eight different spring nights each year and entertained by name bands such as No Doubt and Berlin. By now, a total of over five million students have "graduated" from Grad Nite. Unfortunately, alcohol consumption, minor vandalism, and overly affectionate couples have been persistent problems. To ensure proper conduct, Disneyland has kept a long list of strictly enforced rules, in addition to the usual no drinking and no bad behavior rules. Here are paraphrased selections from that list of Grad Nite regulations.

1. Teenage guests must arrive on school buses before midnight.
2. Nobody can leave before dawn (this rule has been relaxed slightly—students cannot leave the park unattended, but they can leave with a chaperone before 3 AM, with no re-entry allowed).
3. No napping.
4. No smoking.
5. No clothing can be worn that is inappropriate for a family environment (no string bikini tops, no see-through clothing, etc.).
6. No wedding dresses.
7. No hats or bandannas (official Disney hats are okay).
8. No visible tattoos with obscene or offensive language or designs.
9. No skateboards, scooters, skates, unicycles, or pogo sticks.
10. No sporting goods, including baseball bats, hockey sticks, golf clubs, bows and arrows, camping equipment, or Frisbees.
11. No weapons, replica weapons, self-defense equipment, restraining devices, or potentially disruptive items, including water pistols, pepper spray, handcuffs, laser pointers, air horns, megaphones, aerosol cans, tools, or musical instruments (official Disney toy weapons are okay).
12. No cremated remains (this is standard park policy, but grads are given a reminder).

A Dozen Unofficial "Days" at Disneyland

These modern celebrations at Disneyland are unofficial because they're organized by non-Disney groups. Months are approximate, and not all events are always held annually. Attendance ranges from dozens of people to tens of thousands.

1. **Dapper Day** (February and September): Guests wear elegant vintage clothes.

2. **Galliday** (January): Doctor Who fans gather for "the oncoming storm."

3. **Gay Days** (October): So popular that Disneyland sells rainbow-decorated merchandise.

4. **Bats Day** (May): Go goth and show off your tattoos.

5. **Gumball Rally** (May): Teams organized by www.micechat.com compete to ride as many attractions in a day as possible.

6. **Harry Potter Day** (November): Wizards and warlocks roam through the park.

7. **Mad Hatter Day** (October 6): Commemorating the "10/6" on the Mad Hatter's hat.

8. **MouseAdventure** (spring and fall): A scavenger hunt with trivia challenges is held by www.mouseplanet.com.

9. **Raver Day** (June): Guests bring their glow sticks and wear glow jewelry.

10. **Rock Around the Park Day** (November): For retro/rockabilly fans.

11. **Star Wars Day** (late spring): One of the slogans for this event has been "May the 4th be with you."

12. **UEA Days** (October): Fall break for the Utah Education Association (aka "Utahans Entering Anaheim").

MOUSCELLANEOUS

Assorted Tails

50 Projects, Organizations, and Locations That Were Compared to Disneyland

Disneyland is often invoked as an iconic image whenever anyone wants to describe something as being popular, or immaculate, or filled with joyful entertainment (sometimes all three). Over the years, all of the following have been said to be like Disneyland. Books mentioned below are in the bibliography.

1. Adconian Direct: This company is so fun that the "Workplace Feels Like Disneyland," according to a November 2013 headline in the *San Diego Union-Tribune.*

2. Alnwick Garden, England: One of the world's "most extraordinary contemporary gardens" is also, according to www.tripadvisor.com, "the Disneyland of gardens."

3. Amen Wardy: On January 19, 1983, the *Tuscaloosa Times* called this Newport Beach showplace for couture fashions a "clothing store like Disneyland" and "a Disneyland for women."

4. Amphibiville: As noted in O'Brien's *Amusement Park Oddities & Trivia!,* "the *Wall Street Journal* called Amphibiville, a two-acre wetland exhibit at the Detroit Zoo the 'Disneyland for toads.'"

5. Automotive theme park: In March 2013, a columnist for *Automotive News* pitched a concept for a new tourist destination that would be a "Disneyland of cars."

6. Boston College Law School: According to www.top-law-school.com, this institution is "the Disneyland of law schools."

7. Chelyabinsk, Russia: After a stunning meteor strike rocked the Urals region of Russia in February 2013, local officials considered building a commemorative "meteor Disneyland."

8. China City of America: A December 4, 2013 headline in the *New York Post* announced that this proposed multi-billion-dollar Catskills amusement park would be a "Chinese Disneyland."

9. Comet 67P/Churyumov-Gerasimenko: When the European Space Agency's *Rosetta* spacecraft reached this comet in August 2014, the team's senior scientific advisor announced they had finally arrived at a "scientific Disneyland."

10. ComicCon: The *San Jose Mercury News* called this event "Disneyland for Nerds" in a July 10, 2013 headline.

11. Crazy Mountain Ranch: On October 30, 2012, the American Public Health Association's site (www.apha.org.confex.com) posted a description of an 18,000-acre "smokers resort" in Montana that is "a Disneyland

for smokers."

12. **Dog Land:** Reviewing a new app for dog owners, www.appadvicedaily .com had a February 2014 headline that praised Dog Land as "the Disney- land of Dog Apps."

13. **Eataly World:** In February 2014, www.pbs.org reported that the "Disney-land of food," an Italian theme park "dedicated entirely to food," would open in 2015.

14. **Edward M. Davis Driving Training Center:** On April 26, 2005, the *Los Angeles Times* noted that Granada Hills' new police-training facility had been nicknamed "Disneyland for Cops."

15. **Georgia Gun Club:** This organization announced in March 2013 that it was building "the Disneyland of gun ranges."

16. **GoPro Motorplex:** On June 20, 2013, *USA Today* called this Mooresville, North Carolina go-kart track a "racer's Disneyland."

17. **Green Acre Dog Boarders:** On June 25, 2014, the news website www.thedailybeast.com reported on an investigation into Arizona's "Doggie Disneyland" that offered a "free-range, Disneyland-like experience."

18. **Guardians Centers:** Georgia's thirty-acre disaster-training area was called "Doomsday Disneyland" by www.cnn.com in March 2014, "a Disneyland for disaster drills" by the *Wall Street Journal* in May 2014, and "Disaster Disneyland" by CBS News in July 2014.

19. **Hamptons party:** The November 1999 issue of *InStyle* magazine spotlighted Star Jones's party in the Hamptons, which guest Ed Bradley (*60 Minutes*) described as "a champagne Disneyland."

20. **Heritage, U.S.A.:** South Carolina's 2,300-acre theme park was "intended to be a Disneyland for the Devout," says Marshall Fishwick in *The God Pumpers*.

21. **The Hobbit restaurant:** Orange County's *OC Weekly* called this local "homage to Bilbo Baggins" the "Disneyland of dining" on April 26, 2012.

22. **Hsi Lai Temple:** The book *Weird California* includes a chapter called "Buddhist Disneyland" that describes "the largest Buddhist temple in the West."

23. **India:** On February 13, 2012, www.indiawest.com, the site for a leading Indian newspaper, featured an article headlined "Is India a Spiritual Disneyland?" The piece discussed numerous holy locations that had been compared to Anaheim's park.

24. **iPad:** On April 8, 2010, a commentator on www.freedom-to-tinker.com called the iPad "the Disneyland of computers."

25. Jillian's: Writing about this Long Island entertainment center on March 26, 2000, www.nytimes.com said it was "like a Disneyland for evenings on the town."

26. JR Jones Management Group: According to an August 22, 2014 CNN story, working for this company, which has a CEO who's only ten years old, is like "a day at Disneyland."

27. Krakow, Poland: A July 17, 2013 article in *The Jerusalem Post* said that "the Jewish quarter is almost like the Disneyland of Judaism."

28. Kultfrabrik: The Halloween-related site www.funtober.com describes this Munich neighborhood as "a Disneyland for clubbers."

29. Lake Baikal, Russia: The January 27, 2014 edition of *The Moscow Times* announced construction of a new theme park with the headline, "Paper Mill That Polluted Baikal to Become Russian Disneyland."

30. Las Vegas: In 2010, Zappos CEO Tony Hsieh announced an ambitious $350-million project to reinvent the downtown area as an "entrepreneur's Disneyland."

31. Liberty Firearms Institute: An August 27, 2013 *Denver Westword* headline touted Colorado's biggest gun store (which includes an underground shooting range, classrooms, and a full restaurant) as a "Gun Disneyland."

32. Los Angeles International Airport: Though the phrase "Disneyland for adults" is now more commonly applied to Las Vegas, one of its earliest occurrences came in a 1961 *New York Times* article that previewed the forthcoming "jet age" redesign of LAX and compared the airport to Anaheim's park.

33. Henry Mancini: Steely Dan's Donald Fagen imagined in *Eminent Hipsters*, his 2013 memoirs, what Mancini's recording sessions were like in the 1950s—"a kind of Disneyland of Cool." Later in the book, a character calls Las Vegas the "Disneyland of Camp."

34. Media Laboratory: MIT's Media Lab "has been called a Disneyland of multimedia," according to Sharon Seivert's self-help book *The Balancing Act*.

35. Miley Cyrus: According to the *Minneapolis Star Tribune*, Cyrus's March 10, 2014 concert was "a Disneyland of mindless fun" and "her own personal, wild and crazy Disneyland."

36. Pajaro playground: With a new five-acre community park set to open, a January 10, 2014 headline in California's *Santa Cruz Sentinel* declared it was "like walking into Disneyland."

37. Palacio Maya: In November 2014, www.latintimes.com published an article about the abandoned construction of a "Mayan Disneyland" in the Yucatan.

38. Powersports Institute: On January 4, 2011, the motocross site www .racerxonline.com dubbed Ohio's giant training facility a "Disneyland for Gearheads."

39. *Pulp Fiction*: Quentin Tarantino's 1994 film is "a grungy, profane pulp/ *noir* Disneyland," according to Kinn and Piazza's *The Greatest Movies Ever.*

40. Rancho Bonilla: Late in the twentieth century, Jose Luis Bonilla started to build, but didn't finish, what he called a "Mexican Disneyland" in Santa Barbara County's Cuyama Valley.

41. Santorini, Greece: The August/September 2008 issue of *Plenty* magazine described this island as a "Disneyland for honeymooners."

42. SCORE!: "We're combining the Smithsonian with Disneyland," announced the CEO at the ribbon-cutting ceremony of his new interactive sports museum that opened inside Las Vegas' Luxor Hotel in 2012.

43. Sochi Winter Olympics: In December 2013, "The Voice of Russia" radio network called the new Olympic leisure park the "Russian Disneyland."

44. Spirit of California: Announced in August 2012 for a 2024 opening, this park will be located in the rural valley an hour east of the San Francisco Bay Area. It will be "four times bigger than Disneyland" and "a destination entertainment park that will exceed Disneyland," proclaimed developer James Rogers.

45. Temecula Wine Country: A November 29, 2013 headline in Riverside County's *Press-Enterprise* expressed "Concerns Over Creating 'Wine-Themed Disneyland.'"

46. Todd Rundgren's apartment: This rock star's former girlfriend, Bebe Beull, writes in her memoirs (*Rebel Heart*) that the three-story Manhattan apartment they shared in 1973 was a "Rock Disneyland."

47. Tudor Farms: As reported in the December 26, 1993 edition of *The Baltimore Sun*, this hunting lodge/wildlife preserve in Maryland was called a "Disneyland for duck hunters" by Representative Wayne T. Gilchrist.

48. Victoria Falls: In August 2013, Zimbabwe's Minister of Tourism announced a plan to build at the famous waterfall a $300-million theme park he described as "Disneyland in Africa."

49. Waikiki Beach: The Travel Channel show *Bikinis & Boardwalks* had a 2014 episode called "Bikini Shark Dive" that said Waikiki, compared to other beaches, is like "Disneyland compared to a county fair."

50. Wall Street: In an interview posted on www.cnn.com in December 2013, Jordan Belfort (the subject of Martin Scorsese's movie *The Wolf of Wall Street*) said his extravagant lifestyle was "almost like adult Disneyland for dysfunctional people."

Disneyland Compared to One Particular Place

The similarities between two popular locations, over 5,600 miles apart, have been pointed out by many writers. Here are eleven quotes noting the parallels.

1. 1963: "I walked through the silent park . . . I thought of another masterpiece that I had once seen at nightfall. It was the great pleasure ground of Versailles . . . it was a masterpiece of its age. It was built for the amusement of kings and their women. But this one was built for my pleasure and everybody else's. Versailles was copied all over Europe. This one, I think, will be copied all over the world." (Menen, "Dazzled in Disneyland")

2. 1965: "Disneyland is not free. You buy tickets at the gate. But then, Versailles cost somebody a lot of money, too." (Moore, "You Have to Pay for the Public Life")

3. 1968: "It was a projection, on a gigantic scale, of his personality . . . an extension of a man in the way that the pleasant grounds of Versailles were an extension of the Sun King." (Schickel, *The Disney Version*)

4. 1973: "Walt Disney had built the Versailles of the twentieth century—but it was a Versailles designed for the pleasure of the people." (Finch, *The Art of Walt Disney*)

5. 1982: "By far the greatest expression of Disney's world view proved to be his Disneyland amusement park . . . within a year almost four million people had trekked to this $17 million Versailles for the masses." (Kotkin and Grabowicz, *California, Inc.*)

6. 1994: "[Disneyland] was Walt's own Williamsburg, his American Versailles." (Marling, *As Seen on TV*)

7. 1998: At Disneyland, Walt Disney "told a story, as a king or his visionary architect might do in drawing up the master plan for a lovely pleasure garden. First comes the fountain. Then, the statue. And then, the castle. In a modern era of speculative, laissez-faire architecture, with each segment of the urban mix conceived by a different intelligence, each with a different case to plead, Walt's park looked radically different. Some were reminded of Versailles." (Marling, *Designing Disney's Theme Parks*)

8. 2005: "Few noticed the universality of the park format, be it at Versailles or Anaheim." (Jones and Wills, *The Invention of the Park*)

9. 2007: "With its pale blue castle flying pennants . . . its precise gardens and horse-drawn carriages maintained to jewel-box perfection, Disneyland was my Versailles." (Martin, *Born Standing Up*)

10. 2009: "If Versailles is the Disneyland of palaces, then Fontainebleau is the Knotts Berry Farm." (Ewell, *Traveling with Skeptics*)

11. 2014: "Like an eighteenth-century Disneyland, Versailles kept its courtiers so richly entertained they all but forgot the murmurs of discontent brewing back home." (*Fodor's Paris 2014*)

15 Urban Legends About Disneyland

People have been speculating about these topics for years. The urban legends are in quotes, followed by a brief discussion.

1. "The brass spike in the courtyard north of Sleeping Beauty Castle signifies Disneyland's exact center." Many people insist that this is true, and some Disney literature supports them (the *Disney Parks: Disneyland Resort Behind the Scenes* DVD, made with Disney's cooperation, clearly states that the spike "marks the geographical center of the entire park"). However, most experts (including Dave Smith, Chief Archivist Emeritus of the Disney Archives, writing in *Disney Trivia from the Vault*) say the spike is a marker left by surveyors and that it never indicated Disneyland's center. In addition, early park maps suggest that the center was *south* of the castle's moat, not north.

2. "Ghosts have been seen in various locations such as the Haunted Mansion, Space Mountain, and even Walt Disney's apartment in Town Square." Without disputing what people have claimed they saw, we're still waiting for evidence.

3. "Some of the bones on display in Pirates of the Caribbean are real." Now false, but once true. Jason Surrell's book *Pirates of the Caribbean: From the Magic Kingdom to the Movies* states that when the attraction first opened, there were actual bones from the UCLA Medical Center placed in some of the early scenes.

4. "Before it officially opened, the Haunted Mansion was much scarier than it is now; the scares were toned down after someone died during a preview showing." In the planning stages, there were discussions about making the mansion scarier, but ultimately it was built, previewed, and opened as a "happy haunt." The "someone died" part never happened.

5. "That's Walt Disney's face on one of the Haunted Mansion's singing busts." No, the one that resembles him is actually singer Thurl Ravenscroft, who also helped sing the "Grim Grinning Ghosts" theme song heard throughout the attraction.

6. "The horse-drawn carriage in front of the Haunted Mansion was once used in Brigham Young's funeral procession." An interesting idea, but probably false; newspaper accounts from 1877 reported pallbearers, not this particular carriage, bringing Young to his final resting place.

7. "There's a basketball court inside Matterhorn Mountain." Hyperbole runs amuck in this urban legend—photos and eyewitness accounts all define the "court" as just a basketball hoop on the wall of an employee break area up inside the mountain. It's not a full court.

8. "The Skyway was closed after a guest fell out and died." False. Many things fell, spilled, and were tossed out of during flights between Fantasyland and Tomorrowland, but nobody died in a fall.

9. "Feral cats roam Disneyland at night." True, and supposedly they're allowed to roam as a way to help control the rodent population. What's more, in 1956, Walt Disney and two of his Imagineers unwittingly stumbled upon hordes of flea-ridden cats inside Sleeping Beauty Castle, a humorous episode described in Randy Bright's *Disneyland: Inside Story*.

10. "Disneyland's 'official' address makes a reference to Mickey Mouse." Historically, Disneyland's address has been given as 1313 South Harbor Boulevard (on Disneyland's east side; this is the address given out at City Hall, though we've also seen it as 1313 Harbor Boulevard). Searches online, in books, and on Disneyland's information line (714-781-INFO) might also give you the west-side addresses 1313 Disneyland Drive and 1313 South Disneyland Drive (we found all four "1313" addresses while searching and calling around). Anyway, some people say that the number "1313" represents Mickey Mouse, M being the thirteenth letter of the alphabet, thus 1313 = MM. Disney Legend Van France's *Window on Main Street* claims that Walt Disney personally selected the numbers because they're part of Donald Duck's license plate (313) and Disney's wedding anniversary (July 13). The idea that 1313 has some special significance is somewhat supported by Stephen Faessel's *Historic Photos of Anaheim*, which says "Anaheim's civic government took care of . . . arranging the signature address of '1313' South Harbor Boulevard" as Disneyland was being built. Despite all these guesses and authoritative-sounding statements, in 2013 the Anaheim Planning & Zoning Department laughingly said the numbers are "simply a coincidence."

11. "At the end of the original Star Tours film, you can see George Lucas briefly as he ducks under a StarSpeeder 3000 heading toward a fuel tanker." This is most likely false, though the man does bear a resemblance to Lucas. Some experts claim that the man in the film is actually one of Industrial Light and Magic's model makers.

12. "Missouri officially annexed Tom Sawyer Island." As explained by Dave Smith, Chief Archivist Emeritus of the Disney Archives, at www.d23 .com in February 2013, this legend is a reference to a written request

made in 1956 by the Governor of Missouri, jokingly asking to have Frontierland's new island deeded over to the Show Me State.

13. "Club 33 is named for Disneyland's thirty-three original (or biggest) sponsors." When Disneyland's private Club 33 was being created in the mid-1960s, its name, according to an urban legend, acknowledged thirty-three major corporate sponsors (a logical assumption, since entertaining sponsors was one of Club 33's key raisons d'etre). These thirty-three included such famous companies as Atlantic-Richfield (sponsors of Tomorrowland's Autopia), Coca-Cola (Main Street's Refreshment Corner), Kodak (Main Street's Kodak Camera Center), and Timex (Main Street's Watches & Clocks). However, Dave Smith's *Disney Trivia from the Vault* unequivocally debunks this speculation as a "common misperception." According to official Disney publications, Club 33 is named after its address, 33 Royal Street in New Orleans Square.

14. "The clock hanging in the Sleeping Beauty Castle is permanently set to show the exact time Walt Disney died." The truth? The clock doesn't work, and whatever random time it does show (the time is occasionally reset) doesn't correspond to any historical event.

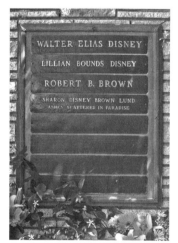

15. "Walt Disney's body is frozen and in storage at Disneyland." Walt Disney was interested in cryogenics, but, as many authoritative biographies have definitively stated, his body was cremated soon after his death in 1966 and is now interred at Glendale's Forest Lawn Memorial Park (*right*).

13 Disneyland-Related Sentences and Phrases That Are 13 Words Long

Anyone with triskaidekaphobia (fear of the number thirteen) might not like this list. Each of these thirteen memorable lines contains exactly thirteen words.

1. "Herbie, I just want it to look like nothing else in the world." (Walt Disney coaching artist Herb Ryman as they worked on a large illustration of Disneyland to be shown to potential investors in 1953; *Walt Disney Imagineering: A Behind the Dreams Look at Making the Magic Real*)

2. "The thing that's going to make Disneyland unique and different is the detail." (Walt Disney to an Imagineer, circa 1956; *Biography* magazine)

3. "Something clean and respectable for all ages was what I was striving for." (Walt Disney; *New York Times*)

4. "Here you leave today and enter the world of yesterday, tomorrow, and fantasy." (Plaques above the entrance tunnels into Town Square)

5. "To all who come to this happy place: —WELCOME— Disneyland is your land." (Dedication plaque in Town Square)

6. "It will grow as long as there is imagination left in the world." (Walt Disney; *National Geographic*)

7. "There's a great big beautiful tomorrow, shining at the end of every day." (Theme song for the Carousel of Progress)

8. "The happy haunts have received your sympathetic vibrations and are beginning to materialize." (Spoken by the Ghost Host inside the Haunted Mansion)

9. "And now, the most dangerous part of our journey: the return to civilization." (Jungle Cruise narration)

10. "Whenever your plans call for intergalactic travel, call on the best—Star Tours!" (Star Tours announcement)

11. Main Street, Adventureland, Frontierland, Fantasyland, Tomorrowland, New Orleans Square, Critter Country, Mickey's Toontown (Disneyland's eight "lands").

12. Town Square, Main Street, Hub, Adventureland, Frontierland, Fantasyland, Tomorrowland, Holidayland, New Orleans Square (eight park areas open during Walt Disney's lifetime).

13. Santa Fe & Disneyland Railroad, Casey Jr. Circus Train, Viewliner, Disneyland-Alweg Monorail (Walt Disney loved trains—these were open at Disneyland in his lifetime).

Ironyland

Here are ten examples of irony in Disneyland.

1. Arcades: Disneyland has had several video game arcades, notably Tomorrowland's Starcade (1977–ongoing), which at its height covered two stories with hundreds of games. Okay . . . but why would anyone pay Disneyland's high admission prices and then spend hours indoors play-

ing air hockey, pinball, and other arcade standards? Back in September 1985, *Mad* magazine parodied this incongruity with a cartoon showing kids being bored inside a Disney park until they finally reach the arcade.

2. Attendance: Everyone's heard (or expressed) complaints about the high prices to get into the park, to dine there, and to shop there, but those complaints sure don't slow down attendance, which (despite a few temporary slumps) has steadily increased from 3.6 million visitors in Disneyland's first full year to around 16 million visitors annually.

3. Autopia: Doesn't it seem ironic that people will make long, sometimes exhausting car trips to Disneyland and then will wait in the Autopia line so they can start driving again?

4. Doritos: Despite all the care and skill that goes into crafting Disneyland's complex, artfully presented meals, desserts, and candies, in the early 1960s, cast members inadvertently invented one of the world's simplest, but most famous, snack foods. Gustavo Arellano's book *Taco USA* credits Disneyland's old Casa de Fritos with spontaneously repurposing its broken, discarded tortilla shells as tortilla chips—a novel concept at the time—which became so popular that Frito-Lay jumped on the idea and officially rolled out its new packaged Doritos ("little golden things") in 1966.

5. The Haunted Mansion: Considering the memorably creepy promotional artwork that ran in the pictorial souvenir books while the Haunted Mansion was under construction in the 1960s, and considering all the rumors and expectations about this being the scariest haunted house ever built, and considering the new standard of excellence set by Pirates of the Caribbean two years before the Haunted Mansion opened, the actual mansion experience turned out to be hardly scary at all. The truly imaginative artistry (*right*) on view inside and outside the building does generate a few chills . . . but terror? Not so much.

6. It's a Small World: The bouncy theme song that perfectly matches the joyous spirit of "the happiest cruise on Earth" was originally composed as a slow, dirge-like ballad.

7. Main Street Cinema: Most of the cartoons played here are shown in silence, though originally they all had music, sound effects, and voices (including Walt Disney's, which sometimes was used for multiple roles). Only *Steamboat Willie*, famous for being the first cartoon with synchronized sound, is

shown with sound. Perhaps listening stations with headphones would enable guests to listen in on one cartoon at a time.

8. Mustaches: For the park's first forty-five years, male cast members were not allowed to have mustaches, even though Walt Disney himself had one.

9. Star Tours: From 1955 onward, Imagineers have incorporated Disney Studios' landmark movies, TV shows, and screen characters into Disneyland attractions. However, in the 1970s and 1980s, when Imagineers were looking for cinematic inspiration as they worked on new Tomorrowland attractions, they couldn't find any recent Disney movies successful enough to warrant development (1974's *Island at the Top of the World* and 1979's *The Black Hole* had both underperformed at the box office). So, Imagineers had to look outside their own company for a blockbuster to pin their plans on—they found it in *Star Wars*, a 20th Century Fox film that became the foundation of the park's thrilling Star Tours flight simulator. This *Star Wars*/Star Tours combination nicely dovetailed George Lucas's past with his present; starting in 1956 (when Lucas was just twelve years old), and continuing all through his teen years, he had been an enthusiastic, dedicated Disneyland visitor.

10. Town Square Realty: Surrounded by a high earthen berm, Disneyland is famously shielded from the outside world. However, in the 1950s the park brought the outside world in by presenting an actual real estate office in Town Square that sold land in Apple Valley, a largely undeveloped area eighty miles northeast of Anaheim (see the "11 Disneyland Giveaways from the Past" list on page 211 for more about Town Square Realty).

7 Ways Disneyland Is Better Than Ever

1. Covered parking spaces: Up until Disney California Adventure construction began in 1998, most guests parked in Disneyland's sprawling hundred-acre parking lot. This lot was easy to access and close to Disneyland's entrance, but virtually all its 15,000 spaces were exposed to full sun, turning cars into furnaces. Nowadays, the colossal Mickey and Friends parking structure nearby offers six levels of parking, so only those cars on the top level feel the heat.

2. Open daily: Today's guests are used to seeing Disneyland open every day of the year, but it wasn't always so. From 1955 to 1957, the park was closed on Mondays in the off-season; from 1958 to 1985, it was closed both Mondays and Tuesdays. On February 6, 1985, the park switched to its current 365-day schedule.

3. Healthier food: For about a decade, Disneyland has been making a concerted effort to offer healthier fare. Vegetarian options are served in most
restaurants, fruits and vegetables have replaced traditional French fries
as side dishes on some menus, sugar-free desserts are frequent options,
and guests can make specific dietary requests. Nutritional information
is also readily available for menu items.

4. No smoking: Except in a few designated smoking areas, lighting up is
prohibited in Disneyland—a restriction that didn't exist for the first four
decades of the park's existence. Naturally, not everyone is happy about
this development, but the majority are breathing easier.

5. Disney California Adventure: When DCA's Cars Land opened in 2012
to rave reviews, for the first time guests had another truly exciting Disney park within walking distance of Disneyland. DCA now siphons off
Disneyland guests throughout the day, thus helping keep Disneyland
crowds a little smaller than they might be if DCA didn't exist at all.

6. Queues are more manageable: The beginning of Disneyland's FAST-
PASS era in 1999 revolutionized the line experience, which has been
further improved by the Hub's information board and line-monitoring
apps that help guests make informed choices.

7. Safety: Recent changes have made the park safer than ever—for example, Space Mountain's new top and safety rails (*above right*) were added
in 2014 to the original structure (*above left*) to make it safer to clean the
exterior.

7 Ways Disneyland Is Worse Than Ever

1. Prices: You could say this almost every year—prices for everything (admission, merchandise, food) are higher than they've ever been.

2. Attractions: Guests used to be able to count on one or more great new
"E-ticket" additions per decade. In 1959, the Matterhorn Bobsleds,
Monorail, and Submarine Voyage all opened on the same day; 1967's
Pirates of the Caribbean and 1969's Haunted Mansion opened just two

years apart. In 2007, the Finding Nemo Submarine Voyage revived an old favorite, but Disneyland's last truly dazzling all-new attraction is 1995's Indiana Jones Adventure.

3. Strollers are multiplying: There are now so many that they have their own parking areas within Disneyland. Not only are there more strollers than ever, they're bigger, too. This is a delicate topic, since Disneyland eagerly embraces families with young children, but what's helpful to some people can be obtrusive to others.

4. The "holiday season" is multiplying: We love the holidays as much as anyone, but the holidays seem to start earlier every year. Sorry, but seeing Christmas treats in the Candy Palace's windows in July (yes—they were there in July 2013) just feels wrong.

5. Generic merchandise is multiplying: Disneyland stores used to sell a much wider variety of merchandise. For instance, long ago, guests on Main Street could buy children's shoes at Blue Bird Shoes for Children, swimsuits at Cole of California Swimsuits, ladies' undergarments at Intimate Apparel, and cigars and cigarettes at Fine Tobacco. See our list called "15 Unique but Extinct Disneyland Shops" on page 188 for some more golden oldies. Check out Frontierland's Bonanza Outfitters for a store that seems to be going a bit more upscale with non-Disney merchandise themed to the surrounding area, which means diverse books, jackets, dresses, belts, bags, and displays celebrating the Old West.

6. Everyone used to dress up: Many Disneyland fans are fascinated by historic photos of the park in the 1950s, when the crowds were filled with women in graceful dresses, men in jackets, and kids in smart-looking play clothes. We're not asking that everyone dress like Haunted Mansion butlers, and we readily admit that today's ultra-casual shorts, tees, and sneakers are more comfortable than vintage fashions (especially in the heat), but sometimes we wish guests dressed up a little more to honor how special every day is at Disneyland.

7. No Court des Anges: When this lovely little New Orleans Square courtyard (*right*) was taken from public use in 2013 and converted into the exclusive Club 33 space for select guests, Disneyland was diminished. This serene oasis within the busy park was the site of uncountable marriage proposals, memorable photographs, and perfect,

quiet moments. While nobody came to Disneyland just for the Court des Anges, they were usually delighted to find it there.

It's Surprising That Disneyland Never . . .

1. . . . Had an official, well-publicized, universally acknowledged theme song. Some consider "When You Wish Upon a Star" (from a movie) to be Disneyland's informal anthem, especially since some of the lyrics encircle the large compass in front of Sleeping Beauty Castle. "The Mickey Mouse Club March" (from a TV show) has been played in many a parade, and various other themes (from attractions such as It's a Small World, the Enchanted Tiki Room, and Pirates of the Caribbean) instantly make everybody think of Disneyland. However, none of these actually includes the name "Disneyland."

2. . . . Had an official Disneyland club for the public to join. There have indeed been clubs associated with the park: the Mickey Mouse Club Headquarters was in Town Square from 1963 to 1964; the Magic Kingdom Club enabled outside companies to sign up their employees for a special discount program from 1958 to 2000; and, of course, there's Club 33, but that's private. What we're suggesting is a club with a modest fee, membership cards, special privileges, a catalog of unique merchandise, occasional meetings or conventions, etc.—you know, an official Disneyland *club*, one you can belong to so you feel like you're part of the park even if you live far away and can rarely visit. Not D23, which showcases the entire Disney company; a D55, just for Disneyland.

3. . . . Anticipated that fishing off the southern tip of Tom Sawyer Island might be a problem. This was tried out early in the island's history when a small sealed area was abundantly stocked and fishing poles were provided to guests. Unfortunately, the odoriferous catches were found abandoned in lockers or stashed elsewhere in the park. When the Disneyland Hotel unveiled its own Fishing Pool in the early 1970s, management had learned to provide cleaning, packing, and shipping services for the guests' fish.

4. . . . Turned Innoventions into a fabulous Disneyland museum. The Carousel of Progress—the original attraction in this enormous Tomorrowland building—showed more of the past than it did of the future, so why not install a Carousel of Disneyland that showcases park history with large exhibits and abundant artifacts? It could end, as the Carousel of Progress did, with a look into the future (thus tying neatly into Tomorrowland). Meanwhile, the Opera House lobby that now exhibits Disneyland artifacts could focus on telling the Walt Disney story in detail.

5. ... Made more of its extinct attractions and structures available to the public by moving them to other locations outside the park. Three things from the past that have been put on view after Disneyland outgrew them: the Midget Autopia, which Walt Disney donated to Marceline, Missouri in 1966, making it the only Disneyland ride ever moved elsewhere; the peripatetic music gazebo that was moved around the park before it settled in the Roger's Gardens nursery in Corona Del Mar; and an engine and cars from the old Mine Train that were loaned to the Carolwood Pacific Historical Society for display in Griffith Park. These are nice starts, but there's so much more that could be made available all over the country. Wouldn't it be cool to visit an old Atomobile or People-Mover on display in your state?

6. ... Standardized the text of Walt Disney's Opening Day dedication speech. His sixty-six-word welcome is memorialized in Town Square at the base of the flagpole:

> TO ALL WHO COME TO THIS HAPPY PLACE
> — WELCOME —
> DISNEYLAND IS YOUR LAND.
> HERE AGE RELIVES FOND MEMORIES
> OF THE PAST ... AND HERE YOUTH MAY SAVOR
> THE CHALLENGE AND PROMISE OF THE FUTURE.
> DISNEYLAND IS DEDICATED
> TO THE IDEALS, THE DREAMS, AND THE HARD
> FACTS THAT HAVE CREATED AMERICA ... WITH THE
> HOPE THAT IT WILL BE A SOURCE OF JOY
> AND INSPIRATION TO ALL THE WORLD.
> · JULY 17, 1955 ·

Disney itself has offered at least three alternate versions (found on the 1958 Fun Map, on a recent plaque inside the Opera House, and in the 1964 edition of *Walt Disney's Disneyland*) that change the punctuation and even one of the words in the speech. Considering that this is one of the most famous statements Walt Disney ever made, it's surprising that there isn't just one universally accepted way of displaying it.

A Dozen Experts on Disneyland

Ever wonder what the experts think about Disneyland? We asked twelve of them to answer the following five questions:

1. What's your favorite place (or attraction or activity) in Disneyland today?

2. What one thing do you miss most that's no longer at Disneyland?

3. Though many people in 1955 predicted its failure, Disneyland has continued to thrive. What is the secret of Disneyland's success?

4. How could today's Disneyland be even better?

5. Give one great tip for other guests.

Josh Agle (Shag)

Shag (real name Josh Agle) is a painter and designer living in Southern California. His widely recognized depictions of cocktail lounges, hedonists, and graceful women have been exhibited on six continents. In 2005, he was selected to be one of three official artists who created work celebrating Disneyland's fiftieth anniversary, and he has continued to work with Disney on various projects to this day. He is currently creating paintings for three exhibitions in Australia.

1. "The Enchanted Tiki Room in Adventureland. Beyond the fact that I love Polynesian pop culture, the Tiki Room is the one thing in Disneyland that has stayed virtually unchanged since it debuted in 1964. It's a well-maintained look at what Walt Disney himself wanted in his theme park."

2. "I miss the Tomorrowland of my childhood, when it was still a forward-looking interpretation of what our future was supposed to look like: gleaming white buildings, undulating concrete, tropical planters, lots of turquoise, red and yellow, and cubist tile murals. We'd get around on PeopleMovers and a rocket trip to the moon would be a regular event."

3. "Through force of will and deep pockets, Walt Disney was able to control and shape every aspect of the experience, and the park continues that to this day. When there are negatives, Disneyland improves or changes them. Don't like the drive down the 5 freeway? They'll widen it. Don't like the long lines? They'll turn them into a visual feast and put entertainment along the way. The company pays a lot of attention to what people like and don't like about Disneyland, and makes decisions accordingly."

4. "The food could be improved. It seems like Disneyland hires a new executive chef every ten years who's going to shake the place up and create new menus, but most of the restaurants serve the same bland, middle-of-the-road food."

5. "After you've been to Disneyland a few times, spend a day seeing the attractions and going on the rides you've never been on. That will probably mean skipping the Haunted Mansion and the Matterhorn, but Great Moments with Mr. Lincoln and the fire truck ride around Main Street are fun and interesting, too."

Siran Babayan

Siran Babayan writes about pop culture and covers Disneyland for the *LA Weekly*. She especially likes Bats Day, a non-sanctioned yet popular event when the park is overrun with mostly black-clad "goths." "It's subversive, counterintuitive, and still good-natured fun," she says. "It's quintessential L.A., and it makes me proud to be an Angeleno." Siran also makes a point of visiting the park on her birthday every year. "Getting older isn't always fun, but when I wear my Disneyland birthday button, and everyone in the park wishes me a happy birthday, it makes me feel special."

1. "Space Mountain, the Cadillac of roller coasters and an icon of theme parks. It's three minutes of dark, dizzying, screaming fun."

2. "*Captain EO*, Michael Jackson's 1986 3-D sci-fi film. The premise was silly, the special effects were cheesy, and the choreography was '80s all the way. But it was the height of the King of Pop's success at a time when music videos were memorable and considered mini-movies."

3. "Disneyland is a distraction from daily life. A suspension of time and reality for both kids and adults."

4. "Provide free stroller rental. A place especially designed for families should have at least one complimentary feature for parents."

5. "Try pairing a churro with a turkey leg. It's a surprisingly tasty flavor combination, much like chicken and waffles."

Steve Barrett

Steve Barrett is the author of the Hidden Mickeys guide book series (Walt Disney World, Disneyland, and the Disney Cruise Ships, the Intrepid Traveler publishers) available in the Disney parks and in book stores, on Amazon, as e-books, and even as iPhone and Android apps. His first *Disneyland's Hidden Mickeys* book was published in 2007; since new Hidden Mickeys appear and are lost at relatively constant rates, he updates the book every two years to stay as current as possible. Steve and his wife Vickie (hiddenmickeygal) are the webmasters of www.hiddenmickeyguy.com.

1. "My favorite attraction at Disneyland is Peter Pan's Flight. In fact, I enjoy all the dark rides in this section of Fantasyland. During my first visits to Disneyland, Peter Pan's Flight helped me leave the stress of my real world job behind like no other attraction could."

2. "It's inevitable that certain Hidden Mickeys are lost from time to time due to refurbishments or to new construction, but I still mourn their loss (some more than others). One of my favorite Lost Hidden Mickeys is the classic (three-circle) Hidden Mickey on a frying pan that hung high on one of the Jungle Cruise boats."

3. "Disneyland has thrived because of the enduring influence of Walt Disney himself. His legacy continues to inspire the folks who create the magic that guests experience every day at Disneyland."

4. "I'm sure Disney Imagineers ponder that question daily. I think it's important that Disneyland stay current with advances in the technology of the entertainment industry. For example, from my point of view, newer Hidden Mickeys tend to be even more compelling, and I hope the Disney Imagineers continue that trend."

5. "Ask cast members about Hidden Mickeys; you may find a new and previously undiscovered one! (Disney doesn't announce new Hidden Mickeys. They just wait for us to find them!)"

Laura Gilbreath

Laura Gilbreath writes for the acclaimed website www.allears.net, and she is a frequent contributor to the "Salute to All Things Disney But Mostly Disneyland" blog. She has been going to Disneyland since she was a small child and remembers when enchanted tikis and hitchhiking ghosts seemed all too real!

1. "The Indiana Jones Adventure. When it first opened, I was amazed by the special effects and the level of detail that made me believe I was in an ancient temple in some foreign land. The technology is a little dated now, but for me this is still one of Disney's best."

2. "America Sings, which replaced the Carousel of Progress and ran from 1974 to 1988. It traced America's history in song, as performed by Audio-Animatronic animals. Just about every scene ended with the weasel popping out of a bag or box and singing, 'pop goes the weasel!' That always made me laugh, and I still smile just thinking about it."

3. "I think it goes back to Walt Disney's famous quote: 'Disneyland will never be completed. It will continue to grow as long as there is imagination left in the world.'"

4. "Disneyland needs to get back to building innovative attractions that use state-of-the-art technology. It's been a long time since it has added an Indiana Jones, or a Star Tours, or a Haunted Mansion."

5. "Be *at* the turnstiles when the park opens. And by this I mean tickets in hand, ready to go. You can ride a lot of attractions in the first couple of hours while most park guests are still arriving for the day."

Chris Jepsen

Local historian Chris Jepsen is a longtime annual passholder and is president of the Orange County Historical Society. He works at the Orange County Archives, writes the "O.C. Answer Man" column for *Orange Coast Magazine*, and runs the "O.C. History Roundup" blog.

1. "Pirates of the Caribbean is still the apex of everything Disneyland does best."

2. "I miss days with lighter crowds. It was more fun, and you'd get lost in the theming."

3. "Disneyland is a beautiful and amazing place, it's well-managed and cared for, and it's marketed to the hilt."

4. "Shorter lines and lower ticket prices would help."

5. "Slow down and admire both the details and the big picture."

David Koenig

David Koenig is probably the theme park industry's best-known outsider, having written five books including *Realityland: True-Life Adventures at Walt Disney World* and *Mouse Tales: A Behind-the-Ears Look at Disneyland*, the first—and best-selling—unauthorized park history.

1. "The Jungle Cruise. It's the one attraction that actually encourages cast members to go off-script and share their real, non-robotic personalities."

2. "Disneyland most sorely misses the PeopleMover, which provided Tomorrowland with wonderful overhead kinetics, sucked thousands of people an hour off the walkways below, and gave them a chance to catch their breath between roller coasters."

3. "Disneyland's initial success came because it took visitors through exotic environments and engrossing adventures unlike any they'd ever experienced before. Where else could you fly an elephant, dodge cannon fire from a pirate ship, and descend to the lost city of Atlantis? Today, you can see quality animatronics at the mall. But Disneyland continues stronger than ever because it's taken care and tweaked its offering just enough to remain fresh for new generations. I can take my kids back to re-live the adventures of my own childhood."

4. "Management should be legally prohibited from removing an attraction unless construction begins immediately on an even better replacement."

5. "Slow down. The best attraction at Disneyland isn't Space Mountain or Indiana Jones Adventure. It's Disneyland itself. Instead of sprinting from one too-long line to the next, take the time to enjoy the roaming entertainers, the tiny themed shops, the beautiful landscaping. The park will feel a lot less crowded."

Jim Korkis

Jim Korkis is an internationally respected Disney historian who has been writing about all things Disney for over thirty years for a variety of websites, magazines, and books. His two latest books are *The Vault of Walt Volume 3* and

Who's The Leader of the Club? Walt Disney's Leadership Lessons, both available on Amazon.

1. "Pirates of the Caribbean captures the joy of the traditional along with appropriate updates for today's generation."

2. "All-American human mermaids frolicking in the submarine's lagoon."

3. "The entire family can enjoy it all together."

4. "Offer more limited interactive live entertainment, like Merlin's Sword in the Stone ceremony."

5. "Take time to just sit and enjoy the park, from the beautiful landscaping to watching guests interact to the intricate details like the musical background."

Karal Ann Marling

Karal Ann Marling is a professor emerita of art history and American studies at the University of Minnesota. In addition to writing twenty-five books on a variety of topics, she planned, organized, and wrote catalogs for several major exhibitions on the architecture and culture of Disney's theme parks (see bibliography). At this writing, she is retired and leaves tomorrow for a week of pure pleasure at Walt Disney World!

1. "Main Street, U.S.A., and the Plaza (aka Hub)—a stroke of genius in the scaling of the architecture to enclose without intimidating even the little ones. The colors are cozy, the awnings are clean, the doorways (like Goldilocks' porridge) are just right. Architects have been known to fall to their knees and measure the width of the pavement. Others among us read the curvy gold script on the upstairs windows to learn the human history of places intimately connected to people and memories. Forced perspective means that high is never too high, enclosure is protective and nurturing. This may be Eden for Americans."

2. "It's hard to actively miss any single thing, what with the rush of new ones. Walt called it 'plussing.' He never feared to step into the waters of change. But if I had to keep anything from disappearing, it might be his apartment, up over the fire station, with its 1950s Victoriana furnishings. After my book *Designing Disney's Theme Parks: The Architecture of Reassurance* appeared, Marty Sklar asked me what they could do for me. I asked for lunch in Walt's little nook; I can see it still."

3. "People did feel the good, safe, happy feelings embedded in the place—the will to please. Disneyland embraces us like a parent's arms."

4. "I have been a little miffed from time to time by the relentless retailing of themed products, especially on Main Street. Until I began to see that people need to take away part of the place: a sweatshirt, a little statue

of Alice in Wonderland, a Mickey watch. Then I see the t-shirts everywhere: in the supermarket, on the street, even in church. I was being a purist and a snob! Shop on, folks!"

5. "Don't take pictures. Take it all in instead. Or buy a souvenir book if you must. Store it away in your heart."

Hugo Martin

Hugo Martin covers the travel industry, including airlines and theme parks, for the *Los Angeles Times*, and he writes the weekly Travel Briefcase column for the Business section. A native Californian, Martin was part of the Metro staff that won three Pulitzer Prizes in 1993, 1995, and 1998. He was also on the Travel section staff that won the Lowell Thomas Award from the Society of American Travel Writers in 2008. He is an avid outdoorsman, gardener, and Lakers fan.

1. "The Haunted Mansion. Even though the ride is forty-five years old, the overall effect is still brilliant. It's scary and fun without being morbid or gory."

2. "The cushioned seats on the Matterhorn Bobsleds. Since the Matterhorn was remodeled a few years ago, the new hard plastic seats have made it one of my least favorite rides."

3. "Disneyland has tied every attraction to a much-loved story or movie. These are stories that appeal to children. Part of the fun of Disneyland is re-living the stories."

4. "Crowd control. Disneyland has to come up with a way to move more people through the rides at a faster pace or limit the number of guests per day."

5. "Disneyland is open on rainy days. Most of the best rides continue to operate in the rain and you will find that lines are shortest on rainy days. I have the most fun visiting Disneyland on rainy days. Rainy days don't happen too often in Southern California, but if you can schedule that, it will pay off."

Kathy McDonald

Kathy McDonald has worked in the offices of both Disney Studios and the Disney Archives. As a kid, she attended Walt Disney World's opening day and visited that park regularly for many years until she moved to California and started studying every detail of Disneyland. She is now a travel writer covering Disneyland for the *Fodor's California* travel guidebook.

1. "The Pirates of the Caribbean, updated with references to the recent movie series and an appearance by Johnny Depp, is my favorite—it starts off quietly, provides laughs and thrills, and is a completely

immersive experience."

2. "I miss the Skyway—a gondola ride between Fantasyland and Tomorrowland that felt like you were floating above the park. It was a great place to relax above the crowds for a few minutes."

3. "Disneyland is expertly managed. The staff is friendly, polite, and helpful—a rarity in today's service industry and the world at large. Guests feel welcomed and appreciated."

4. "The park is so popular now that on some days, it feels overrun. It would be better if they somehow limited attendance, but it's hard to say how that could happen."

5. "Be there before Disneyland opens. Guests at the resort's hotels have an option of an hour's early entrance—take advantage of it. If you're not a hotel guest, be there at 7:45 AM so you're there for the rope drop . . . and then head immediately for the most popular attraction."

Todd Regan

Todd Regan is the executive director of the Walt Disney Birthplace and the Center for Early Childhood Creativity and Innovation. He is currently busy restoring the home Walt Disney was born in and planning museum displays and interactive experiences for the historic house. Todd is also the CEO and Dusty Sage of www.micechat.com, the *uber*-popular Disney and theme park news, history, and discussion site.

1. "Fantasmic! is one of the most magical places/activities to me. During the day, it's just a river and walkways. But at night, it transforms into a massive theater with giant moving props!"

2. "Walt Disney described Tomorrowland as 'a vista into a world of wondrous ideas, signifying man's achievements . . . a step into the future, with predictions of constructive things to come.' With the loss of classic attractions such as the PeopleMover, Adventure Thru Inner Space, Carousel of Progress, and Rocket to the Moon, Tomorrowland seems to have lost its focus over the years and is the one area of Disneyland which feels like it needs an update."

3. "Disneyland's success is in the details. There's nowhere else on earth quite like it. They didn't just build rides, shows and attractions, they created themed environments. Disneyland is at once an adventure and clean and safe—an altered version of reality."

4. "With success comes crowds. Unfortunately, tiny Disneyland struggles to manage the horde of guests that arrive every day to devour Disney's special brand of magic. Limiting attendance or building more ride capacity would be a blessing to Disneyland fans everywhere."

5. "Disneyland is not a list of tasks to be accomplished or checked off a list. Rather than attempting to ride every E-ticket in the park, savor the experience and seek out the side of Disneyland that others frequently miss. Enjoy the shops and shows. Explore the back alleys of New Orleans Square and the Sleeping Beauty Castle Walk-Through. Climb Tarzan's Treehouse and brave the caves of Tom Sawyer Island. In other words . . . enjoy the less-crowded, smaller attractions and see a side of Disneyland that most tourists skip in favor of the long lines of the park's bigger thrills."

Werner Weiss

Werner Weiss is the "curator" of www.yesterland.com, an immensely popular website launched in 1995 and still updated each Friday. Discontinued Disneyland rides, shows, parades, and restaurants live on through historical photos and accompanying descriptions on the site.

1. "This may seem like an odd answer, but I like walking from any place in the park to any other place, taking in the details along the way."

2. "I miss the Mine Train Through Nature's Wonderland—a slow ride through a mountain wilderness, a desert with geysers, and a cave with colorful waterfalls. It was closed for Big Thunder Mountain Railroad. I wish there had been room for both."

3. "Disneyland has thrived since 1955 because Walt Disney's instincts were right. He and his hand-picked team created an environment that many people of all ages find appealing. The park is still guided by their original vision."

4. "Disneyland needs to improve its ability to absorb guests and spread them out. Current attendance levels greatly exceed what the park was designed for. Expanding the park into the area north of Frontierland and adding a few high-capacity attractions would go a long way."

5. "Instead of just running between attractions, enjoy the rich layers of details that are everywhere. Look up. Look down. Turn your head."

A Dozen of the Most-Missed Attractions and Exhibits

The experts in the previous list named their most-missed attractions and exhibits—now it's our turn. Here's our list, originally compiled exactly twenty years ago (1995, the PeopleMover's last year), and listed alphabetically.

1. Adventure Thru Inner Space (1967–1985): This revolutionary ride miniaturized guests to atomic size via Disneyland's first Omnimover ride system.

2. **Carousel of Progress (1967–1973):** Before Innoventions, this show presented an entertaining history of electrical advancements from the 1890s to modern times, culminating with an astonishing Progress City model.

3. **Circle-Vision 360 (1967–1984):** Probably the best version of the amazing 360-degree movie experience.

4. **Disneyland Presents a Preview of Coming Attractions (1973–1989):** A Main Street room (now Disney Showcase) filled with enticing models and art showing future plans.

5. **Flight to the Moon (1967–1975):** A terrific update of Rocket to the Moon with a technologically advanced pre-flight area.

6. **House of the Future (1957–1967):** Innoventions' more recent indoor version paled in comparison to this iconic stand-alone structure with a futuristic interior and lovely landscaping.

7. **Mermaids (1965–1967):** For three summers, beautiful girls in mermaid costumes cavorted in Tomorrowland's lagoon (*right*).

8. **Mine Train (1956–1977):** Slow, relaxed train rides to stunning Rainbow Caverns through Frontierland's Painted Desert (1956–1959) and later through Nature's Wonderland (the Big Thunder Mountain Railroad now occupies this territory).

9. **PeopleMover (1967–1995):** Elevated trains that gave long, scenic Tomorrowland tours.

10. **Skull Rock and Pirate's Cove (1960–1982):** Visual highlights in Fantasyland, especially at night.

11. **Skyway (1956–1994):** Disneyland's best views.

12. **Tomorrowland Terrace:** The terrace is still here today, featuring the *Jedi Training Academy* show, but we miss the exciting terrace of the 1960s and 1970s, when the rising stage still seemed novel and famous pop bands started playing while they were still below ground level.

A Half-Dozen Underappreciated Disneyland Experiences

1. **Big Thunder Trail:** This 800-foot walkway is much more than a shortcut between Frontierland and Fantasyland. There's excitement (the Big Thunder Mountain Railroad roars past the east side), history (remnants

and sounds of the extinct Mine Train), telling details in the walkway (horseshoe prints and cart tracks), a beautiful *Mark Twain* mural on a building at the southern end, a shaded bench with its own mural at the northern end, a tall fence behind the Big Thunder Mountain Railroad that's topped with real barbed wire, a patch of cacti with a Hidden Mickey, access to the Big Thunder Ranch area, fabulous rockwork, a pond with live turtles, and more. Not everyone takes this trail, but they should, at least once.

2. Magnolia Park: In their rush to get to the Haunted Mansion, guests often overlook the small, serene fountain area informally known as Magnolia Park (no sign officially states this name). A much bigger Magnolia Park with paths, a bandstand, and occasional special events (Zorro Days, 1958–1960) stood here until the early 1960s, when the Jungle Cruise expansion, the arrival of the Swiss Family Treehouse, and the construction of New Orleans Square took over. Today's smaller Magnolia Park is still a pretty place to sit and relax awhile (its fountain is on our "15 Fine Fountains in Disneyland" list on page 167).

3. Omnibus: This may seem like just another vehicle on Main Street, but it's not. The other vehicles (a horse-drawn streetcar, a fire truck, horseless carriages, etc.) are quaint, beautiful, and fun, but they don't add any visual perspective different from the one pedestrians get. Since 1956, the stately double-decker Omnibus has been giving guests a second-story moving view, putting them almost at eye-level with Walt Disney's Town Square apartment and Sleeping Beauty Castle's turrets.

4. New Orleans Square's second story: With so much to see on the ground floor, not everyone looks up to notice what's on New Orleans Square's second story. Walk slowly through these narrow streets and above you'll see ornate ironwork, balconies with musical instruments and paintings, hanging flowers, statues, stained glass, seasonal decorations, and more, all adding delightful details to this area's famous atmosphere.

5. Restrooms: Disneyland's restrooms vary from the spacious (at Critter Country's Hungry Bear Restaurant) to the cramped (on Tom Sawyer Island's eastern dock). What never varies, however, is their cleanliness. Even on the busiest days, they're all lightly cleaned every hour and undergo a thorough sanitization every night. Most restrooms include baby-changing stations, and some even sell baby-changing kits (including diapers, wipes, etc.). Themed door signs (aliens in Tomorrowland, for instance) are fun enhancements, and the theming often extends inside the restrooms (wooden walls and antique hurricane lamps in Frontierland). When ya gotta go, ya might as well go with *show*.

6. Sleeping Beauty Castle Walk-Through: In the *Sleeping Beauty* DVD's special features, Disney Legend Tony Baxter describes this wonderful

1957 attraction as "the first application in Disneyland of some artistically brilliant and technically stunning special effects." Unfortunately, many people don't even notice the Walk-Through's entrance off to the side of the castle, so they miss it altogether. Or, once inside, they race through the exhibit to the scary parts and don't study the dioramas long enough to appreciate the ingenuity of the designers and the beauty of their tableaux.

16 Favorite Disneyland Services

Disneyland's extra amenities and services are far too numerous to list here, but we've selected sixteen that are (or were) among our favorites.

1. Birthday surprises: Pre-order through Disneyland Resort Dining (714-781-DINE) to get customized birthday cakes and gifts delivered to tables inside Disneyland restaurants, and visit City Hall to hear congratulatory birthday messages from Goofy on an old-fashioned phone.

2. Brochures: Those free map/info brochures available at the turnstiles come in nine languages—Chinese, English, French, German, Italian, Japanese, Korean, Portuguese, and Spanish.

3. Buy without lugging: You don't have to haul your Disneyland purchases around the park with you. Guests can pick up their purchases later at one of three park locations (including one near the exit), and visitors staying at a Disneyland Resort hotel can have their packages sent there.

4. Charrrggge!: The Main Street Lockers & Storage room includes "charging lockers" where guests can re-charge their electronic devices.

5. City Hall services: As the information center, City Hall is the obvious place to find maps, phone directories, and schedules; but there are also binders here that identify Disneyland's flora and provide recipes for dishes served in the restaurants. Also, throughout Disneyland you'll see signs reading, "Documents related to the Certificate of Compliance for this attraction may be viewed at City Hall in Town Square." It's true—you can see those annually updated safety certificates in City Hall's big binder.

6. Customized music: In its last few years, Tomorrowland's Premiere Shop (1963–2005) had Disneyland Forever kiosks where guests could burn their own customized CDs using a broad selection of Disney songs, sounds from attractions, and other auditory gems.

7. Early admission: Beat the crowds by getting into Disneyland before it even opens—what a concept! Magic Mornings and the Extra Magic Hour enable qualified guests to enter early on certain days.

8. First Aid freebies: At First Aid, headaches, stomachaches, blisters, and more can be treated for free with over-the-counter remedies, ice packs, etc.

9. Flowers by mail: From 1957 to the mid-1990s, guests could shop for beautiful artificial flowers at Main Street's lovely Flower Mart (or Flower Market). The flowers could even be mailed (an orchid corsage, including tax and shipping, was $2.50).

10. Lost and Found: Lose something, complete a form, and the found item will be mailed. (A baseball cap lost on Splash Mountain appeared in our mailbox a week later—totally impressive.) Conversely, guests who find a lost item can turn it in, complete a form, and later claim the item if nobody else does.

11. Mlle. Antoinette's Parfumerie: From 1967 to 1997, New Orleans Square's trained perfumers mixed customized fragrances for guests and kept the formulas on file for return visits.

12. Photography help: There's always been a photo supply/camera center located on Main Street. The awesome variety of photo services has included camera repair/rentals and free battery recharging. In addition, for decades Picture Spot signposts throughout Disneyland have alerted guests to particularly photogenic backgrounds. When Kodak ended its sponsorship in late 2012, Disneyland had seven Picture Spots (one each at the main entrance, Fantasyland, the Hub, Mickey's Toontown, and Tomorrowland, plus two in Frontierland). Nikon started putting up new Picture Spot markers in early 2014.

13. Picnics in the park: There's a picnic area in front of Disneyland in the shadow of the Monorail's beam, but you can also have your own picnic *inside* the park by reserving one of the "happiest picnics on Earth" for yourself and 100 friends. Fully catered meals are presented in the Big Thunder Ranch area and include appearances by Disney characters.

14. Rain supplies: Guest surprised by a rare Anaheim rainstorm can buy inexpensive ponchos and umbrellas from nearly every shop in Disneyland (rain gear isn't displayed, but it's available upon request).

15. Saving with Mr. Bank: Thanks to the Town Square branch of Bank of America that existed from 1955 to mid-1993, guests could do their banking—open genuine B of A accounts, get checks with Disneyland images on them, and more—right inside Disneyland, even on weekends and holidays.

16. Waterworld: It's a simple service, but there are times when it's the only thing we want—free cups of ice water, available at any counter-service restaurant.

It's the Little Things:
16 Small Sights That Generate Happy Sighs

With so many grand things to look at, these little pleasures are easy to miss.

1. Fantasyland: The cast of the yeti footprint along the Matterhorn's western walkway is nice foreshadowing that adds to the bobsled experience.

2. Fantasyland: Infrequently seen swans have gracefully glided across Sleeping Beauty Castle's moat.

3. Fantasyland: Inside the Mad Hatter of Fantasyland, the mirror behind the sales counter holds a nifty trick—periodically, the Cheshire Cat will materialize.

4. Fantasyland: Every twenty-four seconds, the wicked queen peers through the window in the tower above Snow White's Scary Adventures—maybe we're supposed to feel scared, but it's kind of reassuring, too.

5. Fantasyland: Frogs rise up and squirt water into the pond at the Snow White Wishing Well and Grotto.

6. Frontierland: The boot and horseshoe prints (*below, second from left*) in front in front of the Bonanza Outfitters sidewalk, and the cart tracks etched into the Big Thunder Trail, are echoes of the Old West.

7. Frontierland: Wildlife along the Big Thunder Trail includes artificial (but real-looking) fish that leap in the pond and real live turtles that move about on the waterside rocks (*below, far left and far right*).

8. Hub: Tiny magical green lights play along the limbs of the tree across from the Pixie Hollow sign.

9. Hub: At Pixie Hollow's exit is a bank of actual working pay phones (there are about a half-dozen other pay phone locations in Disneyland).

10. Main Street (and other locations): Real mailboxes are scattered throughout Disneyland, reminders of a time when most guests sent letters and postcards instead of emails and tweets (*below, second from right*).

11. Main Street: In the Refreshment Corner, the light bulbs near the ceiling

alternate red and white, but the odd number of bulbs means that one in the middle is half red and half white to keep the color scheme consistent.

12. Mickey's Toontown: Ring the doorbell at Toontown's firehouse, and a Dalmatian puppy will appear in a second-floor window (who doesn't love puppies?).

13. New Orleans Square: Mechanical fireflies drift among the bushes inside the Blue Bayou/Pirates of the Caribbean.

14. New Orleans Square: Faux ship masts peek above the rooftops to the west, suggesting ships at a nearby dock.

15. Town Square: Flying over the train station is the pale blue Disneyland flag (which can also be seen standing in the back of the Imagineering offices on 1965's "Disneyland's Tenth Anniversary" episode of *Walt Disney's Wonderful World of Color*).

16. Town Square: Mounted inconspicuously in City Hall is Disneyland's requisite Business Tax Certificate ("Type of business: Amusement Park").

13 Disneyland Jokes

An Internet and library search for clean jokes and riddles about Disneyland brought up many results, including these.

1. A grandson runs up to his grandfather and asks him if he can talk like a frog.

"Of course not," says the grandfather.

A few minutes later, his granddaughter asks him the same question.

"No, of course not. Why are you both asking me this?"

The granddaughter replies, "Dad said that when you croak, we can go to Disneyland."

2. Q: Why do people go to Disneyland?

A: So they can get a little Goofy!

3. Q: Why did Snow White wait outside the Main Street Photo Supply Co. in Disneyland?

A: She had been told that someday her prints would come.

4. Disneyland—the world's biggest people trap, built by a mouse.

5. Disneyland jobs available. Positions available in the Snow White and the Seven Dwarfs tourist shop due to short staff.

6. Three (insert a plural noun here) were driving to Disneyland when they saw a sign that said "Disneyland Left." So they turned around and went home. (Many sites show variations of this joke putting different groups in the car.)

7. Chevy Chase in the very first episode of *Saturday Night Live* in 1975, delivering the Weekend Update: "Japan emperor Hirohito met Mickey Mouse at Disneyland this week. The emperor presented Mickey with a Hirohito wristwatch." (A photo showed the emperor and Mickey at the park.)

8. Talk show host Craig Ferguson: "Here in Southern California, you can see Mickey Mouse anytime. Just go to Disneyland. All you need is a way to get to Anaheim and about 500 bucks for a ticket to get in."

9. Jay Leno on *The Tonight Show*: "Disneyland celebrated its fortieth anniversary by burying a time capsule. They say it will be dug up in fifty years . . . or when the last person in line at Space Mountain gets to the front, whichever comes first."

10. Talk show host Conan O'Brien: "Disney is coming under fire for raising the price of admission to Disneyland to $92. Even worse, it now costs you $350 just to get out of It's a Small World."

11. In 2009, It's a Small World broke down and a disabled man in one of the boats couldn't be evacuated; he was trapped for over a half hour while the theme song played nonstop. When news broke that the man was suing the park, Conan O'Brien cracked this joke: "A California man is suing Disney because he was trapped on the It's a Small World ride for forty minutes. When they heard it, the Chilean miners said, 'Wow, we got off easy.'"

12. After the man in #11 above won $8,000 in damages in 2013, O'Brien joked again: "A man has won an $8,000 settlement from Disneyland after he got stuck on their It's a Small World ride. The man said he'll use the money to cut out the part of his brain that won't stop playing 'It's a Small World After All.'"

13. Dave Barry in *Dave Barry Turns 50*: "Disneyland was more than just an amusement park: It was an amusement park with *enormous* waiting lines. Americans loved Disneyland because it gave them something good, something decent, something that epitomized a quality that vacationing American families value above all else: clean toilets."

20 More Books of Lists

If you like list books, here are twenty more on a variety of topics (authors are listed in parentheses).

1. *Baseball Top 10* (Buckley and Fischer)
2. *The Beatles Book of Lists* (Spignesi)

3. *The Big Book of Children's Reading Lists: 100 Great, Ready-to-Use Book Lists for Educators, Librarians, Parents, and Children* (Keane)

4. *The Book of Classical Music Lists* (Kupferberg)

5. *David Letterman's Book of Top Ten Lists* (Letterman)

6. *The Book of Rock Lists: A Dell/Rolling Stone Press Book* (Marsh and Stein)

7. *Golf List Mania!: The Most Authoritative and Opinionated Rankings of the Best and Worst of the Game* (Shapiro and Sherman)

8. *Hollywood's Most Wanted: The Top 10 Book of Lucky Breaks, Prima Donnas, Box Office Bombs, and Other Oddities* (Conner)

9. *Listography: Your Life in Lists* (Nola)

10. *List Your Self* (Segalove and Velick)

11. *Mental Floss: The Book, Only the Greatest Lists in the History of Listory* (Trex, Pearson, and Hattikudur)

12. *The Merciless Book of Metal Lists* (Abrams and Jenkins)

13. *The People's Almanac Presents the Book of Lists* (Wallechinsky, Wallace, and Wallace)

14. *Read This! Handpicked Favorites from America's Indie Bookstores* (Weyandt)

15. *The Southern Gardener's Book of Lists: The Best Plants for All Your Needs, Wants, and Whims* (Chaplin)

16. *Super Pop! Pop Culture Top Ten Lists to Help You Win at Trivia, Survive in the Wild, and Make It Through the Holidays* (Harmon)

17. *The 10 Best of Everything: The Ultimate Guide for Travelers* (Lande and Lande)

18. *Top 10 Los Angeles* (Gerber; this slender book includes four general-interest lists covering the entire Disneyland Resort)

19. *The Ultimate Book of Boxing Lists* (Sugar and Atlas)

20. *The Ultimate Book of Top Ten Lists: A Mind-Boggling Collection of Fun, Fascinating and Bizarre Facts on Movies, Music, Sports, Crime, Celebrities, History, Trivia and More* (Frater)

A List of Sources, Research Materials, and Books Mentioned in the Text

Abrams, Howie, and Sacha Jenkins. *The Merciless Book of Metal Lists*. New York: Abrams Image, 2013.

Alarcón, Alicia. "All I Thought About Was Disneyland." *U.S. Latino Literature Today*, ed. Gabriela Baeza Ventura. London, England: Longman Publishing Group, 2004.

Anonymous. "Disneyland Celebrates 50 Magical Years." *PR Newswire*, July 11, 2005.

———. *Disneyland: The First Quarter Century*. Burbank, CA: Walt Disney Productions, 1979.

———. *Disneyland: The First Thirty Years*. Burbank, CA: Walt Disney Productions, 1985.

Arellano, Gustavo. *Taco USA: How Mexican Food Conquered America*. New York: Scribner, 2012.

Bailey, Adrian. *Walt Disney's World of Fantasy*. New York: Everest House, 1982.

Ballard, Donald W. *The Disneyland Hotel: The Early Years 1954–1988*. Riverside, CA: Ape Pen Publishing, 1985.

Barrett, Steven M. *Disneyland's Hidden Mickeys: A Field Guide to Disneyland Resort's Best Kept Secrets*, 4th Edition. Branford, CT: The Intrepid Traveler, 2013.

Barrier, Michael. *The Animated Man: A Life of Walt Disney*. Oakland, CA: University of California Press, 2008.

Barry, Dave. *Dave Barry Turns 50*. New York: Crown Publishing, Inc., 1998.

Beull, Bebe. *Rebel Heart*. New York: St. Martin's Press, 2001.

Birnbaum Travel Guides. *Birnbaum's 2014 Official Guide to the Disneyland Resort*. New York: Disney Editions, 2014.

Bishop, Greg, et al. *Weird California*. New York: Sterling Publishing Co., Inc., 2006.

Bradbury, Ray. *Bradbury Speaks: Too Soon from the Cave, Too Far from the Stars*. New York: HarperCollins Publishers, 2005.

Bright, Randy. *Disneyland: Inside Story*. New York: Harry N. Abrams, Inc., 1987.

Broggie, Michael. *Walt Disney's Railroad Story*. Pasadena, CA: Pentrex Media Group, 1997.

Buckley, James, and David Fischer. *Baseball Top 10*. New York: DK Publishing, 2002.

Carlson, Peter. *K Blows Top*. New York: PublicAffairs, 2009.

Chaplin, Lois Trigg. *The Southern Gardener's Book of Lists: The Best Plants for All Your Needs, Wants, and Whims*. Lanham, MD: Taylor Trade Publishing, 1994.

Childs, Valerie. *The Magic of Disneyland and Walt Disney World*. New York: Mayflower Books, Inc., 1979.

Conner, Floyd. *Hollywood's Most Wanted: The Top 10 Book of Lucky Breaks, Prima Donnas, Box Office Bombs, and Other Oddities*. Washington, D.C.: Brassey's, Inc., 2002.

Crystal, Billy. *Still Foolin' 'Em*. New York: Henry Holt and Company, LLC, 2013.

Cussler, Clive. *Iceberg*. New York: Dodd, Mead & Company, 1975.

DeMarinis, Rick. *Borrowed Hearts: New & Selected Stories*. New York: Seven Stories Press, 1999.

De Roos, Robert. "The Magic Worlds of Walt Disney." *National Geographic*. August 1963.

Disney Miller, Diane. *The Story of Walt Disney*. New York: Henry Holt and Company, 1957.

Disney Parks: Disneyland Resort Behind the Scenes DVD. Lightship Entertainment, 2010.

Doctorow, E. L. *The Book of Daniel*. New York: Random House, Inc., 1971.

Doucet, Clive. *Disneyland, Please*. Ontario, Canada: Fitzhenry & Whiteside, 2010.

Dunlop, Beth. *Building a Dream: The Art of Disney Architecture*. New York: Harry N. Abrams, Inc., 1996.

Eddy, Don. "The Amazing Secret of Walt Disney." *The American Magazine*, vol. 160, no. 2, August 1955.

Eisner, Michael with Tony Schwartz. *Work in Progress*. New York: Random House, Inc., 1998.

Ellroy, James. *L.A. Confidential*. New York: Warner Books, Inc., 1997.

Evans, Morgan. *Walt Disney Disneyland World of Flowers*. Burbank, CA: Walt Disney Productions, 1965.

Ewell, Ken. *Traveling with Skeptics*. Bloomington, IN: iUniverse, 2009.

Faessel, Stephen J. *Historic Photos of Anaheim*. Nashville, TN; Turner Publishing Company, 2007.

———. *Images of America: Anaheim 1940-2007*. Charleston, SC: Arcadia Publishing, 2007.

Fagen, Donald. *Eminent Hipsters*. New York: Viking, 2013.

Finch, Christopher. *The Art of Walt Disney*. New York: Harry N. Abrams, Inc., 1993.

Fishwick, Marshall and Ray B. Browne (eds.). *The God Pumpers: Religion in the Electronic Age*. Bowling Green, OH: Bowling Green State University Popular Press, 1987.

Fodor's. *Fodor's Paris 2014*. New York: Random House, Inc., 2014.

France, Van Arsdale. *Window on Main Street*. Nashua, NH: Laughter Publications Inc., 1991.

Franco, James. *Directing Herbert White: Poems*. Minneapolis, MN: Graywolf Press, 2014.

Frater, Jamie. *The Ultimate Book of Top Ten Lists: A Mind-Boggling Collection of Fun, Fascinating and Bizarre Facts on Movies, Music, Sports, Crime, Celebrities, History, Trivia and More*. Berkeley, CA: Ulysses Press, 2009.

Gabler, Neal. *Walt Disney: The Triumph of the American Imagination*. New York: Alfred A. Knopf, 2006.

Garth, Maureen. *Moonbeam: A Book of Meditations for Children*. Sydney, Australia: HarperCollinsPublishers, 1992.

Gennawey, Sam. *The Disneyland Story: The Unofficial Guide to the Evolution of Walt Disney's Dream*. Birmingham, AL: Keen Communications, 2014.

Gerber, Catherine. *Top 10 Los Angeles*. London, England: Dorling Kindersley Limited, 2012 and 2014.

Gordon, Bruce, and David Mumford. *Disneyland: The Nickel Tour*. Santa Clarita, CA: Camphor Tree Publishers, 2000.

Gordon, Bruce, and Tim O'Day. *Disneyland: Then, Now, and Forever*. Santa Clarita, CA: Camphor Tree/Disney Editions, 2005.

Gowdy, Barbara. "Disneyland." *The Best American Short Stories 1989*, eds. Margaret Atwood and Shannon Ravenel. Boston, MA: Houghton Mifflin Company, 1989.

Green, Amy Boothe, and Howard E. Green. *Remembering Walt*, New York: Hyperion, 1999.

Greene, Richard and Katherine. *The Man Behind the Magic*. New York: Viking, 1998.

Gummerman, Jay. *Chez Chance*. New York: Pantheon Books, 1995.

Hammontree, Marie. *Walt Disney: Young Movie Maker*. New York: Simon and Schuster, 1997.

Handke, Danny, and Vanessa Hunt. *Poster Art of the Disney Parks*. New York: Disney Editions, 2012.

Harmon, Daniel. *Super Pop! Pop Culture Top Ten Lists to Help You Win at Trivia, Survive in the Wild, and Make It Through the Holidays*. San Francisco, CA: Zest Books, 2013.

Hench, John, and Peggy Van Pelt. *Designing Disney: Imagineering and the Art of the Show*. New York: Disney Editions, 2003.

Hillinger, Charles. *Hillinger's California*. Santa Barbara, CA: Capra Press, 1997.

Hollis, Tim, and Greg Ehrbar. *Mouse Tracks: The Story of Walt Disney Records*. Jackson, MS: University Press of Mississippi, 2006.

Hulse, Jerry. "Dream Realized—Disneyland Opens." *Los Angeles Times*, July 18, 1955, B1.

Hurwitz, Sue. *Sally Ride: Shooting for the Stars*. New York: Ballantine Books, 1989.

The Imagineers (text by Kevin Rafferty and Bruce Gordon). *Walt Disney Imagineering: A Behind the Dreams Look at Making the Magic Real*. New York: Hyperion, 1996.

The Imagineers with Melody Malmberg. *Walt Disney Imagineering: A Behind the Dreams Look at Making MORE Magic Real*. New York: Disney Editions, 2010.

The Imagineers (text by Alex Wright). *The Imagineering Field Guide to Disneyland*. New York: Disney Editions, 2008.

Jackson, Kathy Merlock, and Mark I. West, eds. *Disneyland and Culture: Essays on the Parks and Their Influence*. Jefferson, NC: McFarland & Company, Inc., Publishers, 2011.

Jackson, Kathy Merlock, ed. *Walt Disney Conversations*. Jackson, MS: University Press of Mississippi, 2006.

Jones, Karen R., and John Wills. *The Invention of the Park: From the Garden of Eden to Disney's Magic Kingdom.* Cambridge, England: Polity Press, 2005.

Jungk, Peter Stephan. *The Perfect American.* New York: Other Press, 2004.

Karp, Marshall. *The Rabbit Factory.* San Francisco, CA: MacAdam/Cage Publishing, 2006.

Kaufman, J.B. *The Walt Disney Family Museum: The Man, The Magic, The Memories.* New York: Disney Editions, 2009.

Keane, Nancy J. *The Big Book of Children's Reading Lists: 100 Great, Ready-to-Use Book Lists for Educators, Librarians, Parents, and Children.* Westport, CT: Libraries Unlimited, 2006.

Keller, Gary D. *Zapata Rose in 1992.* Colorado Springs, CO: Maize Press, 1992.

Kim, H.C. *Unconditional Election: Poems.* Norwalk, CA: The Hermit Kingdom Press, 2006.

Kinn, Gail and Jim Piazza. *The Greatest Movies Ever.* New York: Black Dog & Leventhal Publishers, Inc., 2008.

Klevin, Jill Ross. *The Turtle Street Trading Co.* New York: Delacorte Press, 1982.

Koenig, David. *More Mouse Tales: A Closer Peek Backstage at Disneyland.* Irvine, CA: Bonaventure Press, 2002.

———. *Mouse Tales: A Behind-the-Ears Look at Disneyland.* Irvine, CA: Bonaventure Press, 1995.

———. *Mouse Under Glass: Secrets of Disney Animation and Theme Parks.* Irvine, CA: Bonaventure Press, 1997.

Kotkin, Joel, and Paul Grabowicz. *California, Inc.* New York: Rawson, Wade Publishers, Inc., 1982.

Krassner, Paul. *Who's to Say What's Obscene?* San Francisco, CA: City Lights Books, 2009.

Kupferberg, Herbert. *The Book of Classical Music Lists.* New York: Facts on File Publications, 1985.

Kurtti, Jeff, and Bruce Gordon. *The Art of Disneyland.* New York: Disney Editions, 2006.

Kurtti, Jeff. *Disneyland: From Once Upon a Time to Happily Ever After.* New York: Disney Editions, 2010.

———. *Disneyland Through the Decades: A Photographic Celebration.* New York: Disney Editions, 2010.

———. *Walt Disney's Imagineering Legends and the Genesis of the Disney Theme Park.* New York: Disney Editions, 2008.

Lande, Nathaniel, and Andrew Lande. *The 10 Best of Everything: The Ultimate Guide for Travelers.* Washington, D.C.: The National Geographic Society, 2008.

Lansdale, Joe R. *High Cotton: Selected Stories of Joe R. Lansdale.* Urbana, IL: Golden Gryphon Press, 2000.

Laurie, Greg. *Lost Boy*. Ventura, CA: Regal, 2008.

Lefkon, Wendy, ed. dir. *Disney Insider Yearbook 2005*. New York: Disney Editions, 2006.

Letterman, David, and the *Late Show with David Letterman* writers. *David Letterman's Book of Top Ten Lists*. New York: Bantam Books, 1995.

Lindquist, Jack. *In Service to the Mouse*. Orange, CA: Chapman University Press, 2010.

London, Roy. *Disneyland on Parade: Three Short Plays*. New York: Dramatists Play Service, Inc. 1985.

Maio, Samuel. *The Burning of Los Angeles*. Kirksville, MO: Thomas Jefferson University Press, 1997.

Maltin, Leonard. *The Disney Films*. New York: Popular Library, 1978.

Markey, Kevin. *Secrets of Disney's Glorious Gardens*. New York: Disney Editions, 2006.

Marling, Karal Ann. *As Seen on TV*. Cambridge, MA: Harvard University Press, 1994.

———, ed. *Designing Disney's Theme Parks: The Architecture of Reassurance*. New York: Flammarion, 1998.

Marling, Karal Ann, and Donna R. Braden. *Behind the Magic: 50 Years of Disneyland*. Oakland, CA: The Henry Ford, 2005.

Marsh, Dave, and Kevin Stein. *The Book of Rock Lists: A Dell/Rolling Stone Press Book*. New York: Dell Publishing Co., Inc., 1982.

Martin, Steve. *Born Standing Up*. New York: Scribner, 2007.

May, Kirse Granat. *Golden State, Golden Youth*. Chapel Hill, NC: University of North Carolina Press, 2002.).

Menen, Aubrey. "Dazzled in Disneyland." *Holiday* magazine, July 1963.

Moore, Charles W. "Creating of Place" (1984). *You Have to Pay for the Public Life: Selected Essays of Charles W. Moore*. Cambridge, MA: The MIT Press, 2001.

———. "You Have to Pay for the Public Life." *Perspecta 9/10: The Yale Architectural Journal*, 1965.

Moore, Charles, Peter Becker, and Regula Campbell. *The City Observed: Los Angeles*. New York: Random House, Inc., 1984.

Moore, Rowan. *Why We Build: Power and Desire in Architecture*. New York: HarperCollins Publishers, 2013.

Mosley, Leonard. *Disney's World: A Biography*. New York: Stein and Day/Publishers, 1985.

Mullane, Nancy. *Life After Murder: Five Men in Search of Redemption*. New York: PublicAffairs, 2012.

Mullin, Michael, and John Skewes. *Larry Gets Lost in Los Angeles*. Seattle, WA: Sasquatch Books, 2009.

Nola, Lisa. *Listography: Your Life in Lists*. San Francisco, CA: Chronicle Books, 2007.

O'Brien, Tim. *Ripley's Believe It or Not! Amusement Park Oddities & Trivia!* Nashville, TN: Ripley Entertainment Inc., 2007.

O'Rourke, P. J. *Holidays in Heck*. New York: Atlantic Monthly Press, 2011.

Price, Harrison. *Walt's Revolution! By the Numbers*. Orlando, FL: Ripley Entertainment Inc., 2003.

Reynolds, Robert R. *Roller Coasters, Flumes & Flying Saucers*. Jupiter, FL: Northern Lights Publishing, 1999.

Richmond, Michele. *The Girl in the Fall-Away Dress*. Amherst, MA: 2001.

Ridgway, Charles. *Spinning Disney's World*. Branford, CT: The Intrepid Traveler, 2007.

Rolle, Andrew. *California: A History*, 5th Edition. Wheeling, IL: Harlan Davidson, Inc., 1998.

Robinson, Adam. *Word Smart*, 5th Edition. Framingham, MA: The Princeton Review, Inc., 2012

Ronstadt, Linda. *Simple Dreams: A Musical Memoir*. New York: Simon and Schuster, 2013.

Samuelson, Dale. *The American Amusement Park*. St. Paul, MN: MBI Publishing Company, 2001.

Schickel, Richard. *The Disney Version: The Life, Times, Art and Commerce of Walt Disney*, 3rd Edition. Chicago, IL: Ivan R. Dee, Publishers, 1997.

Schroeder, Russell, ed. *Walt Disney: His Life in Pictures*. New York: Disney Press, 1996.

Segalove, Ilene, and Paul Bob Velick. *List Your Self*. Kansas City, MO: Andrews McMeel Publishing, LLC, 2008.

Seivert, Sharon. *The Balancing Act: Mastering the Five Elements of Success in Life, Relationships, and Work*. Rochester, VT: Park Street Press, 2001.

Shag. *Shag, Ltd.: Fine Art Limited Editions*. San Francisco, CA: Last Gasp of San Francisco, 2005.

Shapiro, Len, and Ed Sherman. *Golf List Mania!: The Most Authoritative and Opinionated Rankings of the Best and Worst of the Game*. Philadelphia, PA: Running Press, 2011.

Shows, Charles. *Walt: Backstage Adventures with Walt Disney*. La Jolla, CA: Communications Creativity, 1980.

Simpson, Rob. *What We Could Have Done with the Money*. New York: Hyperion, 2008.

Sklar, Martin. *Dream It! Do It! My Half-Century Creating Disney's Magic Kingdoms*. Glendale, CA: Disney Editions, 2013.

———. *Walt Disney's Disneyland*. Anaheim, CA: Walt Disney Productions, 1964.

Smith, Dave. *Disney A to Z: The Official Encyclopedia*, 3rd Edition. New York: Disney Editions, 2006.

———. *Disney Trivia from the Vault*. New York: Disney Editions, 2012.

———, ed. *The Quotable Walt Disney*. New York: Disney Editions, 2001.

———. *Walt Disney Famous Quotes*. Lake Buena Vista, FL: Walt Disney Theme Parks and Resorts, 1994.

Smith, Dave, and Steven Clark. *Disney: The First 100 Years*. New York: Disney Edition, 2002.

Spignesi, Stephen J. *The Beatles Book of Lists*. New York: Carol Publishing Group, 1998.

Starr, Kenneth. *California: A History*. New York: The Modern Library, 2005.

Sugar, Bert, and Teddy Atlas. *The Ultimate Book of Boxing Lists*. Philadelphia, PA: Running Press, 2011.

Surrell, Jason. *The Haunted Mansion: From the Magic Kingdom to the Movies*. New York: Disney Editions, 2003.

———. *Pirates of the Caribbean: From the Magic Kingdom to the Movies*. New York: Disney Editions, 2005.

Thie, Carlene. *Disneyland … the Beginning*. Riverside, CA: Ape Pen Publishing Company, 2003.

Thomas, Bob. *Building a Company: Roy O. Disney and the Creation of an Entertainment Empire*. New York: Hyperion, 1998.

———. *Walt Disney: An American Original*. New York: Simon and Schuster, 1976.

Trex, Ethan, and Will Pearson and Mangesh Hattikudur. *Mental Floss: The Book, Only the Greatest Lists in the History of Listory*. New York: William Morrow & Co., 2011.

Van Maanen, John. *Cultural Collisions: Disneyland Goes to France*. Ann Arbor, MI: Interdisciplinary Committee on Organizational Studies (ICOS), University of Michigan, 1993.

Walker, Derek. *Los Angeles: Architectural Digest Profile*. New York: St. Martin's, 1982.

Wallechinsky, David, and Irving Wallace and Amy Wallace. *The People's Almanac Presents the Book of Lists*. New York: William Morrow & Co., 1977.

Walt Disney Treasures: Disneyland Secrets, Stories & Magic DVD. Walt Disney Video, 2007.

Walt Disney Treasures: Disneyland U.S.A. DVD. Walt Disney Video, 2001.

Walt Disney Treasures: Tomorrow Land DVD. Walt Disney Video, 2004.

Warner, Sally. *Ellray Jakes is NOT a chicken!* New York: Viking, 2011.

Watts, Steven. *The Magic Kingdom: Walt Disney and the American Way of Life*, Boston: Houghton Mifflin Company, 1997.

Weyandt, Hans, ed. *Read This! Handpicked Favorites from America's Indie Bookstores*. Minneapolis, MN: Coffee House Press, 2012.

Williams-Garcia, Rita. *One Crazy Summer*. New York: HarperCollins Publisher, 2010.

Wilson, Eric. *Disneyland Hostage*. Ontario, Canada: Clarke, Irwin & Company, 1982.

Wolfert, Ira. "Walt Disney's Magic Kingdom." *Reader's Digest*, April 1960.

Wong, Janet S. *Minn and Jake's Almost Terrible Summer*. New York: Farrar, Straus and Giroux, 2008.

Zevin, Dan. *Dan Gets a Minivan*. New York: Scribner, 2012.

Zibart, Eve. *This Day in History: Disney*. Cincinnati, OH: Emmis Books, 2006.

Zoglin, Richard. *Hope: Entertainer of the Century*. New York, Simon and Schuster, 2014.

A List of Photo Credits

Any uncredited photos were taken at Disneyland by the author.

Photos courtesy of Orange County Archives: 18–19, 34–35, 76–77, 81, 196–197, 302–303
Lonnie Burr: 42
Bob Gurr: 75 (artist unknown)
Annie Fox: 221
Donnie Osmond: 277
Susan Hoose: 281, 327

Sprinkled throughout the book are photos of signs displayed at Disneyland. Here's where you'll find them: page 12, inside Splash Mountain; page 17, at Big Thunder Ranch; page 273, on the inside of a Frontierland "cast members only" door; page 334, at the Hub's Jolly Holiday Bakery Café; page 335, a door at the extinct Carnation Plaza Gardens; page 343 (*below*), inside Splash Mountain; page 345, at the Harbor Boulevard pedestrian exit; page 359, at the Autopia; and page 360, at the Main Gate turnstiles.

A List of Facts Describing the Author

1. Previous works: *The Disneyland Encyclopedia* 2008 and 2012 (both published by Santa Monica Press), named "Best Reference Book" by *Library Journal*; *The Encyclopedia of Sixties Cool* (Santa Monica Press); *Swingin' Chicks of the '60s* (Cedco Publishing); the children's book *A Sky for Henry*, the young adult adventure novel *Lockerboy*, the comic novel *The Wish Book*, and the story collection *Stories Light and Dark* (all published by Red Hen Press); and articles in numerous periodicals, including *Los Angeles* magazine.

2. Disney employment: None. The author has never worked for the Walt Disney Company and didn't receive free passes or special privileges while performing research and taking photographs for this book.

3. Favorite Disneyland attraction: Skyway.

4. Favorite Disneyland memory: Riding Adventure Thru Inner Space as a teenager with an enthusiastic Grad Nite girl.

5. Favorite Dutch pop singer of the 1960s: Liesbeth List (1941–).

6. Favorite country album: Jimmy Dean's *Dean's List* (1968).

7. Favorite big-band song: Bing Crosby and the Andrews Sisters' "High on the List" (1950).

8. Favorite Hall and Oates song: "Kiss on My List" (1980).

9. Favorite Shakespeare quote: *Hamlet*, Act I, Scene 5, Line 22—the Ghost commands Hamlet to "List, list, O, list!"

10. Favorite TV show based on comedic retellings of real-life celebrity encounters: *Kathy Griffin: My Life on the D-List* (2005–2010).

11. Favorite European location: List Land, a German municipality on the island of Sylt.

12. Favorite classical composer: Franz Liszt (1811–1886), one of the world's greatest piano virtuosos, generated the fan frenzy called Lisztomania (and, eventually, inspired the name of the 1975 movie *Lisztomania* starring Roger Daltrey, as well as the 2009 hit single "Lisztomania" by indie rock band Phoenix).

13. Favorite economist: Georg (with no "e") List (1789–1846), one of the most important economists of nineteenth century.

14. Favorite scientist: Joseph Lister (1827–1912), the British surgeon who began sterilizing instruments, known as the father of antiseptic surgery.

15. Favorite mouthwash: Listerine, invented in 1879 and named after Joseph Lister.

16. Favorite periodical: *The List*, Scotland's monthly entertainment magazine.

17. Favorite foreign word: *Listo*—Spanish for "ready."

18. Favorite European rugby club: SC Germania List, Hanover, Germany.

19. Favorite pianist: New Jersey's Betty Liste.

20. Favorite Christmas song: "Grown-Up Christmas List."

21. Favorite Spanish nobility: Count of Alba de Liste.

22. Favorite young wife of Roger Sterling on *Mad Men*: Jane Sterling (played by Pcyton List)

23. Favorite episodes of *South Park*, *The Office*, and *The X-Files*: "The List."

24. Favorite recruiting poster: The Rebel Alliance's "Enlist Today! You're Our Only Hope!" featuring a sexy Princess Leia.

25. Favorite agent on the '60s TV show *The F.B.I.*: Efrem Zimbalist, Jr.

26. Favorite nineteenth-century French painter: Georges Seurat, the eminent pointillist.

27. Favorite quote: "The list could surely go on, and there is nothing more wonderful than a list." (Umberto Eco; *The Name of the Rose*)

A List of People for Whom the Author Is Thankful

1. So I had this idea of asking various experts to write lists for my list book. A nice idea but, in the words of a wise man, "It takes people to make the dream a reality." To my happy astonishment, these superstars all consented to make this particular dream come true: Josh Agle (Shag), Siran Babayan, Steve Barrett, Lonnie Burr, Rolly Crump, Annie Fox, Laura Gilbreath, Bob Gurr, Susan (Musfelt) Hoose, Chris Jepsen, David Koenig, Jim Korkis, Jack Lindquist, Karal Ann Marling, Hugo Martin, Kathy McDonald, Donny Osmond, Todd Regan, and Werner Weiss. Extra recognition for their extra help goes to Jim and Todd. To all of you, there are no words to express my profound gratitude . . . what am I saying? Of course there are words, including these:

   a. Grateful
   b. Thankful
   c. Appreciative
   d. Admiration
   e. Esteem
   f. Respect

2. As always, I'm profoundly grateful to everyone at Santa Monica Press. Publisher Jeffrey Goldman and his extraordinary team have once again made my own Disneyland dream come true. On the list called "Ranking the World's Coolest Publishing Companies," SMP comes first.

3. Now it's time to say goodbye to you, dear reader. Thank you for coming on this listifying journey with our Disneyland listorian. We know you have many entertainment options, so we're truly grateful that you chose *The Disneyland Book of Lists*.

4. And finally, endless appreciation for Disneyland itself, where people come to a common place that is never commonplace. Disneyland is happiness incarnate; even if Anaheim's weather and your mood are inclement, joy and delight are not just possible at Disneyland, they're imminent.

5. Want to send me ecstatic praise? Thoughtful suggestions? Polite complaints? Ecstatic praise? Visit www.disneylandlists.com for my email address, additional lists, new photos, and more.

6. This book is dedicated to my favorite Disneyland princess. Her name is spelled here in Maraglyphics, the invented alphabet used inside the Indiana Jones Adventure.

A List of 2,242 Proper Nouns in This Book

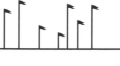

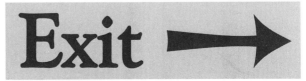